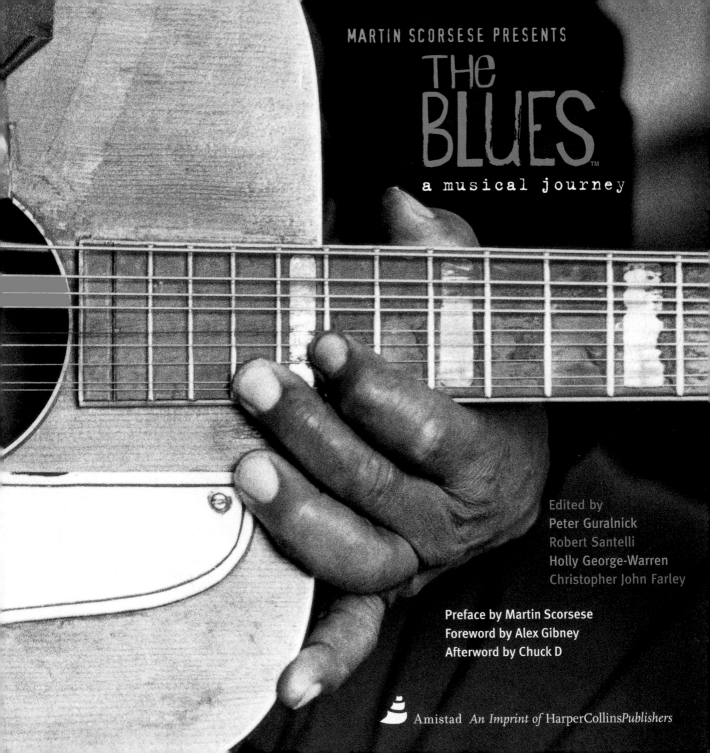

MARTIN SCORSESE PRESENTS

THE BLUES™

a musical journey

Edited by
Peter Guralnick
Robert Santelli
Holly George-Warren
Christopher John Farley

Preface by Martin Scorsese
Foreword by Alex Gibney
Afterword by Chuck D

Amistad *An Imprint of* HarperCollins*Publishers*

CONTENTS

"the blues is the roots...everything else is the fruits" —Willie Dixon

Preface By Martin Scorsese

I'll never forget the first time I heard Lead Belly singing "See See Rider." I was entranced. Like most people of my generation, I grew up listening to rock & roll. All of a sudden, in an instant, I could hear where it had all come from. And I could feel that the spirit behind the music, behind that voice and that guitar, came from somewhere much, much farther back in time.

Many people I know had the same shock of recognition. Rock & roll seemed to just come to us, on the radio and in the record stores. It became *our* music, a very important way of defining ourselves and separating from our parents. But then we uncovered another, deeper level, the history behind rock and R&B, the music *behind* our music. All roads led to the source, which was the blues.

We all like to imagine that art can come from out of nowhere and shock us like nothing we've ever seen or read or heard before. The greater truth is that everything—every painting, every movie, every play, every song—comes out of something that precedes it. It's a chain of human responses. The beauty of art and the power of art is that it can never be standardized or mechanized. It *has* to be a human exchange, passed down hand to hand, or else it's not art. It's endlessly old and endlessly new at the same time, because there are always young artists hearing and seeing work that's come before them, getting inspired and making something of their own out of what they've absorbed.

When you listen to Skip James singing "Devil Got My Woman" or Son House singing "Death Letter Blues" or John Lee Hooker laying down one of his snaking guitar figures, when you *really* listen— and believe me, it's not hard, because this is music

that grabs your full attention from the first note— you're hearing something *very* precious being passed down. A precious secret. It's there in all those echoes and borrowings, all those shared phrasings and guitar figures, all those songs that have passed down from singer to singer, player to player, sometimes changing along the way and becoming whole new songs in the process.

What is that secret? Recently, I was shooting a scene for the film I contributed to this series. I was in a studio with Corey Harris and Keb' Mo', two extraordinary young musicians, and we were talking about Robert Johnson. Corey made a very important point: Throughout the history of African-American music, right up through the present, there's a distinction between the emotions of the singer and the words he or she is singing. The words of "Hellhound on My Trail" may be about a jealous woman sprinkling hot foot powder around her lover's door, but Robert Johnson is singing something else, something mysterious, powerful, undefinable. The words don't contain the emotion, they're a vehicle for it. Corey called this a "language of exclusion," which can be found in the poetry of Langston Hughes just as easily as it can be found in the music of Howlin' Wolf or Lightnin' Hopkins. It was and still is a way of maintaining dignity and identity, both individual and collective, through art; and as we all know (or *should* know), it originated as a response to the very worst forms of oppression: slavery, sharecropping, and the racism that's never left American society. The precious secret is simply that part of the human soul which can never be trampled on or taken away. It's brought more to our culture than any of us ever could have imagined. It's tragic that racism continues to thrive in the western world, but it's also utterly ridiculous, because there's no one who hasn't profited from the spirit that animates this music. Without it, this culture of ours, so rich and varied, would be nothing.

A few years ago, we initiated this project—these films and this book of essays to accompany them—as a celebration of a great American art form. It became many other things along the way: a series of inquiries, tracing the different emotional and geographical paths the music took; a memorial to many great artists who have sadly passed away; a reflection on time and on the many ways the past can both haunt and enrich the present; and for all of us, for Wim Wenders, Charles Burnett, Richard Pearce, Marc Levin, Mike Figgis, Clint Eastwood, and myself, something deeply personal. For my own part, it became a reflection on an essential part of my creative process.

Music has played a key role in my life and my work. When I'm preparing a movie, it's only when I hear the music in my head that the movie comes together for me, when I really start to *see* it. I could picture *Gangs of New York*'s opening scene only after I first heard Otha Turner's hypnotic music. Even when the music doesn't make it into the finished product, it's there behind everything I do. When I look at the wonderful films made by the other directors who took part in this series, I know that it's the same for them. And the blues has always held a special place for me. It's the most physical music I know, with an emotional undertow that's unlike absolutely anything else. When you listen to the otherworldly voice of Robert Johnson hitting those words "blues fallin' down like hail," or Howlin' Wolf riding the rhythm of "Spoonful" with such amazing

ease and more than living up to his name at the same time, or Skip James lamenting love, the worst of all human afflictions, in "Devil Got My Woman," or Son House hugging the memory of his dead lover for dear life in the tightly coiled "Death Letter Blues," you're hearing something from way, way back, something eternal, elemental, something that defies rational thought, just like all the greatest art. You have to let it grab hold of you. You have no choice. When I made *The Last Waltz*, I had the privilege of filming Muddy Waters, and I still get an electric thrill just thinking about his amazing rendition of "Mannish Boy," the pleasure he took in every word, every phrase, the authority he commanded. How many times had he sung that song before that night? And there he was, singing it again, like it was the first time, or the last. I realized that the blues could do that for you, and for us. It gets at the essential.

I hope you enjoy watching these films as much as we all enjoyed making them. And when you read these beautiful essays by all these terrific artists, historians, and writers, you'll feel the passion that this music can arouse. We turned to some of the best writers we could think of— Elmore Leonard, Studs Terkel, David Halberstam, the great biographer and critic Chris Farley, and the wonderful historian Peter Guralnick, among them— and they all came through out of sheer love for the music.

Most of all, we want you to listen to the music. If you already know the blues, then maybe this will give you a reason to go back to it. And if you've never heard the blues, and you're coming across it for the first time, I can promise you this: Your life is about to change for the better.

Foreword

"Ain't but one kind of blues and that consists of a male and female that's in love..."—Son House

It's hard to explain, describe, or write about the blues. Like listening to the sound of sex through a thin motel wall, you know the blues when you hear it, even if you would be hard-pressed to describe *exactly* what is going on. What you do know is that it stirs you and that it keeps you up at night.

From the moment when Margaret Bodde (Martin Scorsese's producer at Cappa Productions) invited me to join this project, I had been giving some thought to what kind of book might accompany the film series. On the one hand, we faced the same problem confronted in *Let Us Now Praise Famous Men*, by James Agee, who agonized over the fact that a literary essay could never capture the pain of rural poverty as much as a collection of weathered shingles, bent lead forks, and torn window blinds. There were also more fundamental questions: What is it about the blues singer and her song that is inextricably linked? Perhaps it's the hardship that so many of these artists had to overcome; perhaps, even further back, is the fact that the roots of the blues trace back to Africa and were born of the horrors of slavery. But the geography of the blues is both a route to a particular time and place as well as a road map to the human soul. That ability of the music to connect with universal feelings of desire, love, loss, and bitter disappointment makes the blues fertile soil for so many of our greatest writers.

The search for that emotional truth brought us back to the parable of the motel room. Being both in the moment and apart from it is the peculiar territory of literature. The quest of the writer seemed to offer the best way to herald both the personal and impressionistic character of the films as well as the music they celebrate. The book would rejoice in the literary power of the blues.

It is a rich tradition. Bluesmen—from the griots of Mali to the itinerant poets of the Mississippi Delta—are more than musicians; they are storytellers. And blues lyrics are underappreciated as poetry. Hearing them in the context of a song, they carry an incantatory, if momentary, emotional power. But on the printed page, a song like Robert Johnson's "Hellhound on My Trail" has the lasting literary impact of a poem that seems as if it were written not just for the elusive pleasures of a juke joint on a Saturday night but to express, in a way that speaks to eternity, a personal reckoning with matters of longing and fear, as well as deep observations about the existential tension of being alive: caught between a restless soul and a hunger for peace.

So, too, there is a great literary tradition of writing *about* the blues. To that end, Peter Guralnick has culled an extraordinary collection of stories and reminiscences from musicians—from John Lee Hooker to Eric Clapton—and authors like Ralph Ellison, Eudora Welty, James Baldwin, Stanley Booth, W.E.B. Du Bois, William Faulkner, Zora Neale Hurston, and many others. In addition, we commissioned original pieces from the likes of David Halberstam, Suzan-Lori Parks, Elmore Leonard, Touré, Luc Sante, John Edgar Wideman, Studs Terkel, and Greg Tate. We did not necessarily seek out music experts; we looked for people who felt passionately about the music and who had a story to tell. We wanted personal impressions. In that quest, we mirrored the goals of Marty's film series: a kind of freewheeling film festival, which, taken together, provides a wonderful sense of the full sweep of the life of the blues. The approach of each film is personal, idiosyncratic, steered by the passions of the individual directors.

This approach is critical to understanding both the films and this book. Neither intends to be the last word on the subject. Rather, they are "first words," agents provocateurs meant to stir audiences and readers to explore the emotional territory of the blues on their own. To aid in that effort, this book offers a series of fundamental and evocative blues portraits by Christopher John Farley (including tips for further listening), as well as a framing essay by Bob Santelli. In filmmaking terms, Bob offers the elegant wide shot that frames the more emotional close-ups. And veteran editors Holly George-Warren and HarperCollins's Dan Conaway have been gracious and indefatigable producers, finding a way,

against all odds, to create something real and lasting out of quixotic expectations.

We have all been alone in that motel room with the thin walls. Hearing the cries of pleasure next door is painful because it is impossible to go to sleep while someone else is having so much fun. Yet those sounds also stir imaginary pleasures. And so this book is a showcase of how the blues has awakened the literary imagination of a group of musicians and writers who have tried to explore that feeling of the blues, an inexorable yearning that, in the words of Muddy Waters, just can't be satisfied. It's not exactly like being in the room next door. But, through the skill of the writers contained herein, it's the next best thing.

Alex Gibney
Series Producer
Martin Scorsese Presents The Blues: A Musical Journey
New York City, May 2003

Writing About the Blues: The Process

It starts before conception, before gestation, before birth. It continues in classrooms (where your history is rarely told), during traffic stops (license and registration please), and job interviews (we're not looking for anyone right now). It carries on at polling places, Supreme Court conferences, and barbershops. There's the music of course—Bessie Smith, Son House, Robert Johnson. There's also the words of those who came before—Langston Hughes, Ralph Ellison, Zora Neale Hurston. Inspiration hangs

on museum walls—Jacob Lawrence, William H. Johnson— and is served up by the plate, with a side of black-eyed peas, at Spoonbread and the Shark Bar. There's the discipline of immersion—knowing the players, the songs, the backgrounds—but there is no process. There is only life, lived, set to music, rendered into words.

Christopher John Farley
New York, May 2003

An Introductory Note By Peter Guralnick

Picking out the pieces for the anthology portion of this book was a labor of love—but it was hard work, too. There wasn't enough room! And as I was forced to leave out one after another of my favorites, in the end I just had to rationalize that after all this was an *introduction* (although what comfort can a rationalization like that ever give?) and that it was intended most of all to give a taste of a world so rich, so alive, so full of what James Baldwin calls "a zest and a joy and a capacity for facing and surviving disaster" that how could it ever be fully contained within the pages of a book?

Well, nice try—but the point for me was to find work that could begin to suggest some of the dimensions of that world, work that could reflect and refract the spirit of the blues. So that whether it is William Faulkner describing the uplifting power of a black church service, literally from the outside, or James Baldwin, a onetime boy preacher, passionately invoking it from within; whether it is Ralph Ellison bringing to broad metaphorical life the already vivid myth of real-life blues singer Peetie Wheatstraw, or Eudora Welty transmuting the experience of seeing pianist Fats Waller perform in a roadhouse in Jackson, Mississippi ("I tried to write my idea of the life of the traveling artist and performer—not Fats Waller himself but any artist—in the alien world"), the reader takes away something far deeper and more *spiritual* than a mere recitation of the facts.

Stanley Booth's brilliantly evocative description of Memphis bluesman Furry Lewis going to work as a street sweeper for the City Sanitation Department at three each morning, coupled with Johnny Shines' poetic portrait of Robert Johnson, with whom he traveled in the thirties; Johnson's own lyrics, along with Langston Hughes' revelatory conjunction of the music and the Movement in "Dream Boogie"; Zora Neale Hurston's uninhibited embrace of "the muck," which in *Their Eyes Were Watching God* amounts to the blues life ("I am not tragically colored," she wrote in a 1927 essay. "I do not belong to the sobbing school of Negrohood who hold that Nature has somehow given them a lowdown dirty deal")—all of these, I hope, suggest just a little of the resilience and diversity, the spontaneity and indomitability of a culture that simply refused to be defined either by what it lacked or by the moralistic judgments of its oppressors.

That culture today remains just as vital and alive as ever, and if the blues seems to have run its course as a twelve-bar form, the blues spirit surely has not. I think much of that spirit comes through here, but more significantly I hope you will find some of that element so uniquely central not just to the blues but to the whole African-American cultural tradition, that unvarnished, unblinking, unapologetic embrace of the human experience in all of its manifold aspects and dimensions.

A CENTURY OF THE BLUES

By Robert Santelli

1903. The place: Tutwiler, a tiny town in the Mississippi Delta, halfway between Greenwood and Clarksdale. It is dusk, and the sky is rich in summer color. The slight breeze, when it visits, is warm and wet with humidity.

William Christopher Handy, better known by his initials, W.C., waits on the wooden platform for a train heading north. Handy, the recently departed bandleader for Mahara's Minstrels, a black orchestra that mostly plays dance music and popular standards of the day, is a learned musician who understands theory and the conventions of good, respectable music. He had joined the Minstrels as a cornet player when he was twenty-two years old and traveled widely with them: the U.S., Canada, Mexico, Cuba. In time, he became their band director. Now, some seven years later, here he is, fresh from agreeing to lead the black Clarksdale band Knights of Pythias.

The train is late, so Handy does the only thing he can do: He waits patiently, trying to stay cool, passing the time with idle thoughts, and scanning the scenery for anything that might prove the least bit interesting. Finally succumbing to boredom, Handy dozes off, only to be awakened by the arrival of another man who sits down nearby and begins to play the guitar. His clothes tattered and his shoes beyond worn, the man is a sad specimen, especially compared to Handy, whose clothes bespeak a black sophistication not often seen in these parts.

The man plays and Handy listens, growing increasingly interested in the informal performance. Handy, of course, has heard many people, black and white, play guitar before, but not the way this man plays it. He doesn't finger the strings normally; instead, he presses a pocketknife against them, sliding it up and down to create a slinky sound, something akin to what Hawaiian guitarists get when they press a steel bar to the strings.

But it isn't just the unusual manner in which the poor black man plays his guitar. What he sings, and how he sings it, is equally compelling. "Goin' where the Southern cross the Dog": Most people around these parts know that "the Southern" is a railroad reference, and that "the Dog" is short for "Yellow Dog," local slang for the Yazoo Delta line. The man is singing about where the Southern line and the

Yazoo Delta line intersect, at a place called Moorhead. But something about the way the man practically moans it for added emphasis, repeating it three times, strikes Handy hard; the combination of sliding guitar, wailing voice, repeated lyrics, and the man's emotional honesty is incredibly powerful. Handy doesn't realize it yet, but this moment is an important one in his life, and an important one in the history of American music as well. The description of this incident, written about by Handy thirty-eight years later in his autobiography, is one of the earliest detailed descriptions of the blues ever written by a black man.

Handy called his book *Father of the Blues*. It's a good title for a book—but not, strictly speaking, an accurate one. What Handy did on that railroad platform in Mississippi a century ago was *witness* the blues, not give birth to it. But there's no disputing that he was forever after a changed man. "The effect was unforgettable," he wrote. Even so, he found it hard to bring the blues into his own musical vocabulary. Wrote Handy: "As a director of many respectable, conventional bands, it was not easy for

me to concede that a simple slow-drag-and-repeat could be rhythm itself. Neither was I ready to believe that this was just what the public wanted."

But later, during a Cleveland, Mississippi, performance, Handy's band was outshone—and outpaid—by a local trio playing blues similar to what he heard in Tutwiler. Shortly thereafter, Handy became a believer. "Those country black boys at Cleveland had taught me something. . . . My idea of what constitutes music was changed by the sight of that silver money cascading around the splay feet of a Mississippi string band," wrote Handy.

In 1909 Handy penned a political campaign song, "Mr. Crump," for the Memphis mayor. He later changed the title to "The Memphis Blues" and published it in 1912. The song was a hit. Entrepreneurially savvy, Handy delved deeper into the music, following it with "The St. Louis Blues," "Joe Turner Blues," "The Hesitating Blues," "Yellow Dog Blues," "Beale Street," and other blues and blues-based compositions. Their commercial success made Handy well-off but, more importantly, solidified the idea that the blues could exist in mainstream music settings, beyond black folk culture. The blues had arrived, thanks to W.C. Handy. American music would never be the same.

⊕ ⊕ ⊕ ⊕ ⊕

No one really knows for certain when or where the blues was born. But by the time of Handy's initial success with the music in 1912, it's safe to say it had been a viable black folk-music form in the South for at least two decades. With a couple exceptions, ethnomusicologists didn't become interested in the blues until later, thus missing prime opportunities to document the origins of the music and to record its pioneers. Still, there are enough clues to indicate that the blues most likely came out of the Mississippi Delta in the late nineteenth century.

Like all music forms—folk, pop, or classical—the blues evolved, rather than being born suddenly. So to understand the origins of the blues, you need to take a look at what came before it. You need to go back to the early part of the seventeenth century, when African slaves were first brought to the New World. Europeans involved in the slave trade stripped as much culture from their human cargo as possible before their arrival in the New World. But music was so embedded in the day-to-day existence of the African men and women caught in this horrific business that it was impossible to tear their songs from their souls. In West Africa, where many of the slaves came from, virtually everything was celebrated with singing and dancing: births, marriages, war, famine, religious beliefs, hunts, death. To eliminate music from an enslaved West African was to kill him.

Not that white slave owners in the New World permitted West African music rituals to exist without condition on early plantations along the Eastern Seaboard. Some slave owners forbade any music made by slaves, fearful that rebellious messaging could be encoded in the rhythms and chants. Other slave owners permitted limited music, particularly in the fields. Singing, the owners eventually realized, produced more and better work from the slaves. More liberal slave owners allowed singing and dancing during days of rest and holidays but often under the watchful eye of a work foreman or field master. Then there were those slave owners, a minority to be sure, who actually trained some of their slaves in Western music theory so that they'd be able to entertain guests at white socials and other plantation events. These slaves played stringed, woodwind, and keyboard instruments and created ensembles that played both popular and sacred music.

The earliest indication that slaves other than those specially trained were able to participate in music celebration beyond their own indigenous strains happened in the church. In the early eighteenth century, during the religious revival period known as the Great Awakening, there existed a desire to make Christians out of the pagan slaves. This missionary zeal swept the American colonies as slaves were taught the teachings of the Bible and spent much of their Sundays in church, albeit a segregated church. While white churchgoers sang hymns with stiff rhythms that required formalized responses from the congregation, Christian slaves sang hymns, too, but were unable to contain their enthusiasm when asked to sing God's praises. Over time, swinging rhythms, hand clapping, foot stomping, and improvised shouts made black Christian music significantly different from the sounds emanating from white churches. The hymns might have been the same, but the singing surely wasn't.

Eventually, black sacred folk songs of redemption and salvation, and of the triumph of hope over

I hate to see the evening sun go down
I hate to see the evening sun go down
It makes me think I'm on my last go
   'round

Feelin' tomorrow like I feel today
Feelin' tomorrow like I feel today
I'll pack my grip and make my getaway

St. Louis woman wears her diamond ring
Pulls a man around by her apron string

Wasn't for powder and this store-bought
   hair
The man I love wouldn't go nowhere,
   nowhere

I got them St. Louis blues, just as blue as I
   can be
He's got a heart like a rock cast in the sea
Or else he would not go so far from me.

despair, created a genre called the Negro spiritual. Songs such as "Go Down, Moses" and "Roll, Jordan, Roll" were sung in the church and in the fields, as slaves seldom regarded the separation of sacred and secular music. The Negro spiritual didn't gain popularity beyond the black community until the 1870s, when Fisk University, a newly appointed black college in Nashville, sought to raise money via a musical tour by its choir. The Fisk Jubilee Singers played not only to white audiences in the United States but also in Europe, prompting attention to the Negro spiritual as a creditable sacred folk-music form.

The blues would borrow from Negro spirituals as well as from field hollers, the most primitive of black music. Field hands didn't exactly holler as much as they whooped, moaned, and sang in sudden and completely improvised ways. A rhythm might come to mind and a melody, too, and then made-up lyrics, perhaps reflecting an approaching storm, a Saturday social, or the resolute stubbornness of a mule. Work songs were more organized musical expressions. Actually, a worker, be it a slave or a post–Civil War sharecropper, could make any song into a work song, if he sang it while working. But many work songs were sung by groups of workers, particularly those picking cotton or laying railroad track or building a levee, who seemed to move in a rhythmic unison. Work songs didn't make the work easier, just a tiny bit more tolerable.

Black folk songs, some of which could be considered work songs, like "John Henry," helped give rise to the blues too. In the song, Henry, a big, strapping black railroad worker, works himself to death trying to outdo a mechanized steel drill. Another song, "Stagolee," (a.k.a. Stagger Lee) tells the tale of a black con man. These musical narratives created characters, outlined plots, and usually contained some kind of lesson for the listener.

Spirituals, work songs, folk songs—these nineteenth-century black music forms were forged with the last of the major blues influences, the minstrel. No other American form is as wrapped in shame as the minstrel, yet there is no doubt of the

"Music did bring me to the gutter. It brought me to sleep on the levee of the Mississippi River, on the cobblestones, broke and hungry. And if you've ever slept on cobblestones or had nowhere to sleep, you can understand why I began ['The St. Louis Blues'] with 'I hate to see the evening sun go down.'" —*W.C. Handy*

music's popularity in the nineteenth century, first with white audiences and then with black. Minstrelsy, born in the years before the Civil War, consisted of white singers and actors in corked blackface coarsely ridiculing black southern plantation life for white audiences, many of which were based up North. They lampooned black slang and superstitions, physical features, and virtually everything else connected to the black man's condition in antebellum America. Dancing and singing songs inspired by black folk music, minstrel entertainers portrayed the typical black slave as little more than a clown or ignoramus. After emancipation and the end of the Civil War, whites grew less interested in minstrel shows. Rather than let minstrelsy die (which, admittedly, had created a canon of black-flavored music from the likes of Stephen Foster and other white composers), black singers and dancers eager for the opportunity to scratch out livings as entertainers adopted the form. Using burnt cork on their already dark-skinned faces, which, looking back today, seems to be the ultimate racial insult, black entertainers re-created minstrelsy by presenting the song-and-dance skits to their own people as a form of musical comedy. Black minstrelsy peaked in the late 1870s, and although the traveling minstrel entertainers were black, as were their audiences, the troupes were owned by whites, including Mahara's Minstrels.

With so many influences, it is surprising that the blues should be such a "simple" music form—at least on the surface. Lyrically, the blues is about repetition. A first line is sung and then repeated with perhaps a slight variation: "My baby, oh, she left me, and that's no lie/Well, I said my baby, oh, she left me, and no way that's a lie." These two lines are followed by a third line that answers the first two: "Wish my baby'd get back to me, before I lay down and die."

Musicologists call this the "A-A-B" pattern. The best blues songwriters pack a whole lot of narrative into such simple lyrical patterns, as the blues has a way of telling its own story. Good love gone bad, evil women and worse men, alcohol, poverty, death, prejudice, despair, hope, the devil, and the search for better days figure into many blues songs. The great bluesman Mississippi Fred McDowell once said, "The blues, it jus' keeps goin' on, goin' on. . . . Know why? 'Cause the blues is the story of life and the spice of life." Mississippi Fred hit it right on the head.

Musically, the blues introduced the "blue" note, one of the most significant contributions to American music made by black culture. These notes are usually made by flattening—lowering by a half step—the third, fifth, or seventh positions of a major scale. Presenting all kinds of emotional possibilities for the musician, blue notes give the blues its special feel, and when they are draped around a blues chord progression, the results can be so rich and *human*, that it satisfies the soul in a way no other music can.

By the late 1890s, it is likely that the blues had taken all its influences and evolved into a form of its own on the plantations that thrived in the Mississippi Delta during this period. Since the blues was born black, the Delta provided the community support necessary for the music to flourish. In the summer, the most tortured of seasons in the Deep South, the large stretch of land known as the Mississippi Delta is as hot as it is flat. During the day, the sun bakes the landscape, much of it below sea level, with nary a rise or hill rump in sight. The seemingly endless fields of cotton, the Delta's principal crop, and the scattered small hamlets, with names like Lula and Bobo, can be paralyzed by the heat and humidity.

The Delta's blues legacy is larger than its physical domain. Only 160 miles long from Memphis to the north, to Vicksburg to the south, and some fifty miles wide, it is not even a true delta, as in the area around the mouth of a river. Rather, it is a remarkably fertile alluvial plain, with soil as dark as the laborers forced to work it. The Delta has its rivers; one of them, the mighty Mississippi, is its western border. One of the more compelling stories of Delta history has to do with man's attempt to keep the Mississippi River out. Long and high levees built by former slaves and sons of slaves in the latter part of the nineteenth and early twentieth centuries kept, more or less, the river from overflowing onto the plantations that grew out of early Delta farms after the land was cleared of its old growth forest.

During the years after the Civil War, known as the period of Reconstruction, the commercial success of cotton made many of the white southern plantation families wealthy. Acres and acres of cotton were planted and picked by black workers and then shipped to Memphis. Having so many fields that needed tending guaranteed work for thousands of black laborers, making the ratio of black to white in the Delta nearly ten to one. Although black workers now had their freedom, in reality they were bound to the plantation, because they worked for a pittance and often owed money to the plantation store for the high-priced goods sold there. Jim Crow laws, the rise of racist organizations such as the Ku Klux Klan, lynchings, and prejudice at every turn made it all but impossible for blacks to enjoy the freedom and dignity that whites did. It was a cruel existence, and the blues documented the black man's woes better than any other form of cultural expression.

The earliest places a person could hear the blues were probably at socials, parties, fish fries, and in juke joints, small shacks on the outskirts of the plantation, where blacks converged on Saturday nights to drink cheap whiskey and dance. The earliest bluesmen were probably local plantation workers who owned a guitar or banjo, had a knack for singing and entertaining, and played for tips. Later, as the blues matured and grew more popular, bluesmen became itinerant entertainers, going from juke to juke, living a life of whiskey, song, women, and wandering.

With its large black population, the Mississippi Delta was the perfect place for the blues to grow, but it wasn't the only place down South where the music thrived. By the turn of the century, the blues had surfaced in west Texas, the Arkansas Delta on the western side of the Mississippi River, Louisiana, and even in Georgia and the Carolinas. The spread of the blues was organic and irregular. The blues pioneers of the late nineteenth and early twentieth centuries had no clue as to the emerging importance of the music they played. There was no way for them to know or even imagine that the blues would have implications far beyond the juke joint, that it would become the foundation for virtually every popular-music form—jazz, rhythm & blues, rock & roll, soul, funk, hip-hop—of the new century. What these blues musicians *did* know was that when they played, people listened, threw some money into their hat, maybe bought them a pint of whiskey. And that was good enough for them.

⊕ ⊕ ⊕ ⊕ ⊕

It's important to note that in the early years of blues history, few of the musicians who played the blues played *just* blues. Most likely interspersed into their collection of songs were spirituals, folk standards, pop favorites, just about anything that would make a crowd of people take note. The idea of specializing in a particular music form and calling oneself a *blues musician* was something that, like the music itself, occurred over time. Early bluesmen were really songsters, musicians who played a variety of *songs,* often in different styles. Their aim was to entertain—and to profit from it in some capacity.

The blues spread throughout the South in the early twentieth century, thanks to itinerant musicians carrying what they learned in one place to another. Traveling medicine and minstrel shows often used musicians who played the blues, thus giving the music a more structured entertainment platform. Not all black folks frequented juke joints, of course, but many showed up in the town square when a traveling troupe came by. They listened, laughed, and danced, and some of them even bought elixirs and potions guaranteed to cure whatever ailed you.

The early blues musician accompanied himself on guitar, or occasionally on banjo or mandolin. Poorer musicians might have played only the harmonica or simply sang. Mostly, the blues musician was a solo artist, though duos were not uncommon. Also, black string bands or small orchestras, the kind led by W.C. Handy, began to play blues as the form grew in popularity. Handy's sheet-music success with tunes such as "The Memphis Blues" and "The St. Louis Blues" enabled the music to expand beyond the poor black community. Black piano players who worked in saloons and whorehouses in southern cities also began adding blues to their repertoire. In New Orleans, where local musicians were more apt to play cornets and piano than guitars or harmonicas, thanks to the popularity of parades, marching bands, and social clubs, blues was one of the bases for "jazzing up" songs. As early as the 1890s, Charles "Buddy" Bolden, a gifted cornet player, had begun "jazzing" songs in New Orleans, as opposed to "ragging" them, which is what you did when you played ragtime, a black-created American music form popular in the 1890s and early 1900s. Bolden influenced a whole generation of horn players to do the same. Blues was a good foundation from which to jazz a song, and the black musicians who followed in Bolden's footsteps—in particular, a young Louis Armstrong—were as much blues musicians as they were experimenters in this new sound, jazz.

Throughout the first two decades of the twentieth century, the blues matured and became increasingly popular in the black community, both rural and urban. Though white musicians, especially down South, knew about the blues and borrowed ideas from the music, the blues didn't truly penetrate white music culture until later, when artists such as Jimmie Rodgers incorporated blues into their hillbilly sound.

The turning point for the blues occurred in 1920. Although the phonograph had been around since the late 1870s—the Edison Speaking Phonograph Company had been established by Thomas Edison in New York in 1878, the same year that Emile Berliner patented his "gramophone"—it wasn't until the turn of the century that entrepreneurs figured out a successful way to market prerecorded music. Columbia Records began selling discs in 1900; three years later the Victor company got into the business. From the outset these companies and others targeted white consumers.

In 1920 a black composer, Perry Bradford, convinced OKeh Records to record a song he had written, "Crazy Blues," with the singer Mamie Smith, an African-American. Prior to 1920, few in the fledgling recording business thought blacks would buy records. Too poor, they reckoned; even if they did have the money, no one knew whether or not they would spend it on music for the home. Bradford's idea paid off—handsomely. "Crazy Blues" was reputed to have sold nearly seventy-five thousand copies in the first month of its release. Other companies noticed, and, almost overnight, the "race" record industry was born, based on the success of the first blues record.

"Crazy Blues" wasn't a *pure* blues record by today's standards. It did, though, contain enough blues strains to warrant calling it a blues record. Mamie Smith's background was vaudeville and cabaret. Based on the success of Smith and "Crazy Blues," the blues soared in popularity. Other recording companies quickly signed black female singers to make blues records; most of the time the women had backgrounds similar to Smith's. It wasn't until a young, Chattanooga-born woman

The first artist to make a blues recording, Mamie Smith cut "Crazy Blues" after its composer, Perry Bradford, got the green light from OKeh Records.

arrived on the scene in 1923 that the blues found its first authentic star. Her name was Bessie Smith.

Smith, no relation to Mamie, didn't just sing the blues—she made you believe the music was the blood running through her veins. A tall, hefty woman, she delivered full-bodied stories of despair and vivid lyrical descriptions of a world where misery was no stranger to the downtrodden. Sung with a voice as big as she was, her blues was profound, and Bessie acquired the title Empress of the Blues. Without question, she was the best and most influential female blues artist of the 1920s, a decade that would become known as the "classic blues era." Just about every blues woman who followed her, and many jazz and gospel singers, too, was touched by her emotional intensity and consuming delivery.

Gertrude "Ma" Rainey would make music history in the 1920s as well. While the younger Bessie was

Ma Rainey was backed by the Georgia Band, led by "Georgia Tom" Dorsey *(third from left)*.

crowned the blues empress, Rainey was called the Mother of the Blues by her record company (and later also by music historians). Rainey's blues was raw, earthy, very authentic—a true link to the blues singers, men and women who pioneered the music, and those, like Bessie Smith, who would make blues records and become blues stars in the twenties.

Many blues historians figured that Rainey was Smith's mentor and that everything Ma knew about the blues she taught to Bessie. More recent accounts of the Rainey-Smith connection describe it as "adversarial," or at least highly competitive. Whatever the case, Smith probably learned some things about singing the blues from Rainey when they

toured together in 1912 with the Moses Stokes Company. Rainey was just too convincing a blues singer to ignore. But what made Smith the bigger-selling (and, ultimately, the more accomplished) artist was her range and versatility. Smith also endeared herself to young women, black and white, with her self-assuredness. When she sang " 'Tain't Nobody's Bizness If I Do," with the lyrics "If I go to church on Sunday/Then just shimmy down on Monday/'Tain't nobody's business if I do . . . "

Smith began her recording career in 1923, the same year Rainey began hers. By this time virtually all of the recording companies of the day were on to "race" records, and talent scouts scampered about looking for black women who could sing the blues. They found none with Smith's pedigree, but singers like Alberta Hunter, Ida Cox, and Clara Smith (no relation to either Mamie or Bessie), among others, made more than competent blues records. Many of these women didn't have Smith's natural talent or the hardened blues edge that Rainey did. Most came from vaudeville and cabaret backgrounds and focused on the blues when it meant better-paying performances and the chance to record.

Bessie Smith recorded for Columbia for ten years, making more than 160 records, often with the likes of first-rate jazzmen such as Louis Armstrong, saxophonist Coleman Hawkins, pianists James P. Johnson and Fletcher Henderson, and clarinetist Buster Bailey. Just about all the records made by classic blueswomen in the 1920s were made with jazz musicians. No musician of note back then considered himself only a "blues" artist. This was the Jazz Age, after all, and the boundaries that historians would use later on to separate blues from jazz didn't exist in the 1920s. Nightclubs in black sections of northern cities like New York's Harlem featured jazz bands and blues singers on the same bill. Both blacks and whites listened to it, danced to it, and made it a vital part of the cultural story of the 1920s.

If the classic blues sound was almost exclusively female driven and urban, the country-blues sound that existed at the same time was male dominated and rural. Country-blues artists often performed solo on a street corner. Some of the earliest country-blues recordings occurred after record company talent scouts traveled south to find new sounds. Companies such as OKeh, Paramount, Gennett, and Vocalion all sent scouts to find artists to record on portable equipment set up in hotel rooms, empty warehouses, or wherever there was enough room and quiet to make the recordings. Record companies also recorded country-blues artists in New York, Chicago, and Grafton, Wisconsin, where recording studios existed. Country-blues musicians unaware of this new business of recording would eagerly record and sign away rights for a few dollars. The chance to hear themselves on a Victrola and earn quick money proved irresistible.

Artists such as Papa Charlie Jackson and Daddy Stovepipe were among the handful of male country artists to record in the early 1920s. But it wasn't until two sightless street musicians—Blind Lemon Jefferson and Blind Blake—recorded their songs that country blues made its mark commercially. Though

Bessie Smith personified the blues diva.

Blind Blake was one of the blues' most spectacular guitar players.

well as cities. When Paramount began recording him in 1925, Jefferson was a seasoned entertainer and musician who had perfected a blues style culled from more than a decade of playing for tips on street corners.

A number of Jefferson recordings, including "Match Box Blues," "Black Snake Moan," and "See That My Grave Is Kept Clean," demonstrate Jefferson's talent for breaking the rhythm dramatically, answering his own vocals with fingerpicked flourishes. His wide use of improvisational twists and turns made his music interesting and unconventional, while his song lyrics, like those of so many other country-bluesmen of his time, centered on hard times, with double entendres spicing things up. Jefferson's popularity made him the best-selling country-blues artist of the 1920s. By the time of his sudden death in Chicago in 1929, he had been traveling with a chauffeur and living more lavishly than just about any other country-blues artist of the time. With a catalogue of more than eighty songs, Jefferson took full advantage of a recording career that lasted only a few years.

Arthur "Blind" Blake came out of the Southeast and began his recording career in 1926. Little is known of his personal life, but musically his blues style told an entirely different story than Jefferson's, suggesting that country blues in general had matured to such a point by the mid-1920s that different geographic regions yielded different blues styles, all of which contributed to a growing blues catalogue.

An exceptional guitarist, Blind Blake's syncopated blues numbers featured some of the most elaborate fingerpicking of the period. Blake, as well as other first-generation southeastern blues guitarists, also infused liberal amounts of ragtime-influenced elements into his music, creating a

country blues in the 1920s seemed richest in the Mississippi Delta (where, later in the decade, nearly a dozen seminal artists would make some of the most powerful country blues in the pre–World War II period), neither Jefferson nor Blake resided there.

Jefferson was a Texas singer/guitar player whose blues repertoire also included robust amounts of hymns and folk standards, plus dance, rag, and pop songs of the day. Despite his handicap, Jefferson's versatility kept him traveling extensively throughout the South, playing country jukes and small towns, as

bouncy and bright sound. Lyrically, Blake mixed his themes. In some songs, particularly "Diddie Wa Diddie," "Skeedle Loo Doo Blues," and "Come On Boys, Let's Do That Messin' Around," Blake lightened things up with the kind of lyrics that would keep a party going and attract sizable tips. However, in other songs, Blake bit down hard on police brutality ("Police Dog Blues"), lynchings ("Rope Stretching Blues"), and black despair ("Bad Feeling Blues").

Because he had thin vocals, Blind Blake's guitar was his primary voice. Blake recorded through most of 1932, with some eighty titles to his credit, many of which remain rag-guitar masterpieces, prompting a whole generation of East Coast blues musicians to be influenced by his style.

The Mississippi Delta's closest contender for the commercial success garnered by Blind Lemon Jefferson and Blind Blake came from Charley Patton. With a gruff, hoarse voice (imagine Tom Waits singing country blues) and an equally rugged guitar style, Patton was the single most influential early Delta bluesman. Distinguished blues writer Robert Palmer put Patton "among the most important musicians twentieth-century America has produced."

In addition to creating a brand of blues featuring complex rhythms, accented by percussive taps on his guitar, elongated melodies, and a slide-guitar technique that cut a path virtually every other Delta bluesmen had to acknowledge, Patton was also a convincing songwriter, often including in his songs astute social commentary. "Mississippi Boll Weevil Blues" told of the plague of insects that destroyed many Mississippi farms in the early 1900s. Both part one and part two of "High Water Everywhere" describe the great Mississippi River flood of 1927. "Dry Well Blues" is about a Mississippi drought; "Moon Going Down" told of the destruction by fire

Early recordings by Patton spelled his first name both as Charley and Charlie; artist Robert Crumb illustrated this anthology of Patton recordings released by Yazoo in 1991.

of a Clarksdale mill. Patton also sang of personal experiences. When he was arrested in the town of Belzoni, he gave his side in "High Sheriff Blues" and "Tom Rushen Blues." He contemplated leaving Mississippi in "Going to Move to Alabama."

Charley Patton also lived the life that mythologized the *idea* of a bluesman. He was a heavy drinker, a carouser, a womanizer, a brawler, once getting his throat slashed in a fight. Mainly Patton clowned around, never giving much thought to getting serious with things other than entertaining people. Living large with little, Patton was known to tear up a juke with performances on guitar that included playing the instrument behind his head or while laying on the floor, or throwing his instrument up in the air, catching it, and resuming playing, never missing a beat.

Despite his popularity in the Delta, Patton didn't get the chance to record until 1929, when Paramount took the suggestion of talent scout H.C. Speir to cut some sides with the Delta bluesman. Despite Patton's huge place in early blues history, his record sales never approached those of Jefferson's or Blake's. One reason might have been that Patton's sandpaper voice and unique guitar style didn't translate as well on record as they did in the juke joint. Or it might have been that Paramount just got to Patton too late.

⊕ ⊕ ⊕ ⊕ ⊕

Like many things in America, the race-record industry came crashing down in late 1929, when the nation said goodbye to prosperity and hello to economic calamity. The Depression killed the Jazz Age and with it the notion that life was one big party. Female blues singers who had become materially comfortable, wearing fancy clothes and acting every part the diva, were soon back living the blues, not just singing them. Nightclubs closed. Theaters featuring revues and vaudeville-styled acts now showed Hollywood films. Performance opportunities disappeared, and recording sessions were scarce. Record sales, even among African-Americans, one of the most loyal music-consumer groups, dropped steadily. There was never any question whether or not the blues would survive. The music, after all, had always dealt with themes of despair and deprivation. It was the most Depression-proof music America had. What was in question was whether the business of the blues would make it through the earliest, most damaging years of the 1930s.

It did, but barely. The classic blues era effectively ended in 1929, although major blues performers such as Bessie Smith continued on. Smith recorded the song "Nobody Knows You When You're Down and Out" that year, a personal and national reflection of the mood that suddenly covered America. Two years later, Columbia Records ended its nearly decade-long association with Smith, although she did record one more time, in 1933, thanks to the persistence of a young talent scout named John Hammond.

Bessie Smith died in a car crash in Mississippi in 1937. Ma Rainey passed on in 1939. Many of the other classic female blues singers resorted to singing in southern tent shows or small clubs up North, or just faded away as demand for their brand of the blues dried up. America had changed, and so, therefore, must its music. The romping sounds of Dixieland, or Traditional Jazz, as twenties jazz would become known, had evolved into swing and big-band dance music. Blues gave up its "classic" sound, ending the only time the musical form would ever be dominated by women. Down South, country blues remained popular, but many artists lost the chance to record because field trips diminished and record companies were less eager to invest in race recordings. Up North, transplanted bluesmen (and a few women, particularly one known as Memphis Minnie) settled in cities like Chicago and began performing together in combos, which would sow the seeds for the electric-blues-band revolution of the 1950s.

One of the few record companies that had managed to survive the economic crash and that continued to record blues artists in the 1930s was Bluebird, a subsidiary of the Victor label. Producer and talent scout Lester Melrose made it the most significant blues record label in the 1930s. Based in Chicago, Melrose and Bluebird favored artists who came out of country blues but who had the vision to alter their sound to make it more urban and therefore more attractive to black Americans living in northern cities like Chicago, Cleveland, Detroit, and Gary, Indiana. These African-Americans, many of whom had come north in the teens and 1920s looking for better economic opportunities, had been introduced to singers and performers who favored thicker, jazzier musical accompaniment in the form of drums and piano. To them, the sound seemed hotter and more exciting than the sound generated by a singer and a single acoustic guitar, the trademark accompaniment of country blues. Transplanted southern black musicians like Big Bill Broonzy easily made the transition from country to city and ended up some of the era's most important recording artists.

Broonzy was born in Mississippi and raised in Arkansas; he served in the army during World War I, making him more aware of life outside the South and making it more difficult for him to return home to the cotton fields and live as a black sharecropper. In 1920, Broonzy moved north, settling in Chicago, where he set aside his original instrument, the fiddle, and picked up a guitar, learning much by hanging around with blues old-timer Papa Charlie Jackson. Broonzy also learned from a bigger blues stalwart, Tampa Red, whose wife rented rooms in Chicago, mostly to young musicians just off the train from Memphis or Mississippi. Tampa Red, whose real name was Hudson Whittaker, first recorded in 1928, with Paramount and then Vocalion. Overnight, Red grew famous for a duet he had recorded with Georgia Tom Dorsey called "It's Tight Like That." The risqué number was a big seller, not only because of its bawdy lyrics but also because of Red's hot guitar licks. One of the seminal songs of the period, it ushered in a blues trend called "hokum" that

featured loose rhythms and cleverly penned, ribald lyrics. Red even formed a combo called Tampa Red's Hokum Jug Band, which artfully defined the hokum style, after his partner, Georgia Tom Dorsey, moved from secular to sacred music. Dorsey found God after the success of "It's Tight Like That" and used his musical genius to help create the modern gospel sound. A pianist, songwriter, and shrewd businessman, Dorsey formed the Thomas A. Dorsey Gospel Songs Music Publishing Company, writing hundreds of gospel tunes, including the monumental "Precious Lord." Over time, Dorsey became known as the Father of Gospel Music, while his old blues partner, Tampa Red, was dubbed the Guitar Wizard.

If Big Bill Broonzy learned the rudiments of the blues from Papa Charlie Jackson, he picked up the music's subtleties from Tampa Red. Broonzy jumped into the hokum craze, recording in 1930 with the Famous Hokum Boys, who cut blues party songs rich with rag-flavored strains and jumpy rhythms.

Broonzy recorded right through the Depression years in a variety of settings: solo, duet, combo. He was, perhaps, the most versatile blues artist of the period and one of its best-selling recording artists. Folk blues, country blues, hokum, prototype urban blues—they were all part of his repertoire. With Broonzy, Tampa Red, Memphis Minnie, guitarist Scrapper Blackwell, and piano player Leroy Carr, the thirties urban-blues sound was rich and lively.

Down South, despite the Depression, country blues served its audience equally well. Memphis, with Beale Street as its nerve center, contained the region's blues heartbeat. Although Memphis lacked its own record company, field recordings were still occasionally done there for the northern record companies, attracting blues musicians harboring the

The Memphis Jug Band, featuring Will Shade

hope of making records like the ones heard on Victrolas in black communities throughout the South.

Located on the eastern bank of the Mississippi River and at the northern edge of the Mississippi Delta, just over the Mississippi-Tennessee state line, Memphis became the mid-South's cotton center in the post–Civil War years. Cotton commerce kept the city busy and flowing with money. A large black population was already in place by the turn of the century, and with Beale Street cooking on Saturday nights, it was no wonder blues musicians flocked to Memphis from the neighboring Mississippi and Arkansas Deltas and from western Tennessee.

Ever since the mid-1920s, when Will Shade's group, the Memphis Jug Band, recorded for the blues talent scout Ralph Peer in Memphis, part of the city's blues scene consisted of jug bands, informal groups of musicians, some of which played homemade instruments like the washtub bass and the whiskey jug. Jug bands also featured banjo, harmonica, and fiddle players mixed with, say, a couple of guitarists, and maybe a kazoo player.

Members came and went. Formalized structure was an anathema to jug bands. Playing hokum and hokum-styled blues with a little of this and some of that thrown in for good measure, jug bands were as popular at parties as they were on street corners, and by the mid-1930s they had become an essential part of the Memphis blues scene. Although other cities down South had their own jug bands, no jug-band scene was ever as lively or as good as the one in Memphis. Other popular Memphis-based jug bands that made records included the Beale Street Sheiks and Cannon's Jug Stompers, with Gus Cannon on banjo.

Memphis also had its share of more traditional blues artists, solo singer/guitarists who wandered the region, worked the corners and alleyways of Beale Street and played parks and parties around town. If they hadn't been born in Memphis, chances are such blues musicians came from the Mississippi and Arkansas Deltas or rural Tennessee towns. Brownsville, Tennessee, for instance, was the home of bluesmen Sleepy John Estes, Hammie Nixon, and Yank Rachell. Some of these places had small blues scenes of their own, but there was greater opportunity in Memphis, and most blues artists at least passed through the city at one time or another.

Memphis might have been the South's urban center, but no region possessed the richness or the number of major blues figures of the Mississippi Delta. From the earliest blues origins in the late nineteenth century through the Depression years and even beyond, the Delta was, in a word, bluesland. The region turned out one great blues musician after another mainly because the blues was an indelible part of black life and owned a significant part of its cultural landscape.

Living and working conditions were harsh in Mississippi, giving blues songsters plenty to write about. Music was a real escape; it took black people away from the drudgery of fieldwork, the poverty of their homes, and prejudice that greeted them practically every time they came in contact with a white man or woman. The juke joint, where blues could be heard either blaring out of a Victrola or played live in the corner of the room, became a black oasis, a place where your guard could be let down, your soul bared, and your feelings of despair lost in a haze of music, kinship, and whiskey.

Thus, the surroundings were indeed right for the blues to flourish in the Mississippi Delta, and they did just that. Charley Patton died in 1934, but he was just one of a number of Delta bluesmen who had perfected a blues style and gotten it onto record before the Depression, or just as it hit. Son House, Tommy Johnson, Tommy McClennan, Skip James, and Mississippi John Hurt, all major Delta blues stylists, unveiled the rich diversity of Delta blues with their late 1920s and early 1930s recordings.

If there was an equal to Patton's blues pedigree, it came from House. He knew Patton, shared a mutual friend in blues guitarist Willie Brown, traveled to Grafton, Wisconsin, in 1930 to record for Paramount Records with them, and worked many of the same Mississippi juke joints and fish fries. Like a few other blues artists from the period, House had always been torn between God's music and the devil's, as blues was often called, even in the black community. The saints and sinners that did battle in House's soul produced some of the most riveting blues of the period. House played guitar with a furious intensity, as if his life depended on it, and he sang with equal conviction. With Son House, the blues possessed an emotional intensity that was not easily replicated.

Skip James owned a similar story. Born into a religious family in Bentonia, Mississippi, James

learned to play piano before he picked up the guitar. The blues came easy to James, and in 1930 he was discovered by H.C. Speir, who sent James to Grafton to record on the heels of House, Patton, and Brown. James' blues sound was like no other. With a falsetto that was at once mysterious, detached, spooky even, James also sang about the inherent conflict between good and evil. Demons and fallen angels floated through James' songs, as did Jesus. You could feel the torment that James struggled with in his music. One moment he sings "Be Ready When He Comes" or "Jesus Is a Mighty Good Leader," while in another he describes how he'd "rather be the devil than to be that woman's man." Add to all this a compelling and original guitar technique, with its lonely notes, finger-picked and eerie minor chords—quite different than the slashing Delta style of Charley Patton and Son House—and you have in Skip James one of the most artistically significant bluesmen of the period.

There were many other singer/guitarists whose work was critical to the development of Mississippi Delta blues in the late 1920s and 1930s, including Bukka White and Big Joe Williams. Their blues, in addition to the music made by Texas bluesmen such as Blind Willie Johnson, Texas Alexander, and Lead Belly, and those musicians playing blues on the East Coast, following the path cut by Blind Blake—Barbecue Bob, Blind Willie McTell, and Blind Boy Fuller—made this the most creatively fruitful period for country blues.

Despite the blues brilliance that came from these artists, none of them achieved the mark or the place in blues history that a skinny singer/guitarist with extraordinarily large hands did. Robert Johnson cut fewer than thirty songs in a recording career composed of just two sessions in two years. Nonetheless, Johnson became the single most

I got stones in my passway
And my road seem dark as night
I got stones in my passway
And my road seem dark as night
I have pains in my heart
They have taken my appetite.

I have a bird to whistle
And I have a bird to sing
Have a bird to whistle
And I have a bird to sing
I got a woman that I'm lovin'
Boy, but she don't mean a thing.

My enemies have betrayed me
Have overtaken poor Bob at last
My enemies have betrayed me
Have overtaken poor Bob at last
And there's one thing certain
They have stones all in my pass.

Now you tryin' to take my life
And all my lovin' too
You laid a passway for me
Now what are you trying to do

I'm cryin' please
Please let us be friends
And when you hear me howlin' in my
    passway, rider
Please open your door and let me in.

I got three legs to truck on
Boys please don't block my road
I got three legs to truck on
Boys please don't block my road
I've been feelin' ashamed 'bout my rider
Babe I'm booked and I got to go.

important artist of the country-blues period and one of the most important blues artists of all time, although none of this came to fruition during Johnson's lifetime. In his biography, fact and fiction are blurred, and wrapped around his legacy are many of the myths and themes that helped give the blues its colorful story.

Johnson, it was believed by some, got his guitar prowess by selling his soul to the devil at a Mississippi Delta crossroads at midnight. More likely, what happened was that Johnson learned by watching Son House and other early Delta bluesmen, by listening to records, and by practicing with a rare fervor that made him an amazing guitarist—seemingly overnight. Johnson didn't develop a new country-blues style; instead, he absorbed most everything he heard, blending styles, picking up nuances, remembering lyrics and song themes—in general, synthesizing almost everything consequential about the blues up to that point. In that way, Johnson created the ultimate country-blues style.

Johnson was born in Mississippi in 1911, making him just old enough in the late twenties to take in the sounds and styles of the great Delta bluesmen who played the dances, socials, house parties, and juke joints all around him. He must have had access to a Victrola because strains of Leroy Carr and other non-Delta bluesmen are woven into Johnson's blues brand, something he could have only learned from their recordings. From Skip James and Tommy Johnson (no relation), he learned to depict in his lyrics the fight against darkness and light, making his music more intriguing. Some of Johnson's best songs—"Me and the Devil Blues," "Cross Road Blues," "Hellhound on My Trail"—detail this never-ending tug-of-war. He also toyed with black hoodoo culture, of which the crossroads, the place where devilish deals were made, figured prominently.

Johnson's voice wasn't pretty or weathered; rather, it was whiny, but in a profound way. It ached, it reached out for comfort, it was dark and lonely, it could stop you in your tracks. But Johnson's guitar playing was even more stunning. No one, not back then, nor today, has been able to fully reproduce Johnson's gift to phrase guitar notes and chords so that they answered oh-so-artfully the lyrics he sang. The size of his hands may have had something to do with the way he played. Listening to Johnson you often swear two guitarists are playing, not one. His long fingers reached for notes other guitarists could only dream of, while his penchant for slide guitar and "walking" bass riffs gave his style a remarkably rich language of notes, tones, and sounds. No wonder people thought he made a deal with the devil.

Precious little is known about Johnson's life; only two photos of him exist. He was born illegitimate, married young, lost his wife during childbirth, traveled widely, was shy yet attracted women wherever he went, and did his share of drinking. He first recorded in a San Antonio hotel room in late 1936. In three days he cut sixteen songs—all of them classics. Less than a year later, this time in a Dallas warehouse, he recorded a second, and final, time. Again the results were legendary. Not long after this session, Johnson was allegedly poisoned in Mississippi by a jealous juke joint owner who accused Johnson of flirting with his wife. Johnson was twenty-seven years old.

Dying so young, Johnson never got the chance to know the importance of his music or his life. His records were not big sellers during the Depression, and when he died he was buried in an unmarked grave. But a quarter century later a collection of his songs put out in album form as *King of the Delta Blues Singers* became one of the most influential

blues albums of all time. Everyone from Eric Clapton to Bob Dylan was moved by Johnson's music.

The country blues of Robert Johnson had to wait until the 1960s before it became more than a mention in the broader span of American pop music. But for other brands of the blues, that wasn't the case. In New York, Kansas City, Chicago, and other urban areas, the jazz-blues connection that began in the 1920s not only survived the Depression years but actually flourished. In New York, Duke Ellington made the transition from the roaring twenties to the swinging thirties without a misstep. Swing contained more controlled improvisation and more tightly defined melodies and rhythms than ragtime, making the music more quickly accessible. With all its "swinging" rhythms, it filled the dance floor. The swing band was larger than the Dixieland band, often possessing upwards of a dozen and a half members. Such size made it important for musicians to have more predetermined roles. With a band of incredibly talented players and an artistic vision as broad and innovative as any of the great composer/bandleaders in the twentieth century, Ellington wrote compositions and arrangements that were steeped in the blues. His was a sophisticated sound, gorgeous in its movement, texture, and arranged phrasing, yet always harkening back to the blues. Graceful and rich in meaning, Ellington's songs dressed up the blues with such style and grace that it would have sounded out of place in country-blues juke joints down South, although, thanks to his incessant touring Ellington and his band were indeed known down South.

Swing had many bandleaders and musicians, black and white, who understood the importance of the blues in this new jazz form. But those who worked out of Kansas City truly made the blues the centerpiece of swing. Walter Page's band, the Blue

Good morning, daddy!
Ain't you heard
The boogie-woogie rumble
Of a dream deferred?

Listen closely:
You'll hear their feet
Beating out and beating out a—

*You think
It's a happy beat?*

Listen to it closely:
Ain't you heard
something underneath
like a—

What did I say?

Sure,
I'm happy!
Take it away!

*Hey, pop!
Re-bop!
Mop!*

Y-e-a-h!

up brand-new blues possibilities within the jazz framework. Together with musicians such as saxophonist Lester Young and singer Jimmy Rushing, Basie put Kansas City on the blues map and kept it there.

Chicago also had its share of piano players who brought new ideas to the blues. But in the Windy City, one of the styles to flourish was less connected to swing and big-band jazz and more a primal root of rock & roll. In 1928 a young piano player, Clarence Smith, whose friends called him Pine Top, moved from Pittsburgh, where he'd been working with Ma Rainey and others, to Chicago. Smith had a song, "Pine Top's Boogie Woogie," that rocked rent parties in local black neighborhoods and lent the latter part of its title to one of the most exciting piano styles of the century. Boogie-woogie featured a romping rhythm, driving melodies, bass notes that jumped instead of walked, and an overall upbeat mood that could heat up a room and fill up a dance floor in record time.

Quickly, Chicago became a hub for boogie-woogie. Smith, plus boogie-woogie piano stalwarts Albert Ammons, Meade Lux Lewis, and Jimmy Yancey, all resided in the city during boogie-woogie's early period; together, they defined the style with their house-rocking sounds.

⊕ ⊕ ⊕ ⊕ ⊕

Devils, was one of the best of the early Kansas City groups that made blues swing hard and hot. Bennie Moten also had a band with strong blues roots. When Moten died suddenly in 1935, William Basie, best known as Count Basie, picked up where Moten had left off. Born in New Jersey, Basie cut his jazz teeth in Harlem in the 1920s before being stranded in Kansas City. A brilliant piano player, Basie emphasized the blues in Moten's style, opening

It wasn't just jazz that cultivated a relationship to the blues in the 1930s. Although Jimmie Rodgers, a white railroad worker and hillbilly singer, died of tuberculosis in 1933, he had already made his mark by writing a number of prototype country songs with strong blues overtones. Rodgers confirmed that the blues, even in its earliest stages, could be explored successfully by white songwriters and performers. Rodgers grew up poor in Mississippi,

0 miles 50

N
W E
S

TENNESSEE

49

West Memphis   Memphis

40

LOUISIANA

Helena

78

Clarksdale

Cleveland

ARKANSAS

Greenwood

49

61

Dallas

20

Vicksburg   Jackson

MISSISSIPPI

Mississippi River

55

TEXAS

LOUISIANA

New Orleans

10

Houston

where he was early on exposed to the blues. When he started working on the railroad, his blues education continued, prompting him to pen what music historians call some of the earliest country songs—in actuality blues songs written and played by a white man. "Mississippi Delta Blues," "Long Tall Mama Blues," and "TB Blues" were just some of the blues songs in Rodgers' growing repertoire. Rodgers created the "blue yodel" to make his music more distinctive, leading to one of his nicknames, the Blue Yodeler. (Rodgers had a knack for landing nicknames; he was also called the Singing Brakeman and the Father of Country Music.)

Blues strains even began appearing in the music of George Gershwin, one of America's most distinguished composers. Gershwin's instrumental composition "Rhapsody in Blue" (1924) became an instant classic in the American music lexicon, and although his opera "Porgy and Bess" (1935) wasn't directly about the blues, it bore blues themes. Charles Ives and Aaron Copland were among the American classical composers who spoke of the influence blues and other American vernacular music forms had on their own music. In literature, Langston Hughes, Zora Neale Hurston, and Ralph Ellison brought the blues into their poetry, prose, and essays.

The fascination for blues finally spread into the conventional worlds of academia and governmental institutions. Beginning in the late 1920s and continuing through much of the Depression era, John Lomax, with eventual help from his son, Alan, collected American folk music, mostly for the Library of Congress. For the Lomaxes, music was the pathway into the soul of America. Together they traveled throughout the South, driving the back roads with a tape recorder, searching for songs that told stories and revealed something about the national character. Churches, fields, back porches,

even prisons were all places they visited in search of American music.

At the Angola Prison Farm in Louisiana they discovered a convicted murderer, Huddie Ledbetter, better known as Lead Belly, who could play guitar and sing songs that reflected African-American culture precisely the way the Lomaxes thought they should. In 1934 Lead Belly earned a pardon from prison after writing a song about Louisiana governor O.K. Allen, in which Lead Belly pleaded for his release. It is not certain how much influence, if any, John Lomax exerted on Allen, but upon going free, Lead Belly began a more formal association with the Lomax family, moving to New York and becoming the elder Lomax's chauffeur. Lead Belly also began a recording career in the mid-thirties, and although his music seemed out-of-date and too "downhome" for urban blacks, the folk-blues singer struck a warm chord with white audiences, which viewed Lead Belly as an authentic black blues and folk specimen. Young left-leaning radicals in New York embraced him, and Lead Belly gave them back the kind of music that often attacked the bourgeois.

Interest in authentic black music was best represented in 1938 and '39 by John Hammond's From Spirituals to Swing concerts at Carnegie Hall, which brought together black artists from all walks of sacred and secular music. One of the artists he sought most was Robert Johnson; Hammond was fascinated with the sides that Johnson had cut for producer Don Law and hoped to present this mysterious Mississippi bluesman to New York's urbane music audience, much like an anthropologist might share artifacts from an exotic culture. Hammond, however, was too late. The first concert was slated for December 1938; Johnson had been murdered a few months earlier.

Despite his disappointment in not featuring Johnson, Hammond presented a number of amazing black artists in his From Spirituals to Swing event, which was a great critical success, prompting Hammond to stage a second show the following year. But 1939 would be more remembered as the start of World War II. And even though Germany's aggression in Poland and later the Low Countries occurred thousands of miles away from the flatlands of the Mississippi Delta, east Texas, and the Carolinas, blacks, and the blues, would be seriously impacted by the events. The world grew darker with each passing month, as war spread through Europe and the threat of war grew stronger in Asia. America was on the sidelines in this brewing epic battle between democracy and fascism, but not for long. On December 7, 1941, the Japanese bombed Pearl Harbor, forcing the U.S. to declare war on Japan. Two days later, America also went to war with Germany and Italy. The world would never be the same, and neither would the blues.

⊕　⊕　⊕　⊕　⊕

The story of the blues in the 1940s is the story of a people and a music on the move. The war years created opportunities for African-Americans that had never been presented before, and thousands were eager to take advantage. Beginning in 1940, black sharecroppers, farm hands, and laborers, often with their entire families in tow, left the South for northern cities where work in war factories was plentiful—and profitable. Nearly three million blacks left the South between 1940 and 1960. The migration was one of the largest shifts of people in twentieth-century America, and cities such as Chicago, Cleveland, Gary, Detroit, Pittsburgh, Philadelphia, Newark, and New York saw a dramatic rise in their black population. Out west, Los Angeles, San Francisco, Oakland, and Seattle saw similar changes.

This wasn't the first black exodus from the South, just the largest. During World War I factories up North were faced with a shrinking work force as young white males joined the armed services to fight in Europe. Northern black newspapers such as the *Chicago Defender* and the *Pittsburgh Courier* persuaded black workers to leave the fields for factories. Thousands came, despite the hardships that went with the journey north, including cases of discrimination that were nearly as bad as those they had fled. The onset of the Depression dampened the prospects for economic opportunities up North, but still a steady stream of black workers made the trek anyway.

World War II quickly put an end to the last vestiges of the Depression. Trains bound for Chicago were filled with young blacks looking for a chance to break out of the poverty that prevailed back home. They brought with them their music—the blues. And as black workers settled into a new, urban life, they relied on their music to see them through. Listening to the old country-blues sounds was a way to cure—or bring on—homesickness. But eventually, country blues began to sound out of place in the big city. For the blues to remain an important part of black culture, it had to absorb new ideas, new sounds, new ways of delivering the emotional highs and lows of black country folk in the big city. And that's exactly what happened.

The quest for volume resulted in one of the biggest changes in the blues. An acoustic guitar and accompanying voice sounded plenty loud in a juke joint or on a back porch in Mississippi. But up North, the acoustic guitar and vocals were frequently overwhelmed by the din of a nightclub and the busy sounds of a street corner. Beginning in the mid-

1930s, some jazz guitarists began experimenting with the electric guitar, transforming the instrument from one that was full-strumming and rhythmic to one on which single-string solos could be played and heard. The electric guitar also broadened the possibilities for new tones and textures.

One of the earliest blues musicians to make a musical statement using an electric guitar was Aaron "T-Bone" Walker, who began playing the instrument in the late 1930s. Walker's sound was smooth, richly complex, and very jazzlike. Little of what he played had hard connections to country blues. Electrifying country blues so they could survive in an urban setting fell to a young Mississippi transplant to Chicago by the name of McKinley Morganfield, whose friends called him Muddy Waters. In the process of modernizing country blues, Waters created a sound that was bigger, louder, and hotter than practically anything that had come before it.

The roots of the early electric blues that Waters played came out of the country-blues sounds of Charley Patton, Son House, and Robert Johnson. In 1941, just a couple of years before Waters moved to Chicago, Alan Lomax had come across him in Rolling Fork, Mississippi, where Lomax recorded the young bluesman for the Library of Congress. Waters sang and played as if he were the natural descendant of Johnson and the rest of the early blues greats. He carried this classic country-blues sound, with its slashing slide guitar and raw chords, to Chicago. Once there, Waters began to adapt the blues and his delivery of the music to what he heard around him.

Waters wouldn't have made the impact he did without the means to get his music out. Fortunately, two brothers, Phil and Leonard Chess, Polish Jews who had gone into the nightclub business in Chicago, decided to broaden their reach. Believing bigger money was possible in the making and selling of records, the Chess brothers bought into the nascent Aristocrat label in 1947, which had been issuing jazz discs, and began looking for blues talent to record. The Chess brothers hit pay dirt when they brought Waters into the recording studio to cut "I Can't Be Satisfied" and "I Feel Like Going Home," with bass accompaniment by Big Crawford in 1948. It wasn't the first time that Waters recorded in Chicago. In 1946, two years after he had begun using an electric guitar, Waters recorded for Lester Melrose, but his performance was less than convincing. In February 1948, Waters first recorded for Leonard Chess, but Chess was not impressed, either. Nonetheless, Chess brought Waters back into the studio in April of that year. The session began with a couple songs that included Sunnyland Slim on piano and Crawford on bass. There was little magic. Unfazed, Waters decided to play a pair of songs that he had recorded for Lomax back in Mississippi. But there were differences: Waters was seven years older and more mature as a bluesman, and where he once recorded the songs with an acoustic guitar, this time it was with an electric, an instrument that now felt right at home in Waters' rugged hands.

Waters' sound was steeped in country blues, which would appeal to those blacks just up from Mississippi and homesick. "I Feel Like Going Home" was all about longing for a familiar place. But when the song was performed on the electric guitar, Waters gave it a new vitality. It *sounded* like it was recorded in Chicago, even though it had been written in Mississippi. It was old *and* new, country *and* urban. As for the A side, "I Can't Be Satisfied," Waters sang and played it with an urgency and a vigor that smacked of sexual frustration. It was a one-two punch, and although Leonard Chess had not yet understood what made for a great blues performance—he was irritated by his inability to understand what Waters sang—he reluctantly agreed to put out the record and see what happened.

What happened was that nearly all three thousand copies of the song sold in one day. Waters' success caused a number of things to happen. First, it put him on a path to blues stardom and solidified his career as a recording artist. Second, it began the transformation of Aristocrat from a jazz to a blues label. Third, it regained for Chicago the attention of the blues fans; the city now shared the spotlight with Memphis, at a time when equally exciting things were happening blueswise in that city. And fourth, it announced that a new blues sound and a new blues era were dawning. Muddy's record had an effect that would continue to resonate unlike any blues recording of its era.

Despite the success of his first record, Waters continued to search for a richer and fuller sound. Waters had begun to play black clubs and beer joints on the South Side of Chicago with a band that included Little Walter Jacobs, a harmonica player; drummer Elgin Evans; and another guitarist, Jimmy Rodgers. Amplification wasn't just an asset with Waters. Little Walter deftly played his harmonica into the microphone, which he used as an extension of his instrument rather than merely as a means to increase its volume. And when Evans punctuated this new blues sound with a steady backbeat, dance floors got crowded—and fast. Soon other blues bands began forming in Chicago, permanently transforming the music and its place in American history.

Blues bands were reshaping the music in Memphis, too. In addition to its Delta connection and Beale Street, Memphis also had WDIA, the nation's first all-black-format radio station that hired upstarts like a young Riley King to spin blues records and plug Pepticon, a cure-all tonic. A guitar player and aspiring bluesman, King had moved from Mississippi to Memphis, where he met Sonny Boy Williamson, a blues singer and harmonica player who understood the value of radio.

In 1941, Williamson and guitarist Robert "Junior" Lockwood (who had been taught to play by Robert Johnson when Johnson was living with Lockwood's mother) approached KFFA, a station in Helena, Arkansas, about doing a live blues show on the air. The manager agreed, sensing the opportunity for the duo to push King Biscuit Flour to black listeners. Each day at noon the group, which would eventually include Peck Curtis on drums and Dudlow Taylor on piano, played for fifteen minutes on the KFFA King Biscuit Flour Time, with the Interstate Grocer Company as its sponsor.

King Biscuit Flour Time was a big success; sales soared and Sonny Boy and his blues buddies grew more popular than they'd ever been in the Delta, since the station blanketed the region. The show eventually also featured Sonny Payne, a white announcer and friend of Lockwood's, who gave the show stability when Williamson got the itch to wander—which, after 1944, was often. After cutting a series of seminal sides for the Jackson, Mississippi–based Trumpet label that proved Williamson's talent

"Of all the blues artists that we love, our favorites would probably be Son House, Blind Willie McTell, and Skip James—but it's Robert Johnson who inspired and influenced us most. He was a full-ranged, truly beautiful singer; good and evil are equally present in his songs. A tagalong to Charley Patton, Son House, and Willie Brown, Johnson in most ways surpassed them all. He outsang, outplayed, and outperformed all of the greats of his time in that area of Mississippi, even though he wasn't as popular as them."

—Jack White, The White Stripes

Willie Dixon, Muddy Waters, and Buddy Guy *(from left)* cut some sides in the Chess studio, 1964.

not only as a harmonica player but also as a singer, songwriter, and bandleader, Williamson left another mark in Chicago in the 1950s, cutting sides for Chess and rivaling Little Walter as the city's most innovative blues harp player.

Riley King, who on the air in Memphis was known as "Blues Boy" or "B.B." King, used his time at WDIA to build a reputation in the blues community and to study the many records he had at his disposal. King might have been a cotton picker and tractor driver in Mississippi, but his taste in music was very cultured, and he preferred jazz as much as he did downhome blues. King was struck by the elaborate guitar musings of Charlie Christian and T-Bone Walker and loved a lush big-band blues sound that a hot horn section could provide.

King also admired Louis Jordan, one of the most popular black recording artists of the day. Jordan had scaled down the big-band idea to a more economical "combo" in the years after World War II, when black America seemed to be searching for a fresher sound that was a bit different from the swing bands. Using fewer musicians and insisting on driving dance rhythms with bluesy strains, Jordan created a new "jump" blues sound that would fall under the banner of rhythm & blues in the late 1940s. Jordan also had a knack for spicing up his songs with humor and jive, thus giving "Ain't Nobody Here but Us Chickens," "Is You Is, or Is You Ain't (My Baby)," "Five Guys Named Moe," and "Caldonia" an irresistible charm.

Jump blues replaced swing as the music of choice in black nightclubs, and there were dozens of black bands, singers, and musicians creating the sounds. Jump blues bands featured "honking" saxophones and "shouting" singers. At times the music was rowdy and raw, but the insistence was always that the blues "jump." This was feel-good music: The war was over, the nation's economic footing was firmer than ever, and there existed hope that the gains made by African-Americans in the 1940s would not only stick but enable still more progress to be made in eliminating racial prejudice in America. So the feeling up North and on the West Coast, where jump blues was particularly popular, was best summed up by Jordan when he sang, "Let the good times roll!"

B.B. King took what he learned from Charlie Christian, T-Bone Walker, and Jordan, fused it with his experiences gained by playing and hanging with other Memphis blues musicians like Bobby "Blue" Bland, Rosco Gordon, and Johnny Ace (known loosely as the Beale Streeters), and turned it all into a sound that made a big impact in the blues community. King began his recording career in 1949; two years later he had a Number One hit on the fledgling rhythm & blues charts with "Three O'Clock Blues." King was as good a singer as he was a guitarist, always stressing a gospel influence. And with his penchant to get the most out of his band, King and company crisscrossed the country in a bus playing one-night stands in nightclubs and roadhouses, becoming one of the most popular blues bands in 1950s America.

Despite the popularity of the music in the postwar years, the business of the blues was shaky, shady, exploitative, and driven almost entirely by the chance to make a quick buck at the expense of naive musicians. More times than not, blues musicians received a single payment for a recording session; royalties were unheard of in the blues world. Similarly, songwriters were paid a fee for their songs and often had to share credit for composing the music with a producer or record company owner. By

B.B. King *(far left)* and his band spent endless days and nights on the road beginning in the late 1940s.

the late 1940s, most of the major record companies had lost interest in the blues. This gave a chance for a slew of small, independent record labels like Chess, RPM, Modern, Bullet, and others to gain control of the blues market.

A Memphis recording service owned by Sam Phillips, conveniently called the Memphis Recording Service, cut tracks by a number of blues artists, including B.B. King, James Cotton, Walter Horton, Little Junior Parker, and a big strapping hulk of a bluesman known as Howlin' Wolf, who had arrived in West Memphis in 1948, leaving behind the life of a Mississippi sharecropper. Phillips understood black music, wasn't afraid to record it (even though Memphis was one of the mid-South's most segregated cities), and believed the blues was an important American music form, though at the time it was made by black artists for black audiences. Phillips' outfit leased blues recordings for release by other small labels, eventually releasing some on his own label, Sun, until a young white singer named Elvis Presley showed up one day in 1954. With Phillips' encouragement, Presley revolutionized popular music by taking a blues song, Arthur "Big Boy" Crudup's "That's All Right," hyping its rhythm with a nervous, youthful energy, and singing it like no one had sung a blues song before. Unknowingly, Presley created a brand-new hybrid sound: rock & roll.

Presley had everything in place to make history. For starters, he stumbled into Sun Records, where Phillips was looking for someone white who could sing convincingly in a black style. Going anywhere else to make a record, like, say, Nashville, a few hours east of Memphis, where white singers made the city the capital of country music, would have probably meant Elvis would have never been discovered. Second, not only had Elvis absorbed the sounds of black gospel and blues growing up in

Tupelo, Mississippi, before relocating to Memphis, but he genuinely loved black music, which gave his music honesty and sincerity. And finally, Presley was young (not yet twenty years old when he first recorded for Phillips), remarkably handsome, sexy but in a safe, innocent way, and white. Also, being musically astute, he had a firm grasp of country music, white gospel, and the pop music of the day as exemplified by crooner Dean Martin.

Elvis Presley blended the best elements of white and black music and culture and, with Phillips' guidance, turned the mix into rock & roll and a musical explosion, the power of which had never been felt before, not even in the 1920s, when blues and jazz captured the imagination of young America. The blues was also impacted by the sudden birth of rock & roll in the early 1950s. Black artists began looking more to rock & roll and less to the blues for musical success, especially those who had been singing a very blues-based, black rock & roll prototype—Little Richard, Fats Domino, Ike Turner, Big Joe Turner. So did rhythm & blues singers like Wynonie Harris and Roy Brown, both of whom had big-selling records in 1948 with a song called "Good Rockin' Tonight." The young white audience that embraced rock & roll was larger and richer than the black blues and rhythm & blues communities.

A young black man from the St. Louis area with looks as striking as Presley's and an equal understanding of the formula that mixed black blues with white country, guitarist Chuck Berry wrote his own songs and was just brash enough to think his sound could appeal to both black and white audiences. Berry went to Chicago in 1955 to see about recording his music for Chess. Later that year Chess issued Berry's "Maybellene," a song with even more musical significance than Presley's "That's All Right," since it was an original composition

(though inspired by a country standard, "Ida Red"), not a cover of an already existing song. And it was performed by a black man.

Music historians may argue that Berry's history-making record was predated by Ike Turner and Jackie Brenston nearly four years earlier in Memphis

Little Walter played harmonica with Muddy Waters' band and became a solo blues star with the hit "My Babe."

at the Sun studio, when they recorded a song called "Rocket 88," which was released by Chess in 1951. Depending on one's definition of rock & roll and interpretation of who gave birth to it and where, a good case can be made for Turner and Brenston as being the first rock & roll artists, black or white. But all historians and critics would agree that neither Turner nor Brenston had the social and cultural components in place in 1951 to cause the stir that Presley and Berry did a few years later. With Berry, Chess broadened its catalogue to include black rock & roll artists, making an impact on American music that rivaled Sun's.

In addition to Berry, Chess scored commercially with Bo Diddley, a black artist whose signature guitar sound featured a rhythm that bounced and boogied and whose songs often contained a beat— the "Bo Diddley" beat—built on a previous black beat described as "shave 'n' a haircut, two bits." Born Otha Ellas Bates in McComb, Mississippi, in 1928, Bo Diddley was adopted as a child, and his name became Ellas Bates McDaniels when his family moved to Chicago in 1934. After playing around the Windy City in blues bands in the early 1950s, Diddley signed a recording contract with Chess in 1955. His debut record—the self-titled "Bo Diddley," backed by the bluesy "I'm a Man"—made him nearly as big a star as Chuck Berry. But Berry was able to follow up the success of "Maybellene" with nearly two dozen other Chess hits.

Chess Records released its share of rock & roll records in the 1950s, but it ruled the blues during the music's golden decade. No other label produced as many seminal artists or recordings or did as much to bring the blues into the modern era. Muddy Waters was the label's first—and biggest— blues artist. But he was surrounded by a group of other artists, some of whom played in his bands

(Little Walter, Jimmy Rogers, Junior Wells, James Cotton, Otis Spann) and later became stars in their own right, some of whom were recording rivals (Howlin' Wolf, Sonny Boy Williamson), and some of whom were critical behind-the-scene players, vital to Waters' success (Willie Dixon).

That Chess was a Chicago-based recording company cannot be underestimated. During the black migration north in the 1940s, which continued unabated in the fifties, hundreds of blues artists settled in the Windy City, as did hundreds of thousands of transplanted black blues record buyers, in effect creating a fertile field of blues talent *and* a large enthusiastic audience for the records Chess issued. Detroit also had a thriving blues scene in the postwar years. New York had become the home not only of Lead Belly but also of Reverend Gary Davis, Josh White, Sonny Terry, Brownie McGhee, and other bluesmen relocated from the Carolinas and the Piedmont region along the Eastern Seaboard as early as the thirties and forties. The Memphis blues scenes continued to thrive in the 1950s, as did the scene in St. Louis and East St. Louis, the nearly all-black community across the Mississippi River in Illinois. Out on the West Coast, Los Angeles and Oakland contributed a blues sound that often was smoother and softer than the sounds back east, courtesy of artists such as singer/pianist Charles Brown. But none of these cities could match Chicago's blues power. In the 1950s, Chicago became "home of the blues," and Chess was the kitchen where the music was made.

The chef was Willie Dixon. In the studio he produced records, played bass on them, wrote and arranged songs, oversaw session musicians, befriended artists and offered advice, and acted as talent scout. He also made his own records, although, as a recording artist, he never could match the success of Muddy Waters and Howlin' Wolf, the two Chess bluesmen who benefited most from Dixon's many talents. Both Waters and Wolf relied on Dixon for songs, in particular. Two of Waters' best records—"Hoochie Coochie Man" and "I Just Want to Make Love to You"—were written by Dixon, while Wolf scored with such Dixon numbers as "Spoonful," "Little Red Rooster," "I Ain't Superstitious," and "Back Door Man." Dixon also gave Little Walter "My Babe," which was a big hit for the singer/harmonica player; and to Sonny Boy Williamson went "Bring It On Home."

Dixon had arrived in Chicago from Vicksburg, Mississippi, as early as 1936, not to play the blues but to pursue a career as a prizefighter. He won the Illinois State Golden Gloves heavyweight championship and turned pro, but after only a few fights he hung up his gloves and picked up the bass. After serving prison time as a conscientious objector for refusing to serve in the armed forces, Dixon played bass in a number of groups, most notably the Big Three Trio, which recorded blues and pop from 1947 to 1952. During this time Dixon met Phil and Leonard Chess at a popular blues club they owned, the Macomba Lounge, and began working for their label in 1948. Hiring Dixon would be one of the Chess brothers' smartest moves. By 1954, Dixon's input was critical to the success of the Chess sound.

In addition to Chess, there were many other independent record companies that were part of the postwar blues story—Atlantic and Fire in New York; the aforementioned Sun in Memphis; Modern, RPM, Aladdin, and Specialty in Los Angeles; Peacock and Duke out of Houston; Trumpet from Jackson, Mississippi; Nashville's Excello and Bullet; Newark's Savoy; King from Cincinnati; and Vee Jay and Cobra from Chicago. Together, these and other

labels made more blues available to the record-buying public than ever before.

And it wasn't just Chess artists who made the most exciting blues statements on record. In addition to B.B. King, there were dozens more major blues artists who played a part in the golden age of electric blues. John Lee Hooker moved to Detroit from Mississippi in 1943, finding opportunity on Hastings Street, Detroit's version of Memphis' Beale Street. Hooker's brand of boogie-blues and his dark, low-slung, sexually provocative vocals made him one of the most popular of the non-Chess recording artists. Hooker's landmark record "Boogie Chillen" captured the music's primal energy and simplicity; the one-chord boogie drone was hypnotic. In the song Hooker tells how he heard "Papa tell Mama, let that boy boogie-woogie," which is exactly what Hooker did, becoming the dark prince of boogie blues.

By most accounts, Jimmy Reed could drink just as effectively as he could sing and play the blues. Recording mostly for Vee Jay, Reed created a slow-drag, easygoing blues sound that was downright irresistible. Eighteen of Reed's records made it onto the *Billboard* R&B charts from 1955 to 1961, including such blues chestnuts as "Honest I Do," "Big Boss Man," and "Bright Lights, Big City." Working with boyhood friend Eddie Taylor, who taught Reed how to play guitar, and his wife, Mary Lee "Mama" Reed, who helped Reed compose his songs and get him through recording sessions despite his penchant for drink, Reed was one of the blues' most popular artists in the 1950s. As compared to Muddy Waters and Howlin' Wolf, who confronted their listeners with gritty, urgent blues, Reed stroked his audience with laid-back blues grooves that hit a responsive chord almost immediately. With his nonthreatening vocals, soft

Slide guitar stylist Elmore James

harmonica riffs, and walking bass lines, Reed and his blues were impossible not to like.

Elmore James brought new excitement to the slide guitar style that had been a staple of the blues since the 1920s. Using Robert Johnson as his main inspiration, James created a riveting slide technique first heard in "Dust My Broom," his epic 1952 reinvention of the Robert Johnson classic "I Believe I'll Dust My Broom" for the label Trumpet that featured slurred, hell-raising notes that whooped with emotion. The main slide riff in the James

version was used time and again by the guitarist in future recordings and became so identifiable that any blues slide guitar player worth his salt had to master it and include it in his or her guitar vocabulary.

Like so many other bluesmen, James was born in Mississippi. After learning the rudiments of the guitar, playing with Sonny Boy Williamson, and serving in the navy during World War II, James returned to Mississippi, where he played in a series of makeshift bands before getting the chance to record for Trumpet in 1952. Riding the success of his Trumpet recordings, James moved to Chicago, formed a group, the Broomdusters, and recorded for the Meteor label. By the late fifties he had struck a deal with Bobby Robinson's New York–based Fire Records, which released some of his best post-Trumpet recordings, including "The Sky Is Crying" and "Done Somebody Wrong." Unfortunately, James died of a heart attack in 1963, never having quite reached the level of acclaim enjoyed by Muddy Waters, Howlin' Wolf, and other Chess artists.

Ever since Blind Lemon Jefferson became one of the most important country-blues artists of the 1920s, Texas had been a state with a remarkably rich blues tradition. Texas Alexander, Sippie Wallace, and T-Bone Walker all hailed from the Lone Star State, as did Sam "Lightnin' " Hopkins, one of the most prolific and consistently popular blues musicians of the twentieth century. Hopkins was a cousin of Texas Alexander, one of the best pre-war blues singers to come out of Texas, and his earliest blues connection was with Blind Lemon Jefferson, who influenced Hopkins' emerging blues guitar style. Just after World War II, Hopkins began his recording career, which, when it finally ended in the late seventies (Hopkins died in 1982), amounted to hundreds of recordings with nearly two dozen labels.

Hopkins recorded as a solo artist, as part of a duet, and with a band. He was a master improviser, making up songs on the spot, reshaping melodies and lyrics to fit a particular moment or audience, and cutting one song into another. "Depending on how he felt or what day it was or whether the moon was full, Lightnin' was just totally unpredictable," recalled Chris Strachwitz, who recorded Hopkins for his Arhoolie label in the sixties. Many of Hopkins' songs were autobiographical; humor was an element that could often be found in his music. In the end, Lightnin' Hopkins was a blues machine, producing one good blues record after another.

In the 1950s the blues went international. From its inception, jazz was viewed by Europeans, particularly the British and French, as something exotically American and therefore, alluring. Beginning as early as the last quarter of the nineteenth century, when the Fisk Jubilee Singers toured England and parts of Europe, African-American music began to be embraced by European and British art crowds. In the early twentieth century, bandleaders such as James Reese Europe and, later, singer Josephine Baker, made their marks overseas. Louis Armstrong, Duke Ellington, and other jazz artists toured there in the 1930s. After World War II, the appetite for American recordings broadened. Merchant seamen would trade or sell records in ports such as Liverpool and London before distribution agreements with American record companies were in place. Collectors and American music fans there treasured rare copies of Chess recordings and knew well the excitement created by the blues, even if it was experienced only on vinyl.

The first country-blues singer to perform overseas was Lead Belly, in France in 1949, shortly before his death, and then Josh White and Lonnie Johnson the following year. In 1951, and then again a year later, Big Bill Broonzy played Great Britain and France. Knowledge of Broonzy and other African-American folk-blues artists came from musicologist Alan Lomax and his frequent music shows on BBC radio and television. Adventures in Folk Song and Patterns in American Song were two of Lomax's most popular radio shows that aired on the BBC. They cultivated a small but growing audience for American folk and blues music in England. Thanks to the encouragement of Lomax and Hugues Panassie, a French jazz fanatic and the editor of the publication *Jazz Hot*, Broonzy played a series of dates that introduced live American folk blues from the concert stage to French and British audiences.

Broonzy had had trouble maintaining his popularity with African-American blues fans in the years just after World War II. Smartly, Broonzy had seen how young white intellectuals, especially in New York City, had embraced the blues as a treasured folk music from a disenfranchised people. Lead Belly, Josh White, and others had done well with whites by playing folk blues. Broonzy decided he would do the same. He began playing college coffeehouses and small folk-music clubs in the States; his success there gave him the courage to try Europe with its equally white audiences. The trip paid off, as Broonzy in the 1950s became one of the best-known American blues artists outside America.

Other artists followed in Broonzy's path, most notably Sonny Terry and Brownie McGhee, followed by Muddy Waters in 1958, Champion Jack Dupree in 1959, and Memphis Slim, Roosevelt Sykes, James Cotton, Little Brother Montgomery, Willie Dixon, and Jesse Fuller in 1960. The arrival of the new decade saw interest in electric Chicago blues recede in the

American black community. Record sales stopped growing. Waters' near-decade run of hits had slowed down; there was little in the way of new ideas or energy coming from Waters and Wolf, though they continued to make exemplary recordings. The sound was somewhat stale, if the songs weren't.

But there was something else happening in the black community in the mid-1950s: a new determination to gain self-respect and equality in white-dominated America. A young preacher from Atlanta, Reverend Martin Luther King Jr., pushed for reform through nonviolence. On December 1, 1955, a tired housewoman, Rosa Parks, refused to sit in the back of a Montgomery, Alabama, bus, prompting a boycott of the city's transit system by blacks. Suddenly, it seemed as if African-Americans all over had gained the courage to speak out, step out, cry out in frustration—and do something about it. For a growing number of young black activists, the blues was music from another era.

The African-American civil rights movement caused monumental change, not just in black culture but in all America. The blues stood by while African-Americans, mostly young, took to the streets and demanded justice. A new music form suddenly seemed to appear out of nowhere. It was called soul music.

Soul counted blues and rhythm & blues among its roots, but it also drew heavily from gospel and pop. There was more melodic freedom in soul; the traditional A-A-B blues form was only acknowledged, not followed as if it were the main musical source. Improvised vocalizing, the kind that made gospel so dynamic, was an important soul ingredient, as was the call-and-response delivery, a standard strategy in most forms of gospel. And where in blues the guitar was a primary means of expression, in soul the human voice knew no competition.

Ray Charles is often considered to be the author of the first big-selling soul song. In 1959 his "What'd I Say" topped the *Billboard* rhythm & blues charts. Though the song had as many R&B roots as it did prototype soul sounds, it did mark a change in black music. By the time a young, ambitious assembly line worker from the automotive factories of Detroit started a record company called Motown, soul was on its way to redefining black music, much the way Muddy Waters and Chess Records did a generation earlier. To young black ears, soul sounded in sync with the times. People were moving forward in their thinking and actions, dreams suddenly seemed possible, the world could be changed, things could happen. For many young African-Americans, soul music reflected all of these feelings.

The blues, though, didn't dry up and die. On the contrary: The music came to a crossroads and took a different turn. Along the way the music picked up a new audience—white people. In England in the early sixties interest in the blues and blues culture took off with young musicians absorbing every blues recording that came their way. Bands formed and dedicated themselves to replicating the blues. The early British blues advocates had also been fans of American folk music and jazz. They enjoyed skiffle, a homegrown hodgepodge of English and American folk and traditional music, with a nod toward pop. Lonnie Donegan, skiffle's most popular recording artist, recorded Lead Belly's "Rock Island Line" in 1954 and turned it into a huge hit in England. Chris Barber and Alexis Korner collected jazz and blues records and played the music as well. It was Barber who organized the tour with Sonny Terry and Brownie McGhee in the U.K. and who arranged for Muddy Waters to follow shortly thereafter. Together with Cyril Davies and John Mayall, Barber and

Korner laid the foundation for the sixties British blues movement, inspiring young musicians such as Eric Burdon (the Animals); Eric Clapton (the Yardbirds); Jack Bruce (Cream); Graham Bond and Long John Baldry (Blues Incorporated); Mick Jagger, Keith Richards, Brian Jones, Bill Wyman, and Charlie Watts (the Rolling Stones); Mick Fleetwood and Peter Green (Fleetwood Mac); and many others to form blues-based bands and give the music a new path.

The 1961 release of *King of the Delta Blues Singers* made Robert Johnson's music available to blues fans and musicians. Aspiring guitarists on both sides of the Atlantic threw themselves into *King of the Delta Blues Singers* as if it unveiled the blues' deepest secrets. Many tried, but few mastered Johnson's guitar style. Eventually, the best of the young British blues players picked up enough riffs to acceptably interpret the blues. What they lacked, of course, was authenticity. Not being American, their life experiences did not have the cultural and racial underpinnings to express blues nuances. The blues evolved out of a distinctively black tradition that even many white Americans had trouble

Big Bill Broonzy found a new audience in coffeehouses in the 1950s.

identifying with. Being British and white was a double disadvantage.

Still, bands like the Rolling Stones, who had formed around 1962, persevered. Named after "Rolling Stone," a popular Muddy Waters song, each member of the band shared an adoration for the blues that seemed to know no bounds. An early sixties performance by the Stones might have included interpretations of such American blues gems as Elmore James' "Dust My Broom," Muddy Waters' "I Want to Be Loved" and "Tiger in Your Tank," and Jimmy Reed's "Bright Lights, Big City."

European blues fans were fortunate that two Germans, Horst Lippman and Fritz Rau, decided to launch an American blues tour of the Continent in 1962 that featured the likes of T-Bone Walker, Willie Dixon, John Lee Hooker, and others. First calling their endeavor the American Negro Blues Festival, the promoters later changed it to the American Folk Blues Festival and kept it going annually through 1971. Attending the festival was like going to blues college for aspiring British and European blues musicians. Dozens of major blues artists toured with the American Folk Blues Festival during its tenure, giving bluesmen and blueswomen new audiences and enabling blues fans beyond the States to experience and enjoy the music firsthand.

The American Folk Blues Festival opened up other English and European possibilities for the blues. When Sonny Boy Williamson toured England in 1963, he wore an English bowler's hat and a dapper pinstripe suit, and worked in front of the Yardbirds, with Eric Clapton on guitar. Williamson didn't think much of the band or British blues audiences, but he didn't mind the paycheck. It was considerably more than he could earn in America at the time. When bluesman Big Joe Williams received his money after the end of an English tour,

he cried. It was much more than he had ever earned in his life.

Back home, however, black audiences, particularly young ones, continued to move away from the blues and closer to soul. All but abandoned was acoustic-driven country blues, which simply summed up too many painful memories of Jim Crow, sharecropping, and lynchings. The genre was saved, however, by young white kids, many of them in college, who had grown bored with the current crop of homogenized rock & rollers, or teen idols. Bobby Rydell, Fabian, and Bobby Vee eschewed the rebellious, sexually overt sounds and styles of such pioneering rockers as Elvis Presley, Chuck Berry, Jerry Lee Lewis, Eddie Cochran, Gene Vincent, and others for a teen sound that was as dangerous—and as exciting—as white bread.

On college campuses across America in the early sixties, folk music, with its heady lyrics and authentic sounds, attracted listeners eager for a more meaningful music experience. Country blues fit right in with the growing fascination with bluegrass, hillbilly, Cajun, and traditional music from Appalachia and the Ozarks. Suddenly, a full-fledged folk music revival was in swing in America.

The first major folk festival of the "folk revival," a term most folkies hated since they believed folk music never went away in the first place, was in Newport, Rhode Island—on the surface, an unlikely setting since it was a vacation community for the rich. But with a jazz festival already in place there, music impresario George Wein used its infra-structure and introduced a prototype folk festival in 1959, the weekend after the Newport Jazz Festival.

Among other roots music artists, the Newport Folk Festival featured Robert Pete Williams, a country-blues singer from Louisiana, found at

Angola Prison Farm by Dr. Harry Oster, a folklorist in the Lomax mold. Lomax was still such a powerful figure in American folk music that it was only a matter of time before others would venture off in search of undiscovered music talent in the hills, bayous, fields, and prisons of America. Oster was a certified folklorist; he had the Ph.D. to prove it. Another roots music enthusiast and aspiring musician, Ralph Rinzler, worked for the Smithsonian. But others, amateurs, really, set out to do the work of folklorists in the early and mid-sixties based on their passion for the music. Young white country-blues fans, such as Dick Waterman, Phil Spiro, Nick Perls, guitarist John Fahey, and later Chris Strachwitz, bought tape recorders, hopped into cars, and headed south for Mississippi, Tennessee, and other southern states to mine music gold. And they did. Son House was rediscovered (in Rochester, New York, of all places); so were Skip James, Mississippi John Hurt, Mississippi Fred McDowell, Sippie Wallace, Little Brother Montgomery, Sleepy John Estes, Bukka White, Furry Lewis, Mance Lipscomb, and others. Pulled from poverty and obscurity, many of them having given up performing and making records long ago, these country-blues artists were now playing the Newport festival in one of the wealthiest communities in America for northern white audiences who adored their authentic sounds. Few of these bluesmen minded, though it was obvious to them that the atmosphere was circuslike and their new fans viewed them curiously, like relics. House and James and a few others had their recording careers resuscitated by the folk revival. Many of the other blues artists who were invited to play Newport in the early sixties also found work on city concert stages and the college coffeehouse circuit, as well as the other folk festivals that were sprouting up all over the country.

"PRISONER'S TALKING BLUES"
By Robert Pete Williams

[*Spoken:*] Lord I feel so bad sometime,
Seem like that I'm weakenin' every day
You know I begin to get gray since I got here
Well, a whole lot of worry cause that.
But I can feel myself weakenin',
I don't keep well no more
I keeps sickly.
I takes a lot of medicine, but it look like it don't do no good.
All I have to do is pray, that's the only thing that'll help me here,
One foot in the grave look like
And the other one out.
Sometime it look like my best day gotta be my last day
Sometime I feel like I never see my little ole kids anymore
But if I don't never see 'em no more, leave 'em in the hands of God.
You know, my sister, she like a mother to me
She do all in the world that she can
She went all the way along with me in this trouble 'til the end.
In a way, I was glad my poor mother had [de]ceased
Because she suffered with heart trouble,
And trouble behind me sho' woulda went hard with her.
But if she was livin', I could call on her sometime.
But my old father's dead, too,
That make me be motherless and fatherless.
It's six of us sisters, three boys
Family done got smaller now, look like they're dyin' out fast.
I don't know, but God been good to us in a way,
'Cause ole death have stayed away a long time.

[*Sung:*] Lord, my worry sure carryin' me down,
Lord, my worry sure is carryin' me down.
Sometime I feel like, baby, committin' suicide. [*repeat*]
I got the nerve if I just had somethin' to do it with.
I'm goin' down slow, somethin' wrong with me [*repeat*]
I got to make a change whilst that I'm young,
If I don't, I won't never get old.

Mississippi blues greats Skip James *(left)* and Son House were both rediscovered in 1964.

Electric blues would be thrown a life preserver by whites, too. In 1960 Muddy Waters brought his band to play the Newport Jazz Festival. As Robert Gordon remarked in *Can't Be Satisfied: The Life and Times of Muddy Waters,* "The terms of Muddy's personal acquaintance with white America were established at the Newport Jazz Festival . . . he dropped in on the folk scene like a museum exhibit from the wild—jungle music authenticated by jungle

men." Waters and his band ripped up Newport, demonstrating that the fervor and ferociousness of electric blues remained and proving that although electric blues might have lost its luster with young blacks, the music still owned a vitality that could match that of soul or rock.

Black Chicago didn't abandon the blues the way other cities did; the music was just too embedded in the culture and day-to-day survival there. On the South Side, black clubs and joints like Pepper's and Theresa's continued to feature blues, giving older musicians a place to perform and socialize and younger players a place to learn. By the mid-sixties, the Chicago blues scene had produced a brand-new crop of musicians who guaranteed that electric blues would continue to thrive. Guitarists Buddy Guy, Freddie King, Otis Rush, Earl Hooker, and Magic Sam forged a more modern blues guitar sound. Their talent was such that, on occasion, you'd never think there was any other black music but the blues attracting young black music talent. All five guitarists cut their blues teeth in Chicago clubs, learning from the Chess blues masters, yet creating a style of their own that had little to do with country blues save the inspiration that was a given. Guy, Rush, and company were the first generation of blues players who didn't have much memory of the pre–World War II years, when the acoustic guitar still played the dominant role in the blues. To them, the blues was best electrified.

Oddly, the man who had inspired everyone to pick up the electric guitar, Muddy Waters, returned to his acoustic roots in the early sixties. Hoping to capitalize on the folk and country-blues revival, Waters recorded a convincing album, *Folk Singer,* in 1964, followed by *The Real Folk Blues* and *More Real Folk Blues,* both of which contained tracks recorded earlier in Muddy's career. Chess released a pair of country-blues albums by Howlin' Wolf with the same two latter titles. But live, both Wolf and Waters continued to play electric blues in Chicago clubs, prompting young white aspiring blues guitarists to begin to venture into the black ghetto to hear the masters. A few of them became all-absorbing students. Eventually, the studying began to pay off.

Harmonica player and Chicago native Paul Butterfield built his harp style and attitude toward the blues from the firsthand inspiration he drew from Little Walter and the other blues harp players heard in the South Side blues clubs he frequented. Not all of the white kids who came looking for blues authenticity were welcomed in these all-black clubs, but Butterfield was, and he took full advantage of it. Quickly, Butterfield became the best white blues harmonica player in the city. In 1963 he formed the Paul Butterfield Blues Band. The group included a young white Jewish guitar player, Mike Bloomfield, who played with the same kind of blues passion expressed by Butterfield and with at least the same amount of talent, and Elvin Bishop, a second guitarist. The group also featured a black rhythm section—Sam Lay on drums and Jerome Arnold on bass, two veterans from Howlin' Wolf's band—making the Butterfield band a fully integrated outfit when such a concept was rare, not just in Chicago blues but in any kind of black music. (In Memphis, Booker T. and the MGs also sported a black-white mix. Booker T. Jones on organ and Al Jackson on drums were black musicians; guitarist Steve Cropper and bassist Donald "Duck" Dunn, white.)

The Paul Butterfield Blues Band released its first album in 1965 and proved that a mostly white band could play the blues—and play it well. Its success sparked the creation of other white blues bands and made Chicago a place to come to learn from the legends. Boz Scaggs and Steve Miller, two young guitarists who would make their mark in San Francisco later in the decade, came to Chicago hoping to hear the blues musicians they knew only from listening to records. Harmonica player Charlie Musselwhite had arrived in 1962 from Memphis and became as adept at playing his instrument as Butterfield, and equally accepted in the city's blues community. From England came the Rolling Stones, whose dream it was to meet some of their Chicago blues heroes and to record at Chess Records, which they did.

Paul Butterfield (*left*) and Michael Bloomfield played together in the Paul Butterfield Blues Band.

According to Chuck D, "Hendrix was able to take the blues and put it on steroids."

With traditional country blues finding a new audience with young white kids in the early sixties, it was only a matter of time before electric blues had also made the shift from black audiences to white. The success of the Paul Butterfield Blues Band certainly helped, giving white blues fans a few white blues heroes of their own. But the real thrusts came from England and from San Francisco. In the former, not only was black blues, country and urban, embraced by the best young musicians in London and other cities, but experiments in blending blues with rock were becoming the most exciting sounds of the music scene there. The same interest in a blues-rock hybrid was occurring around 1966–67 in San Francisco with bands like the Steve Miller Blues Band, Quicksilver Messenger Service, Grateful Dead, and Big Brother and the Holding Company (which featured Janis Joplin, a rousing singer recently arrived from Austin, Texas). These groups used the blues form to engage in long, drug-laced jams that took the blues to a new psychedelic high.

By 1968, a second influx of British bands had arrived in America, the first having occurred four years earlier with the explosion of the Beatles and the Rolling Stones. In the late sixties, virtually all of the new British bands were, at least originally, blues based. Fleetwood Mac, Cream, Pink Floyd (the band took its name from American bluesmen Pink Anderson and Floyd Council), Ten Years After, Savoy Brown, Jethro Tull, and Led Zeppelin all began as British blues bands before they either became psychedelicized, drawing influence from the drug revolution going on in San Francisco rock thousands of miles away, or traveled into art-rock territory. In Texas, an albino, Johnny Winter, became the great white blues hope. Down in Georgia, the Allman Brothers Band whipped up a blues frenzy with their elongated versions of blues standards that gave the music a brand-new feel, courtesy of Gregg Allman's wailing vocals and his brother Duane's incredibly fluid slide guitar solos. In California, Canned Heat's boogie blues was a welcomed sound. A black Seattle-born guitarist, Jimi Hendrix, had to go to London to be discovered, forming the Jimi Hendrix Experience, who were as bluesy as they were psychedelic.

With blues, rock, and blues-rock bands all vying for the same white audiences in the States, England, and Europe, it wasn't surprising that touring blues acts sought to make the transition from black clubs and festival stages to rock halls like the Fillmore Auditorium and later the Fillmore West in San Francisco, the Fillmore East in New York, and the Armadillo World Headquarters in Austin. In the late sixties and early seventies, the lineups for concerts in these rock halls often included traditional black blues bands as well as white blues-rock bands. Muddy Waters, B.B. King, and Howlin' Wolf, along with Memphian Albert King, and Big Mama Thornton (who, in 1953, cut the original version of the Presley hit "Hound Dog") all counted on playing white rock venues, making decent pay at the same time they were giving blues lessons to white kids anxious to hear the real thing. The Rolling Stones, eager to share the stage with their blues heroes, invited some to open their concerts, thus enabling Waters, B.B. King, Ike and Tina Turner, and others to play to crowds that might otherwise have never seen them. The Stones even got Howlin' Wolf on national television, when the band refused to perform on *Shindig!* unless Wolf was also on the program.

The late sixties were a high-water mark for the blues. For more than twenty years, the music enjoyed unprecedented artistic and commercial growth. The blues was remarkably resilient; it exchanged one fan base for another without missing a beat. Its most important artists, Muddy Waters,

Howlin' Wolf, Willie Dixon, Little Walter, Sonny Boy Williamson, Elmore James, Jimmy Reed, B.B. King, Albert King, and Big Mama Thornton, among them, had paved the way for a new generation of visionaries. The blues had been an essential part of perhaps the most creative period in rock history—the sixties—and had influenced virtually every major rock artist, British and American, of that period. The music had even made it to near the top of the pop charts; in 1970 B.B. King's "The Thrill Is Gone" rose to Number Fifteen on the *Billboard* charts. In short, the future seemed big and bright for the blues.

It wasn't. Although rock's late-sixties love affair with the blues carried over into the first years of the 1970s, the rock world's interest in the blues began to wane. By 1973, the blues-rock hybrid sounded stale;

Big Mama Thornton taught white audiences the original version of "Hound Dog."

Koko Taylor first recorded for Chess in the sixties and moved to Alligator Records in the seventies.

was killed in a street brawl in 1968. Magic Sam died of a heart attack in 1969; he was just thirty-two years old. Skip James and Leonard Chess died that same year. Earl Hooker succumbed to tuberculosis in 1970 at age forty. Mississippi Fred McDowell died of cancer in 1972. Howlin' Wolf, Jimmy Reed, and Freddie King passed on in 1976.

Chess Records was sold in 1968, and Phil Chess went into radio. Leonard's son Marshall moved to another label, Rolling Stone Records. There was little profit left in turning out blues records. Without blues-rock bands continuing to produce exciting music, the white audience drifted and it too eventually abandoned the blues. Young black audiences, now tired of soul, moved on to a new sound, funk. The success of the civil rights movement in the sixties had brought significant change for African-Americans, and no one wanted to look back.

Despite its dire predicament in the 1970s, the blues hung on, and in some pockets even thrived. The southern chitlin' circuit, that motley collection of black clubs, jukes, bars, and roadhouses, continued to feature blues bands doing one-night stands from Texas to Georgia. The audiences weren't large, the money was barely enough, but black singers and musicians committed to the music played on, just scraping out a living, and longtime fans who still felt connected to the music's emotional intensity turned out to hear them perform. Europe, with its seemingly endless fascination with American music, particularly black music, provided work for blues artists. But even that, too, was spotty, and available only for the biggest names. The blues and the business of the blues had come full circle by 1973. After enjoying a twenty-five-year period of unprecedented growth and popularity, the blues slid quietly out of the spotlight, finding refuge in the remaining

many rock bands that built their sound on the blues either broke up or moved on. Cream crashed after only a couple of studio albums. Quicksilver Messenger Service faded out. Steve Miller and Fleetwood Mac went in a pop direction. Led Zeppelin delved into heavy metal, as did a number of other sixties blues-rock bands. Drugs and booze took some of the best blues-rock performers and advocates: Janis Joplin, Jimi Hendrix, Jim Morrison, Brian Jones of the Rolling Stones all died too young. Eric Clapton, Johnny Winter, Mike Bloomfield, and Paul Butterfield also battled drug demons. Clapton and Winter survived; Bloomfield and Butterfield did not.

The blues also lost its own key figures, more from hard living than heroin, which in the seventies ran rampant through the rock world. Little Walter

blues clubs on the South Side of Chicago and in clubs in other cities where the aging black blues crowd continued to congregate, and in the occasional summer blues festival.

All was not lost, however. In Chicago, a young blues fanatic, Bruce Iglauer, started a blues record company, Alligator Records, and sold his music the old-fashioned way: out of the trunk of his car. Iglauer had worked with another Chicago blues and jazz label, Delmark, which, in the mid-sixties, had released one of the greatest Chicago blues albums of all time—Junior Wells' *Hoodoo Man Blues*—along with Magic Sam's classic effort *West Side Soul*. After hearing a six-fingered slide guitarist named Hound Dog Taylor in Florence's, a small Chicago club, Iglauer pleaded with Delmark owner Bob Koester to record Taylor. Koester, a longtime advocate of black music, refused, figuring the venture was not a wise one, given the state of the blues record business. Iglauer, who dreamed of one day running his own label, recorded Taylor and his band the Houserockers with his own money, in 1971. The self-titled album became the very first release on the Alligator label.

Encouraged by his success with Taylor—the artist and his record received positive reviews in the music press and sold well enough—Iglauer decided to make Alligator a permanent entity and began looking for more blues talent to record. Iglauer moved slowly, careful not to overextend himself in the depressed blues market. By the end of 1977, he had released just nine albums. But his persistence paid off. In 1978 Alligator released *Ice Pickin'*, an album by veteran blues guitarist Albert Collins, who had begun his career in the early fifties, developing along the way a reputation for playing in a "cool" blues style. Collins had enjoyed some success in the late fifties with a record called "The Freeze," followed by "Frosty," "Frost-Bite," and other similarly

named songs. Although the Alligator album, *Ice Pickin'*, continued Collins' familiar cool connection, the work featured freshly "chilling" guitar work and inspired vocals. *Ice Pickin'* was just what Collins needed to resuscitate his career and just what Iglauer needed to take Alligator to the next level. The album was nominated for a Grammy, and another Alligator album, *The Earthshaker*, by longtime blues singer Koko Taylor, also garnered favorable attention. Taylor, who had been discovered by Willie Dixon in the early sixties, recorded a best-selling single for Chess in 1966, "Wang Dang Doodle," written and produced by Dixon. A hard-working performer with a gritty blues growl for a voice, Taylor toured regularly in the seventies,

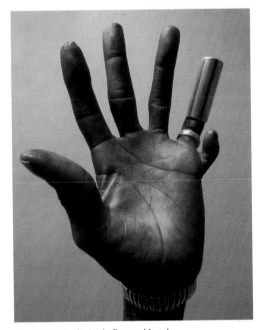

Hound Dog Taylor's six-fingered hand

gradually rebuilding her career, with lots of help from Iglauer.

The year 1978 was the turning point for Alligator. In addition to *Ice Pickin'*, the label garnered three other Grammy nominations, making Alligator the most important Chicago blues label since the sale of Chess nearly ten years earlier. Iglauer's strategy was simple: sign up veteran blues talent with name recognition who still had exciting music in them. By the early eighties, Alligator had added to its roster Johnny Winter and James Cotton, along with zydeco king Clifton Chenier and Arkansas guitarists Roy Buchanan and Son Seals. Alligator's success enabled Iglauer to search out and then cultivate new blues talent such as Lucky Peterson, William Clarke, and the female blues group Saffire, becoming the number one blues label in America.

Alligator wasn't the only small, independent label releasing blues records in the seventies and early eighties. Delmark continued its steady flow of quality blues releases. Hightone, Testament, and Tomato released blues albums with some success. And the major record companies continued to release the occasional blues and blues-influenced album. Warner Bros. kept the blues alive on its roster by issuing records made by the Texas boogie band ZZ Top and the talented, red-headed slide guitarist Bonnie Raitt. Warners also signed Taj Mahal, who began his career in the late sixties with Columbia, making some of the most innovative blues of the period; in the seventies he continued his quest for new blues sounds by blending, among other things, Caribbean music with the blues. A Columbia subsidiary, Blue Sky, permitted Johnny Winter (before his exodus to Alligator) to produce a series of critically acclaimed Muddy Waters albums that represented the best work Waters had done since his fifties heyday with Chess.

Nonetheless, the business of the blues continued to suffer throughout the seventies and early eighties. A commercially successful blues album was the exception, not the rule. The music needed more than the small but dedicated core of record buyers to support it and foster growth. The blues also needed a brand-new artist who could garner the kind of excitement and media attention normally owned by rock and pop artists, as well as a new scene to complement Chicago. The blues got what it needed in the mid-eighties, and then some.

Texas had always been a state blessed with blues talent. In the music's formative years, Dallas, particularly the Deep Ellum section of the city, fostered a busy blues scene with the likes of Blind Lemon Jefferson playing on street corners. Later on, Houston became an important blues city with Johnny "Guitar" Watson, Albert Collins, Johnny Copeland, Clarence "Gatemouth" Brown, and others gigging at blues clubs there, and with Don Robey's Peacock and Duke Records recording both home-grown and outside blues talent in local studios. By the sixties, the blues scene in Austin, home to the University of Texas, heated up. But it wasn't until the late seventies and early eighties that Austin truly came of age as an important blues city, one that could—and would—rival Chicago.

Because of a steady stream of college kids, there existed a vibrant music club scene in Austin, and more than a couple of them were not averse to featuring touring blues acts. Threadgill's was where a young Janis Joplin sang. The Armadillo World Headquarters imitated the booking style of the old Fillmore venues, putting established blues artists on the same bill as featured rock bands. In the mid-seventies, Antone's, a club owned by Clifford Antone, a music fan with an insatiable blues appetite, began booking Muddy Waters and other traveling blues greats, eventually starting a blues record label and touring company. Solid fan support enabled Antone to bring in local talent, in effect, cultivating an exciting homegrown blues scene that would soon break nationally.

The Fabulous Thunderbirds, led by guitarist Jimmie Vaughan and singer/harmonica player Kim Wilson, was the first blues-based band to graduate from the new Austin blues scene. The Thunderbirds formed in 1974 and released their self-titled debut album on the Takoma label in 1979. The following year they moved to Chrysalis Records and quickly issued three critically acclaimed but marginally successful albums, saleswise: *What's the Word*, in 1980, *Butt Rockin'*, in 1981, and *T-Bird Rhythm*, in 1982. The band's breakthrough occurred in 1986 with *Tuff Enuff*, its debut album for the Epic label. The title song made it as a single into the Top Ten of the *Billboard* pop charts, not only establishing the Fabulous Thunderbirds in blues and rock circles but also drawing important attention to Austin.

But it was Jimmie Vaughan's kid brother who really put Austin on the blues map. Stevie Ray Vaughan followed his big brother to Austin from Dallas, their hometown, in 1972 and joined the Nightcrawlers, followed by the Cobras, before forming a blues-rock group, Triple Threat Revue, with singer Lou Ann Barton. In 1978 Barton left and Vaughan re-formed the group as Double Trouble. With Stevie Ray now doing all of the singing, and with his guitar blazing through blues standards and a growing batch of originals, the trio, which included former Johnny Winter bass player Tommy Shannon and drummer Chris Layton, tore up the Austin music scene. At the invitation of legendary Atlantic Records producer Jerry Wexler, Stevie Ray Vaughan and Double Trouble performed

Brothers Stevie Ray *(left)* and Jimmie Vaughan reinvigorated the national blues scene.

at the Montreux Jazz Festival in Switzerland, scoring the same results registered nightly back home in Austin. Shortly thereafter, Vaughan and his band signed a recording contract with Epic. Vaughan was finally poised to make blues history.

Vaughan's debut album for Epic, *Texas Flood*, was released in 1983, the same year the world lost the great Muddy Waters, who passed away in Chicago. Keeping the sound alive, Vaughan wowed critics with his scintillating guitar work and incredible blues command. He continued to garner fans via his live shows, which exploded with his potent interpretation of Jimi Hendrix's "Voodoo Chile." The Hendrix link attracted curious rock fans eager to find a new guitar god in the swamp of synth-pop and Michael Jackson/Madonna dance music that was filling up the charts in the mid-eighties.

Vaughan's success brought new fans—and new meaning—to the blues. Suddenly, magazines like *Rolling Stone* and *Musician* began paying attention to the music form again. Vaughan followed the success of *Texas Flood* with the equally acclaimed

John Lee Hooker *(left)*, who electrified the blues in the 1940s, and Robert Cray, who did the same thirty years later.

couple of R&B-influenced blues albums before participating in an Alligator project, *Showdown!*, which featured, in addition to Cray, guitarists Albert Collins and Johnny Copeland. Released in 1985, *Showdown!* was one of the most important blues albums of the decade. Not only did it showcase Cray to a broader audience, pump life into Copeland's career, and further Alligator's mission of remaking Collins' career, this guitar summit sold nearly a quarter million units, an unheard-of number for a blues album, and earned a Grammy Award in the blues category.

Cray, who considered both Collins and Copeland blues mentors, gained the most from *Showdown!* The exposure from the album and the critical acclaim that went with it led to critics taking seriously his *Strong Persuader* album, which was released the following year. The record contained the hit single "Smoking Gun" and got Cray his second Grammy in as many years.

By the mid-eighties, these two new exciting and important blues artists, as well as a pair of veteran performers, Albert Collins and Koko Taylor (now dubbed Queen of the Blues), had spearheaded the music's sudden revival. But there was one other element that needed to be added to the mix, something that would push record sales and reconnect sixties blues fans who had lost touch with the music. Technology came to the rescue in the form of the compact disc. By the late eighties, the CD had become the perfect alternative to the vinyl album and to the cassette. Music fans who got tired of playing their old blues albums—with all the scratches, pops, and crackles that accumulate on worn vinyl—began replacing them with CDs.

When record companies realized this new buying trend, most of them began to reissue old, long-out-of-print albums. It was easy money.

and commercially successful *Couldn't Stand the Weather* (1984), *Soul to Soul* (1985), *Live Alive* (1986), and *In Step* (1989). He toured endlessly, growing his audience as he went along and upping his guitar talent seemingly every time he took the stage. Vaughan was the first blues superstar of the post-modern blues period; that he was white made little difference to record buyers or even purists. He had given the music a long-awaited shot in the arm, without sacrificing integrity or a commitment to the music's storied past.

Equally important to this blues revival was Robert Cray, a black Pacific Northwest blues artist who had a cameo in the 1978 comedy *National Lampoon's Animal House,* which starred John Belushi. Cray had made a

Nothing new needed to be recorded; it was simply a matter of transferring music from the master tape onto this new medium. Sometimes selling just a few thousand albums meant profit. Blues artists had been making records since the 1920s, so, as with jazz, there was a lot to reissue. Record companies both big and small began mining their vaults for old chestnuts. Beginning in the late 1980s and carrying on right through the next decade, thousands of old blues recordings saw the light of day again on compact disc. In addition to reissuing old albums, record companies created compilations and then a new concept, the box set, all of which sent very healthy revenue streams into the coffers of labels with any kind of back catalogue.

At Columbia Records, a persistent A&R man who loved the blues, Lawrence Cohn, persuaded the label to release all of Robert Johnson's recordings in a special set. Despite the rise in CD reissue sales, label executives were skeptical that a full collection of recordings made nearly a half-century earlier would make sense to release. Who would be interested in such music, especially in the case of Johnson, where the master tapes of his recordings had never been found? Recording engineers would have to take Johnson's music from the best 78s they could find, scratches and all. Cohn insisted that the box set's release would make economical sense since Johnson was one of the most important American artists of the twentieth century, and that music fans wanted his recordings. Columbia executives hoped to sell ten thousand units, recoup the investment, and move on. Everyone at the label, even Cohn, was stunned when the set sold half a million units, garnered a Grammy, and inspired dozens of magazine pieces.

Such was the state of the blues in 1990. Interest in the music was part of a greater fascination in American roots music that would continue through the decade. There were more blues recordings available than ever before, thanks to CD reissue campaigns that just about every label participated in. Equally important, these same labels also began to search out new talent, something that hadn't happened in earnest since the 1960s. Traditional country-blues artists such as Keb' Mo', Corey Harris, and Alvin Youngblood Hart made debut recordings in the mid-nineties and settled into careers that would have been impossible without the roots music revival in full swing. Young white blues guitarists—Kenny Wayne Shepherd, Jonny Lang, and Susan Tedeschi, among them—secured record deals and attracted not just blues but also roots-rock audiences. Lang even toured with the Rolling Stones as an opening act.

In 1991, Buddy Guy attained the kind of commercial heights and critical acclaim that had always eluded him in the past when he released the Grammy-winning *Damn Right, I've Got the Blues*. In the nineties, Guy's elevated blues status meant he shared the same spotlight enjoyed by B.B. King, John Lee Hooker, and other longtime stalwarts. After a decade and a half of pop and rock albums, Eric Clapton returned to the blues in 1994 with *From the Cradle*, his first full blues album since his mid-sixties days with John Mayall's Bluesbreakers. An acclaimed tour followed. At the decade's end, he collaborated with B.B. King on the Grammy-winning effort *Riding With the King*, released in 2000.

"All my early years I worked in the fields picking cotton with black people. We were the only white family sharecroppin' on this one farm. I remember that late in the evening when the sun was getting low, you would hear these wonderful voices start to sing out. The music of these people would be flooding the air after a while. To this day, I can hear that music in my soul, the rhythm, the feeling it gave." —*Carl Perkins*

Robert Johnson won the acclaim of a rock star when this box set garnered a Grammy and went gold.

By then, King's stature was such that he had become blues music's elder statesman and ambassador, its true spiritual leader. He had spent the nineties playing nearly two hundred dates a year, releasing album after album, and making television commercials with blues as the soundtrack. John Lee Hooker had not been left out of the blues revival either. In 1989 the small Chameleon label issued *The Healer,* a Hooker album that featured guest appearances from Carlos Santana, Robert Cray, Bonnie Raitt, and others. It won a Grammy and set in motion a 1991 followup, *Mr. Lucky,* that this time featured cameos by such fans as Van Morrison, Keith Richards, and Ry Cooder. Not as articulate as King, Hooker nonetheless enjoyed elder statesman status in the blues and American roots music in general until his death in 2000.

The blues had also suffered a loss ten years earlier with the tragic and shocking death of Stevie Ray Vaughan, in the early years of the blues revival. After successfully beating a debilitating drug and alcohol dependency and making *Family*

Style, a much-anticipated album with his brother Jimmie, Stevie Ray died in a helicopter crash after a Wisconsin concert where he'd appeared with Jimmie, Clapton, Cray, and Guy. His death on August 27, 1990, stunned the music world. No one artist had done more to revitalize the blues and bring on its revival than Vaughan. Despite the strength of the music in the 1990s, Vaughan's presence was missed at every turn.

With the blues approaching something of a centennial at the turn of the century, it seemed as if every inch of blues territory had been explored and mined for talent. Yet in the early part of the nineties, Fat Possum, a small independent blues label out of Oxford, Mississippi, issued recordings by local bluesmen R.L. Burnside and Junior Kimbrough. Although Burnside had recorded much earlier, few others than the deepest blues enthusiasts had taken notice of his unique blues style. Like Kimbrough, Burnside hailed from the hill country of Mississippi, just east of the Delta lowlands. His and Kimbrough's blues styles, although not really similar, nonetheless had some common elements, such as the influence of Mississippi Fred McDowell. The north Mississippi hill country became the final frontier of the blues. Kimbrough played an amazingly hypnotic, almost dronelike blues that could put both listeners and dancers in a trance, while Burnside's bristling vocals and hyped rhythms recalled the best acoustic recordings of Muddy Waters and John Lee Hooker. Both Burnside and Kimbrough were featured in the Robert Mugge documentary *Deep Blues,* which introduced music fans to hill country blues. Musicologist, author, and musician Robert Palmer wrote and narrated the film, and his enthusiasm for the music resulted in the music's release on Fat Possum.

Buoyed by the commercial and critical success enjoyed by Burnside and Kimbrough, Fat Possum dug deeper into the Mississippi blues scene and released a number of other long-undiscovered bluesmen in the 1990s. In effect, Fat Possum became the new Alligator Records, issuing consistently intriguing blues that was unschooled, raw, and riveting. None of the other artists Fat Possum recorded in the nineties matched the success of Burnside or Kimbrough, but artists such as T-Model Ford, Robert Belfour, and especially CeDell Davis brought new sounds to old blues styles. In the meantime, hill country bluesman Otha Turner kept alive the sound of centuries-old, African-born fife and drum music, performing on his fife at his annual picnic-cum-music festival. Young white musicians, such as local boys Luther and Cody Dickinson (sons of producer/sessionman Jim Dickinson), started bands inspired by the music. The Dickinsons' North Mississippi All-Stars became one of the most compelling blues-rock bands of the late nineties.

As the millennium approached and the twentieth century—America's music century—gave way to the twenty-first, the blues, along with virtually every other roots music form, had carved out an impressive piece of the pop music landscape for itself. Summer music festivals that featured blues, Cajun, zydeco, jazz, country, and bluegrass music were seemingly everywhere. The Delta Blues Museum had opened in Clarksdale, Mississippi. The Blues Foundation, a Memphis-based organization that supported blues education programs and advocated for the blues in general, each year featured the W.C. Handy Awards, the blues equivalent of the Grammys. Madison Avenue discovered the blues; the music helped sell beer, cars, blue jeans, and even medicine for diabetics.

There were three places, however, where the blues lacked. One was the hole left by the death of Stevie Ray Vaughan. Despite the influx of new artists in the nineties, none of them filled Vaughan's shoes, leaving the music without a charismatic superstar other than the aging King. The second was the blues' inability to bring back black audiences. Hip-hop was the most dominant pop music form of the last two decades of the twentieth century, and it completely consumed young black record buyers, leaving no room for the blues revival to touch them. It was a rare young black face at a blues concert in the 1990s. Finally, despite the decade-long success of the blues and its reestablishment with white baby boomers, the music still failed to reach young white music fans. Most of the blues CDs sold in the nineties were purchased by white blues consumers over thirty-five years old. Without new music-buying blood pumped into the business of the blues, it would be only a matter of time before sales figures for blues discs dropped, leaving the blues scene in a dangerous position in the early part of the twenty-first century.

Despite these weaknesses, the blues moves on. The oldest and most resilient of all American roots music forms, the blues has found a way to remain relevant, despite the endless changes that occur in pop music and the uncertainty of the business of music—the advent of downloading free songs from the Internet and the competition from other forms of entertainment (video games, DVDs). In 2002 Congress passed a resolution making 2003 the Year of the Blues, providing long-overdue official recognition of the blues. A century earlier, W.C. Handy had come across an itinerant musician playing blues music that at once captured Handy's heart and soul. One hundred years later, the blues still possesses the power to touch people and impact the nation's rich music heritage. As B.B. King once mused, "The blues? It's the mother of American music. That's what it is—the source." ☛

When I was growing up, there always seemed to be music in the air. It drifted up from the street, from the radios of passing cars, from the restaurants and corner stores, from the windows of apartments across the way. At home, my mother often sang to herself—I have vivid memories of her singing while she was doing the dishes. My father loved to play his mandolin, and my brother Frank played the guitar. Actually, it was my father who was the guitar enthusiast, and the first music I remember hearing was by Django Reinhardt and his Hot Club of France Quintet. At that time, you could always hear an incredible range of music on the radio, everything from Italian folk songs to country & western. And my uncle Joe, my mother's brother, had an amazing record collection, which ranged from Gilbert and Sullivan to swing. He was one of the first people I could really talk to, and I think we related to each other because of our shared love for music.

One day, around 1958, I remember hearing something that was unlike anything I'd ever heard before. I'll never forget the first time I heard the sound of that guitar. The music was demanding: "Listen to me!" I ran to get a pencil and paper and wrote down the name. The song was called "See See Rider," which I already knew from the Chuck Willis cover version. The name of the singer was Lead Belly.* I got up to Sam Goody's on Forty-ninth Street as fast as I could, and I found an old Folkways record by Lead Belly, which had "See See Rider," "Roberta," "Black Snake Moan," and a few other songs. And I listened to it obsessively. Lead Belly's music opened something up for me. If I could have played guitar, *really* played it, I never would have become a filmmaker.

At around the same time, my friends and I went to see Bo Diddley. That was another milestone for me. He was playing at the Brooklyn Paramount, in one of the rock & roll package shows. He always had great stage moves, and he was a mesmerizing performer. I remember Jerome Green, on the maracas, dancing out from one side of the stage and Bo Diddley dancing out from the other, and that they kept meeting in the middle and passing each other by. But Bo Diddley also did something unusual: He explained the different drumbeats and which parts of Africa they came from. It gave us a sense of the

LEADBELLY'S EARLY RECORDINGS **LEGACY VOLUME 3**
PIGMEAT • BLACK SNAKE MOAN •
ROBERTA PARTS 1 and 2 •
FORT WORTH AND DALLAS BLUES •
SEE SEE RIDER • DADDY I'M COMING BACK TO YOU •
Edited by FREDERIC RAMSEY JR. FOLKWAYS RECORDS N. Y. FA 2024

This Folkways anthology of Lead Belly recordings introduced Martin Scorsese and other young music lovers to the blues in the 1950s.

* Over the years, Lead Belly's name often has been spelled "Leadbelly"; his family prefers the spelling of his name to be two words, so that is the spelling used throughout this book.

history behind the music, the roots of the music. We all found this very exciting, and it gave us a thirst for more knowledge. We wanted to dig deeper.

In the early Sixties, my preference was for Phil Spector, Motown, and the girl groups, like the Ronettes, the Marvelettes, and the Shirelles. Then came the British Invasion. Like everyone else, I was floored by this music, and struck by its strong blues influence. The more I understood the history behind rock & roll, the more I could hear the blues behind it. With some of the new British music, the blues came to the forefront, and the bands were paying homage to their masters in the same way that the French New Wave filmmakers were paying homage to the great American directors with their films. There was John Mayall and his Bluesbreakers. There was the first installment of Fleetwood Mac, with Peter Green on guitar, basically a blues band. There were the Stones, whose music had a heavy blues accent right from the start, and who did cover versions of "Little Red Rooster," "I'm a King Bee," "Love in Vain," and many others. And, of course, there was Cream. I still love to sit alone in a room and wrap myself up in that music. They created an amazing fusion of blues and hard rock, and some of their most beautiful songs were covers: "Rollin' and Tumblin'," the old Delta classic, which I first heard on volume one of *Live Cream;* Robert Johnson's "Crossroads," which was one of their biggest hits; and "Sitting on Top of the World," which was on *Goodbye Cream.* When I heard that song I went back and found the original, by the great Mississippi Sheiks.

Around the end of the Sixties, this urge to find the roots of the music really started to spread. People all over the country were discovering the blues, and it went way beyond a specialized audience. At that time, the music wasn't as readily available as it is now.

You would have to search for certain titles, and others you could find in reissues and package collections. The blues had such a powerful mystique, such an aura around it, that certain names would suddenly be in the air, and you just *had* to have their records. Names like Son House, which I heard for the first time when we were editing *Woodstock.* It was Mike Wadleigh, the director, who brought in the record. Someone who once heard Caruso sing said that he was so moved that his heart shook. That's the way I felt the first time I heard Son House. It was a voice and a style that seemed to come from way, way back, from some other, much earlier time and place. About a year later, there was another name: Robert Johnson. Another ancient voice, another soul-stirring experience.

It was my love for music, which has never stopped growing, that led me to do *The Last Waltz.* I wanted to make it more than just a document of the Band's last concert. Because it was more than just a musical tribute: It was a tapestry of music history, the Band's music history. And every one of those performers—one legend after another—made up a thread in that tapestry. But when Muddy Waters walked onto that stage and sang "Mannish Boy," he took control of the music, the event, the history, everything. He electrified the audience, took it all up to another level and back to the source at the same time. He gave a phenomenal performance, and I will always consider myself privileged to have been there to witness it, to film it, and to give it back to millions of people with the finished film. It was a defining moment for me.

Over the last ten years or so, this search for historical roots has found its way into my movie-

"The blues—it's kind of like religion, really." *—Peter Green*

"The blues—there's no black and no white— it's the truth." —*Van Morrison*

making. I've made two documentaries on the history of cinema—one on American movies, then another on Italian cinema. And I decided early on that I wanted them to be personal, rather than strictly historical surveys. It seemed to me that this was the best way to work: The teachers from whom I learned the most were always the most passionate, the ones with a deeply personal connection to the material. For the blues series, I decided to do something similar.

The project began when Cappa Productions producer Margaret Bodde and I were working on a documentary with Eric Clapton called *Nothing but the Blues,* where we intercut footage of Eric performing blues standards with archival footage of older blues musicians. We were all struck by the elemental power and poetry of these juxtapositions—it seemed like such a simple yet eloquent way of expressing the music's timelessness. It also gave us a way of approaching the history of the blues in cinematic terms. So it seemed like a natural progression to ask a number of directors whose work I admired, each with a deep connection to the music, to make his own personal exploration of blues history. By having each of them come at the subject from his own unique perspective, I knew we'd come away with something special, not a dry recitation of facts but a genuinely passionate mosaic.

For my own film, which was the first in the series, the idea was to take the viewer on a pilgrimage to Mississippi and then on to Africa with a wonderful young blues musician named Corey Harris. Corey isn't just a great player, he also knows

the history of the blues very well. We filmed him in Mississippi talking to some of the old, legendary figures who were still around and visiting some of the places where the music was made. This section culminates in a meeting with the great Otha Turner, sitting on his porch in Senatobia with his family nearby and playing his cane flute. We were also fortunate to film Otha's magnificent November 2001 concert at St. Ann's in Brooklyn, which I believe was his last performance captured on film. It seemed natural to trace the music back from Mississippi to West Africa, where Corey met and played with extraordinary artists like Salif Keita, Habib Koité, and Ali Farka Toure. It's fascinating to hear the links between the African and American music, to see the influences going both ways, back and forth across time and space.

The links between Africa and the blues were always very important to Alan Lomax, and that's one of the reasons I wanted to include him in my film. I relate strongly to Lomax's instinct, his need to find and record genuine sounds and music before the originators died away. It's hard to overestimate the importance of what he accomplished—without him, so much would have been lost.

Otha Turner's music was one of those links to Africa that Lomax spent so much time searching for. That elemental music, made with nothing but a fife and drum, has always fascinated me. When I first heard it, I was editing *Raging Bull* by night. I was enthralled: It sounded like something out of eighteenth-century America, but with an African rhythm. I never even imagined that such a music could exist. I found an audio tape of Otha's music, and I listened to it obsessively over many years. I always knew that it would play a key role in *Gangs of New York*. That project went through many false starts, and it changed quite a bit over the years, but

Corey Harris *(left)* plays with Ali Farka Toure in Niafunké, Mali.

one thing that never changed was the idea that it would include that music. When I finally did get to make the picture, we were lucky enough to be able to use a piece by Otha and his Rising Star Band, and I used it as playback on the set to propel the action—it gave the film an energy and power it would have lacked otherwise, and it helped to create a world we had never seen before. When the picture came out, many people understandably thought they were listening to "Celtic" music and were surprised to discover that it was by Otha Turner, from north Mississippi.

The sense of continuity and transformation in the blues, the way past, present, and future are joined as one dynamic creative entity, never ceases to amaze me. Earlier this year, there was a Salute to the Blues concert here in New York, which Antoine Fuqua filmed for our series. It was an event I'll never forget, and the spirit of that night was summed up memorably by Ruth Brown, who said: "It's so great that we're all here together—and it's *not* for a funeral!" The sheer range of music that night was something to marvel at, and the beauty of

"There are happy blues, sad blues, lonesome blues, red-hot blues, mad blues, and loving blues. Blues is a testimony to the fullness of life." —*Corey Harris*

Otha Turner's young granddaughter, Sharde Thomas, carries on a centuries-old hill-country music tradition, playing a cane fife her grandfather made for her.

of the playing and singing was incomparable. There were some musicians who completely transformed the music, and made a kind of twenty-first-century blues. Chris Thomas King did a version of Son House's "John the Revelator" with drum machines and a synth bass guitar. He kept piling layers of sound on top of one another, and managed to create something completely modern and surprising but very much in keeping with the *voice* of the blues.

This idea of continuity and transformation runs through all the films in the series. Charles Burnett made a poetic and personal drama about blues life seen through the eyes of a young boy. Wim Wenders made an evocative film that moves in a dreamlike fashion through past, present, and future, in order to "conjure" three different bluesmen. Dick Pearce made a terrific film about Memphis, with Bobby Rush and the great B.B. King. Marc Levin did Chicago blues, featuring Chuck D and Marshall Chess in the studio with the *Electric Mud* band recording great new tracks with members of the Roots—once again, you get a strong sense of ongoing transformation in the blues here. Mike Figgis, who is himself a musician, made a film about the British blues scene, in the form of a story told by many of its creators. Clint Eastwood paid a very elegant tribute to the great blues piano players, Jay McShann, Pinetop Perkins, and others. All of these wonderful films are like pieces in a mosaic, in the end a moving and dynamic portrait of a great American art form.

People like to think of the great blues singers as raw, instinctive, with talent and genius flowing from their fingertips. But John Lee Hooker, Bessie Smith, Muddy Waters, Howlin' Wolf, Blind Lemon Jefferson, and so many other amazing talents, more names than I have space for here, are some of the greatest artists America has ever had. When you listen to Lead Belly, or Son House, or Robert Johnson, or John Lee Hooker, or Charley Patton, or Muddy Waters, you're moved, your heart is shaken, you're carried and inspired by its visceral energy, and its rock solid emotional truth. You go right to the heart of what it is to be human, the *condition* of being human. That's the blues.

—Martin Scorsese

"What Muddy Waters did for us is what we should do for others. It's the old thing, what you want written on your tombstone as a musician: HE PASSED IT ON." —Keith Richards

SON HOUSE: SATURDAY NIGHT AND SUNDAY MORNING
BY CHRISTOPHER JOHN FARLEY

Son House killed a man at a party on a Saturday night.

That's the way the story goes, anyway. It was at a gathering in Lyon, Mississippi, in 1928. House had learned how to play the guitar only a few months before but had already landed a couple of gigs performing at juke joints. House's primary audience of black laborers, after hard, hot days in the field working for white landowners, needed to release some tension, had to cut loose, and the Saturday night parties could get dangerous. On this particular Saturday night at this particular juke joint, a man opened fire. History hasn't recorded the man's name, and we don't know why he started firing or even at whom he was aiming. But it's said that House was hit in the leg. That's when he returned fire, killing the man.

Son House—whose given name was Eddie James House Jr.—is said to have pleaded self-defense but was convicted of manslaughter and sentenced to fifteen years at Parchman, a penal work farm. Parchman's main purpose, from its founding in 1904 until reform came around in the 1970s, was not to rehabilitate its prisoners, or even to punish them—Parchman was a state-run seventeen-thousand-acre cotton farm, and it used its inmates to make money, which went directly into the coffers of the state legislature. The Parchman work farm, according to many accounts, was run like a pre–Civil War plantation, with prisoners substituting for slaves. Men who didn't follow the rules were quickly introduced to Black Annie, a four-foot leather strap used to administer discipline. Luckily for House, a judge is said to have reviewed his case and freed him after less than two years—but with a warning that he never set foot in Clarksdale again.

According to the records of the Mississippi State Penitentiary, only one inmate with the surname House was incarcerated during that period—an Ed House who was sentenced on September 8, 1930, in Clark County for manufacturing liquor, received by Parchman on September 16, 1930, and released on April 28, 1932. Is Ed House really Son House? Was Son House a killer or merely a bootlegger? Son House never liked to talk about his time on the penal farm and would brush off the subject when it came up. One thing is for certain: Son House's murky, vaguely felonious past added to the mystery and shadowy allure of his art. It also helped set the biographical tone for all the bluesmen, rockers, and hip-hoppers who would come after him: This was music for people who wanted to break rules, not follow them.

Son House grew up with religion; he was "churchified" as he put it. He was born in Mississippi, "a little past Riverton," as he once said; his birth certificate lists the date as March 21, 1902, but he may have been born much earlier. He indicated to folklorist Dick Waterman, who managed House's later career, that he was born in 1886. Waterman also says he has an application for social security that Son House filled out in 1943, in which House lists his birth year as 1894. Later in life, House may have adjusted his birth date so he wouldn't be too old to work for the railroad.

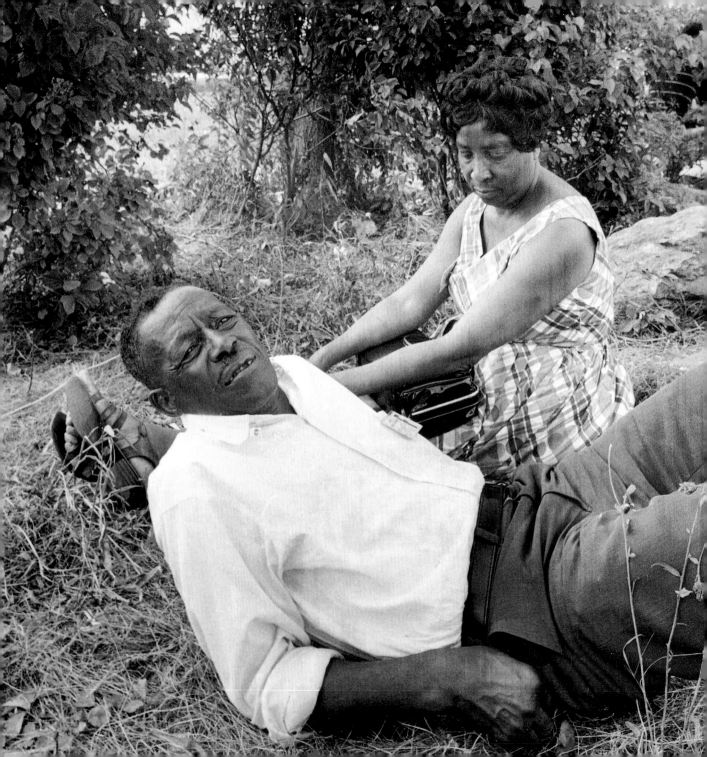

House attended Sabbath School at the Morning Star Missionary Baptist Church, but, when he was a youngster, religion didn't touch him, at least not deeply. He'd see the old folks holler and "squall 'round," possessed by the spirit, but House didn't feel it, and he didn't want to fake it. So he began to pray—harder and harder, trying to feel what the others were feeling. One night he went out to an old alfalfa field, one that was full of snakes and weeds, and he fell down on his knees and reached out to God in supplication—and finally, feeling the spirit, he hollered out, "Yes, it is something to be got, too, 'cause I got it now!"

House, when he was just a teenager, strove hard to establish himself as a church man and a family man. He preached his first sermon at age fifteen, and became a pastor at age twenty. When he was in his early twenties, he married Carrie Martin, who was then in her early thirties. House's mother, Maggie, and his father, Eddie James House Sr., separated when he was young and so, when he got to be "some size"—around twenty or twenty-one— he went to work. He gathered moss in Algiers, Louisiana, pulling the gray strands down from the trees (it was shipped out and used for mattresses). He also worked other jobs—raising horses with a friend, picking cotton in the fields, driving a plow. The wages were low: "Well, people kind of suffered a little during some of those years," said House. "Suffered right smart." Music helped people get by. House heard music all around him, the work songs of men in the cotton field, the hollers of mule drivers echoing across the fields at dusk, singing what House called "the old corn songs, old long-meter songs." He also heard the blues—from guitar-picking street musicians and the like—but at first, at least, he didn't like the sound. Said House, "I just figured that was one of the wrongest things in the world to be doing, you know. Wasn't no other way you could get to heaven—not fooling with them things. Just putting your hands on an old guitar, looked like that was a sin. To me." But the music kept calling. House's father played in a band with his seven brothers, and although the elder House didn't play the blues, his son was exposed to music close-up at an early age. "He played a bass horn," House recalled about his father. "He had been a church man, but he had gotten out. Finally, he went back to church and laid it all down, quit drinking, and became a deacon. He went pretty straight from then on."

Son House finally got the idea to start playing music in the late 1920s. He had been living in Louisiana, but after only a few years of marriage, decided to walk away from it all and return to Clarksdale. A year later, in 1927, he had a streetside epiphany. As House told the story: "I saw a guy named Willie Wilson and another one named Rubin Lacy. All before then, I just hated to see a guy with a guitar. I was so churchy! I came along to a little place they call Mattson, a little below Clarksdale. It was on a Saturday, and these guys were sitting out front of a place, and they were playing. Well, I stopped, because the people were all crowded around. This boy, Willie Wilson, had a thing on his finger like a small medicine bottle and he was zinging it, you know. I said, 'Jesus! Wonder what's that he's playing?' I knew that guitars hadn't usually been sounding like that. So I eases up close enough to look, and I see what he has on his finger. 'Sounds good!' I said. 'Jesus! I like that!' And from there, I got the idea and said, 'I believe I want to play one of them things.'"

House paid $1.50 for "an old piece of guitar" with only five strings. Said House, "It was nearly all to pieces, but I didn't know the difference." Wilson helped House tape the guitar up, add the missing sixth string, and even showed him a few chords. House immediately set to work on developing what would become his famous slide guitar technique, slipping the neck of a bottle around his ring finger to slip along the strings. Said House, "I got me an old bottle. Cut my finger a couple of times trying to fix the thing like his, but finally I started zinging, too." Even after the repairs, though, the guitar must not have sounded right to House's ears. He thought back to when he was a church-choir leader and was singing "do-re-mi." He tuned the guitar to sound like the choral church voices in his head, and in a few weeks he had taught himself a number that he had heard Willie Wilson play called "Hold Up Sally, Take Your Big Legs Offa Mine." He must have been excited because the next time he saw Wilson, he played it for him.

It was a Saturday night, and Wilson had an idea. "Come on and play with me tonight," said Wilson.

"I ain't good enough for that," said House.

"Oh, yes, you is. You just play that. I'll back you up."

So House launched his musical career with a repertoire of one song. Wilson left the area, but House kept practicing, focusing on improving his guitar playing and rhyming words. He realized he didn't need to learn more songs by other people. Said House, "I can make my own songs." He was interrupted in his musical exploits by his incarceration at Parchman, but soon after his release he set off for Jonestown, Mississippi, catching a ride to the Lula train station. After his performances drew a crowd, a woman named Sara Knight invited him to perform on her café porch and also introduced him to Charley Patton. Patton was already well known in those parts—he had recorded a couple of 78s. House and Patton soon became drinking buddies and, after teaming up with another local bluesman,

Willie Brown, a short, wrinkly faced brown-skinned man with watery eyes, the trio began to hit the juke joints around the region.

They had some wild times, those three. They would sling their guitars over their shoulders and walk four or five miles to their next gig. Saturday night was money night: They'd line up three straight-back chairs right next to each other at a juke joint, and they'd play and play and go outside to cool off and let the sweat dry and come back in and play some more. Patton would do tricks with his guitar—spinning it round, strumming it behind his head, throwing it into the air and catching it again—and Brown sometimes would stomp his bare foot and slap his guitar to keep the beat. All three would take turns singing the verses to the songs, and with just a look they'd know when to change off. On record, blues songs are often around three minutes long, but at parties, House and his buddies would sometimes make tunes last nearly a half-hour. Listeners would dance to the music—slow-drag, two-step—they'd "lope all night long," House said. The crowd was wild, crying out, "Say it again!" to lyrics that they liked, or shouting out, "Yes!" if they liked the way the music was going. You had to sing loud and you had to have a strong voice, if you wanted to be heard over the crowd. House and his friends would perform for three, four, five dollars, "no big money," but good enough for that time. Sometimes Son would play birthday parties for two or three dollars and a slice of cake. Other times he'd perform until the whiskey was gone.

House—his style nurtured at these very secular parties—transformed the blues into a spiritual experience. When he played, he sometimes seemed to fall into a trance—his head would rock, his eyes would roll back into his head, he'd strum the same chords over and over. He worked the slide like no one did before him, using it to give his guitar a voice of its own—a siren's song of emotional turbulence, spiritual longing, and raw seuality. House's singing employed a full range of vocal effects that would be much copied by the bluesmen, soul stars, and rock & rollers who would come after him: his thoughtful melisma, his spontaneous use of falsetto to emphasize certain lines, his growls and whoops and moans. House's performances seemed inner-directed—as if he was playing for himself and not a crowd. Songs like "Dry Spell Blues" offer up a kind of intimate theater of suffering and endurance. His singing voice was also that of a man—not a minstrel currying favor, not a clown courting an audience, not a field hand trying to get in good with his boss. House's bold, dark voice was that of a man expressing himself to the world—without compromise, and his aggressive guitar attack was a fitting complement. House's best songs—the immortal "Death Letter Blues" and the aching "Pearline"—have an emotional force that has echoed through the decades and made them standard fare for artists to cover—even in the twenty-first century.

House's music had an impact on his contemporaries, as well. At some of the Saturday-night balls, House started noticing a young boy who would come around to watch. The boy—sometimes called Little Robert—played some harmonica, and he wasn't bad as far as that goes, but he really wanted to play the guitar. His mother and stepfather didn't like him hanging around the rough juke joint crowd, but every Saturday night Little Robert would slip out through a window and come to where House and his crew were playing. He'd sit right down on the floor and watch House and Brown and Patton, his eyes going from one to the other to the other. Whenever the fellas took a break to cool off,

"HELLHOUND ON MY TRAIL"
By Robert Johnson

I got to keep movin'
I got to keep movin'
Blues fallin' down like hail
Blues fallin' down like hail.

Ummmmmmmmmmmmmmmmmmmm

Blues fallin' down like hail.
Blues fallin' down like hail.

And the days keeps on worryin' me
There's a hellhound on my trail
Hellhound on my trail
Hellhound on my trail.

If today was Christmas Eve
If today was Christmas Eve
and tomorrow was Christmas Day
If today was Christmas Eve
and tomorrow was Christmas Day
(Aw, wouldn't we have a time baby)
All I would need my little sweet rider just to pass
    the time away
Uh huh to pass the time away.

You sprinkled hot foot powder
Mmmmm, around my door, all around my door
You sprinkled hot foot powder all around your
    daddy's door
Mmmmmm mmmm mmmm
It keep me with a ramblin' mind, rider, every old
    place I go.
Every old place I go.

I can tell the wind is risin'
The leaves tremblin' on the trees
Tremblin' on the trees
I can tell the wind is risin'
Leaves tremblin' on the trees
ummm hmmm hmmm hmmm
All I need my little sweet woman
And to keep my company
Mmm hmm hey hey hey
My company

Little Robert would run up and fool around with their guitars. The sound he would make was far from sweet.

"Why don't y'all go in there and get that guitar away from that boy," people would say. "He's running people crazy with it."

So Son House would talk to Little Robert.

"Don't do that, Robert," he'd say. "You drive the people nuts. You can't play nothing. Why don't you blow the harmonica for 'em?"

After a while, Little Robert disappeared for about a year. One Saturday night, Brown and House were playing a little place east of Robinsonville called Banks, Mississippi, when the boy—now a man—reappeared, swinging through the door with four or five harmonicas stuck in a broad belt around his waist and a guitar slung over his back.

"Bill!" Son House said. "Look who's coming in the door."

"Yeah, Little Robert."

"And he's got a guitar," said House.

The two men laughed about it as the man made his way though the crowd and came up to them.

"Well, boy, you still got a guitar, huh?" said House. "What do you do with that thing? You can't do nothing with it."

The man replied, "Well, I'll tell you what."

House said, "What?"

"Let me have your seat a minute."

"All right, and you better do something with it," House said, and he winked at Brown.

Little Robert proceeded to put on a performance that left House and Brown stunned. Little Robert—his full name was Robert Johnson—was finally showing his true genius. House would say later, "That boy could play more blues than [any] of us."

Johnson hung around for a week or so, and House gave him a "little instruction"—probably in slide guitar technique and the like, much as House had gotten some tips from Willie Wilson years before. House also gave Johnson some advice: He told him he was a little crazy when it came to women; and corn liquor and Saturday-night balls and women saying, "Daddy, play it again, Daddy" were a dangerous mix. Said House, "Don't let it run you crazy. You liable to get killed." Johnson laughed it off. Not long afterward, House heard some of Johnson's records. The first one was "Terraplane Blues." Son House thought, "Jesus, it was good." Other songs would follow, and they would all become classics: "I Believe I'll Dust My Broom," "Hellhound on My Trail," "Love in Vain," "Come On in My Kitchen," "From Four Until Late," "32-20 Blues." House thought Johnson was going places. But the trip turned out to be a short one. Said House, "The next word we heard was from his mother, who told us he was dead. We never did get the straight of it. We first heard that he got stabbed to death. Next, a woman poisoned him, and then we heard something else. Never did just get the straight of it."

After that, death followed Son House like a shadow. His pal Patton died in 1934 in Indianola, Mississippi, of a long-standing heart condition that probably wasn't helped much by his itinerant ways and constant drinking. House moved to Rochester, New York, in 1943 and tried to settle down with his wife Evie. His friend Brown joined him in

Rochester but eventually moved back down South and died in 1952. House got a letter from Brown's girl about his passing—he died, she said, "of the effects of alcohol." House, depressed and discouraged, and wondering if his lifestyle wasn't to blame for all the tragedy around him, mostly gave up the blues after that but kept drinking. He worked odd jobs around Rochester: a grill cook at a Howard Johnson, a porter on the New York Central Railroad, a veterinary assistant who shaved animals before surgery.

Now, Son House had been discovered and rediscovered throughout his career. In 1930 Son was "discovered" by H.C. Speir, who hooked him up with Paramount; House traveled from the Delta to Grafton, Wisconsin, to record with his pals Brown and Patton, and was paid forty dollars for his trouble. In 1941, he was discovered working as a tractor driver by Alan Lomax, who recorded a series of House's songs for the Library of Congress, including "Death Letter Blues"; House was given a cold Coca-Cola for his work. In 1964 three folklorists, Dick Waterman, Phil Spiro, and Nick Perls, drove from the Delta to Rochester and rediscovered House, just in time for the folk boom of the mid-1960s. Most people thought House—like the rest of the original Delta bluesmen—was dead. He hadn't played a guitar in five years and his hands had a senile tremor, but he could still sing. In 1965 House's comeback was underway and he recorded for Columbia. But bluesmen are not objects to be lost and then found. Having vast talent, and having it go unrecognized, takes a toll. One winter morning in 1966, House was found by a Rochester snow-plowing crew—numb, drunk, and almost lifeless in a pile of snow. In 1976 he moved to Detroit; he died in obscurity in 1988. He might have been 86 years old or he might have been 94 or he might have been 102.

One thing is for certain, though: He wasn't a tragedy. House's protégé Robert Johnson sang about coming to the crossroads, but it was House who drew the map that led him there. House, in his music and in his life, brought together the sacred and the profane; he found the musical moment where Saturday night meets Sunday morning. House's lyrics, which were personal and emotional, made the blues about more than suffering, more than celebration—he imbued the form with an introspective quality, exploring the torments of the soul without choosing sides or making easy judgment. "Ain't no heaven, ain't no burning hell/Where I'm going when I die, can't nobody tell," House sang in "My Black Mama." Many churchmen and bluesmen saw the world in black and white; Son House sang in shades of blue—dark, rich, varied hues that could capture the range of human experience. "I wish I had me a heaven of my own," he sang in "Preachin' the Blues." House got a little piece of paradise every time he played his guitar. 🎸

RECOMMENDED LISTENING:
Son House, *The Original Delta Blues* (Columbia/Legacy, 1998). The definition of the form.
Robert Johnson, *King of the Delta Blues* (Columbia/Legacy, 1997). Every song on this set is a masterpiece.
Various Artists, *Roots of Robert Johnson* (Yazoo, 1990). A survey of the artists who blazed a trail for Johnson.
Various Artists, *Son House and the Great Delta Blues Singers* (Document, 1994). A rough, intriguing collection of early blues songs.
The White Stripes, *Der Stijl Original Recording Remastered* (V2/BMG, 2002). This alternative-rock duo's cover of Son House's "Death Letter" injects new life into the blues.

THE BLUES AVANT-GARDE BY LUC SANTE

The country blues was a form of music created by the children and grandchildren of slaves, in settings that ranged narrowly from plantations to small towns, in some of the most remote, least modern, and least cosmopolitan areas of the Deep South. Because of this, latter-day listeners with a glancing acquaintance, even if they do not consider the music to be "primitive," often suppose it to be traditional, folkloric, a craft more than an art in everything but its emotional content. But the blues was radical in its very manifestation—as much an expression of modernism as anything hatched in Paris or Berlin or New York—and its individual practitioners included explorers working in the far reaches of the form, experimenting with harmony, rhythm, structure, voice, stance, and arrangement. These early-twentieth-century adventurers could properly be considered avant-garde, especially in the context of the period, when radical experimentation flourished in every city and in every art form. But all were unschooled, many were illiterate, many were itinerant—they worked under a daunting set of disadvantages—and their exchange of ideas occurred strictly by word of mouth.

We know nothing about how the blues came to be, only that it was first noted just after 1900, in the vicinity of the lower course of the Mississippi River, and that the sophisticated observers who noted it—W.C. Handy, Ma Rainey, and Jelly Roll Morton, all found it strange, haunting, startling. It was something more than an evolutionary development of earlier African-American music. Something had happened very suddenly: a moment of discovery, a "paradigm shift"—but everything else about it is a mystery. Making matters even more needlessly

mysterious is the fact that the first blues was not recorded until 1920 (Mamie Smith's "Crazy Blues"), the first country blues roughly five years later. On the scale of folklore, a quarter-century is a blink, but on the scale of modernism, it is an eon. In that same twenty-five years (1903–1928), for example, Cubism came and went. It would now be difficult to gauge the paintings of 1926 without some knowledge of those of 1913 and 1922—it would be like coming into a heated conversation well into its third hour and trying to determine by inference what had transpired before one's arrival. So it is with the blues.

Given the hit-or-miss nature of the recording industry's coverage of the country blues between 1924 or so and the early 1930s, when most recording was curtailed by the Depression, the range of what did come down to us is startling. We have recordings by the most popular and ambitious artists, of course, but much else is due to chance alone. We can assume, then, there is an equivalent number of significant artists who were excluded by the same process of chance. What you would expect from the documentation of a widespread phenomenon of musical ferment in a fairly circumscribed time frame is something geometric and hierarchical: a row of major influences succeeded by increasing ranks of derivative followers, with a handful of eccentrics on the fringes. Instead, the blues of the period, if mapped on a grid, would look like many disparate clumps—separated by spaces—of a vast jigsaw puzzle. The alternative possibility, no less real, is that the quotient of originality ran disproportionately high.

By the time Charley Patton was recorded, in 1929, he had been playing for a good twenty years.

He was a celebrity in the Mississippi Delta, probably more for his antic stage presence than for his music per se. That music, however, was of astonishing complexity and formal daring. Not only did he achieve the sound of a small band by playing lead, rhythm, and bass lines on his guitar all at once but he cut and folded songs into other songs, made collages of fragments, took on a dizzying variety of personae in his lyrics ("A Spoonful Blues" has a different narrator in every line), and, from the evidence of a pair of unissued alternate takes, seldom played a song the same way twice. His recorded work represents the equivalent of a midcareer retrospective—two decades' worth of experimentation, still in progress, alas cut short by his death in 1934.

Patton was a star, and his influence would only become more noticeable over subsequent decades—he was king of the Delta blues. Of quite a different profile, though, was Joe Holmes, an itinerant from Louisiana who went by the name of King Solomon Hill. Only four sides are known by him (a third record has recently been discovered but not yet made public), and they are among the strangest in the blues. The beat of "The Gone Dead Train," for example, varies constantly—each vocal line is of a different length, as are the guitar fills—and the whole thing constantly threatens to break down into formlessness. But it has its own logic, at once musical (the changes of the fills effectively correspond to those of the vocals without merely echoing them) and conversational; or maybe the word would be *poetic*—his metric anarchy, startling in popular song, evokes the kind of unscannable but audibly dynamic music you find in the most rigorous free verse. And Holmes was a hobo. You almost have to believe in providence to account for his being admitted into a recording facility.

Holmes is perhaps an extreme case, an individualist who came from no identifiable school and left no immediate progeny. But originality in the early blues is often highly subjective. The originality of Blind Lemon Jefferson is sometimes overlooked, maybe because of the physical deterioration of his recordings, but much more on account of his massive influence: He was indisputably the most popular of the early rural bluesmen. On the other hand, the man who worked the corner across from him in Dallas' Deep Ellum was Blind Willie Johnson, who has been far less-often copied and remains evergreen. His wordless moan on "Dark Was the Night" sounds like nothing else in music, period. As for Johnson's trademark guttural rasp, who can even say, at this remove, whether he originated the sound or transmitted an element of a tradition of which we have no other trace? We can be fairly certain that nobody but the extraordinarily delicate gospel bluesman Washington Phillips played the dulceola—a massive, harplike thing that's been referred to as a "plucked piano"—since no other recordings of it are known. We can be reasonably sure that no recorded blues player employed "Spanish" tuning, capoed to a different absolute key in every one of his eight recordings, quite like the Alabama street singer Buddy Boy Hawkins. We can search in vain for anyone employing the surrealist lyrical imagery of Funny Papa Smith.

But then, we don't know who their friends and rivals and teachers were, either. Nevertheless, it is far less likely that these men had forgotten doubles than that there were many such self-determined explorers of sound and sense who were working within the physical conventions of traditional, premodern popular music but who must have been aware that they were contributing to the invention of something wildly new. ☛

THE LEVEE-CAMP HOLLER By Alan Lomax
[From *The Land Where the Blues Began*, 1993]

In spite of [certain] villainies, levee work was attractive to the men of the Delta. Years of plowing had given them the skills required to get work out of a mule team in any weather. On the river, payday came once every week or two, rather than once a year, and in a month a man could pocket more gambling and drinking money than he might earn in a season on the farm. Split away from their little home places and families, these itinerant muleskinners knew the pain of alienation and anomie, yet they enjoyed the freedom of roaming from job to job and woman to woman. If they had to knuckle under to a bullying boss, then they could take out their anger on their weaker fellows. Meantime, they were creating their own culture of racy lingo, humor, tall tale, custom, and song, in which their sociable and ebullient African temperaments could flower. The swampland and the sordid streets of their tent cities became the stage for new acts in the African-American drama, where they could test their manhood, cement their friendships, and enlarge their collective culture. They sang multiple melodies until their mules—all of whom had nicknames—joined in the chorus, sometimes grew so excited that they literally worked themselves to death.

In the thirties, when my father, John A. Lomax, and I were recording across the South, levee camps existed not only along the Mississippi but also on the White River in Arkansas, the Red River in Louisiana, the Brazos and Trinity rivers in Texas, and a score of lesser streams in the vast alluvial plains of the lower South. In these swampy lowlands, indeed wherever land was to be drained, foundations laid, or dirt moved, the black muleskinner appeared with his scoop pulled by a team of lusty mules, and the high lonesome levee song would soon rise in the air.

Got up in the mornin, so doggone soon,
So doggone soon,
I couldn see nothin, good podner,
But the stars and moon—
Oh-oh-oh-oh-oh, but the stars and moon.

The singer is explaining why he's late to work, but like a good worker, he also complains about working conditions in an outfit where all the mules have sore shoulders. The humane law forbade working a mule with a bad shoulder, forcing the animal to grind an open sore against its stiff leather collar. Most outfits disregarded this law, and its constant and flagrant violation became the subject of the muleskinner's perennial complaint.

Well, I looked all over the whole corral,
The whole corral,
And I couldn find a mule, good podner,
With his shoulder well—
Oh-oh-oh-oh-oh, with his shoulder well.

We found this song not only in the Mississippi Valley and the flood plains to the west into Texas, but in every other Southern state as well. Lately, I have looked up all these non-Mississippi levee-holler variants, and every one of them was sung by a Mississippian on his travels or by someone who had learned it from somebody from the Delta.

Charles Peabody, a young archeologist working a site in the Delta, was the first to report on the levee-camp holler. In his journal of 1903 he comments on the difficulty of describing the strange songs his muleskinners were singing:

As to the autochthonous music, unaccompanied, it is hard to give an exact account. Our best model for the study of this was a diligent Negro living near called by our men "Five Dollars" (suggestive of craps), and by us "Haman's Man," from his persistent following from sunrise to sunset of the mule of that name. These fifteen hours he filled with words and music. Hymns alternated with quite fearful oaths addressed to Haman. Other directions intoned to him melted into strains of apparently genuine African music, sometimes with words, sometimes without. Long phrases there were without apparent measured rhythm, singularly hard to copy in notes. When such sung by him and by others could be reduced to form, a few motives were made to appear, and these copied out were usually quite simple, based for the most part on the major or minor triad. The long, lonely sing-song of the fields was quite distinct from anything else, though the singer was skilful [sic] in gliding from hymn-motive to those of the native chant.

Peabody also transcribed the free-flowing melody Haman sang, and there is no question that it contains the cadences peculiar to the levee-camp holler that my father and I so frequently recorded all across the Deep South during the thirties and forties.

The levee-camp holler therefore seems definitely to be Delta or at least Western in provenance. In fact, repeated recording trips into the area revealed the existence of an extensive genre of songs, called hollers,

Alan Lomax recording the Pratcher brothers (Miles and Bob) in Como, Mississippi, in 1959

in the Delta region. For example, every black prisoner in the penitentiary, we discovered, had a holler that was, in effect, his personal musical signature. Heard at a distance, another prisoner could say, "Listen at old so-and-so. Don't he sound lonesome this morning."

All these hollers share a set of distinctive features. They are solos, slow in tempo, free in rhythm (as opposed to the gang work songs), composed of long, gliding, ornamented, and melismatic phrases, given a melancholy character by minor intervals as well as by blued or bent tones, sounding like sobs or moans or keening or pain-filled cries, even when they were performed with such bravura that they resounded across the fields. Because they were seldom sung except on the job, even the aficionados of black music have little acquaintance with this wondrous recitative-like vocalizing through which black labor voiced the tragic horror of their condition. "Cap'n, doncha do me like you do po Shine/Drove him so hard till he went stone blind."

The style of these solo, unaccompanied, idiosyncratic, melancholic hollers runs directly counter to the mainstream of black song in the South and generally round the Caribbean, where song is for the most part on-beat, brisk, merry, sensuous, integrated, choralizing, and accompanied, if not by drums or some other instrument, at least by hand clapping and/or foot stomping. Most black song, both post- and antebellum, even when its mood is somber and serious when the song begins, usually picks up tempo and is transformed into music that can be danced to before it has been sung to a conclusion. Indeed, the bulk of black song, unlike that of Europe, which is usually lyrical, can be danced to—in the case of work songs, making work into a sort of dance.

Major exceptions to this rule are two: the long-meter hymns and the work hollers of the Delta and the lowland Southwest. Both these forms came into prominence at the time of the decay of the plantation collectivity and the emergence of individualized effort as the main source of survival for Delta blacks. Both mark a sharp stylistic turn away from the on-beat collective song style of most earlier African-American genres and the adoption of a highly individualized solo attack. The favorite long-meter hymn is an ego-oriented appeal for help from God: "Lord, in my trouble I stretch my hand to thee,/Lord, in my trouble no other help I know."

The usual levee-camp holler is a personal appeal to Mister Cholly, the white boss who hires, fires, pays, or doesn't pay him: "Mister Cholly, Mister Cholly, just gimme my time./Gwan, old bully, you are time behind."

It was in the Delta that blacks entered the levee and land-clearing crews, often forcibly organized, and became for the first time anonymous units of labor instead of being owned by somebody or belonging on some plantation and to an extended family. In this new condition they could see themselves being used up and flung aside, often actually worked to death, alongside the mules they drove. In the earlier plantation situation, under slavery and later on as renters or field hands, they still had some feeling of identification with the bosses they worked for and the place they lived. These relationships were usually attenuated in the levee camps and on the penal farms. There, "a nigger wasn't worth as much as a mule." In most societies the individual can look to organized authority as in some sense beneficient or protective, can ask for mercy and help in times of distress and expect to receive it. But increasingly, the laborers of the Deep South, floating from camp to camp, often from prison to prison, came to feel that they had nowhere to turn.

There was, as usual in black tradition, a musical response. It came in the sudden emergence of the lonesome holler, and later the blues, notable among all human works of art for their profound despair. They gave voice to the mood of alienation and anomie that prevailed in the construction camps of the South. In creating these new, critical genres, American blacks called upon ancient African resources, for complaints of this very type existed in the traditions of African kingdoms. Indeed, our Cantometric survey has found very similar songs in Northwest Africa and the Lake States, among the Wolof and the Watusi, for example. A broader look finds that such ornamented, unaccompanied singing is commonplace in the kingdoms and empires of North Africa, of the southern Mediterranean, and of the Middle East. It seems, in fact, that this song type, which we might call the high, lonesome complaint, is one undercurrent of music in the whole of civilized Eurasia—the ancient world of caste, empire, exploited peasantry, harem-bound women, and absolute power—from the Far East to Ireland. A related and ultimately derivative string-accompanied solo style is also present in this same region. It turns up in West Africa, and in the Americas gave rise to the blues. ☞

"If it ain't about what's real, what's happenin' right now, it ain't the blues." —*Chris Thomas King*

MUDDY WATERS: AUGUST 31, 1941

By Robert Gordon

[From *Can't Be Satisfied: The Life and Times of Muddy Waters*, 2002]

By the early 1940s, Muddy [Waters] was famous in his "circle we was going in," the skinny strip of Delta that fanned out from Clarksdale to the Mississippi River along Number One Highway. There were plenty of little back-road juke houses along there—he'd never want for a job—but it wasn't exactly international fame.

Muddy Waters' first real break into the outside world came in the summer of 1941, during a field recording trip under the combined auspices of Nashville's Fisk University and the Library of Congress in Washington, D.C. He made his first recordings that summer and then several more the following summer when the group returned; a year after that, with the courage of a recording veteran, he would leave the Delta for Chicago. These encounters were perhaps the most crucial to his future career. . . .

Searching for funds to finance the trip, Fisk contacted the Library of Congress. Their Archive of American Folk Song, in the person of folklorist Alan Lomax, recognized the strength of the project and agreed to collaborate. His father, John Lomax, had been associated with the Archive since soon after its founding in 1928. Alan became the Archive's first full-time employee in 1937. [Fisk's] study jibed with the Lomax family's perception of "folklore," a more malleable notion than the reigning tradition in which the oldest songs—dating prior to the Industrial Revolution (indeed prior to the printing press) and unchanged by time—were considered purest; Alan and his father believed that the living folk and their input were as vital as the original source of the material. . . .

On Sunday, August 31, 1941, Lomax and Fisk professor John Work arrived early and unannounced on the Stovall Plantation. They sought Captain Holt, the friendly, pipe-smoking overseer, and gained permission to mix with the black population, especially one "Muddy Water." The singer, suspicious of being busted by a conniving moonshiner, came to the commissary before this stranger could find him at home. The trust between them was established by Lomax's guitar, sealed with a whiskey, and then Lomax began setting up the equipment that Muddy had helped bring in. Lomax did not like for Work to handle the equipment. Son Sims had appeared by the time the bottle was being uncorked, and he accompanied Muddy on their original song "Burr Clover Blues" so recording levels could be set. While Lomax made final adjustments with the knobs, John Work conducted a brief interview with the two musicians. Asked to state their names, Muddy identified himself as "Name McKinley Morganfield, nickname Muddy Water," then added, "Stovall's famous guitar picker."

And so, after lunch and before supper, Muddy Waters recorded one of the songs for which he was known in his neck of the Delta and for which he would later become known throughout the world. "Country Blues" was the name Lomax appended to it; "I Feel Like Going Home" was the title in John Work's notes and the title when it took Chicago by storm a few years later. These first recordings were quite different from the electric versions Muddy would later record. They were about the marriage of acoustic space created by the human voice and a wooden guitar. "You get more pure thing out of an acoustic," Muddy later reflected. "I prefer an acoustic." The power in Muddy's playing is comparable to the way a blade cuts rows into a field; his music is informed and

Photographer Dorothea Lange captured this Mississippi plantation overseer and his crew of sharecroppers in 1941.

defined by the immediacy of touching a string and the knowledge of how it affects the air around it.

After Muddy completed "Country Blues," the recording captured him leaning back in his chair, a creaking, and then a bassy rumbling that becomes recognizable: footsteps crossing a wooden floor. It was Lomax, not stopping until he was right next to Muddy; he was speaking into the microphone when he said, "I wonder if you can tell me, if you can remember, when it was that you made that blues, Muddy Water?"

Muddy answered straight away, a bit anxious and almost stepping on Lomax's question. "I made that blues up in '38."

"Do you remember the time of the year?"

"I made it up about the eighth of October in '38." Muddy clustered his words together, with a halting nervousness between them.

Lomax inquired in a comfortable, almost intimate voice. By this point, he, Work, and Muddy had been together several hours, during which Muddy had seen this untold dream unfold and assemble itself in his very living room. Lomax, realizing he could capture Muddy while the mood still hung, got close and casual.

"I remember thinking how low-key Morganfield was, grave even to the point of shyness," Lomax wrote in his field notes. "But I was bowled over by his artistry. There was nothing uncertain about his performances. He sang and played with such finesse, with such a mercurial and sensitive relation between voice and guitar and he expressed so much tenderness in the way he handled his lyrics that he went right beyond all his predecessors—Blind Lemon, Charley Patton, Robert Johnson, Son House, and Willie Brown. His own pieces were more than blues, they were love songs of the Deep South, gently erotic and deeply sentimental."

Lomax's questions continued: "Do you remember where you were when you were doing your singing, how it happened?"

"—No, I—"

"No, I mean, where you were sitting, what you were thinking about?"

"I was fixing the punction [puncture] on a car, and I had been mistreated by a girl and it looked like that run in my mind to sing that song."

"Tell me a little of the story of it if you don't mind, if it's not too personal. I want to know the facts, and how you felt and why you felt the way you did. It's a very beautiful song."

This white man complimented the field hand, and he answered like an artist: "Well, I just felt blue, and the song fell into my mind, come to me just like that song I started to sing and went on with it."

Muddy may not have been in the boisterous voice he'd have when frying Saturday fish sandwiches and laughing with friends, but he was loosening up. Things were working out. 🎸

A RIFF ON READING STERLING PLUMPP'S POETRY BY JOHN EDGAR WIDEMAN

Blues announces the end of the world—the old world you've known or thought you knew till the blues jumps up and grunts, Huh-huh, no-no-no, boy, it ain't like that at all. Here's something more for you to learn, to cry over or grin about or celebrate or mourn. Don't you ever forget there's always the break, the hesitation, hitch between one beat, one word, one note, one line, one breath and the next. Slide and glide as best you can, my friend, there's still the unexpected you got to deal with— falling down, falling up, Lawd, Lawd-shit. Great-googa-mooga—turn me on, turn me down, turn me all around, turn me loose. The world ain't what it used to be, spozed to be, only exactly what its Big Bad Wolf self wants to be—so lissen up and don't be getting too far ahead of yourself, uh-huh.

No essay here—rather, a riff on reading Sterling Plumpp's poetry, on reading any words on a page that want to sing the blues, any writing aspiring to attain the metaphorical, spiritual, and material complexities of blues music.

Three abiding qualities distinguish Plumpp's best work (and recapitulate blues tradition). Focus: intense, compressed (becoming even more clipped, enigmatic, dense, and cryptic in his most recent writing), blues a sort of navel or blade of grass he gazes at to see the entire universe. Discipline: He contains his ambitious project within a single idiom of African-American musical style. Variety: In spite of intense discipline and focus, he manages to swing—to range widely, freely, and achieve, like blues, an amazing allusiveness, capaciousness of tone, subject matter, form, scene, voice within his chosen realm. Bluesmen and classical composers have been inspired to set his lyrics to music.

And one—bluesmen and women and songs and themes and attitudes as ways of figuring, modeling, representing a reality the poetry seeks to communicate.

And two—the effort to wring from the music a philosophic inquiry with blues as worldview, as consolation and rumination, a long quarrel and tentative reconciliation with godhead or god-long-gone. Blues (through paraphrase, analysis, contradiction, dialogue) as a path for coming to terms with existence.

And three—blues forms, translated or paralleled or suggested through the techniques of written poetry; blues as poetry/poetry as blues; to what degree are their structures and rhetoric mutually intelligible—are they wary, compatible, welcoming— how/why/when. Think about the multidimensional singing space—how it implicates all the senses, how performing a song employs time as duration and rhythmic beat and intimate, shared presence. How is time embodied in reading, in written poetry's line breaks, line length, stanzaic patterns, refrains, spacing (is space silence), rhyme, meter, repetition, direct address, the mimicking of vernacular dialect. Can typography capture melisma, slurring, noises, rolling eyes, call and response, sing-along choruses, the showmanship and foolishness acted out onstage.

Hit it—ain't nothing but a party, so let's just play—play the blues—blues always a fugue of tradition, dream, impossibility, invention—changes sometimes successful, sometimes disastrous. Plumpp attempts print analogues of characteristic blues devices such as the repeated, cumulative urgency of a "shout"—an unchanging (yet always different because of context) word or refrain beginning each line of a poem. He tells stories simply, directly, and no matter how personal the subject, tells them with minimal particularizing clutter so they stand for, invite the collective drama as echo, affirmation. Can I hear somebody say, Amen.

Technical craftsmanship and taking chances saturate Sterling Plumpp's work in the blues medium. Just as important is his formidable sense of self. Whether in Mississippi or Capetown, South Africa, the poet writes with profound assurance of being rooted. He knows exactly who he is, where he's from—even when (especially) he poses as somebody else. Not that he uncritically approves or romanticizes. Or brags. Or is blasé. Not that he doesn't brag or profile or strut or seem quite satisfied with himself. Point is he doesn't stand still. He owns up to paradoxes and inconsistencies, the flat-out wars within his heart, soul, body, and mind. Because that's the portable place he really comes from. His unfinished business on the planet. The song he keeps on singing.

Paradox: Part of what he knows about himself is, of course, the blues—the blues forever mysterious, irreducible, open-ended, Promethean, in-progress, questions not answers. You never get the sense the poetry or poet claims to know what's coming next, nor that the past, intimidating as it can be, is a done deal. Performance embodies tension—the troubadour moving on down the line. The mode of discovery of blues is checking what might work this time out. The poet or singer shares with the audience the particulars of a fragile truce he or she has achieved at some moment or another and seeks to reanimate the feel of that experience.

Though blues depends on an established tradition, and we can predict (foretaste) the 4/4 time, percussive polymetric rhythms, gravelly gut-bucket tonalities, falsetto shrieks, field hollers, anticipate rimes and formulaic lines from the standard repertoire, the tags beginning or ending songs if they ask you who sang this song, tell 'em, Sterling, been here and gone, each time we step on board, the blues, our destination's uncertain. We're suspended in the medium, by the medium. We won't know there till we go there.

Yes, plenty of oft-used couplets, familiar patterns, sounds. Then here come Skip James, Son House, Robert Johnson, bending and extending notes till they're eerie and haunted; disruptive intrusions that gradually turn solid and shapely;

"In 1965, as a twenty-year-old poet living in a rooming house in Pittsburgh, I discovered Bessie Smith and the blues. It was a watershed event in my life. It gave me history. It provided me with a cultural response to the world as well as the knowledge that the text and content of my life were worthy of the highest celebration and occasion of art. It also gave me a framework and an aesthetic for exploring the tradition from which it grew. I set out on a continual search for ways to give expression to the spiritual impulse of the African-American culture which had nurtured and sanctioned my life and ultimately provided it with its meaning. I was, as are all artists, searching for a way to define myself in relation to the world I lived in. The blues gave me a firm and secure ground. It became, and remains, the wellspring of my art." —*August Wilson*

sure-handed as fists gripping the wooden handles of an old-time plow must be to dance metal and mule in directions they don't want to go or know better than to go, won't go unless there's a boss driving, digging, holding on for a long, steady furrow, for a good groove cutting so deep it's not exactly man nor mule nor plow in charge but the earth saying, "Yes, I'll let you go there this time." Blues voices sculpting sound like Giacometti elongates the human body, worries his people's bronze skin, pinching, gouging, twisting, compressing a freshly roughened surface to bear the ruins of its history.

Plumpp's poems conduct a kind of research upon the body of blues tradition—research in which he tests himself, tests his body to determine how it responds to the knowledge, the challenge blues transmits. Letting go. Getting it on. I feel something large at stake when I engage his poems. A simple utterance, bare and skimpy-looking on the page, seizes my attention; its spareness and immediacy makes me believe he wants me to hear what he's saying. The seeming transparency of the utterance complicates it. A piece of business, bigger, more concrete than either of us. A sense of sharing, of common ground is palpable. Together we're figuring out something important.

> The
> birth of chaos
> is the embryo of my songs
>
> voices I collect bits of nights
> crushed by blind winds
> [from Plumpp's *Blues Inside His Breathing* (1997)]

I'm a prose writer, so when I talk about Sterling Plumpp's poetry, I'm also thinking about what I demand from all kinds of good writing: surprise, subtlety, style, a self-consciousness of language as medium. I search for proof that words can be reeducated, revitalized, saved. The best writing suggests implicitly or explicitly how readers must participate in the making of words/worlds. For abundant evidence that Plumpp's writing accomplishes these tasks, see for instance: "Turf Song," "Blues From the Bloodseed," or "Sander's Bottoms" (from *Johannesburg and Other Poems*).

Plumpp makes me feel he feels—feels powerfully about something he's willing and able to express with eloquence. I'm hit again and again by the tenacity of his spirit's questing, the single-minded pursuit, unrelenting importance and urgency he projects about the task of identifying, locating, then squeezing truth and pleasure from his blues roots. As I read, I'm learning about a person, a stance, a bottom line—inherited, internalized, recreated, extended to poetry.

Many of his poems are dedicated to famous blues artists, others to anonymous blues people. Some celebrate well-known heroes of various third world and domestic liberation struggles, many are addressed to family members, friends, and acquaintances, a few to the art of blues itself. Dedications are signs of generosity. Poems become a means of saying thanks, of returning bounty for bounty, replenishing the sources, the tradition. Poems are political in the best sense because they honor debts, commemorate the necessity of conscious struggle, of paying dues, paying back. I'm grateful for the gift—beguiled, intrigued, enlightened by Plumpp's project so far—how he takes and gives.

Finally, and maybe most important, his blues poems make me want to write. ✒

THANK GOD FOR ROBERT JOHNSON BY ELMORE LEONARD

Son House said there was only one kind of blues: something between a man and a woman, one deceiving or walking out on the other. Any situation different than that, Son House said, was "monkey junk." My experience with the blues goes back to the early 1930s, when I was a little kid in Memphis, and the voices of Mildred Bailey and Billie Holiday caught my ear. It was only about ten years ago that I learned Mildred Bailey was white, and I could not believe it. In my memory of her voice and phrasing, she never sounded like a white woman.

In 1941 we paid Woody Herman seven hundred dollars to bring his herd to the University of Detroit High School for Gala Night. He closed with his theme song, the dirgelike "Blue Flame," and it's been my favorite big-band blues number ever since, placing it just above Earl Hines' "After Hours" and the Basie Orchestra behind Joe Williams doing "Every Day I Have the Blues." During high school I was into black bands almost exclusively, and I saw Earl Hines, Jimmie Lunceford, Fletcher Henderson, Lucky Millinder, Andy Kirk and his Clouds of Joy with Mary Lou Williams—all of them at

the Paradise Theatre in Detroit— on their way to or from New York's Apollo. What used to be the Paradise is now the home of the Detroit Symphony Orchestra.

In January 1946 I got off a Navy ship at Treasure Island, had my first glass of milk in over a year—couldn't finish it, too rich— and raced over to a ballroom in Oakland to see Stan Kenton. The high point was standing close to the stage and staring up at June Christy doing "Buzz Me."

In the late forties, following the war, my favorite spots for jazz and blues in Detroit were the Flame Show Bar, Sportree's, and one or two others. I saw Anita O'Day, Red Allen, J.J. Johnson and Kai Winding. It was at Sportree's that I met T-Bone Walker and joined him for drinks later, at an after-hours club.

In 1955 in New York, I told Wild Bill Davison I'd always wanted to play the cornet but now, at thirty, felt I was too old to learn. Wild Bill said, "I can teach you how to play the fuckin' horn in ten minutes." I went home and bought a used cornet but never learned. A friend who was with me on the trip bought a new

cornet and learned to play it but was never any good.

About 1985, I heard Dizzy Gillespie up close at an outdoor venue and was moved to go home and write, practice my craft. Other jazz performers had the same effect on me. I was listening to Ben Webster one time and named a character in the story I was writing after him: a bull rider turned Hollywood stuntman. I make these references to jazz because, according to Count Basie, the blues is what jazz came out of, what it's all about.

The last time I saw Basie perform was in '69 at the Whiskey in L.A., sitting in with Carmen McRae, who prompted Eddie "Lockjaw" Davis during his solos to "Go, Jaw, Go!" Later, listening to Lorez Alexandria at another club, we sat close to the bandstand, and I got to watch Carmen nodding to the beat, chewing her gum in rhythm with Lorez' timing.

And in 1987 in a club in Detroit called All That Jazz, Kris Lynn, who sat at her piano turning show tunes into jazz, invited an older black guy to take the mike, and I heard "Tishamingo [sic] Blues" for the first time.

I'm going to Tishamingo
to have my hambone boiled
These Atlanta women done
let my hambone spoil.

The song was recorded by Peg Leg Howell in Atlanta, November 8, 1926. In *Freaky Deaky*, published in '88, I wrote the song into a jazz club scene. Two years ago I began writing a book set in Mississippi and saw the chance to use "Tishomingo Blues" as the title; the main reason being I like the sound of it—*Tisho-mingo*.

The rationale at first: A Civil War battle in the book is based somewhat on the Battle of Brice's Cross Roads, a Confederate victory that took place in the vicinity of Tishomingo Creek, not far from Tishomingo County, Mississippi. But for the book's setting I needed a town that would attract criminal activity, and for that I chose Tunica, "the Casino Capital of the South," almost forty miles down Highway 61 from Memphis. What I didn't realize—until my researcher for the past twenty years, Gregg Sutter, pointed it out—was the story took place in the heart of the Mississippi Delta, where blues styles were fashioned and fooled with until the 1930s when country blues had become a tradition, an American institution.

Gregg said, "And you want Robert Taylor, the coolest guy in the book, to be driving around in his Jaguar, listening to jazz?" He was right. I told Gregg I'd better add some blues for color, and maybe some of its history.

The next step was to become familiar with the lineage: how Charley Patton's riffs influenced Son House, and Son House was the man until Robert Johnson "sold his soul to the Devil" and came up with a sound that got everybody excited, influencing not only the bluesmen who followed, but also the Rolling Stones, Led Zeppelin, Eric Clapton. Listen to Robert Johnson's "Love in Vain" and then the Stones' coverage of it on their hit album of thirty years ago, *Get Yer Ya-Ya's Out!*, and Clapton with Cream taking off on Johnson's "Cross Roads Blues."

I came to the legend of Robert Johnson selling his soul at the famous crossroads in Clarksdale, where Highways 61 and 49 intersect, not far from Tunica, and for the first time in thirty-seven novels I detected a theme. Until now I'd had to wait for Scott Frank, an A-list Hollywood screenwriter, to tell me what my novels—SOON TO BE A MAJOR MOTION PICTURE!—were about. This time, during the actual writing of the book, the theme of

Tishomingo Blues was staring me in the face.

In reference to Robert Johnson's "I Believe I'll Dust My Broom," along with Elmore James dusting his, I gave the character Robert Taylor a grandfather named Broom Taylor, a bluesman who moved his family to Detroit with John Lee Hooker.

Writing the book took me into Delta blues for the good part of a year. On a video of a 1960s documentary called *Legends of Bottleneck Blues Guitar*, I saw the distinctive styles of Son House and Mississippi Fred McDowell, of Johnny Shines, Jesse Fuller, Mance Lipscomb, Furry Lewis. I listened to the recordings of Peg Leg Howell, Charley Patton, Robert Johnson, Elmore James, B.B. King, Muddy Waters, Howlin' Wolf, Willie Dixon, Buddy Guy. These bluesmen played with soul and you could feel it and have to nod, *yeah*, at spellbinding combinations of riffs.

It's the music that evolved to become the inspirational sounds that have played in my head. Anita O'Day letting me off uptown, or the Diz' cool bop, or Brubeck's "Take Five," his piano enticing the drums to kick out, or the way Basie's band comes in low on "Sweet Lorraine" and rises with one sound to blast you out of your chair. 🖝

HOWLIN' WOLF BY GREG TATE

His was not a city sound. He never being one to be easily domesticated or taken out of his elementalness. He never being one to be so engaged with the cosmopolis as to lose sight of the outback's verities or the sexual cornucopia of the barnyard. Therefore his bluesongs display the worst features of an amoral ark—an erotically amok animal farm of roosters, dogs, backdoor men, and coons shot to the moon. A countrified vision of morality and mortality. I asked for water, she gave me gasoline. He is speaking, really, of frontier romances, the kind handily capable of dispensing frontier justice. And that Wolferine yodel, a libertine's sigh of release, which in actuality reflects a faith only in that lone gift of absolute comfort in this world. The only one we were left with after the fall and therefore worth every disaster that might ensue in, say, tasting the forbidden fruit of another man's wife. Like the preachers say: On your tombstone will

"I was three years old and they started callin' me Wolf. My grandfather gave me that name. He used to sit down and tell me tall stories about what the wolf would do. Because I was a bad boy, you know, and I was always in devilment. I'd say, 'Well, what do the wolf do?' He'd say, 'Howl.' You know, to scare me, you know, and I'd get mad about this. I didn't know it would be a great name." —*Howlin' Wolf*

read two dates and a dash, and it's only what you did with the dash that matters. So this man Chester Arthur Burnett, also known as Howlin' Wolf, took to air on wings of song, grunt, and hoodooed holler, let the whole world know what a bad boy he had been, the kind of women he loved whether they were betrothed to him or another, and the mad dash from her married bed to leaping out the nearest window, and the gittin' up the road apiece.

There are all kinds of blues for all kinds of men, some regular in length and form, and others irregular and maybe more circular than anything. The Wolf favored those forms you could ride around in forever, like a well-built vehicle, and never feel trapped in a vicious cycle of recycled sentiments or mindless repetitions. There was room to breathe in his songs and all kinds of manly secrets got traded between the two guitars and the loping bass, the detonating drums, and the cavernous body of his lungs.

He was known to crawl the floor in search of a note others might consider too raw for the human esophagus. Here we have a singer driven by the moonlight mile to acts too devilish in design for other men to even contemplate. So that there are times when you hear in him something of a kinship with Nietzsche—one man going it alone and wantonly shouldering the burden of surgically extracting the desire for hell's gate from the human soul, only to then force us all to feast liberally on his hunger for the taboo, tawdry, unchristian, and transgressive.

JIM DICKINSON AND HIS SON LUTHER ON COMING OF AGE IN THE NORTH MISSISSIPPI HILL COUNTRY

Producer, session keyboardist, singer, and songwriter Jim Dickinson started his career in the 1950s, playing in rock & roll bands in Memphis. He became a member of Atlantic Records' esteemed rhythm section in the 1960s, and has played piano on sessions by the Rolling Stones, Aretha Franklin, and Bob Dylan. He produced albums by Big Star and the Replacements, among other bands, collaborated on recording projects with Ry Cooder, and has released several solo albums. His two sons, guitarist Luther and drummer Cody, formed the blues-rock combo the North Mississippi All Stars in 1997. Luther also produced two albums by Otha Turner, who died (the day before the death of Fred Rogers) a few months after this November 2002 conversation.

JIM DICKINSON: I guess your memory all starts with seeing Otha Turner on *Mister Rogers' Neighborhood.*

LUTHER DICKINSON: That's the first thing I remember. Every day we'd watch *Mister Rogers* on TV, and one day they announced Otha Turner and the Rising Star Fife and Drum Band were going to be on.

JD: And I said, "*Whoa! We gotta check this out!* These guys live just down the street."

LD: We grew up east of Memphis, in rural Tennessee, right on the state line, and our neighbors further down were in Marshall County, Mississippi. It was great because there was a juke joint—Parks' Spot—a little ways down.

JD: I liked to think y'all could hear the music in the night coming from Parks' Spot.

LD: I could. I remember. But I wish I could say that I snuck down there and peeked in the window.

Jim Dickinson, 1956; Luther Dickinson, 2001

There was a lake across the street where they'd have baptismal services.

JD: A church next to the honky-tonk. They would walk down the gravel road from the church for baptism fully robed. They would have baptism in the stock pond, a farm lake, near Rossville, Tennessee, where Fred McDowell was born.

LD: I remember way before I knew anything about country blues, I always liked Fred McDowell, because I read it on the back of your record that he was from Rossville. I was about thirteen when we moved to Mississippi, and Cody was ten. That summer we were really getting into music, and that was when Cody got his first drum kit. Dad borrowed an old drum kit from Stax—the second kit that belonged to Al Jackson [of Booker T. and the MG's]. And we've been rockin' ever since.

JD: I had a great blues experience at our house. It was pretty isolated, on a gravel road. One time we were snowed in and they didn't clear the roads. I was out there in the front yard digging snow and I heard somebody singing, somebody black, and it was getting closer. Finally, I saw an old black man walking down the middle of the road in the snow singing to himself. And I stood there; he never did see me. It was an existential moment, like Jean-Paul Sartre sitting alone feeling the burden of being alone, then he turns and sees somebody watching him. I didn't violate the guy's space. But I thoroughly enjoyed every note he sang. And I thought, We're at the right place. This is where I want to be, where I want my family to be raised. In terms of you learning to play the guitar, you taught yourself. As I told you as a child, I think rock & roll is self-taught.

LD: I remember. You showed me the chords, but you told me to teach myself. I was eighteen or nineteen when I met Otha Turner, and down the street is Junior Kimbrough's juke joint and there's R.L. Burnside playing shows in punk clubs in Memphis, and the whole world opened up to me. Of course, Fred McDowell was the godfather of the hills. He was a great influence on R.L. Burnside, Otha, and Junior Kimbrough. Right then I was just taken over. For a long period of time we still had our rock band, but all I was playing and studying was hill-country guitar music.

JD: What you have to learn from somebody else, somebody black, if you wanna play the blues, is how to *feel* it. And that's what Otha Turner taught you. I've heard those tapes of you playing for Otha where he'd just say, *"No, no, no."* And then he'd throw his hat down on the floor and say, *"That's it! That's it!"* And there's no apparent difference except that he could hear you feel it. That's what he taught you. You were playing songs by Fred McDowell—who had been his friend—and you can hear the joy in his voice. That's the thing you've got that nobody can ever take from you—what Otha taught you. The limited ability I have, I got from somebody black showing me.

LD: Playing with Sleepy John Estes and Bukka White . . . ?

JD: Before that. Butterfly and Dish Rag showed me when I was a little kid. It was like magic. My mother was a great piano player and she tried to teach me, but she couldn't teach me what I wanted to know. *They* could. As limited as it was. It was the thing I needed, to know what I wanted to do.

LD: Alec, the yardman you grew up with, he brought his friends over to teach you.

JD: He couldn't play an instrument but was a great singer. When he realized I wanted to play, he brought over musicians.

LD: I remember when I got my first guitar. You tuned it to open E, then showed me Bo Diddley. You said, "Here ya go, this is it."

JD: Bo Diddley is the heart of the hill-country rhythm. Bo Diddley was from Greenville, Mississippi. As far as I'm concerned, Bo Diddley and John Lee Hooker are playing hill-country music because they're outside the chord changes. And Bo Diddley—if that's not the hypnotic groove or, as Jessie Mae Hemphill called it, the endless boogie, I don't know what is.

LD: It's even in the fife-and-drum rhythm. They got a snare with the maracas.

JD: The hill-country rhythm of fife and drum has changed and modernized. There's three generations of musicians in Otha's band, and when the older guys play the drums, they're playing the old country version of the second line—Bo Diddley rhythm, hambone, body slappin', all the way back to Africa. But when the kids play, they bring in the contemporary boogaloo pattern they heard in the high school football games. And it's still all the same thing, a different beat emphasis but still the same polyrhythmic, all-the-way-back-to-Africa trip.

LD: Otha's grandsons are kinda hip-hop influenced, then there's his granddaughter Sharde, who plays fife and is the future queen of the hill-country cane fife. When she gets on the drums, she brings her own thing. The blues here—the juke-joint, house-party foot-stompin' blues—that's what it's about, enjoying yourself.

JD: Celebration of life. Traditional music is either worshipful music in reverence of a deity, or it's a celebration of life.

LD: That's what the hill-country blues is about. R.L. Burnside said blues is nothin' but dance music. And that's what it comes down to: You're playing for Otha Turner or at Junior Kimbrough's back in the day on Sunday nights sittin' in, or if you're at R.L. Burnside's wife's birthday party playing on the porch.

JD: Juke joint music is about empty glasses and shakin' asses. The first time I heard R.L., it was this wonderful thing. He was doing "Bottle Up and Go." It was definitive crazy blues—electric guitar and vocal, nothing but. I thought, This is so good, but maybe ten people on earth will ever get to hear this. And since then, R.L. Burnside opens for the Beastie Boys, plays for ten grand a night. That's a miracle. Though I don't agree with the marketing philosophy of his label, Fat Possum, it is nonetheless a miracle what they have done. And whether he wants to take the credit or not, Jon Spencer had an awful lot to do with it. And Robert Palmer, who I'd known since we were teenagers. When he moved to Holly Springs, I thought he was crazy. But he knew there was something going on there; he felt it first. And in his film, *Deep Blues,* there's a lot of people who were all saying the blues is dead. But that was crap. It was alive in the hills. That's what Robert Palmer figured out. There's a spirit in Memphis that comes and goes. Right now that spirit is in north Mississippi.

LD: Yes, Otha is a teacher. He's so encouraging—passin' it on, makin' it happen. His music is not juke joint blues. It's working songs, behind-the-mule

Godfather of the Mississippi hill country, Fred McDowell

cornfield blues, field hollers. But he can definitely rock the party. It wasn't until I played guitar in Otha's house or on his porch that I realized how an acoustic guitar juke joint party could happen. Acoustic guitar in any modern environment is gonna die, but if you're in an old-fashioned house. . .

JD: A wood-frame house with a hollow floor . . .

LD: Up on cinder blocks, and a tin roof.

JD: In a juke joint you couldn't hear the lyrics. The loudest thing you'd hear would be the feet stompin'. You're not gonna be in there fingerpickin', you're gonna be thrashin' it—like Son House or Bukka White, who literally beat it like a drum.

JD: The relationship you and Otha had . . . one of the things he felt he needed to do in his life was teach young white boys, and that comes straight from plantation life. It's a miracle to me that in this century a young white boy in the South can have that kind of relationship with an older black man, literally from another century. Maybe it's bad, but to me it's a beautiful thing. I know my life wouldn't have very much meaning without it. And it brings up pictures of Uncle Remus, no doubt, and some people are offended by it.

LD: I tell you what Otha Turner is offended by: tractors. Modernization.

JD: What made life in the Delta bad was the damn mechanized cotton picker that put 'em all out of business.

LD: Otha says when you plant by hand, you plant a good foot into the ground and the soil is damp and fertile, but when the tractors came by, everybody started messin' up the soil. He hates tractors. He remembers the first tractor he ever saw. It was a John Henry–like showdown in the D.C. area. A man and a mule and a plow against a tractor. And they went head to head. He saw that. Before the days of the tractor, he says, the mule was man's best friend—your partner. You did everything together. You took care of your mule. But once the tractors came out, they put the mules out to pasture, and it was the saddest thing he ever saw. A whole country full of abandoned mules.

JD: Otha Turner is a master. I believe he's the most complete human being I've ever met because his art and his life and his family and his existence as a farmer—it's all one thing.

LD: We were young children growing up when a lot of the great blues guys were still around. I do remember going to the Memphis Blues Festivals and seeing Mud Boy and the Neutrons, which was you and Lee Baker, a great guitar player and protégé of Furry Lewis; Sid Selvidge, a great singer; and Jimmy Crosthwait, washboard player extraordinaire.

JD: We were the white boys from the Memphis Country Blues Festivals. We were exposed to these great men. I used to play with Sleepy John all the time, and Furry got to where he couldn't play without Lee. There was definitely a real special symbiotic relationship between the Memphis bohemian underground and these old men. I used to play for Bukka White a lot. We used to open for each other . . . if it was the two of us, he'd play piano and make me play guitar because he thought that was funny. Toward the end, there was a honky-tonk biker bar where Mud Boy first started playing—a place called Hot Mama's. I used to play there with Bukka pretty regularly. We were teaching him to play "Sunshine of Your Love" and "Born to Be Wild."

LD: These four young guys—Mud Boy and the Neutrons—were having the same kind of relationship that I ended up having with R.L. Burnside and Otha Turner.

JD: Twenty years earlier . . . But back to *Mister Rogers'*. On the show with Otha was Jessie Mae Hemphill, the "She-Wolf" playing the bass drum—legends of the blues. And Fred Rogers, gentleman and genius that he is, interviewing. Called Otha Mr. Turner. If there was to be an introduction to the way I feel about the blues for me to show my son—it was perfect. A gift from Mister Rogers. From his neighborhood to our neighborhood. 🖛

WHY I WEAR MY MOJO HAND *By Robert Palmer*

[From the *Oxford American* music issue, 1997]

Blues and trouble, that's the cliché. The reality is: blues and chaos. Blues is supposed to be—what?—*nurtured* by trouble? So is most art that reaches deep inside and demands unflinching honesty. Is blues *about* trouble? No more than it is about good-time Saturday nights and murder most foul, sharecroppers' servitude, and sweet home Chicago. Is blues a *cause* of trouble? Not directly. But what sort of thing almost inevitably causes trouble in our oppressively regimented world? You guessed it: chaos.

The blues-and-chaos equation first presented itself to me in the mid-sixties, when a bunch of us—musicians, artists, and a smattering of smugglers and dealers—organized and presented the first Memphis Blues Festival in the Overton Park Shell. For years I believed the remarkable levels of chaos in everything remotely connected with those festivals resulted from a bunch of hippies trying to turn elderly blues singers into anarchist father-figures.

Now I'm not so sure. In any case, that was before I met R.L. Burnside.

R.L. was an outstanding disciple of one the greatest of all bluesmen, Mississippi Fred McDowell, who had been a Memphis Blues Festival regular. By the early 1970s, R.L. had really come into his own. The juke joints he ran in the north Mississippi hill country were as famous for their level of violence as for R.L.'s outstanding music, which rolled out of his jacked-up guitar amp in dark, turbulent waves—sometimes punctuated by gunshots, especially on Saturday nights. In fact, R.L. has been reported waving a (presumably loaded) pistol in at least one crowded joint. If that strikes you as akin to yelling "Fire!" in a crowded theater, well, that's R.L. The man is a connoisseur of chaos; he attracts it, admires it, and then absorbs it, like a black hole sucking reality itself into the chaos of Nothing.

Back in 1993, when I found myself producing a Burnside session for the album *Too Bad Jim,* a succession of chaotic eruptions seemed to threaten the entire project. A string bass fell to pieces in the studio. Then the drum kit collapsed into kindling after being given a single light tap. A glass door fell out of its mounting and gave me a skull-rattling knock upside the head. Out of the corner of my eye I glanced over at R.L.—he was enjoying himself

like a kid at a Disney movie. The performances he recorded that day were highlights of the album.

I decided, out of near-desperation, to fight fire with fire. Using objects and materials you can find in any good botanica, and dedicating them with a simple, made-up ritual I thought appropriate, I made myself a chaos-buster, a post-Heisenberg-Uncertainty-Principle Mojo Hand. The next time I went in the studio with R.L., the mojo was secreted on my person. The session went well. Toward the end we were taking a break when it happened again: A tall screen began to tip over, as usual for no apparent reason. It fell and hit engineer Robbie Norris on his head. This time, I was all smiles. "It works!" I crowed, giving my mojo charm a surreptitious rub. Robbie was gingerly rubbing the top of his head. "Yeah," he said, "it works *for you.*"

But of course, that's just what you expect from magic: If it affects the practitioner's reality, and in the way desired, it *works.* Chaos theory is one way of explaining the mechanics involved. Another, more poetic, and perhaps wiser way of explaining it is called "the blues." Rarely have chaos and uncertainty been so *listenable;* and I'll almost certainly be listening for the rest of my life. If I choose to pack my mojo, well, once again the blues says it best: "Ain't Nobody's Business If I Do." ✍

ALI FARKA TOURE: SOUND TRAVELS BY CHRISTOPHER JOHN FARLEY

Griots, in West Africa, are history set to music. They embody every story ever told, or worth knowing, anyway; they are every legend and every fable; they are schooled in the lore of kings and in the chronicles of wars. And, of course, there is a story told about how the line of storytellers was born. Griots sing of a time during the life of the prophet Mohammed when a man named Sourakata heard Mohammed's message and mocked him. But each time Sourakata's wicked words left his mouth, he found himself frozen in his tracks. Three times he mocked the Prophet, and three times he was held in place. Sourakata then recognized the power of Mohammed and the grace of his message, and his taunting words became songs of praise. Afterward, whenever Mohammed would visit a new place, Sourakata would go with him and implore, "Come out! Come out! People of the village, the Prophet of God has come!"

Time passed, Mohammed's message spread, and the Prophet and his followers continued their travels. Sourakata became so beloved by the Prophet, the story goes, that Mohammed's other followers became jealous. They began to wonder why, when the pair came to villages and received offerings, that Sourakata was always granted by the Prophet the largest share when the bounty was divided.

"Why do you favor Sourakata?" the jealous followers asked Mohammed.

"It's because of Sourakata that we receive anything," the Prophet answered. "If you want nothing else, I will tell him to be quiet."

And so, when they entered the next village, Sourakata was silenced. He did not sing the praises of the Prophet, he did not announce his coming to the town, and he did not call the people to come out. And because he said nothing and sang nothing, no one came to hear the Prophet speak and no gifts were given. Immediately, Mohammed's followers recognized their error, and Sourakata was asked to call to the people again.

"People of the village, the Prophet of God has come!" And thus was the line of griots started.

Ali Farka Toure, who is known by many as the "Bluesman of Africa," was born in 1939 but not with that name and not into that profession. His birthplace was the village of Kanau, which is on the banks of the river Niger in Mali, just north of Niafunké, the town he would move to when he was four years old and where he now makes his home. He was his mother's tenth son, and every male son she had given birth to before him had died in infancy. But he had lived, and it was an occasion worth marking. The name he was given was Ali Ibrahim, but it was a local custom to give a child an unusual nickname if the child's parents have had other children who have died. The moniker that was selected for Ali was Farka, which means donkey— an animal known for its strength and stubbornness, traits he had displayed by clinging to life. "But let me make one thing clear," Toure would tell an interviewer later. "I'm the donkey that nobody climbs on!"

From an early age, Toure was summoned by music. He came from a noble family, and the members of his clan were farmers—patiently working the land, praying for favorable weather and good harvests. But something called to him beyond the fields. He would hear local musicians playing in the spirit ceremonies on the banks of the Niger and he would watch, fascinated. The musicians would sing and play a variety of instruments: the *njurkle* (a single-string guitar), the *ngoni* (a four-string lute), and the *njarka* (a single-string violin). Something in Toure longed to join them, but members of his family did not consider music a suitable profession.

Music in Mali can be a closed profession. Some are born to it, others are not. The griots of the region—also known as *jelis*—are a kind of spiritual trade union: Only those who are members are trained and encouraged to practice the craft. The griot tradition is a long one, spanning from the thirteenth century all the way to the twenty-first. A griot is like a library with an instrument, the *kora*, telling the tales of their people and setting them to music. Griots—like the American blues musicians who would come after them—are often on the move, from one place to the next, from one village to another. Their songs are not written down but passed from one generation to the next. Some of the songs are simple; others are complex, taking two days or more to perform. Becoming a griot without being born into a griot family is like becoming a lawyer without attending law school. One might have the talent for it, but there is a history to be learned before the tradition can be mastered, there are contacts that must be made before one can earn a living, and there are credentials one must possess before being taken seriously. And the boy who was named after a donkey was on the outside of it all. Still, when he was twelve years old, Toure fashioned his first instrument, a njurkle guitar, and taught himself how to play. Says Toure, "My family weren't griots, so I never got any training. This is a gift I

have; God doesn't give everybody the ability to play an instrument. Music is a spiritual thing—the force of sound comes from the spirit."

Toure, like 90 percent of his countrymen, is a devout Muslim. But there are other traditions in Mali, and there are other powers that are said to hold sway over the people in the region. The river Niger is one of them, and some believe that between its banks, beneath the surface of the water, exists a world of spirits, supernatural beings with the power to influence events—from illnesses and diseases, to earthquakes and floods. The *djinns* are summoned through spirit ceremonies, and the world of men can communicate with their world by means of music and dance.

When Toure was thirteen years old, he had a spiritual encounter in Niafunké. He was walking along playing songs on his njurkle guitar. It was about 2 a.m. Suddenly, before him he saw three little girls, each one taller than the last. They were lined up next to one another, like the steps of a staircase. He found himself frozen in place, unable to move any further. He stood there, unmoving, until 4 a.m.

The next day Toure was again walking, this time along the edge of the fields, without his instrument. There before him he saw a black-and-white snake with a strange mark on its head. The snake wrapped itself around Toure's head. He extricated himself, and the snake fell into a pit. Toure ran away, but the incident wasn't over. Shortly after that he began to have "attacks," he later reported, saying that he felt as if he entered a new world. He was no longer the person he once was. He felt he could resist pain, he had a new conviction that he could even withstand fire. He was beyond the physical world. He was sent to the village of Hombori to be cured, and he stayed there for a year. He eventually came back to Niafunké, but as a musician. He may not have been

Ali Farka Toure, 2000

born into it, but now he was born again. He began to play his instrument with new passion and focus and began his career as a musician. He could feel the spirits welcoming him. Says Toure, "I have all the spirits. I work the spirits, and I work with the spirits. I was born among them and grew up among them." He was not born a griot, but like a griot, he began to travel around Africa.

In 1968 he heard a recording of John Lee Hooker and was entranced. Initially, he thought Hooker was playing music derived from Mali. Several Malian song forms—including the musical traditions of the Bambara, Songhai, and Fulani ethnic groups—rely on minor pentatonic (five-note) scales, which are similar to the blues scale. Toure would later come to understand in greater depth the connection between African music and American

blues. Also in 1968 Toure bought a six-string electric guitar. Armed with that instrument, Toure has since journeyed around the planet: to America, England, France, Japan, and many other nations. He has collaborated with American blues performers such as Taj Mahal and Ry Cooder, the British-Indian musician Nitin Sawhney, and won a Grammy. Now he is at home in the town he grew up in and feels little reason to leave it again. In 2001, he announced that he was retiring from touring.

These days, Toure stays close to home. Niafunké is a small village where fishermen cast nets into the Niger, cattle roam the countryside, and where some of the buildings are constructed of mud brick. "I know everywhere in the world," Toure says. "I prefer it here." Toure's home has no telephone, and he likes it that way. "There's nothing here— that's why I'm here," he says. "If there were a phone, you have to listen to people talk: *'Yah, yah, yah, yah, yah.'"*

Toure confirmed his commitment to his native region by naming his 1999 album *Niafunké* and recording it at home. He didn't want to make music that was purely a commercial venture—he wanted whatever he did to draw on his environment and reflect his social and spiritual values. "Music in Africa is not just a simple pleasure," Toure says. "It's a culture. It's the culture in which we are born. We've grown up in it, we've lived it, and it's what we know. For me, music is not something that comes from the university or the conservatory. What God gives you is worth more than what man gives you." A recording facility was set up in an abandoned building in Niafunké; Toure worked the fields of his large rice farm during the day, and at night he settled in with his friends and band mates to record. Says Toure, "The albums I recorded before were recorded in rooms with enormous amounts of machinery. This album was not. I recorded it in my own village. It's more authentic, like honey. I've tasted both sugar and honey, and I prefer honey. Now I'm allowing you to taste the honey."

Toure has been dubbed the Bluesman of Africa by the western press, but he doesn't feel that he plays the blues. He says American blues performers play African music. The blues, he says, was a false name given by Americans to traditional African music that was brought to North America by slaves. Toure feels that Americans are lost, cut off from the source of their culture and language, and that they don't know the correct names for the things that they left behind and half-remembered in their new land. Because Toure is African, because he is still in touch with the source of black culture, he feels he, and his fellow African musicians, know the right names for things. When he hears the blues, he hears the burbling of the Niger; he hears the spirit ceremonies on the riverbank; he hears the buyers and sellers calling out at the marketplace and the muezzin calling the people to prayer at the mosque. When he hears the blues, he hears Africa.

American blacks did take much of their musical culture from Africa. A French text dating back to 1810 documents the music that Africans brought to the West. It reads, "As to guitars, which the Negroes call *banza,* see what they consist of: They cut lengthwise through the middle of a calabash. . . . This fruit is sometimes eight inches or more in diameter. They stretch upon it the skin of a goat, which they adjust around the edges with little nails; they make two holes in its surface; then a piece of lath or flat wood makes the handle of the guitar; they then stretch three cords of *pitre* . . . and the instrument is finished. They play on this instrument tunes composed of three or four notes, which they repeat endlessly; this is what Bishop Grégoire calls

sentimental and melancholy music, and which we call the music of savages."

Nearly two hundred years later, Africans hear American music and hear themselves, and Americans hear Africa and hear the blues. Call and response. It is one of the oldest elements of black music. A river-spirit calls out to a young boy on the banks. In the belly of a slave ship, the imprisoned cry out to one another through the long middle passage. In a cotton field, workers call out to each other through a long sweltering workday. A guitarist sings and her guitar answers back with a twang. A preacher exhorts his flock and they answer in sweet celebration. Africa calls out to North America, and the latter calls back to the former in the form of John Lee Hooker and Robert Johnson and Son House and Bessie Smith. The whole world hears and responds as Manu Dibango hears Miles Davis, and Salif Keita listens to Cuba's Orquesta Aragón, and Miriam Makeba hears Harry Belafonte, and the Roots hear Fela Anikulapo Kuti, and all the music mixes and matches, and just who is the caller and who is the responder is somehow lost in a tangle of blue sound.

Africa gave America some of what is now called the blues, but America gave Africa and the world back something else: a music that was something more than it once was. America gave back a sound tempered by hundreds of years of incarceration, a music energized by electric strings, a culture baptized by blood and by sweat and by the mud of the Mississippi. Africans may hear it and call it their own, but it isn't. The blues is something that Africans and Americans now share. Toure certainly understands that the flow of music—its sharing and its spread—are important. Says Toure, "Honey is not sweet when tasted by one lone mouth. In my life I have only one ambition. . . . Everything I do, everything I have, must be shared with others."

FRENCH TALKING BLUES BY CATHERINE NEDONCHELLE

How did the love of African-American music in France turn into a passion for African music—from the blues to world music?

The raspy voices of James Brown and Wilson Pickett, the seductive vocals of Marvin Gaye had added heat to the parties of our teenage years. We were slow-dancing, barely moving, paying close attention to the heavy breathing of Percy Sledge's "When a Man Loves a Woman" and Solomon Burke's "Cry to Me." We squeezed each other, hugged even tighter, hearing the first notes of Otis Redding's "These Arms of Mine." In the sixties and seventies, the blues, rhythm & blues, and soul intoxicated us: "Shake, Shake, Shake," "Chains, Chains, Chains." We were stunned and ravished by African-American music. It gave our political revolts a depth, an existentialist inspiration. And all of a sudden, in the early eighties, a new wave took us by surprise: the music of the African diaspora—majestic music, both happy and melancholic, that set our Parisian rainy days on fire.

We were moved, but also unable to make up our minds about which we liked better: Afro-American music or African music? The plaintive, falsetto voices of Youssou N'Dour, Ismael Lo, Salif Keita, or the smooth sounds of Stevie Wonder, the pounding heavy funk of the Gap Band, of Maze, or the luminous incantations from Ladysmith Black Mambazo of South Africa? But little by little, we could see some connections, some ties; we didn't have to choose after all, we could gobble it all up.

Black American music had in a way psycho-analyzed us. James Brown was screaming, "I'm black, I'm proud," and in a self-imposed reversal of fortune, a kind of metaphysical self-hatred, we idealized the suffering and the struggle of the oppressed; feeling ill at ease, we wanted to be black. We discovered our fascination for exile and suffering present in the dramatic and simple "Dock of the Bay," by Otis Redding, with the last notes drowning in the sad murmur of the waves.

Flash back to Paris in the eighties: A funky, brass band of a magazine, *Actuel,* defines those ten years for us. Fast, cheeky, inquisitive, *Actuel* was like an oracle, with its intuitions that would make a mark on its time. Jean-Francois Bizot, who started *Actuel,* is a big gruff guy full of big gruff ideas, a walking encyclopedia, crazy about jazz and blues, someone who didn't hesitate to champion African music that came out raw and against the grain.

Just as happiness, or sorrows, never come alone, along with the African music wave came the pirate-radio movement. Bizot, never one to miss a beat, started his own, Radio Nova, a truly original station that brings together and fosters multiple worlds of sound. I worked there, in the elegant seven-story building of *Actuel*-Radio Nova. We would see lots of fascinating people passing by, who made it hard to concentrate. The magazine and the radio were for West Indian, Jamaican, and African musicians, a place of anchorage, of recognition—they were at home there. There was a DJ from Guadeloupe, Socrates, his record collection of blues and soul music particularly impressed us. He turned us on to the Staples Singers' emblematic "I'll Take You There" and also the music of Joe Tex, Bobby Womack, Ernie K-Doe, Eddie Floyd, and Arthur Conley. There was also DJ Bintou, from Burkina Faso, a beautiful, commanding presence who orchestrated numerous tumultuous gatherings, full of laughter and smoke in the corridors and the studios of Radio Nova. We thought history was happening right here, happening and spinning outward, worldwide, orbit-wide, a future that would last forever, and we were getting a kick out of being seated in the first row.

In those days, we were always scheming to top off the days with jazzy nights. The best address for this, of course, was the most secret one: We would sneak out for a party at the Rex, on Boulevard Sebastopol, where African and West Indian artists would meet, where we could count on a rainbow swirl of sounds, dances, and encounters. There was Mamadou, the smooth talker who would organize hilarious contests among the best-dressed *sapeurs,* those Congolese dandies who liked to show off in patent-leather shoes and wear crisp designer clothes by Armani or Miyake. Oh yeah, can't forget the energetic West Indian DJ named Sydney, who would hook up funk and African music on the Rex turntable.

Actuel nicknamed us *"les jeunes gens modernes."* It was truly a renaissance, a newly found humanism. We believed in multiculturalism, cultural cross-fertilization, bricolage, merging, citizens of the world, world music, a global village. It happened like that, like falling in love or love at first sight, and we could not live without it, without African music or Afro-American music; yet, the interplay between the two confused us. Africans in France had issues with Afro-American artists, whose huge popularity would irritate the Africans but also would challenge them. There were a lot of quarrels among schools and cliques, some real, some pure hype.

Through the nineties, we witnessed great lessons of reversibility and hybridization: Papa Wemba and his moving, playful, Africanized version of Otis Redding's "Fa-Fa-Fa-Fa-Fa (Sad Song)"; Ali Farka Toure and his blues recorded in Memphis; Youssou N'Dour in a duet with Wyclef Jean.

What is left today of our love stories, where are our mentors, the pioneers? What happened to Bonga, Bongo, or Zao? Zao, from the former Zaire, a prophet, serious and droll, who had written in 1985 the great antiwar song "The Veterans": Did we really believe once that a song could change the world, that to love people's songs was to love the people in their songs? Were we fools? Was it fake, the worshipping of difference in the suddenly reconciled differences? Did world music fail us?

While waiting for the answers in France, like elsewhere, to get down, we replay the blues, even the globalized versions, a thousand times redone, electrified, Africanized, Arabized, distilled, cyberspaced, and worked through the grinder of disco, ragamuffin, techno, ambient, house, garage, acid, trip-hop. Blues Frenchified also by our nostalgic French singers, Bernard Lavilliers, Alain Souchon, or by Patricia Kaas, who sings the blues a la Edith Piaf, or Francis Cabrel, who in a dignified way talks about slavery and the blues: "Son House and Charley Patton, Blind Blake and Willie Dixon, Ma Rainey and Robert Johnson, Howlin' Wolf and Blind Lemon" in his tune "100 More Years."

As for the children of the African and West Indian diaspora, Princesses Nubiennes, Zap Mama, Princesse Erika, Oxymo Puccino, MC Solaar, and many others in France, caught in between all these trends and fashions, from hip-hop to Afro-European pop, it's not always easy for them to know where they stand.

"When I get the blues, awake at night, I find myself," sing the Nubiennes. Perhaps, that's one thing the blues means, going back to the roots, listening to the sonic ocean, while "sitting on the dock of the bay." *[Translated by Brigitte Engler]*

WARMING BY THE DEVIL'S FIRE

Directed by Charles Burnett

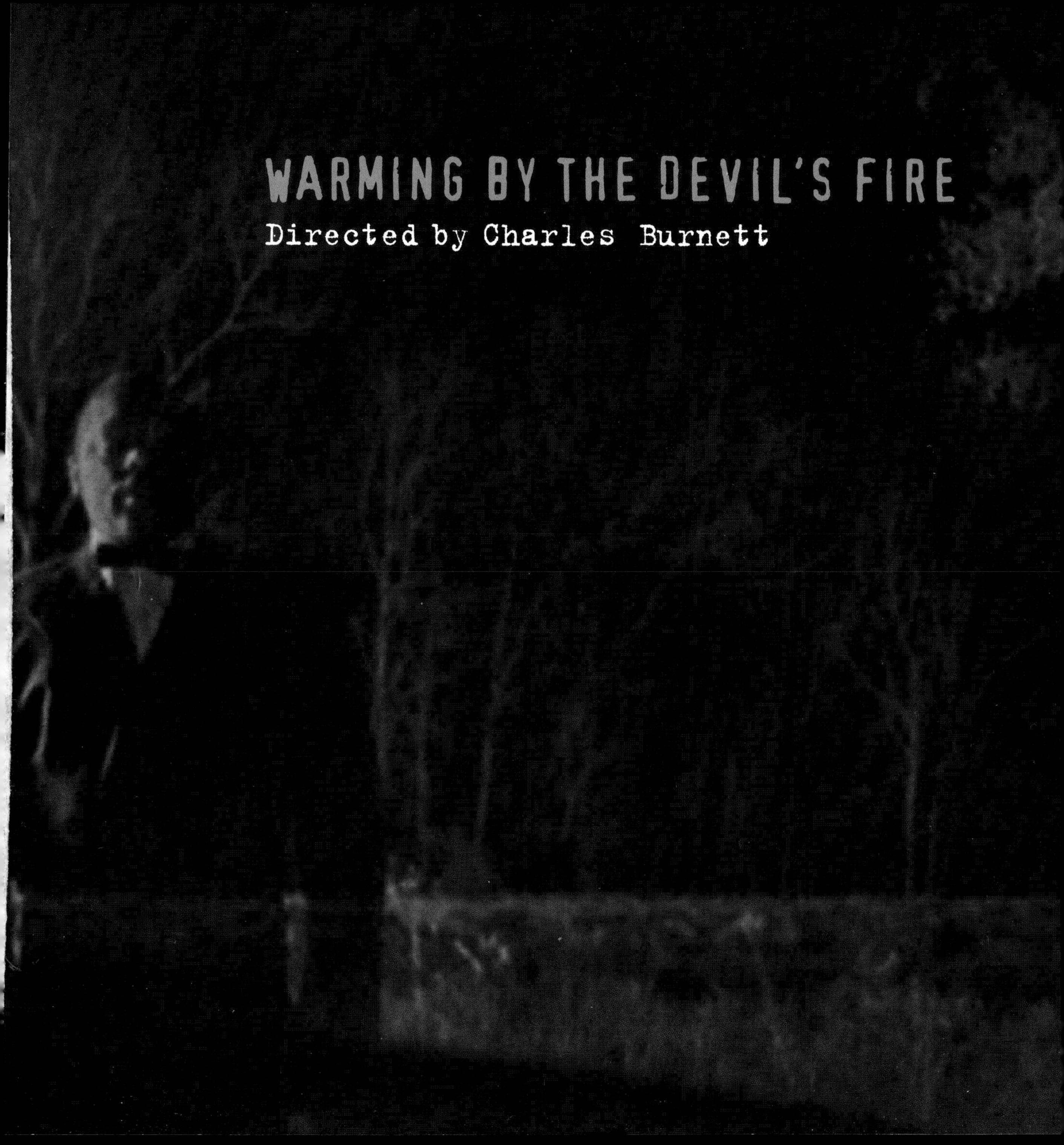

Historically, there's a complex, even antagonistic, relationship between the blues—the devil's music, Satan's music—and the church in the black community. A lot of blues players, many of them women, left the church to pursue a career in the blues, and ended up going back at the end of their days. In *Warming by the Devil's Fire,* we mentioned how Son House, who was a preacher at one time, went to jail for murder in self defense, came out, tried to be a preacher again, then went back to playing the blues. "Georgia Tom" (whose real name was Thomas A. Dorsey) wrote sexually graphic songs for Bessie Smith and others, then he went and wrote some wonderful, lyrical religious compositions later on. Sister Rosetta Tharpe and Reverend Gary Davis did the same thing.

This relationship between the sacred and the profane is the theme of *Warming by the Devil's Fire.* It tells the story of a young kid going back to Mississippi before he's twelve to get baptized. To get *saved.* But then he's kidnapped by his uncle Buddy—a *blues person*—who takes him around to experience what he's gonna be saved *from.* At the end, his other uncle, a preacher named Flem, finds him and puts him on the road to the mourner's bench. And years later, Uncle Buddy also ends up becoming a preacher.

When we started this project, I screened a lot of footage on the blues; if I hadn't, I probably would have made a relatively conventional documentary. But after seeing so many others, I began to think what could I add? How is this going to be different? I also had to consider how to frame the film—because there's so much *to* the blues, what do you include, who do you exclude? It took quite a while for me to sort these questions out, which must have frustrated Marty Scorsese.

The story I chose for *Warming by the Devil's Fire* isn't strictly autobiographical, but everything in the film happened to a certain extent, and I used these experiences as guideposts to come up with a story that everyone could identify with. I had an uncle who was very much like Buddy. Like the trickster figure in folklore, Buddy awakens things in his nephew and gives him experiences that will help him become a complete person. At the same time, I wanted to tell a story about the blues that echoed the form. There's play within the material; it tries to be loose. And the character played by Tommy Hicks—Uncle Buddy—personifies the feeling of the blues and embodies all of its contradictions.

The story's told from the perspective of the narrator, the young kid who returns to Mississippi and becomes aware of the blues as an art form. It's through his eyes that we, the audience, meet the blues. It's through his ears that we listen to the blues and come to appreciate them. The film includes a wide range of music, from raw gutbucket blues to the more sophisticated R&B, and is representative of both male and female singers.

I wanted to put the music in context, too. The blues came out of the South, and the South has its history of struggles, and it seemed to me you can't really separate the blues from their historical context: how people lived, the hardships they experienced, the texture of their daily lives—it was all related. I was looking for things that spoke to that period, that conveyed the harshness, the humor, and the contradictions. For example, we use a lot of footage of the horrible flood that devastated that part of Mississippi. Lives were lost. The whole economy was damaged. We showed the levee camps that sprang up as a result—another tragic period in the history of black labor. We used chain-gang images. For a black person in the South at the time, it didn't take very much to go to jail. You didn't have to do a serious crime—just look the wrong way. Out of those experiences came the elements for the blues.

The blues encompasses every emotion; people listen to the blues because the blues allows one to come to terms with basic instincts. And they speak to the circumstances for blacks of an earlier time. When you look at the atmosphere surrounding the blues—racism, hard work and little to show for it; exploitation, humiliation, and the explosive life at the juke joint, where shootings and knife fights were not uncommon—you get a picture of survival and the will to live and self-destruct at the same time.

I also wanted to include images that were in themselves moving, visual, cinematic. I really admire a work by James Agee called *Now Let Us Praise Famous Men*. He and Walker Evans went across the South and documented workers—black and white—during the Depression. What made that book remarkable was that it provided this sense of history told from a certain perspective. Yet Agee was also concerned about exploiting the subject; he wanted to be as objective as possible. The result was a document that gives a feeling of the period that would have been lost otherwise. That's one of the things I was trying to achieve—to go beyond information and convey a *feeling* for how these people lived and how they felt.

I grew up playing the trumpet, so W.C. Handy's music was the beginning; his were the first blues I learned how to play. Handy wasn't your typical vagabond blues player, like Robert Johnson and Blind Lemon Jefferson, traveling with a guitar on his back to find work on the street corners. Handy came from a middle-class family, which was unusual. His father wanted him to go to college and didn't think music was any way to make a living. But Handy had a lot of things going for him—he was one of the first African-Americans to write and publish his own

A young W.C. Handy, circa 1898

material. He followed his own dreams, went against his parents' wishes, and ended up being successful.

Handy went blind, then his sight came back, and finally he went permanently blind. I've always been interested in people who have to overcome a handicap like blindness, like Blind Lemon Jefferson,

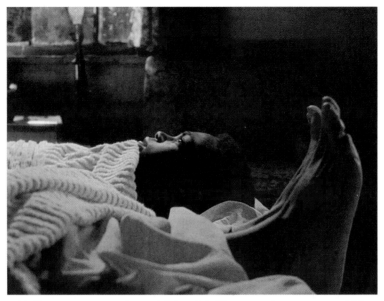

In his film, Burnett portrays the rough living of the blues. Here, the narrator, as a child, shares a bed with his uncle Buddy.

who managed to survive, hopping trains and singing in levee camps, the worst and most dangerous places to work, where there wasn't any law. That he was able to be imaginative and creative and have a sense of poetry under those circumstances is remarkable. His music and lyrics are incredibly moving, but the things he sings about are things you only want to experience vicariously.

During one scene, Buddy plays a record by Lucille Bogan, a singer whose lyrics were very graphic sexually. Her records should be double X-rated. [In fact her first release was too raw to be released.] When she sings about "nipples on my titties as big as the end of your thumb" and on and on, you get a clear sense of why the church was so opposed to the blues. On the other hand, Lucille

Bogan can be seen as an important figure in that she was unabashed about her sexual desire at a time long before the so-called "sexual revolution." Bogan, Mamie Smith, Ma Rainey, Bessie Smith—these were women at the top of their game creatively who dealt openly with women's themes and issues.

Choosing the music was the hardest part—because there was so much great material to choose from. Every time I came back to the film, I'd wind up choosing another piece of music. To *really* get a sense of the blues, you'd need to do the impossible, by putting *everything* in. I chose a Sonny Boy Williamson song, for example, because he's a great singer/harmonica player, of course—but also because he was a character himself, someone with a great screen presence. When you do a film, you

Burnett's narrator remembers going to Mississippi to get baptized, or "saved." Uncle Buddy shows him what he's getting saved from.

always have to consider casting. There were some wonderful musicians we could have used who, unfortunately, weren't as cinematically engaging. A lot of people who were essential to this era probably should have been included for historical reasons, but for dramatic reasons I wound up leaving them out. Movies don't allow for any lulls. So you go for the personality, what works well on the screen.

I wanted to have more of Bessie Smith and Billie Holiday in the film, in fact more of everyone. Especially the women, who came from vaudeville, which meant they had more professional training, as opposed to someone like Robert Johnson, who migrated and picked up things as he went. The early women singers had a big impact on the blues, particularly because of their record sales. They had huge audiences and helped spread the blues. The women had a unique role.

—Charles Burnett

BESSIE SMITH: WHO KILLED THE EMPRESS?
BY CHRISTOPHER JOHN FARLEY

The only thing clear about that September night was the night itself. It was nearly 2 a.m, ten miles north of Clarksdale, Mississippi. There was no rain, just the open air, the stars, and the shadowy ribbon of Highway 61 stretching into the Delta distance.

Bessie Smith was on that road, traveling in an old Packard with a wooden frame. The date was September 26, 1937. Bessie—known as the Empress of the Blues—was a bit down on her luck around that time. She wasn't flat broke, but she was no longer music royalty. She was, in a way, living the life she had sung about in her song "Nobody Knows You When You're Down and Out." Time was, she would blow into town, traveling in her own private train car, heralded by adoring articles in black newspapers such as the *Pittsburgh Courier* and the *Chicago Defender*, her many minions passing out flyers announcing that the Empress had arrived. Now she was playing smaller joints, some half filled, and she was lucky to get the work. Her driver was a man named Richard Morgan, and by most accounts he was also her lover. Bessie had a gig set for later that day in Darling, Mississippi; to get a head start, she and Morgan had left Memphis early. They had traveled around seventy-five miles and figured they'd spend the night in Clarksdale before heading on.

Bessie never made it to her gig. But the story about how she died has kept traveling on, like a car on a dark highway, picking up truths and half-truths, exaggerations, and outright fabrications along its journey. A *Down Beat* magazine article published two months after her death asked, "Did Bessie Smith Bleed to Death While Waiting for Medical Aid?" Another *Down Beat* article printed just a month later retracted the claims made in the first and announced, "Southern Whites Did Not Turn Dying Bessie Away," but the earlier charges had already entered popular lore. The story that Smith had been turned away from a hospital by racist whites got more mileage from the 1959 play *The Death of Bessie Smith,* by Edward Albee. Then in 1972, Chris Albertson published the biography *Bessie* that was widely interpreted as debunking the story that Smith's death resulted from segregation and prejudice. Still, there may be some substance to the claims that bigotry, and not just bad luck, played a part in ending the reign of the Empress of the Blues.

⊕ ⊕ ⊕ ⊕ ⊕

Bessie Smith's life began with loss. She was born on April 15, 1894 (or possibly 1895) in the Blue Goose Hollow section of Chattanooga, Tennessee; her father, a part-time Baptist preacher named William, died when she was still a small child, and her mother, Laura, passed away before Bessie was ten. Bessie's brother Clarence, the oldest surviving man in the family, joined a traveling minstrel show in 1904, working as a comedian and dancer. When Clarence passed through town in 1912—with the Moses Stokes troupe—Bessie grabbed her chance, auditioned, and left with them, initially as a dancer.

The troupe's premier singer at the time was none other than Ma Rainey, one of the earliest, and most influential, blues singers. Rainey was as colorful a character as there's ever been in American music—which is saying a lot—and was given to wearing wild costumes, getting her way, and living an openly bisexual life. Some music writers discount Rainey's impact on the young Bessie, but black newspapers from the period testify to her influence. The April 10, 1926, edition of the *Baltimore Afro-American,* noted " . . . it was [Ma Rainey] who first started on their way to fame and fortune [vaudeville stars] Butterbeans and Susie . . . and Bessie Smith." Maud Smith Faggins, Bessie Smith's sister-in-law, said that even after Bessie left Rainey's troupe, the two singers remained friends. Said Faggins: "Ma Rainey used to come on our show car, and she used to talk about how she used to spank Bessie and how she used to make Bessie sing. Ma Rainey and Pa Rainey is the one [*sic*] that really put Bessie on the road."

Bessie and Ma Rainey hit the road together, but the former's career went on to places the latter only dreamed of. In the beginning, Smith was rejected as "too rough" following early record-label auditions. But Columbia took a chance on her, and in 1923 she cut her first record: "Down Hearted Blues," with the flip side of "Gulf Coast Blues." A huge success, the record sold 780,000 copies. Between 1924 and 1929, according to a 1937 article in the *Pittsburgh Courier,* she sold four million records. She also influenced a generation of blues and jazz instrumentalists who played as her sidemen, including Louis Armstrong and Benny Goodman.

Bessie Smith was brown skinned, big boned, and an orphan. With so many strikes seemingly against her in a world that lusted after thin, light-skinned, demure fairy princesses with good pedigrees, how did she become such a big star? Of course, the answer is in her voice. Bessie hit notes like a boxer—no, perhaps boxing is too inelegant a term for the melodious precision with which she

spun out her songs. Boxing is sometimes called the sweet science, and that poetic euphemism better captures the essence of her musical style—she was not like some singing street brawler or some brawny pugilist; she jabbed through songs with economy, with grace, with power, with a wink and a kiss. Right hooks, uppercuts, growls, and bent phrasing that could break your heart. Louis Armstrong once said, "She used to thrill me at all times, the way she could phrase a note with a certain something in her voice no other blues singer could get. She had music in her soul and felt everything she did. Her sincerity with her music was an inspiration."

There was an empathic quality to her music, as well; after hearing a Bessie Smith song, you didn't just feel like you knew where she was coming from, you also felt as if she knew where *you* were coming from. Especially if you had ever been in a love affair that went wrong, or been wronged by a lover who had an affair, or been in love at all. Bessie, like Rainey before her, sang about women in trouble, women in need, women who had been turned on or turned out by their men. She also sang about fighting back, about shooting and slashing and hunting down men who had done her wrong. Some of her songs were addressed to other women—as if, with her performances, she wanted to create a community of caring.

"When I was a little girl," singer Mahalia Jackson once remembered, "I felt she [Bessie] was having troubles like me. That's why it was such a comfort for the people of the South to hear her. She expressed something they couldn't put into words." This was at a time when lynchings were common (the *Afro-American,* on March 7, 1926, reported that "seventeen lynchings were recorded in 1925, showing an increase of one over the preceding year") and ads for skin bleaching creams were plentiful

"MA RAINEY"
By Sterling Brown
[1932]

I

When Ma Rainey
Comes to town,
Folks from anyplace
Miles aroun',
From Cape Girardeau,
Poplar Bluff,
Flocks in to hear
Ma do her stuff;
Comes flivverin' in,
Or ridin' mules,
Or packed in trains,
Picknickin' fools. . . .
That's what it's like,
Fo' miles on down,
To New Orleans delta
An' Mobile town,
When Ma hits
Anywheres aroun'.

II

Dey comes to hear Ma Rainey from de little
    river settlements,
From blackbottom cornrows and from
    lumber camps;
Dey stumble in de hall, jes a-laughin' an' a-
    cacklin',
Cheerin' lak roarin' water, lak wind in river
    swamps.

An' some jokers keeps deir laughs a-goin' in
    de crowded aisles,
An' some folks sits dere waitin' wid deir
    aches an' miseries,
Till Ma comes out before dem, a-smilin'
    goldtoofed smiles
An' Long Boy ripples minors on de black an'
    yellow keys.

III

O Ma Rainey,
Sing yo' song;
Now you's back
Whah you belong,
Git way inside us,
Keep us strong. . . .
O Ma Rainey,
Li'l an' low;
Sing us 'bout de hard luck
Roun' our do';
Sing us 'bout de lonesome road
We mus' go. . . .

IV

I talked to a fellow, an' the fellow say,
"She jes' catch hold of us, somekindaway.
She sang Backwater Blues one day:

> 'It rained fo' days an' de skies was dark
>   as night,
> Trouble taken place in de lowlands at
>   night.

> 'Thundered an' lightened an' the storm
>   begin to roll
> Thousan's of people ain't got no place
>   to go.

> 'Den I went an' stood upon some high
>   ol' lonesome hill,
> An' looked down on the place where I
>   used to live.'

An' den de folks, dey natchally bowed dey
    heads an' cried,
Bowed dey heavy heads, shet dey moufs
    up tight an' cried,
An' Ma lef' de stage, an' followed some de
    folks outside."

Dere wasn't much more de fellow say:
    She jes' gits hold of us dataway.

(the same issue of the *Afro-American* featured an ad for Nadinola Bleaching Cream, which, claimed the manufacturer, "is the one bleaching cream and skin whitener that never fails . . . men admire you— women envy you"). Bessie Smith stood up for black people in general, for brown-skinned women in particular, and for down-and-out people everywhere (her song "Poor Man's Blues" lamented the mistreatment of the poor by the rich), and she raised the spirits of the downtrodden simply by lifting her voice.

Although some observers depicted Smith as a loud, lewd singer, accounts in the black press from the 1920s tell a different tale. The *Afro-American*, in an interview with Smith dated March 27, 1926, wrote that "Miss Smith says her greatest ambition now is to carry her marvellous voice into the small towns and villages so that young people of our race may be inspired to use their talent and develop themselves." The article goes on to describe her fashion style: "Miss Smith might best be described as buxom. Her clothes are made and fitted well, and together with her smooth brown skin, which is not rouged, she presents a very attractive appearance." In a review of her show at the Royal Theatre from the same issue, the critic writes, "It is impossible to describe or imitate the eerie moaning quality of Miss Smith's 'blues' voice." The review goes on to note: "Indeed, the whole show is clean and ought not offend so many folks as its predecessors have." Smith was the Empress of the Blues, but she didn't have to work blue.

⊕ ⊕ ⊕ ⊕ ⊕

But a mere decade later, tastes had changed. The Empire State Building had opened, and Al Capone had been closed down; talking pictures were all the rage, and Joe Louis was the new heavyweight champ. Prohibition had been tried and repealed; the Nazis were on the march across Europe, and a second world war was brewing. In music, the blues was waning, and swing was swinging.

By the late 1930s, newer, younger jazz stars were replacing the aging blues queens. On October 23, 1937, less than a month after Bessie Smith's death, the *Afro-American* ran an interview with the next rising singing star, Billie Holiday, dutifully noting that the young vocalist did her own hair, her own nails, and wore "a black satin underslip trimmed with rhinestones at the neck." Another article in the same issue reported that Holiday's success was considerable given her age: "To do this at twenty-one is no small feat, but Billie Holiday is intelligent, she has a splendid disposition, she's unaffected, and it's a ten-to-one bet that there are even bigger things in store for Billie Holiday." The press had a new darling; she could sing as well as Bessie, and people cared about her undergarments.

Still, when Smith died, the black press and the music press turned their attention back to the Empress. The rumors about her death—about racism and refusal of care, of shadowy doings down South, and a blues diva left bleeding by the side of Highway 61—started with an article that the highly respected music journalist and producer John Hammond published in *Down Beat* in November 1937. Wrote Hammond, "A particularly disagreeable story as to the details of her death has just been received from members of Chick Webb's orchestra, who were in Memphis soon after the disaster. . . . When finally [Bessie] did arrive at the hospital, she was refused treatment because of her color and bled to death while waiting for attention."

That's the part of *Down Beat*'s coverage of Bessie's death that tends to get replayed. But Hammond, in that same article, actually went on to say,

"Realizing that such tales can be magnified greatly in the telling, I would like to get confirmation from some Memphis citizens who were on the spot at the time. If the story is true it is but another example of disgraceful conditions in a certain section of our country. . . . " In December 1937, *Down Beat* ran a front-page followup, stating, "Bessie Smith did not bleed to death from lack of medical attention."

The generally agreed-upon facts of the Bessie Smith accident are these: While being driven by Morgan, Smith's car ran into a large truck whose driver had apparently pulled off Highway 61 to check his tires and had just started to pull back on. A white surgeon, Dr. Hugh Smith, traveling along that same road with a man named Henry Broughton (the two were on a fishing trip), came upon the wreck of Bessie's car; Morgan waved them down. It was approximately 2 a.m.

Dr. Smith gave the following account to the *Clarksdale Press Register* on September 26, 1957, the twentieth anniversary of the crash: "My associate and I jumped out of the car, and I examined the colored woman in the light of my headlights. Her left arm, at the elbow, had been torn completely loose at the joint . . . in essence, a traumatic amputation, except that the main artery was still intact. She was bleeding profusely. A tourniquet was applied. Obviously, this woman had severe internal injuries to her chest or abdomen but she was conscious."

After Dr. Smith and his companion got out to help, another car, carrying a white man and a white woman, crashed into Dr. Smith's car. Dr. Smith told the *Clarksdale Press Register* in an interview published on October 3, 1957: "Now we had three patients on our hands, all lying on the grass beside three wrecked automobiles. At approximately this time, traffic began to pile up a bit, but simultaneous with this, the ambulances began to appear, and all three injured people were promptly dispatched to Clarksdale in two different ambulances."

Albertson, in *Bessie,* suggests that the stories about the white hospital turning away Bessie Smith are probably false, largely based on what Dr. Smith told him. He quotes Dr. Smith as saying, "The Bessie Smith ambulance would not have gone to a white hospital, you can forget that. Down in the Deep South cotton country, no colored ambulance driver, or white driver, would even have thought of putting a colored person off in a hospital for white folks. In Clarksdale, in 1937, a town of twelve to fifteen thousand people, there were two hospitals— one white and one colored—and they weren't half a mile apart. I suspect the driver drove just as straight as he could to the colored hospital." In fact, according to the October 2, 1937, *Defender* and other news reports from the period, Bessie Smith was taken to the G.T. Thomas Afro-American Hospital; the hospital closed in 1940 and was re-opened a few years later as the Riverside Hotel. Frank Ratliff, the hotel's owner, says his establishment has a Bessie Smith Room on the first floor to memorialize and pay tribute to the singer, but no documents relating to her time in the hospital have been kept, if any were ever there.

According to Frank Bolden, who was starting his career as a journalist for the *Pittsburgh Courier* in the late thirties and is now considered an expert on the subject of the black press, black newspapers routinely covered stories of black patients being turned away by white hospitals during that period and for years afterward. The book *Patterns of Negro Segregation,* by Charles Spurgeon Johnson, also says that in rural and small towns at the time, blacks were systematically banned from white hospitals, as well as from white libraries, swimming pools, and drinking fountains. Charles Tisdale, the longtime publisher of the *Jackson Advocate,* a black newspaper based in Jackson, Mississippi, said in a February 2003 interview that "in Clarksdale in the 1930s, they didn't let black people in the hospitals at all."

Dr. Smith's account also seems to suggest that at least one potential Good Samaritan passed on a chance to come to Bessie's aid. Dr. Smith told the *Clarksdale Press Register* on September 26, 1957, that the truck that had pulled over and set off the chain accident drove away without helping the wounded singer. Dr. Smith said, "The truck driver had informed the injured people that he was carrying U.S. mail and was also carrying the Sunday morning *Commercial* and had a time schedule and had to go on, but he told the colored man that he would go on into Clarksdale and send an ambulance back to pick them up. He had departed the scene for two or three minutes when we arrived." Was race a factor in the trucker leaving the accident scene and going about his business? If that driver had seen a white woman lying by the side of the road, her left arm nearly ripped off, would he have carried her for help? Would a load of Sunday newspapers and the U.S. mail have been more important than a white female victim? And might Bessie Smith have lived had the truck driver taken her for help immediately instead of speeding off to complete his mail run?

Jack Gee Jr., the adopted son of Bessie Smith and her estranged husband, Jack Gee, charged in the *Baltimore Afro-American* in 1938 that he had heard that Dr. Smith told a spectator at the scene that the reason he didn't transport Bessie Smith in his own car (a brand-new Chevrolet) is that he didn't want his car to get "too bloody." The younger Gee tells this story about the moment transportation finally arrived: "About this time Morgan came back with

Bessie Smith, Empress of the Blues

the ambulance. As the men were about to take the stretcher out to take my mother, somebody in the crowd said, 'Wait, let's see what's the matter with this white woman first.' The doctor then administered first aid to the white woman, and then put her in the ambulance and sent her back to town. Morgan protested but could do nothing."

Jack Gee Jr., in the article, supported the story that his mother was denied medical care: "We have never found out accurately yet how my mother was taken back to town, but we do know that she was taken first to a white hospital, which refused to administer first aid or take her in. She was then taken to the Afro-American hospital, a colored institution. This hospital didn't have the proper equipment with which to operate. Physicians had to run all over town to get the proper equipment."

The younger Gee went on: "It was about 11:30 a.m. before they administered ether to her. She died at 11:45 a.m. No reason was given as to why she died, but we know clearly that she died from loss of blood and neglect. I believe that if the ambulance had taken my mother back to town, as it was proper for the doctor to have instructed the driver, since the ambulance was sent for her case, she might be alive today."

Certain aspects of Jack Gee Jr.'s story are contradicted by other witnesses. The ambulance driver who transported Bessie was located by the *Clarksdale Press Register* twenty years later, in 1957. The man, Willie George Miller, worked for the L.P. Gibson Funeral Home in Clarksdale. (According to Robert Birdsong, a local historian and tour guide in Clarksdale, black accident victims at the time weren't allowed in ambulances and were instead driven in hearses sent by black funeral homes.) Miller said his memory of the event was "hazy" but believed that Smith "passed" while en route to the black hospital and that she wasn't taken to a white hospital.

Another player in the night's events also contradicts the younger Gee's take on the accident. Dr. W.H. Brandon, the man who signed Bessie Smith's death certificate, told John Lomax in 1941 that the charge that Smith was refused treatment was an "absolute untruth." Brandon also made a charge of his own, claiming that the man who was driving her "was apparently very drunk." But Dr. Smith, who was on the scene, told reporters that the driver of the Bessie Smith car appeared to be sober.

Dr. Smith died in 1989, but his widow, Mimi Smith, told me in early 2003 that her late husband believed that Bessie Smith's injuries would have been fatal no matter what kind of care she had received or how quickly it had been administered. Said Mimi Smith, "The one thing he wanted people to understand is that if the accident had happened outside of the city hospital, she wouldn't have survived. Her injuries were that great." But at least one news report from the time of the accident seems to contradict the claim that Bessie was beyond help. The October 2, 1937, *Chicago Defender* reported that "even in her last minutes Miss Smith maintained that real trouper spirit. She made a valiant fight against death and smilingly told friends at the bedside that she was certain she would be able to make the evening performance of the Winsted Broadway Rastus minstrels show in Memphis."

If the *Chicago Defender* anecdote is true, or partially true (it does sound apocryphal that a woman whose arm is half-missing would talk about going through with a gig), if Bessie did have some life left in her after the accident, that would lend more weight to the argument that the assistance she didn't get (perhaps because of her race) but that she should have gotten—help from the truck that sparked the accident, a ride from Dr. Smith, even if it meant bloodying his Chevrolet (though, in fairness, the doctor's vehicle was probably totaled before he could use it), or help from the white ambulance that may have arrived on the scene first, or care from the white hospital to which she may have never been taken but that was probably better equipped than the black hospital she was eventually brought to—all of those might-have-beens and should-have-beens could have saved her life.

✦ ✦ ✦ ✦ ✦

But something survived that night. Something that was bigger than Bessie and beyond music. Something that, instead of confirming the continuing presence of racism in American society, showed that perhaps the future held out some possibility of racial reconciliation after all. Since the late nineteenth century, an alliance had been brewing in America between black women and white women, between abolitionists and the activists who would form the core of the feminist movement in the twentieth century. There was empathy on both sides. As Angelina Grimké, who, along with her sister, Sarah, was one of the leading white abolitionists of the nineteenth century, said in 1837: "They are our country women—*they are our sisters*— and to us, as women, they have a right to look for sympathy with their sorrows, and effort and prayer for their rescue." Decades later, in the 1960s, the white female social activists who worked on civil rights campaigns took the energy and stratagems they had seen on display in the South and transplanted them to the growing feminist movement in the North. Sara Evans, in her book *Personal Politics: The Roots of Women's Liberation in the Civil Rights Movement and the New Left,* writes in a chapter with the heading "Black Power—Catalyst for Feminism" that "thus the fullest expressions of conscious feminism within the civil rights movement ricocheted off the fury of black power and landed with explosive force in the northern, white new left."

Blueswomen, chief among them Bessie Smith, played a role in creating the new activist woman of the twentieth century. Bessie Smith, by living by her own rules, by singing about working women and their loves and struggles in public places, gave women a voice—a voice that was big and assertive and unafraid to explore any issue, from the bed-room to the barroom, from the poorhouse to the jailhouse. Her death—especially, perhaps, because of the controversy and publicity her end inspired— was confirmation that a woman could live a bold life, dictate her own rules, set her own sexual boundaries, and go down in history as a woman of consequence to whom attention must be paid. She became an icon, a lodestar, whom black women, and eventually women of all colors, could follow. Daphne Duval Harrison, in her book *Black Pearls: Blues Queens of the 1920s,* asserts that blues divas helped create "an emerging model for the working woman—one who is sexually independent, self-sufficient, creative, assertive, and trend-setting." Activist Angela Davis, author of the book *Blues Legacies and Black Feminism,* also argues that the work of pioneering blues women Bessie Smith, Ma Rainey, and Billie Holiday has been instrumental in the formation of the core values of feminist thought. Bessie's voice has echoed, through the decades, louder and longer than the crash that took her life. ☞

RECOMMENDED LISTENING:

Bessie Smith, *Bessie Smith: The Collection* (Columbia, 1989). The best sampling of Smith's work.

Bessie Smith, *The Essential Bessie Smith* (Columbia, 1997). A fairly comprehensive two-disc set with most of Smith's greatest numbers. If you want a hefty helping of Smith, this is the set to get.

Bessie Smith, *Martin Scorsese Presents the Blues: The Definitive Bessie Smith* (Columbia/Legacy, 2003). The companion CD to the documentary series.

Janis Joplin, *Martin Scorsese Presents the Blues: The Definitive Janis Joplin* (Columbia/Legacy, 2003). This companion CD to the documentary series showcases Smith's powerful spiritual heir of the rock era.

A NIGHT WITH BESSIE SMITH

By Carl Van Vechten

[From "Negro 'Blues' Singers," *Vanity Fair,* 1926]

A trip to Newark is a career, and so I was forced to rise from the dinner table on Thanksgiving night shortly after eight o'clock if I wished to hear Bessie Smith sing at the Orpheum Theatre in that New Jersey city at a quarter of ten. I rose with eagerness, however, and so did my guests. Bessie Smith, the "Queen of the Blues," whose records sell into figures that compete with the circulation of the *Saturday Evening Post*, was to sing in Newark, and Bessie Smith, who makes long tours of the South where her rich voice reaches the ears of the race from which she sprang, had not been heard in the vicinity of New York, save through the horn of the phonograph, for over a year.

The signs and tokens were favorable. When we gave directions to the white taxicab driver at Park Place, he demanded, "Going to hear Bessie Smith?" "Yes," we replied. "No good trying," he assured us. "You can't get in. They've been hanging on the chandeliers all the week." Nevertheless, we persevered, spurred on perhaps by a promise on the part of the management that a box would be reserved for us. We arrived, however, to discover that this promise had not been kept. It had been impossible to hold the box: The crowd was too great. "Day jes' nacherly eased into dat box," one of the ushers explained insouciantly. However, Leigh Whipper, the enterprising manager of the theater, eased them out again.

Once seated, we looked out over a vast sea of happy black faces—two comedians were exchanging jokes on the stage. There was not a mulatto or high yellow visible among these people who were shouting merriment or approval after every ribald line. Were did they all come from? In Harlem the Negroes are many colors, shading to white, but these were all chocolate browns and "blues." Never before had I seen such an audience save at a typical camp-meeting in the far South.

The comedians were off. The lights were lowered. A new placard, reading BESSIE SMITH, appeared in the frames at either side of the proscenium. As the curtain lifted, a jazz band, against a background of plum-colored hangings, held the full stage. The saxophone began to moan; the drummer tossed his sticks. One was transported involuntarily, inevitably, to a Harlem cabaret. Presently, the band struck up a slower and still more mournful strain. The hangings parted and a great brown woman emerged—she was the size of Fay Templeton in her Weber and Fields days, and she was even garbed similarly, in a rose satin dress, spangled with sequins, which swept away from her trim ankles. Her face was beautiful, with the rich, ripe beauty of southern darkness, a deep bronze brown, like her bare arms.

She walked slowly to the footlights.

Then, to the accompaniment of the wailing, muted brasses, the monotonous African beat of the drum, the dromedary glide of the pianist's fingers over the responsive keys, she began her strange rites in a voice full of shoutin' and moanin' and prayin' and sufferin', a wild, rough Ethiopian voice, harsh and volcanic, released between rouged lips and the whitest of teeth, the singer swaying slightly to the rhythm.

Yo' treated me wrong;
I treated yo' right;
I wo'k fo' yo' full day an' night.

Yo' brag to women
I was yo' fool,
So den I got dose sobbin' h'ahted blues.

And now, inspired partly by these lines, partly by the stumbling strain of the accompaniment, partly by the power and magnetic personality of this elemental conjure woman and her plangent African voice, quivering with pain and passion, which sounded as if it had been developed at the sources of the Nile, the crowd burst into hysterical shrieks of sorrow and lamentation. Amens rent the air. Little nervous giggles, like the shivering of Venetian glass, shocked the nerves.

It's true I loves yo', but I won't take
mistreatments any mo'.

"Dat's right," a girl cried out from under our box.

All I wants is yo' pitcher in a frame;
All I wants is yo' pitcher in a frame;
When yo' gone I kin see yo' jes' duh same.

"Oh, Lawdy! Lawdy!" The girl beneath us shook with convulsive sobbing.

I'se gwine to staht walkin' cause
I got a wooden pah o' shoes;
Gwine to staht walkin' cause I got
a wooden pah o' shoes;
Gwine to keep on walkin' till I lose
dese sobbin' h'ahted blues.

The singer disappeared, and with her her magic. The spell broken, the audience relaxed and began to chatter. The band played a gayer tune.

Once again, Bessie Smith came out, now clad in a clinging garment fashioned of beads of silver steel. More than ever she was like an African empress, more than ever like a conjure woman.

"I'm gwineter sing dose mean ornery cussed 'Wo'khouse Blues,'" she shouted.

Everybody's cryin' de wo'khouse
Blues all day,
All 'long,
All 'long . . .

A deep sigh from the gallery.

Been wo'kin' so hard—thirty days
is long,
long, long,
long, long . . .

The spell once more was weaving its subtle sorcery, the perversely complicated spell of African voodoo, the fragrance of china-berry blossoms, the glimmer of the silver fleece of the cotton field under the full moon, the spell of sorrow: misery, poverty, and the horror of jail.

I gotta leab heah,
Gotta git du nex' train home . . .

Way up dere, way up on a long lonesome
road;
Duh wo'khouse ez up on a long lonesome
road . . .

Daddy used ter be mine, but look who'se got
him now;
Daddy used ter be mine, but look who'se got
him now;
Ef yo' took him keep him, he don't mean no
good nohow. 🖝

BILLIE HOLIDAY BY HILTON ALS

What can we offer her by way of recompense for the various messes made of Her Story? The pop vulgarizations, the dry-mouthed academicism of technical writers without benefit of ear or compassion, the gaseous memoirs by overinflated egos who once caught a glimpse of the famous bad temper, the unimpeachable style, and yet remember nothing of the woman but what they felt once she left the room to do God knows what?

She was trouble and looked for it. She was a changeling who found her true shape in an atmosphere of disaster. She was intent on having things her way because that is the only way an artist knows how to tell it: her way, and ruthlessly, with not a modicum of decency tainting the surface of her sound or stage appearances, since that is the mark of the bourgeois, the tidy-minded, something to get over if you are intent on doing the do and realizing your own genius.

"Here was a woman who had never been a Christian," Elizabeth Hardwick wrote in her 1977 novel, *Sleepless Nights,* which remains the best account we have of this "bizarre deity." What made her so strange? Well, she never compromised—the better to be loved by many instead of the few. She was not interested in the American way of the public validation of a private preoccupation. And she suffered for it.

She embodied the self as myth. She was witty no matter what the context, meaning no matter how trite the song she sang, or tiresome the context she sang the song in. Women are not like that. They are socialized to make things better, not worse, often by not acknowledging "the worse."

She couldn't help seeing what was wrong and saying something about it. Her mind would not shut up. She was born in 1915 and died forty-four years later. She saw the South, and Europe, and should have lived abroad, where she was adored, but adoration is no kind of life if you're interested in life. And despite her horror at what it could do, and had done to her, she lived her life because she had a sense of humor about life's horrors, but maybe not such a great sense of humor about herself. Maybe she was curious about this dichotomy. At times.

She was a documentation, interested in her own version of the facts. She mythologized her sound. She said that Bessie Smith and Louis Armstrong influenced her sound. And yet one hears a great deal of Ethel Waters in her early recordings—the high-pitched wail that has more than a bit of the smart aleck in it. Sometimes, it's all one can do not to laugh right along with her. The joke she's telling is about our square-ness. She exposes our silly and conventional lives with the asperity of her vision, which tells us that love and respectability are fiction, as much a fiction as anything else. That's the story she wanted to tell. And she did.

You can see her telling it in her various appearances on film, on TV. She knew what the camera was for. In front of it, she projected volcanic emotion disciplined by subtlety and intellection. She was a motion-picture star who dared us to look at her while we listened. Some of us did. Still do. 🖐

EARLY DOWNHOME BLUES RECORDINGS
By Jeff Todd Titon
[From *Early Downhome Blues: A Musical and Cultural Analysis,* 1977]

As early as 1923, Black Swan and OKeh thought there might be a market for [downhome] blues, or blues less sophisticated than the vaudeville variety [that they had been releasing]. A Black Swan advertisement for Josie Miles' "Love Me in Your Old Time Way" read: "Have you ever heard the snatches of songs sung by Negro section hands on Southern railroads? Do you recall how their plaintive melodies struck a responsive chord in you? Generally termed blues, yet how strongly contrasted are these songs springing from the depths of the laborer's soul to the commonplace dance tunes that we are accustomed to call BLUES. LOVE ME IN YOUR OLD TIME WAY is in the vein of the laborer's songs."

Miles was a vaudeville singer, and her song was merely "in the vein of" the "songs springing from the depths of the laborer's soul." . . . [Her] record, released on the Black Swan label in 1923, a year after it was made, and reissued on Paramount in 1924, when the latter company absorbed the former, evidently was successful, but it did not lead to imitations. In 1923, OKeh A&R director Ralph Peer took portable equipment to Atlanta, ostensibly to record hillbilly musician Fiddlin' John Carson. Atlanta's OKeh jobber, Polk Brockman, thought Carson's records would be successful locally. They were. But neither Peer nor Brockman predicted what happened next: Carson's record opened a hillbilly market as lucrative as the race market. And though Peer had recorded Birmingham blues singer Louise Bogan on the Atlanta trip, the idea of making field trips to record blues singers in Southern cities was forgotten in the rush to capitalize on the new hillbilly market.

The downhome impulse [though] was undoubtedly responsible for Paramount's promotion of Ma Rainey as a Southern-styled singer. It was also responsible for the publicity surrounding that company's "discovery" of Papa Charlie Jackson—"the only man living who sings, self-accompanied, for Blues records"—who was introduced in a [*Chicago*] *Defender* advertisement as if he were a relic of a bygone era. Since his records sold well, he is a likely candidate to honor as the first downhome blues singer, but others have classified him a vaudeville singer because he accompanied his songster's repertoire (which did include some blues) on six-string banjo-guitar, which gave it an unmistakable minstrel-show sound. Although he was a minstrel-show veteran, his downhome blues credentials are at least as good as those of some, such as Jim Jackson, who had the good fortune to record after Blind Lemon Jefferson. . . .

Local record dealers in the South had been suggesting downhome singers for some time before Sam Price sent a letter to Paramount recommending Jefferson, who was already well known throughout Texas. A.C. Laibley, Paramount recording director, claimed that he found Jefferson on the streets of Dallas and late in 1925 invited him to Chicago. The music of the vaudeville blues singers was close enough to Tin Pan Alley for the record companies to feel familiar with it; and the music of singers like Papa Charlie Jackson and Daddy Stovepipe was close enough to the common stock of folk and minstrel song shared, at the turn of the century, by Anglo- and Afro-Americans for the record companies to recognize *that*. The inescapable conclusion is that Jefferson's music confused them. Unsure at first what to do with the blind singer, Paramount had him record a spiritual under the pseudonym "Deacon L.J. Bates," but its release was delayed. In March 1926, he recorded four blues songs. For the first release, "Booster Blues" and "Dry Southern Blues," Paramount introduced him in an April 8, 1926, *Defender* advertisement as "a real, old-fashioned Blues singer" singing "a real, old-fashioned Blues." The point was emphasized in succeeding sentences, which called his songs "old-time tunes" and his guitar playing "in real Southern style." It is difficult to imagine a better word to describe Paramount's judgment of Jefferson's songs than the one they used continually in their publicity about him: *weird*. They could not understand his words; they had never heard anyone play the guitar as he did. Even his appearance must have been startling—a blind, black street-singer of enormous girth with tiny, steel-rimmed glasses perched on his nose. So striking was his appearance that the advertising illustrators forgot their rule of avoiding cartoon caricatures of the singer's likeness when it came to his advertisements.

Yet Jefferson's downhome style was familiar to almost anyone from the Black Belt. His first record sold moderately well, but his second, "Got the Blues" and "Long Lonesome Blues," became [a] best seller. Paramount's success with Jefferson led the other record companies to work [in] the same vein, and they quickly sent scouts south looking for downhome blues talent. The naïveté of the companies' scouting behavior indicates unfamiliarity with the music; they sent their representative directly to Dallas, Jefferson's home city. Dallas pianist Alex Moore described this activity: "Specialty Records, OKeh, Vocalion, Decca Records, Columbia Records, all had talent scouts in Dallas . . . [they] were in and out of Dallas every fifteen to thirty days. You can't imagine how they were, savaging [*sic*] up songs for recordings. Dallas was a noted town for piano players and guitarists, blues and boogie-wise, good ones like Blind Lemon Jefferson. . . . "

In the early twenties, OKeh courted a new group of record buyers as it pushed the downhome blues, sold as "race records."

The first major period of downhome blues recording extended from 1926 until 1930. (The second occurred from 1947 until 1955.) Talent scouts secured primarily local and regional Southern blues singers who had been entertaining in juke joints, in barrelhouses, and at suppers, picnics, and country dance parties. Most of these entertainers were songsters whose repertoires included many kinds of songs besides blues, but the scouts were looking for original blues songs. Many of the singers had just one recording session, in a makeshift studio in a Southern city. Others, like Blind Blake, were so successful that they were invited to make records on a regular basis.

Race record sales fell as the decade drew to a close. Although about five hundred blues and gospel titles

Black Swan's marketing approach was more refined than that of OKeh, who incorporated urban jive lingo into its ads.

were released each year from 1927 until 1930, the number of copies of each record pressed declined sharply toward the end of that period. The sales decline has been attributed to black poverty in the Depression, but this explanation is insufficient, for the Depression came to the Black Belt farm country at least six years before the stock market crash of 1929. Rather, as the industry retrenched it adopted several economy measures that worked against securing a continuing supply of downhome blues singers—measures that initiated a self-fulfilling prophecy. The expensive field trips were cut back severely. Professional singers with wide repertoires and practiced efficiency promised to be the most productive, as studios came to operate on assembly-line techniques, processing songs very quickly. Under these circumstances, for example, one take instead of two became normal procedure. As long

as their records sold reasonably well—Leroy Carr and Scrapper Blackwell, Tampa Red and Georgia Tom, Memphis Minnie and Kansas Joe were selling consistently in the early 1930s—it was foolish to take chances on unknown singers or to keep issuing records of established performers, like Blind Blake, whose sales figures suddenly dropped. Although the industry continued to issue downhome blues records, and although new singers like Big Bill Broonzy, Bumble Bee Slim (Amos Easton), and John Lee "Sonny Boy" Williamson established their reputations in the 1930s, the intense activity was over.

There was a redefinition of the downhome style, as the younger singers felt the influence of recordings and as jukeboxes began to displace live entertainment in the juke joints. Solo singers accompanying themselves on guitar seemed archaic, though some (like Blind Willie McTell) would continue to record, and others (like Robert Johnson, Tommy McClennan, and Robert Petway) would break into the race market. If the guitar had been the major downhome blues instrument in the recordings of the 1920s, the piano replaced it in the following decade. As Bessie Smith's generation of vaudeville blues singers aged, the featured spot they had held was taken over by the jazz band itself, and singers became attached to bands, instead of the reverse. There was a sharp decline in race titles issued, both in overall quantity and as a percentage of all records issued. But in the Black Belt, juke parties continued, and downhome musicians with portable instruments were still in demand to provide entertainment at them. When, after World War II, small record companies sprang up, breaking the major companies' virtual monopoly, they found plenty of black singers accompanying themselves with guitars. And some of the more successful ones, like Lightnin' Hopkins and John Lee Hooker, sounded very much like their counterparts twenty years earlier—after their electric guitars were unplugged by folk music enthusiasts.

LET'S GET DRUNK AND TRUCK: A GUIDE TO THE PARTY BLUES
BY JAMES MARSHALL

Since that immortal day in 1927 when Blind Lemon Jefferson decided the critter his pud most resembled was a black snake—and got the biggest hit record of his career out of it, "That Black Snake Moan"—sex has sold plenty of blues discs. In the years before World War II, blues records concerning sex, a.k.a. "party blues," possibly comprise the largest portion of the recorded body of blues. (Sociologists theorize this is because many of the parents of blues singers actually may have engaged in the sex act—but this is merely a hypothesis.)

The biggest blues hit of the late 1920s was a stompin' ode to pussy entitled "It's Tight Like That" (1928) by Tampa Red (Hudson Whittaker) and Georgia Tom (a.k.a. Thomas A. Dorsey, who a few years later would zip up his pants for Jesus and invent modern gospel music, composing "Precious Lord" among other valuable, tax-free copyrights). "It's Tight Like That" was covered by dozens of blues and jazz artists, ranging from Louis Armstrong to female impersonator Frankie "Half Pint" Jaxon. In addition, it inspired such answer songs as the Mississippi Sheiks' "Loose Like That" (1930) and Tampa Red's own "It's Tight Like That #2" (1929), among others. That same year, Georgia Tom teamed with Jane Lucas for "Terrible Operation Blues," one of the strangest and most flagrantly obscene party blues of all time.

New Orleans–born guitar virtuoso Lonnie Johnson always knew how to make a buck, and in the early years of his six-decade career he cut "It Feels So Good" (1929) and "Wipe It Off" (1930), both of which are as bawdy as the titles sound. Bo Carter (né Chatmon), a member of the Mississippi Sheiks (whose "Sitting on Top of the World" was one of the biggest blues hits ever), was responsible for the Sheiks' "Ramrod Blues" (1930) and "Bed Spring Poker" (1931). Post-Sheiks, Carter pursued a career based on single-entendre smut like "Banana in Your Fruit Basket" (1931), "Pin in Your Cushion" (1934), "My Pencil Won't Write No More" (1935), "Pussy Cat Blues" (1936), "Your Biscuits Are Big Enough for Me" (1936), and, of course, "The Ins and Outs of My Girl" (1936). The guy was shameless!

Blind Boy Fuller, one of the greatest and most popular of the rural-blues singers, recorded "Truckin' My Blues Away" (1936) and "She's a Truckin' Little Baby" (1938), coining a clever double entendre (with *truckin'* standing in for *fuckin'*). Fuller also cut the downright blunt "I Want Some of Your Pie" (1929) and the rhetorical number "What's That Smells Like Fish" (1938), as well as others equally focused below the belt. Even tortured soul Robert Johnson took time out from playing hide-and-seek with Satan long enough to invite his honey to "squeeze my lemon, baby, till the juice runs down my leg" in "Traveling Riverside Blues" (1937); his lines later were appropriated by Robert "Percy" Plant of Led Zeppelin, who sounded quite stupid singing them.

Kokomo Arnold, a moonshiner and guitar player, cut some truly fine dirty discs, including an intense reading of "the dozens," the African-American folk game that consists of insulting one another's family. He called his 1935 number "Dirty Dozens." Earlier, in 1929, the similar tune "The Dirty Dozen" had

Double entendres abound in the party blues.

and recorded it as "Keep a Knockin'" in 1958. Arnold's version included the lines: "I heard you knockin' about twelve o'clock/But I had your mammie on the choppin' block/Keep a knockin' but you can't come in/I'm busy bootin' and you can't come in."

Women, especially the classic blues singers of the twenties and thirties, were not immune to recording party blues. In one of her most memorable performances, the great Bessie Smith bemoaned the fact that "I need a little sugar for my bowl," inviting the men folk to indulge in her bowl of jelly ("I Need a Little Sugar in My Bowl," 1931). Also for Columbia, she cut "Do Your Duty" and "I'm Wild About That Thing," both of which were equally uninhibited. In 1929, Clara Smith waxed her version of "It's Tight Like That," as well as a ditty entitled "Ain't Got Nobody to Grind My Coffee." Needing no further explanation is Barrel House Annie's "If It Don't Fit (Don't Force It)."

The bawdy and prolific Lil Johnson recorded several versions of "Hot Nuts (Get 'Em From the Peanut Man)," not to mention such 1929–1937 sticky classics as "Rock That Thing," "Sam the Hotdog Man," "Was I Drunk?," "Let's Get Drunk and Truck," "Rug Cutter's Function," "Meat Balls," "Take It Easy Greasy No. 2 (You Got a Long Way to Slide)," "You Stole My Cherry," and "My Stove's in Good Condition."

The majority of blues record buyers in the twenties and thirties were reportedly women, and judging from the numerous discs directed specifically at the "sportin' woman" market, we can assume that many of these records ended up in houses of ill repute. Among them: Little Laura Dukes' "Jelly Sellin' Woman"(1929); the aforementioned Lil Johnson's "Anybody Want to Buy My Cabbage?" (1935); and Georgia White's "I'll

been a hit for Speckled Red, who recorded "The Dirty Dozen No. 2" and "No. 3" in successive years. Leroy Carr and Scrapper Blackwell, as well as Lonnie Johnson, also cut "The Dirty Dozen," in 1930, and Memphis Minnie did "New Dirty Dozen," but none were as great or as graphic as Arnold's later version. Perhaps Arnold's finest moment—certainly his most tasteless—was his 1935 recording of "Busy Bootin'," a tune that would eventually find its way into rock & roll's repertoire via Little Richard, who cleaned it up

Keep Sittin' on It (If I Can't Sell It)" (1936) and "If You Can't Get Five, Take Two" (1936). Adding to the canon, Bessie Smith recorded two tunes about pimps: "My Sportin' Man" (1929) and "Hustlin' Dan" (1930).

For my money, the pinnacle of both the classic-blues form and the party-blues style is an unreleased (until the mid-seventies) version of "Shave 'Em Dry" by Lucille Bogan (a.k.a. Bessie Jackson and also attributed to Lucille Brogan), cut in 1935, which includes the following truly inspired couplets:

I got nipples on my titties
As big as the end of your thumb
I got something between my legs
Make a dead man come.
Oh daddy
Baby won't you shave 'em dry
Won't you grind me baby
Grind me till I cry
I fucked all night and the night before
And I feel like I want to fuck some more . . .
Oooh daddy
Baby won't you shave 'em dry
Ohhh fuckin' is the thing that takes me to
* heaven*
I'll be fuckin' in the street till the clock strikes
* eleven*
Baby, shave 'em dry
Grind me, daddy, grind me til I cry
Now your nuts hang down like a damn bell
* clapper*
And your dick stands up like a steeple
Your goddamn asshole stands open like a church
* door*
And the crabs crawls in like people
Oooww . . . shit!

Baby won't you shave 'em dry
A big sow gets fat from feedin' corn
And a cow gets fat from suckin'
If you see this pork
Fat like I am
Goddamn I got fat from fuckin'
Weeoow—shave 'em dry
My back is made of whalebone
And my cock* is made of brass
And my fuckin' is made for workin' men's
Two dollars
Great God you can come around and kiss my
* ass!*

[*In the vernacular of the day, *cock* was female genitalia.]

The most popular party blues of the 1920s was "It's Tight Like That," written by Georgia Tom (Thomas Dorsey) and Tampa Red (Hudson Whittaker) in 1928.

"She Wouldn't Give Me None"

1576—SHE WOULDN'T GIVE ME NONE & MY MARY BLUES
Vocal Duet with Guitar Acc.
Memphis Minnie-Kansas Joe 75c

Memphis Minnie and her husband Kansas Joe bemoan hard times of a different sort, in an advertisement for their record "She Wouldn't Give Me None."

Bogan seemed to have had a one-track mind, also cutting "Bed Rollin' Blues," "Skin Game Blues" (both 1935), and the sapphic "Women Won't Need No Man" (1927).

In the years following World War II, as the blues market evolved from race records to rhythm & blues, and the electric-blues style was forged in Northern cities by John Lee Hooker and Muddy Waters, the nature of party blues changed, from blatant to coy; the years 1946 to 1954, which directly preceded the rise of rock & roll (cleaned-up R&B), represent the golden age of the double entendre.

The rock & roll era ended even the more subtle dirty blues—at least for a while—since record labels didn't want to expose their new audience, middle-class white teenagers, to such gutter-minded material. In 1955, for example, Little Richard took "Tutti Frutti," an old tent-show standard about sodomy (original lyrics: "Tutti Frutti/Good bootie/If it don't fit/Don't force it/Just grease it/And make it easy"), and turned it into a raucous but innocent teenage nursery rhyme, ushering in the new era.

Though the party blues went underground during the rock & roll years, it survived into the sixties and seventies, occasionally surfacing, as with Chick Willis' "Stoop Down Baby" (1971) and Willie Dixon's "Pettin' the Baby" (1972).

It resurfaced with a vengeance in the eighties with Clarence Carter's surprise smash hit "Strokin'" (1986), which sold a million copies just as the CD began supplanting the 45-rpm record. Hip-hop has proudly continued the party-blues tradition, with highlights including 2 Live Crew's "We Want Some Pussy" (1987) and "Me So Horney" (1988) and Khia's "My Neck My Back," and Too $hort's answer record "My Balls My Sack" (both 2002).

Today, the party blues are alive on what's left of the chitlin' circuit and on Southern radio stations like New Orleans' WODT, which plays nothing but filthy blues records. Unfortunately, radio conglomerate Clear Channel recently purchased WODT and dozens of other tiny blues stations in the South, leaving one to wonder how long these stations will keep such earthy sounds on their playlists. One thing's for sure: Just as people will never stop having sex, recording artists will never stop singing about it. ✏

REMEMBERING ROBERT JOHNSON *By Johnny Shines*

[From *The American Folk Music Occasional,* 1970]

I met Robert in 1935 in Helena, Arkansas, through a friend of his and mine who had played piano with me in Hughes, Arkansas. I never did know this fellow's right name, but everybody called him "M.&O." He often talked to me about Robert and how good he was, and he wanted the three of us to get together and jam some. So we went to Helena to meet Robert. M.&O. had heard that Robert was in Helena.

It was a worthwhile trip—I met a friend, someone who liked to travel and play music as well as I did. When Robert and I first met, I was twenty years old, and I would say that he was about twenty-two or twenty-three.

Now, we didn't decide to team up. We just went places together and played together. The fact of it was that I was the bad penny. I stayed on Robert's heels, and at that time I would follow anyone who had a run, a riff, or a chord that I wanted until I got it, if they were anyways friendly at all.

Through M.&O. we struck up a good friendship, but while we were there Robert left town. He went over into Mississippi and, if it hadn't been for M.&O.'s knowing how Robert was, I would still be waiting for him to come back!

Then I met him again in Memphis. That was my home and I wanted to be anywhere but there. So Robert was telling me about how he had to go to Dallas to make some records, and I told him "let's go," but he had a ticket and I didn't. We went as far as Texarkana, Arkansas, and I told him to go on, I would catch up to him soon, and I did. I caught him in a place called Red Water, Texas. Robert had made his records (Note: This would have been in 1937, as Johnson recorded in Dallas on June 19 and 20 of that year),

and we had a lot of fun. He would play them for me and I would learn them.

We worked Texas until the cold weather began to set in, then we headed for the southern part of Texas. That's when I found out that Texas was a cotton country; I had thought Texas was only a cow country. Robert and I came back into Arkansas as far as Little Rock. I can't recall just what happened, but my mother was in Arkansas not too far from Hughes and I ended up there. Robert went on, but I stayed on in Hughes. One night I came in and was putting my guitar away when a girl came up to me and told me that a fellow was in my bed who said he knew me real well and could play like she had never heard before. I asked, "What did he play?" When she said guitar, that did it! I knew it was Robert.

We worked around there together, and most of the time individually. What I mean by that is that there were very few songs that Robert wanted to play with anyone, so we mostly played in turns. Hughes was a small town, but if anything was going on anywhere it was there. We made the paydays at Stuttgart, Cotton Plant, Snow Lake, and many other places, together and sometimes separately. If we both were in Hughes at the same time we shared the room, or whoever was there on Monday paid the rent. . . .

Since Robert was the peculiar person that he was, you would have to say that his love life was very slack, or open. You see, no woman really had an iron hand on Robert at any time. When his time came to go, he just went. I never could see how a man could be quite so neutral. I have seen him treated so royally that you would think he would never depart from this kindhearted woman that would do anything in this world for him. But how wrong can you be?

There were two guys over [to] Jersey that had heard about Robert and me being in New York, and by some magic they found us and wanted us to go over in Jersey to play for them. That was right up Robert's alley. At the time Robert and I were going with two girls in New York.

So we—Robert and I—left New York and went to New Jersey with these guys to play for them, and for two weeks we didn't think to write, but by the same magic the girls found Robert and me. Being the silly ones that they were, they wanted us to go back with them. Robert would have no part of this: He was ready to go South, North, or West, but not back to New York—and the way we were living, you would think any person in his right mind would want to get away from that place. Don't get me wrong. We were making good money; the people were going for what we were putting down, and we were really unloading. But these girls, they were loaded and offering us everything we wanted, but Bob treated them like they were just two old friends we once had known.

Now, look, please don't let the way this is being said disillusion you at all. Robert was far from being a sissy, and sometimes was too forward. Even men's wives were fair game for him.

Let us change the scene to Arkansas.

We were having quite a time in this little town where people gathered every night to gamble, drink, and dance, or whatever employed their minds to do for their pleasure. We were playing regularly in this get-together joint every night, and this specific night Robert saw this girl and wanted to meet her. He found another girl who knew her and got this girl to introduce them.

Robert didn't lose any time, even though she told him she was married. Robert would not let her out of his sight the rest of the night. And when we left there a couple of days later she was with us, and she stayed for quite a while. Her name was Louise, and she was everything that Robert wanted: She could sing, dance, drink, and fight like hell. Oh, yes, she could play a little guitar too. She and Robert used to get on until she hit him on the head with a hot stove eye. I don't think that was part of Robert's plan at all, because they never got along well after that.

I only know two women who might have been near as close, and they were Shakey Horton's sister and Robert Lockwood Jr.'s mother. I have heard Bob talk more about Shakey's sister than anyone else. Robert's mother must have meant quite a bit to him too, because he called her his wife. I am sure that you've noticed I call these ladies "girls," but that is just a figure of speech, because there was only one girl in the bunch, and that was Horton's sister. She was in her early teens, but the rest were thirty and older. Robert spent a lot of time getting the attention of girls without knowing it himself, and he spent the rest of the time trying to get away from them.

Robert's route was: Memphis, Tennessee; Mississippi; Helena, Arkansas; Missouri; and sometimes Texas. He was a guy that could find a way to make a song sound good with a slide, regardless of its contents or nature. His guitar seemed to talk—repeat and say words with him like no one else in the world could. I said he had a talking guitar, and many a person agreed with me.

This sound affected most women in a way that I could never understand. One time in St. Louis, we were playing one of the songs that Robert would like to play with someone once in a great while, "Come On in My Kitchen." He was playing very slow and passionately, and when we had quit, I noticed no one was saying anything. Then I realized they were crying—both women and men.

Things like this often happened, and I think Robert would cry just as hard as anyone. It was things like this, it seems to me, that made Robert want to be by himself, and he would soon be by himself. The thing that was different, I think, was that Robert would do his crying on the inside. Yes, his crying was on the inside.

As I have already said, Robert was far from being a sissy, and he proved it without trying. He could do the darnedest things. Women, to Robert, were like motel or hotel rooms: Even if he used them repeatedly, he left them where he found them. Robert was like a sailor—with one exception: A sailor has a girl in every port, but Robert had a woman in every town. Heaven help him, he was not discriminating—probably a bit like Christ. He loved them all—the old, young, fat, thin, and the short. They were all alike to Robert.

We were in West Memphis, Arkansas, staying at the Hunt Hotel, and playing for a fellow called "City." There was a girl not more than a midget in height and size who also lived in this Hunt Hotel that we all took for granted because she was always running errands for the three of us as well as everyone else in the neighborhood. When she would make a run for us, the change that was left, we would give it to her because we thought she was just a very nice girl.

One day we missed Robert and thought he was on Eighth Street with a girl that he gave quite a bit of attention to. We were satisfied with this explanation until the girl we thought he was with came over with food for Robert, and the rest of us too, but when she didn't find Robert we had to make a quick guess as to where he was, regardless of what we really thought. So we said he was in Memphis, but she wanted no part of this and was getting quite angry. So somebody had to find him. Well, I knew this little girl always was up and around early and she might just know where Robert was—and she did. One guess, and I bet you are right! He was there in her bed. She only had one room, and since it would have looked kind of foolish to ask her to go out of her own room so I could talk to Robert, I told her what had happened, and she was very broad-minded about the whole thing. She in turn told Robert as though he weren't listening and showed him a way to get out of the hotel without being seen, and it worked. After that,

Robert used this exit quite often, but he was not always coming from the little girl's room!

One time we were in Wickliffe, Kentucky, and met some girls that I liked very much. They were a dance team that had never been no place and wanted to be seen and heard. I should have said a song-and-dance team of four people. They could really go to town, and I wanted to take them with us when we left and had it all arranged, but Bob, he would slip from one girl to the other until he had them all fighting among themselves. Now he was ready to give them the slip, and we did.

Did Robert really love? Yes, like a hobo loves a train—off one and on the other.

Robert had all kinds of moods—singing, playing, drinking, fighting, rambling, sometimes talking (which was the shortest mood of all, except playing with other men in a playful manner). It seems to me that where there were no women around, that's where Robert would find the woman he liked best, and had to have her or go to hell trying to get her. And he got her.

Robert left me in Chicago. He went to St. Louis, to the state line—that is where Arkansas and Missouri join—and from there to Blythesville, Arkansas, then Memphis, Tennessee, and then back to Hughes, Arkansas. I caught up with him in Helena, Arkansas.

If you want to guess, you can score yourself a hundred: Yes, he was back with Robert Lockwood's mother again. He spent lots of time going between her house and another house that I won't name at this time. Yes, Robert was quite a ladies' man, but he was always running from one, to learn a new face, or to get where another woman was that he already knew. Then Robert went over into Mississippi. I didn't like the thought of Mississippi, so I didn't go with him, and I never saw Robert again.

This was the Robert Johnson that I knew and the good things that I knew about him. 🖊

THE DEVIL'S SON-IN-LAW

By Ralph Ellison

[From *Invisible Man*, 1952]

It was a clear, bright day when I went out, and the sun burned warm upon my eyes. Only a few flecks of snowy cloud hung high in the morning-blue sky, and already a woman was hanging wash on a roof. I felt better walking along. A feeling of confidence grew. Far down the island the skyscrapers rose tall and mysterious in the thin, pastel haze. A milk truck went past. I thought of the school. What were they doing now on the campus? Had the moon sunk low and the sun climbed clear? Had the breakfast bugle blown? Did the bellow of the big seed bull awaken the girls in the dorms this morning as on most spring mornings when I was there—sounding clear and full above bells and bugles and early workaday sounds? I hurried along, encouraged by the memories, and suddenly I was seized with a certainty that today was the day. Something would happen. I patted my brief case, thinking of the letter inside. The last had been first—a good sign.

Close to the curb ahead I saw a man pushing a cart piled high with rolls of blue paper and heard him singing in a clear ringing voice. It was a blues, and I walked along behind him remembering the times that I had heard such singing at home. It seemed that here some memories slipped around my life at the campus and went far back to things I had long ago shut out of my mind. There was no escaping such reminders.

> She's got feet like a monkey
> Legs like a frog—Lawd, Lawd!
> But when she starts to loving me
> I holler Whoooo, God-dog!

> Cause I loves my baabay,
> Better than I do myself . . .

And as I drew alongside I was startled to hear him call to me:

"Looka-year, buddy . . ."

"Yes," I said, pausing to look into his reddish eyes.

"Tell me just one thing this very fine morning—Hey! Wait a minute, daddy-o, I'm going your way."

"What is it?" I said.

"What I want to know is," he said, "is you got the *dog?*"

"Dog? What dog?"

"Sho," he said, stopping his cart and resting it on its support. "That's it. *Who—*" he halted to crouch with one foot on the curb like a country preacher about to pound his Bible—*"got . . . the . . . dog,"* his head snapping with each word like an angry rooster's.

I laughed nervously and stepped back. He watched me out of shrewd eyes. "Oh, goddog, daddy-o," he said with a sudden bluster, "who got the damn dog? Now I know you from down home, how come you trying to act like you never heard that before! Hell, ain't nobody out here this morning but us colored—Why you trying to deny me?"

Suddenly I was embarrassed and angry. "Deny you? What do you mean?"

"Just answer the question. Is you got him, or ain't you?"

"A *dog?*"

"Yeah, *the* dog."

I was exasperated. "No, not this morning," I said and saw a grin spread over his face.

"Wait a minute, daddy. Now don't go get mad. Damn, man! I thought sho *you* had him," he said, pretending to disbelieve me. I started away and he pushed the cart beside me. And suddenly I felt uncomfortable. Somehow he was like one of the vets from the Golden Day . . .

"Well, maybe it's the other way round," he said. "Maybe he got holt to you."

"Maybe," I said.

"If he is, you lucky it's just a dog—'cause, man, I tell you I believe it's a bear that's got holt to me . . ."

"A bear?"

"Hell, yes! The bear. Caint you see these patches where he's been clawing at my behind?"

Pulling the seat of his Charlie Chaplin pants to the side, he broke into deep laughter.

"Man, this Harlem ain't nothing but a bear's den. But I tell you one thing," he said with swiftly sobering face, "it's the best place in the world for you and me, and if times don't get better soon I'm going to grab that bear and turn him every way but loose!"

"Don't let him get you down," I said.

"No, daddy-o, I'm going to start with one my own size!"

I tried to think of some saying about bears to reply, but remembered only Jack the Rabbit, Jack the Bear . . . who were both long forgotten and now brought a wave of homesickness. I wanted to leave him, and yet I found a certain comfort in walking along beside him, as though we'd walked this way before through other mornings, in other places . . .

"What is all that you have there?" I said, pointing to the rolls of blue paper stacked in the cart.

"Blueprints, man. Here I got 'bout a hundred pounds of blueprints and I couldn't build nothing!"

"What are they blueprints for?" I said.

"Damn if I know—everything. Cities, towns, country clubs. Some just buildings and houses. I got damn near enough to build me a house if I could live in a paper

The only known picture of Peetie Wheatstraw, taken in 1935

house like they do in Japan. I guess somebody done changed their plans," he added with a laugh. "I asked the man why they getting rid of all this stuff and he said they get in the way so every once in a while they have to throw 'em out to make place for the new plans. Plenty of these ain't never been used, you know."

"You have quite a lot," I said.

"Yeah, this ain't all neither. I got a coupla loads. There's a day's work right here in this stuff. Folks is always making plans and changing 'em."

"Yes, that's right," I said, thinking of my letters, "but that's a mistake. You have to stick to the plan."

He looked at me, suddenly grave. "You kinda young, daddy-o," he said.

I did not answer. We came to a corner at the top of a hill.

"Well, daddy-o, it's been good talking with a youngster from the old country but I got to leave you now. This here's one of them good ole downhill streets. I can coast a while and won't be worn out at the end of the day. Damn if I'm-a let 'em run *me* into my grave. I be seeing you again sometime—And you know something?"

"What's that?"

"I thought you was trying to deny me at first, but now I be pretty glad to see you . . ."

"I hope so," I said. "And you take it easy."

"Oh, I'll do that. All it takes to get along in this here man's town is a little shit, grit, and mother-wit. And man, I was bawn with all three. In fact, I'maseventhson-ofaseventhsonbawnwithacauloverbotheyesandraisedon-blackcatboneshighjohntheconquerorandgreasygreens—" he spieled with twinkling eyes, his lips working rapidly. "You dig me, daddy?"

"You're going too fast," I said, beginning to laugh.

"Okay, I'm slowing down. I'll verse you but I won't curse you—My name is Peter Wheatstraw, I'm the Devil's only son-in-law, so roll 'em! You a southern boy, ain't you?" he said, his head to one side like a bear's.

"Yes," I said.

"Well, git with it! My name's Blue and I'm coming at you with a pitchfork. Fe Fi Fo Fum. Who wants to shoot the Devil one, Lord God Stingeroy!"

He had me grinning despite myself. I liked his words though I didn't know the answer. I'd known the stuff from childhood, but had forgotten it; had learned it back of school . . .

"You can hear . . . richness and complexity in Robert Johnson's music. . . . He's an incredible figure, and he always sparks my imagination. . . . There's an incredible complexity I'm drawn to in his guitar playing. He's really playing the drum. It's amazing to listen to him with that in mind. I imagine that movement from the drum to no drum, having to play all of the parts without the drum, including the polyrhythms that are beginning to happen in his music. He's singing on top of all that, which adds still another layer. His music is what I mean when I say 'thick.' " —*Cassandra Wilson*

"You digging me, daddy?" he laughed. "Haw, but look me up sometimes, I'm a piano player and a rounder, a whiskey drinker and a pavement pounder. I'll teach you some good bad habits. You'll need 'em. Good luck," he said.

"So long," I said and watched him going. I watched him push around the corner to the top of the hill, leaning sharp against the cart handle, and heard his voice arise, muffled now, as he started down.

She's got feet like a monkeeee
Legs
Legs, Legs like a maaad
Bulldog . . .

What does it mean, I thought. I'd heard it all my life but suddenly the strangeness of it came through to me. Was it about a woman or about some strange sphinxlike animal? Certainly his woman, *no* woman, fitted that description. And why describe anyone in such contradictory words? Was it a sphinx? Did old Chaplin-pants, old dusty-butt, love her or hate her; or was he merely singing? What kind of woman could love a dirty fellow like that, anyway? And how could even *he* love her if she were as repulsive as the song described? I moved ahead. Perhaps everyone loved someone; I didn't know. I couldn't give much thought to love; in order to travel far you had to be detached, and I had the long road back to the campus before me. I strode along, hearing the cartman's song become a lonesome, broad-toned whistle now that flowered at the end of each phrase into a tremulous, blue-toned chord. And in its flutter and swoop I heard the sound of a railroad train highballing it, lonely across the lonely night. He was the Devil's son-in-law, all right, and he was a man who could whistle a three-toned chord . . . God damn, I thought, they're a hell of a people! And I didn't know whether it was pride or disgust that suddenly flashed over me. ✒

HOBOING WITH BIG JOE
By David "Honeyboy" Edwards
[as told to Janis Martinson and Michael Robert Frank]

[From *The World Don't Owe Me Nothing,* 1997]

I stayed by my daddy's for a while when one day Big Joe Williams come through there hoboing. There was a woman staying on our plantation at Fort Loring called Black Rosie and she run a juke house. Black Rosie gave a dance one Saturday night. It was a little before Christmas in 1932. And Big Joe Williams was playing at Black Rosie's dance. Joe wasn't nothing but a hobo then, running down the streets. I went over to Rosie's and there he was playing. He was in his thirties, had a red handkerchief around his neck, and was playing a little pearl-necked Stella guitar; he was playing the blues. He played "Highway 49" and I just stood and looked at him. I hadn't heard a man play the blues like that! I was standing up in the corner looking at him and he said, "Why you lookin' at me so hard? Can you play?" I said, "A little bit!" He got a drink of whiskey and said, "Play me a little." I was ashamed and shy but I strummed a little. I played a little number or two for him. He said, "I can learn you." Just like that! So I hung with him then, I wanted to play so bad. I stayed with him all night that night. All night till daylight.

I come home Sunday morning and Joe come up with me, with his guitar on his shoulder. My dad was a musician and he would take [*sic*] with musicians. I brought Joe to him and said, "This is my father." I said, "He used to play, too." So Joe sat down and played the blues for my father, and my sister cooked a big chicken dinner for him. After Joe got through eating, he wanted to go out to Greenwood [Mississippi] where he could stop at the whiskey house, make a little money around the bootlegger's house. He asked my daddy, "Well, Mr.

Henry, can I carry Honey with me? It looks like he's taken a likin' to me. I can learn him how to play." My daddy said, "He can go if he want to. It's cold and dead out here in the wintertime. There ain't nothin' to do on the farm. Just come back when the weather breaks." My sister's man, the one we called Son, had that little old guitar with the neck broke on it. We fixed that guitar and that's the guitar I played with Joe. Son said, "Honey, take it on with you." Joe tuned it up for me. I was playing in the key of E, low, and he was playing high.

So I went to Greenwood with him and we played at a good-timing house on Avenue F. Man, we played. Women was flocking, giving us nickels and dimes and quarters, and we kept the house lively.

Fridays, Saturdays, we'd be on Carrolton Street, at a white man's grocery store called Mr. Russell's. That's where all the people come out of the country in their wagons to buy their groceries. That's where they do all their trading, at that store; that was a meeting point for the people. Me and Joe would sit in the back on cottonseed sacks and play our guitars. All them country people coming into town to buy their groceries gave us money.

Saturday nights we'd go out to different whiskey houses. We'd go out with our guitars, try to get a good shot of that white whiskey and feel good. Then we'd start to holler the blues. People would be pouring in. We done had a good time around there.

Then one day we left down the river, me and Joe left there, hitchhiking and hoboing. Back then when a musician was on the road with a guitar, cars would stop and pick you up. "Where y'all goin'? Play me some music, y'all!" We'd fall in the back and play the blues. Sometimes they'd stop and get us a drink, buy us a sandwich.

And Joe Williams would catch trains. Joe wasn't nothing but a hobo! He couldn't write his name! But he had a lot of sense, mother wit sense. He could go to any town, get off at a corner and look around. He'd say, "Well, let's go to such and such a place." And when we come back there and you think, "Hell, was this where we was?" he'd say, "Uh-uh. You go down further." He knew. He couldn't read or write, he didn't know his name hardly when he saw it. That's right! But he knowed the spots that he went by. And he'd be right, too.

Me and Joe stayed together about eight or nine months. We come to Jackson, Mississippi, and we come to Vicksburg. I met quite a few musicians. Frank Haines, he was a guitar player; he was in Jackson. Johnny Young was down in Vicksburg, playing the mandolin. He was real young, working with a fellow named Blue Coat who played violin. We stayed with a guy who run a riverboat and sold whiskey, he kept a good-timing house. We left Vicksburg, crossed the Mississippi River to Tallulah. Went to Rayville, a little town that stayed up all night and all day barrelhousing. Then we went to West Monroe, played over there. They had a big paper mill over there, and we went to the paper mill quarter and played. And when we left there we went to New Orleans.

I stayed with Joe till I got plumb good. Joe Williams would play in high Spanish with a capo on his guitar, and he run me down in E, open key. When I played open key behind that high Spanish, it sounded just like a bass behind a mandolin or something because of that high tone of his with the capo. And I got a low tone in the key of E, but it's the same key. Nine strings, he always had those nine strings on his guitar. That's something he invented himself. He bored holes at the top of the neck of the guitar and made himself a nine-string guitar. That's the way he played all the time.

He was playing "Brother James," all them old numbers like that. "Brother James," "Highway 49," "Stack O'Dollars." "Stack O'Dollars, keep a-knockin', you can't come in. Stack O'Dollars, you can't come in." "Baby, Please Don't Go," "Milkcow Blues." He played all them old numbers. Some songs he made up, and I just played second guitar behind him. He'd just make up songs on the spot, and they'd be good songs, too. And we got pretty good; we made money. Because there wasn't a whole lot of blues players in the streets then. They was scattered around; it was hard to find a good blues player. You could find anybody to sit up and holler and go on. But to find something with life and a sound, you couldn't run up on that every day.

Joe was the first man that learned me how to hustle on the road. He could go anywhere, and he knew how to hustle with that guitar. I was following Joe, because Joe was like a dog. He knew everywhere, knew every train. Joe was the laziest man you ever saw; he wanted to work no way. I don't think he'd work in a baker's shop if you gave him a cake every time the pan came out. He played that guitar and made enough nickels and dimes and quarters to get rooms.

At that time, you could get rooms anywhere for three dollars a week. It wouldn't be a nice, classy room, but you had somewhere to sleep and eat at. Sometimes we'd pay six dollars a week and get board, room and board. The woman would cook you two meals a day. You get your breakfast, hot biscuits, bacon. Most of the people then raised hogs and had all that ham hanging in the smokehouse. Them old womens would put a couple big slices in the skillet, make the rice, put that ham gravy on the rice. Have bacon and rice and biscuits. That's six dollars a week. And that didn't cost them much because they raised that meat.

We could go on a Friday night, get two dollars apiece at a little country dance. In the daytime, in a set on the streets, we pass the hat around and sometimes we'd make up five or six dollars apiece. That was natural money. With a couple of dollars in them country towns, you could do alright. Nickel and dime, go and change it up for some greenbacks. We hustled—we gambled with them guitars.

He learned me how to go on the road, he learned me how to stand on the streets and make nickels and dimes and learned me how to hustle in barrelhouses. I learned under Big Joe. He'd take me in them places when I wasn't old enough to go in there and people let him bring me in.

When he wasn't playing, Joe would be messing around with the women, getting drunk, having fun. I remember one time he was in a room with a woman and he broke her bed down! That woman was saying, "Mister, don't tear my bed up," and he said, "Well, this bed just ain't no damn good!" Joe, he didn't gamble too much but he drank and played with the women. I'd be out shooting marbles with some boys on the streets. I loved to play guitar but I was still young; I had childish ways. He'd say, "Come on, Honey, get your guitar. Let's go." And he fed me, gave me a little money to keep in my pocket. I appreciate that, he kept me out of the field. He changed my life and I'm glad of it.

In New Orleans, that was good hustling there. I always did want to come to a big city. We stayed with a Creole woman of Joe's in the French Quarter. It was something to see them bright lights. There was streetcars and the Canal Ferry was running then, men loading banana boats on the river, people everywhere on wagons and in old cars and on horses. It was beautiful.

We was the only ones playing blues around there then. New Orleans always been a jazz town. But the people got excited over the blues we was playing. Me and Joe would play around Rampart Street at the little joints, go in the bars, get chairs, and set down and play. In New Orleans in them bars people didn't drink white whiskey. They'd sit at a table and get a gallon of wine and a pitcher of ice. They let me play in the bars even though I wasn't but a boy. Things wasn't so strict and I'd sit behind Joe. We'd play in them bars, serenade in the streets, play for the whores, play at the train station, different places all over New Orleans.

Joe started drinking heavy in New Orleans, started drinking heavy on the pint. I was young, I didn't weigh but 110 pounds, and Joe started wanting to fight me. So I slipped off and left there walking. Slipped off one day and left Joe sleeping. And I come out of New Orleans and hit number 90 Highway, coming down the coast. I had my guitar on my shoulder and I'm wondering what I'm going to do because I hadn't been by myself before. I caught a ride to Bay St. Louis and got out on a bridge where there was people catching crabs. Some guy stopped me. He said, "Can you play that guitar?" And I said, "Yeah, I can," and I started to play it a little bit. "You're good!" I didn't know how good it was, but I was trying to play like Joe. This man starts to throwing me dimes and I thought, Hell, I don't need Joe.

I come into Gulfport and I went to the music store there and found a little old harp rack. I started playing the harp and guitar and that was sounding alright.

I hitched a ride from Gulfport to Columbia, Mississippi, with two white men in a old black Ford. Friday come up and I played at the mill quarters there, at a big sawmill. All the people lived at the mill, in those section houses. I got up at the barrelhouse, playing my guitar, and them old women got drunk and started to hollering, going on, chunking that money at me. I played there for about a week, made a little money, and finally pulled up for home.

I lit out hitchhiking and got to Greenwood in a couple of days. When I got there, all of them, my sisters and them, was standing around me like somebody they never seen before. They said, "Honey can play now!" 🖝

THE LITTLE CHURCH
By William Faulkner
[From *Soldier's Pay*, 1926]

. . . The road dropped on again descending between reddish gashes, and across a level moon-lit space, broken by a clump of saplings, came a pure quivering chord of music wordless and far away.

"They are holding services. Negroes," the rector explained. They walked on in the dust, passing neat tidy houses, dark with slumber. An occasional group of negroes passed them, bearing lighted lanterns that jetted vain little flames futilely into the moonlight. "No one knows why they do that," the divine replied to Gilligan's question. "Perhaps it is to light their churches with."

The singing drew nearer and nearer; at last, crouching among a clump of trees beside the road, they saw the shabby church with its canting travesty of a spire. Within it was a soft glow of kerosene serving only to make the darkness and the heat thicker, making thicker the imminence of sex after harsh labor along the mooned land; and from it welled the crooning submerged passion of the dark race. It was nothing, it was everything; then it swelled to an ecstasy, taking the white man's words as readily as it took his remote God and made a personal Father of Him.

Feed Thy Sheep, O Jesus. All the longing of mankind for a Oneness with Something, somewhere. Feed Thy Sheep, O Jesus. . . . The rector and Gilligan stood side by side in the dusty road. The road went on under the moon, vaguely dissolving without perspective. Worn-out red-gutted fields were now alternate splashes of soft black and silver; trees had each a silver nimbus, save those moonward from them, which were sharp as bronze.

Feed Thy Sheep, O Jesus. The voices rose full and soft. There was no organ; no organ was needed as above the harmonic passion of bass and baritone soared a clear soprano of women's voices like a flight of gold and heavenly birds. They stood together in the dust, the rector in his shapeless black, and Gilligan in his new hard serge, listening, seeing the shabby church become beautiful with mellow longing, passionate and sad. Then the singing died, fading away along the mooned land inevitable with to-morrow and sweat, with sex and death and damnation; and they turned townward under the moon, feeling dust in their shoes.

DOWN AT THE CROSS
By James Baldwin
[From *The Fire Next Time,* 1962]

I was saved. But at the same time, out of a deep, adolescent cunning I do not pretend to understand, I realized immediately that I could not remain in the church merely as another worshipper. I would have to give myself something to do, in order not to be too bored and find myself among all the wretched unsaved of the Avenue. . . .

The church was very exciting. It took a long time for me to disengage myself from this excitement, and on the blindest, most visceral level, I never really have, and never will. There is no music like that music, no drama like the drama of the saints rejoicing, the sinners moaning, the tambourines racing, and all those voices coming together and crying holy unto the Lord. There is

Mother's Day in Shaw, Mississippi, 1974

still, for me, no pathos quite like the pathos of those multi-colored, worn, somehow triumphant and transfigured faces, speaking from the depths of a visible, tangible, continuing despair of the goodness of the Lord. I have never seen anything to equal the fire and excitement that sometimes, without warning, fill a church, causing the church, as Lead Belly and so many others have testified, to "rock." Nothing that has happened to me since equals the power and the glory that I sometimes felt when, in the middle of a sermon, I knew that I was somehow, by some miracle, really carrying, as they said, "the Word"—when the church and I were one. Their pain and their joy were mine, and mine were theirs—they surrendered their pain and joy to me, I surrendered mine to them—and their cries of "Amen!" and "Hallelujah!" and "Yes, Lord!" and "Praise His name!" and "Preach it, brother!" sustained and whipped on my solos until we all became equal, wringing wet, singing and dancing in anguish and rejoicing, at the foot of the altar. . . .

Being in the pulpit was like being in the theater; I was behind the scenes and knew how the illusion was worked. I knew the other ministers and knew the quality of their lives. And I don't mean to suggest by this the "Elmer Gantry" sort of hypocrisy concerning sensuality; it was a deeper, deadlier, and more subtle hypocrisy than that, and a little honest sensuality, or a lot, would have been like water in an extremely bitter desert. I knew how to work on a congregation until the last dime was surrendered—it was not very hard to do—and I knew where the money for "the Lord's work" went. I knew, though I did not wish to know it, that I had no respect for the people with whom I worked. I could not have said it then, but I also knew that if I continued I would soon have no respect for myself. . . .

In spite of everything, there was in the life I fled a zest and a joy and a capacity for facing and surviving disaster that are very moving and very rare. Perhaps we were, all of us—pimps, whores, racketeers, church members, and children—bound together by the nature of our oppression, the specific and peculiar complex of risks we had to run; if so, within these limits we sometimes achieved with each other a freedom that was close to love. I remember, anyway, church suppers and outings, and, later, after I left the church, rent and waistline parties where rage and sorrow sat in the darkness and did not stir, and we ate and drank and talked and laughed and danced and forgot all about "the man." We had the liquor, the chicken, the music, and each other, and had no need to pretend to be what we were not. This is the freedom that one hears in some gospel songs, for example, and in jazz. In all jazz, and especially in the blues, there is something tart and ironic, authoritative and double-edged. White Americans seem to feel that happy songs are *happy* and sad songs are *sad,* and that, God help us, is exactly the way most white Americans sing them—sounding, in both cases, so helplessly, defencelessly [*sic*] fatuous that one dare not speculate on the temperature of the deep freeze from which issue their brave and sexless little voices. Only people who have been "down the line," as the song puts it, know what this music is about. I think it was Big Bill Broonzy who used to sing "I Feel So Good," a really joyful song about a man who is on his way to the railroad station to meet his girl. She's coming home. It is the singer's incredibly moving exuberance that makes one realize how leaden the time must have been while she was gone. There is no guarantee that she will stay this time, either, as the singer clearly knows, and, in fact, she has not yet actually arrived. Tonight, or tomorrow, or within the next five minutes, he may very well be singing

"Lonesome in My Bedroom," or insisting, "Ain't we, ain't we, going to make it all right? Well, if we don't today, we will tomorrow night." White Americans do not understand the depths out of which such an ironic tenacity comes, but they suspect that the force is sensual, and they are terrified of sensuality and do not any longer understand it. The word *sensual* is not intended to bring to mind quivering dusky maidens or priapic black studs. I am referring to something much simpler and much less fanciful. To be sensual, I think, is to respect and rejoice in the force of life, of life itself, and to be *present* in all that one does, from the effort of loving to the breaking of bread. It will be a great day for America, incidentally, when we begin to eat bread again, instead of the blasphemous and tasteless foam rubber that we have substituted for it. And I am not being frivolous now, either. Something very sinister happens to the people of a country when they begin to distrust their own reactions as deeply as they do here, and become as joyless as they have become. It is this individual uncertainly on the part of white American men and women, this inability to renew themselves at the fountain of their own lives, that makes the discussion, let alone elucidation, of any conundrum—that is, any reality—so supremely difficult. The person who distrusts himself has no touchstone for reality—for this touchstone can be only oneself. Such a person interposes between himself and reality nothing less than a labyrinth of attitudes. And these attitudes, furthermore, though the person is usually unaware of it (is unaware of so much), are historical and public attitudes. They do not relate to the present any more than they relate to the person. Therefore, whatever white people do not know about Negroes reveals, precisely and inexorably, what they do not know about themselves.

REDEMPTION SONG
By W.E.B. Du Bois

A great song arose, the loveliest thing born this side of the seas. It was a new song. It did not come from Africa, though the dark throb and beat of that Ancient of days was in it and through it. It did not come from white America—never from so pale and thin a thing, however deep these vulgar and surrounding tones had driven. . . . It was a new song and its deep and plaintive beauty, its great cadences and wild appeal wailed, throbbed, and thundered on the world's ears with a message seldom voiced by man. . . . America's one gift to beauty; as slavery's one redemption, distilled from the dross of its dung.

"I (TOO) HEAR AMERICA SINGING"
By Julian Bond
[1960]

I, too, hear America singing
But from where I stand
I can only hear Little Richard
And Fats Domino.
But sometimes,
I hear Ray Charles
Drowning in his own tears
or Bird
Relaxing at Camarillo
or Horace Silver doodling,
Then I don't mind standing a little longer.

THE ROAD TO MEMPHIS
Directed by Richard Pearce

The interesting thing about making a film about Memphis is that it was an extraordinarily fertile ground for the development of a whole musical style that emerged from the Delta. The artists who came to Memphis and then went on the radio suddenly had a huge audience—initially a black audience—which created a life for these guys who went out on the road to play. That is what became the chitlin circuit. That's how they became stars: All of a sudden, the audience out in the Delta got to know them, and they went out and played these clubs. B.B. King represents a generation that came out of the cotton fields and became major figures, major stars on a world stage. And they're not gonna be around that much longer. It's extraordinary to have been able to tell B.B.'s story—a guy who was a tractor driver and heard music and went to Memphis to become part of a world that he'd only dreamed of.

B.B. went on to play a much bigger circuit. Bobby Rush is still playing the old circuit that B.B. played back in the early fifties.

Bobby Rush and one of his stage dancers get down.

Bobby Rush wasn't actually from Memphis, but he was a living embodiment of what Howlin' Wolf and all those guys had lived in the 1950s. Filming Bobby was a chance to show the world that circuit and do it in present-tense terms. The film crew loved Bobby. We made an arrangement to hook up with his band and his bus, and we had no idea what we were gonna get. We'd just had a couple phone conversations. We arrived at this gas station in Mississippi, and we just piled on the bus, took off, and he started telling stories and introducing us to the band members. This was a relief after dealing with musicians who were insulated by managers and handlers. This was a guy on his own, running his own show, and he loved the idea of us being on the bus with him.

It was a world I'd never before had any experience with. I grew up in Louisville, Kentucky. Like a lot of kids, by thirteen, I was playing a guitar, learning blues from other white boys. Bobby Rush plays to black audiences by going town to town through the South—it's actually wider now than just the South. He goes from club to club, and audiences love him; they come back every night he plays. He has a huge loyal fan base. It doesn't have anything to do with the recording industry as it currently exists.

At one point we met Bobby outside Jackson, Mississippi, to ride the bus together to Tunica, Mississippi. If we had taken the interstate, it would've taken us two hours, but we asked Bobby if it was okay to instead go up Highway 61, and he said sure, and it took us an extra six or seven hours. We arrived at the concert about five minutes before it was to begin. It represented no problem to Bobby whatsoever. He said 61 is the right road, the road we should take. If we're late, they'll still be there. We were on the bus for an hour or two, and we just looked at each other and thought, This is why we want to make this movie. This is great; it beats dealing with managers. We're in the middle of the real thing. It was exciting.

Personally, I can remember in 1963 as a college student setting off with a bunch of friends in an open convertible to Mexico, and we got stopped and given a ticket somewhere outside Bowling Green and ended up in the courthouse waiting to adjudicate this fine. In back of the courthouse was this jail, near where we were sitting for hours, and suddenly out of this jail window came this singing. I'll never forget it: some inmate singing his heart out.

I always loved the blues: Jimmy Reed, Howlin' Wolf. I remember in the mid-sixties hearing Jimmy Reed play. So it was exciting to be asked to make this film. I remember we saw Jeff Scheftel's film *Sounds of Memphis* and said, "Uh-oh. It's already been made. What're we gonna do that's different than telling a history of Memphis?" That's why we decided to try to keep everything as much in the present tense as possible. That's why Bobby was so great. You felt you could go back and tell the history, and yet Bobby's still living that today. And someone like Rosco Gordon coming back to Memphis for the W.C. Handy Awards—he was someone who'd been a star in the 1950s, then was a dry cleaner in New York for twenty years. To see the blues world through his eyes today: That was our attempt to try to tell this story in a different way than most historical films usually tell stories.

With B.B. King, his story includes his becoming an American institution. Part of the problem is: How do you get inside? How do you see the man beyond the handlers, managers, beyond the 250 concerts a year? B.B. is a lovely human being who likes to please people. We really tried to get an inner voice from B.B., and it's not easy, because B.B. has

Rosco Gordon rehearsing for the W.C. Handy Awards in Memphis, 2002

been asked the same questions for fifty years. Sometimes you remember telling the stories more than you remember the stories themselves. It was difficult breaking through to get to an inner B.B., but I think our persistence paid off.

Another challenge was: How do you limit the story you're going to tell? Ultimately, you can only tell so much. Blues music, in effect, really told the story of the early fifties, so that's the period we focused on. The blues, in a way, is extraordinarily simple. What makes it complicated is the character and the life experiences of the person who is singing it.

—Richard Pearce

"I've been doing this forty-nine years: 250, 300 shows a year. I've been off work six weeks, I think, in forty-one years. That make me be either hungry, crazy, or in love with the music." —*Bobby Rush*

FURRY'S BLUES (1966)
By Stanley Booth
[From *Rythm Oil,* 1991]

After the Civil War, many former slaves came in from the country, trying to find their families. There were only about four thousand Negroes in Memphis in 1860, but by 1870 there were fifteen thousand. Beale Street drew them, it has been said, "like a lodestone."

The music the country Negroes brought, with its thumping rhythms, unorthodox harmonies, and earthy lyrics, combined with the city musicians' more polished techniques and regular forms to produce, as all the world knows, the Beale Street blues. Furry [Lewis] cannot remember when he first heard the blues, nor is he certain when he started trying to play them.

"I was eight or nine, I believe," he said, "when I got the idea I wanted to have me a guitar." We were at the Bitter Lemon now, Furry, [his wife] Versie, [my pal] Charlie, and I, waiting for the crowd to arrive. The waitresses, pretty girls with long straight hair, were lighting candles on the small round tables. We sat in the shadows, drinking bourbon brought from the liquor store on the corner, listening to Furry talk about the old days.

He was coatless, wearing a white shirt with a dark blue tie, and he was smoking a wood-tipped cigar. "I taken a cigar box, cut a hole in the top, and nailed a piece of two-by-four on there for a neck. Then I got some screen wire for the strings and I tacked them to the box and twisted them around some bent nails on the end of the two-by-four. I could turn the nails and tune the strings like that, you see. I fooled around with it, got so I could make notes, but just on the one string. Couldn't make no chords. The first real guitar I had, Mr.

Cham Fields—who owned a roadhouse, gambling house—and W.C. Handy gave it to me. They brought it out to my mother's and I was so proud to get it, I cried for a week. Them days, children wasn't like they are now." His cigar had gone out; he relit it from the candle on our table, puffing great gray clouds of smoke. "It was a Martin and I kept it twenty years."

"What happened to it?" Charlie asked.

"It died."

Furry put the candle down and leaned back in his chair. "When I was eighteen, nineteen years old," he said, "I was good. And when I was twenty, I had my own band, and we could all play. Had a boy named Ham, played jug. Willie Polk played the fiddle and another boy, call him Shoefus, played the guitar, like I did. All of us North Memphis boys. We'd meet at my house and walk down Brinkley to Poplar and go up Poplar to Dunlap or maybe all the way down to Main. People would stop us on the street and say, 'Do you know so-and-so?' And we'd play it and they'd give us a little something. Sometimes we'd pick up fifteen or twenty dollars before we got to Beale. Wouldn't take no streetcar. Long as you walked, you's making money; but if you took the streetcar, you didn't make nothing and you'd be out the nickel for the ride."

"That was Furry's wild days," Versie said. "Drinking, staying out all night. He'd still do that way, if I let him."

Furry smiled. "We used to leave maybe noon Saturday and not get back home till Monday night. All the places we played—Pee Wee's, Big Grundy's, Cham Field's, B.B. Anderson's—when they opened up, they took the keys and tied them to a rabbit's neck, told him to run off to the woods, 'cause they never meant to close."

I asked Furry whether he had done much traveling.

"A right smart," he said. "But that was later on, when I was working with Gus Cannon, the banjo player, and Will Shade. Beale Street was commencing to change then. Had to go looking for work." He rolled his cigar ash off against the side of an ashtray. "In the good times, though, you could find anything you could name on Beale. Gambling, girls; you could buy a pint of moonshine for a dime, store-bought whiskey for a quarter. We'd go from place to place, making music, and everywhere we'd go, they'd be glad to see us. We'd play awhile and then somebody would pass the hat. We didn't make too much, but we didn't need much back then. In them days, you could get two loaves of bread for a nickel. And some nights, when the people from down on the river came up, we'd make a batch of money. The roustabouts from the steamboats, and *Kate Adams,* the *Idlewild,* the *Viney Swing*—I've taken trips on all them boats, played up the river to St. Louis, down to New Orleans—white and colored, they'd all come to Beale. Got along fine, too, just like we doing now. 'Course, folks had they squabbles, like they will, you know. I saw two or three get killed."

There were enough squabbles to make Memphis the murder capital of the country. In the first decade of the century, 556 homicides occurred, most of them involving Negroes. Appeals for reform were taken seriously only by those who made them. When E.H. Crump ran for mayor on a reform ticket, W.C. Handy recorded the Beale Streeters' reaction: "We don't care what Mr. Crump don't allow, we goin' barrelhouse anyhow."

But as the self-righteous Crump machine gained power, the street slowly began to change. Each year the red-light district grew smaller; each year, there were fewer gambling houses, fewer saloons, fewer places for musicians to play.

Then came the Depression. Local newspapers carried accounts of starving Negroes swarming over garbage dumps, even eating the clay from the river bluffs. Many people left town, but Furry stayed. "Nothing else to do," he said. "The Depression wasn't just in Memphis, it was all over the country. A lot of my friends left, didn't know what they was goin' to. The boy we called Ham, from our band, he left, and nobody ever knew what became of him. I did have a little job with the city and I stuck with that. I had been working with them off and on, when there wasn't anyplace to play. They didn't even have no trucks at that time. Just had mules to pull the garbage carts. Didn't have no incinerator; used to take the garbage down to the end of High Street, across the railroad tracks, and burn it."

Before Beale Street could recover from the Depression, World War II brought hundreds of boys in uniform to Memphis; and, for their protection, Boss Crump closed the last of the saloons and whorehouses. It was the final blow.

Furry sat staring at the end of his cigar. "Beale Street really went down," he said after a moment. "You know, old folks say, it's a long lane don't have no end and a bad wind don't never change. But one day, back when Hoover was president, I was driving my cart down Beale Street and I seen a rat, sitting on top of a garbage can, eating a onion, crying."

⊕ ⊕ ⊕ ⊕ ⊕

Furry has been working for the City of Memphis Sanitation Department, since 1923. Shortly after two o'clock each weekday morning, he gets out of bed, straps on his artificial leg, dresses, and makes a fresh pot of coffee, which he drinks while reading the

Furry Lewis hanging out at his home in Memphis

Memphis *Press-Scimitar*. The newspaper arrives in the afternoon, but Furry does not open it until morning. Versie is still asleep and the paper is company for him as he sits in the kitchen under the harsh light of the ceiling bulb, drinking the hot, sweet coffee. He does not eat breakfast; when the coffee is gone, he leaves for work. . . .

The cafés, taverns, laundries, shoe-repair shops, and liquor stores are all closed. The houses, under shading

trees, seem drawn into themselves. At the Clayborn Temple A.M.E. Church, the stained-glass windows gleam, jewel-like against the mass of blackened stone. A woman wearing a maid's uniform passes on the other side of the street. Furry says good morning and she says good morning, their voices patiently weary. Beside the Scola Brothers' Grocery is a sycamore, its branches silhouetted against the white wall. Furry walks slowly, hunched forward, as if sleep were a weight on his shoulders. Hand-painted posters at the Vance Avenue Market: CHICKEN BACKS 12 1/2¢ LB.; HOG MAWS, 15¢; RUMPS, 19¢.

Behind Bertha's Beauty Nook, under a large, pale-leafed elm, there are twelve garbage cans and two carts. Furry lifts one of the cans on to a cart, rolls the cart out into the street, and, taking the wide broom from its slot, begins to sweep the gutter. A large woman with her head tied in a kerchief, wearing a purple wrapper and gold house slippers, passes by on the sidewalk. Furry tells her good morning and she nods hello.

When he has swept back to Vance, Furry leaves the trash in a pile at the corner and pushes the cart, with its empty can, to Beale Street. The sky is gray. The stiff brass figure of W.C. Handy stands, one foot slightly forward, the bell of his horn pointing down, under the manicured trees of his deserted park. The gutter is thick with debris: empty wine bottles, torn racing forms from the West Memphis dog track, flattened cigarette packs, scraps of paper, and one small die, white with black spots, which Furry puts into his pocket. An old bus, on the back of which is written, in yellow paint, LET NOT YOUR HEART BE TROUBLE, rumbles past; it is full of cotton choppers: Their dark solemn faces peer out the grimy windows. The bottles clink at the end of Furry's broom. In a room above the Club Handy, two men are standing at an open window looking down at the street. One of them is smoking, the glowing end of his cigarette can be seen in the darkness. On the door to the club, there is a handbill: BLUES SPECTACULAR, CITY AUDITORIUM: JIMMY REED, JOHN LEE HOOKER, HOWLIN' WOLF. . . .

When Furry has cleaned the rest of the block, the garbage can is full and he goes back to Bertha's for another. The other cart is gone and there is a black Buick parked at the curb. Furry wheels to the corner and picks up the mound of trash he left there. A city bus rolls past; the driver gives up a greeting honk and Furry waves. He crosses the street and begins sweeping in front of the Sanitary Bedding Company. A woman's high-heeled shoe is lying in the sidewalk. Furry throws it into the can. "First one-legged woman I see, I'll give her that," he says and, for the first time that day, he smiles.

At Butler, the next cross street, there is a row of large, old-fashioned houses set behind picket fences and broad, thickly leafed trees. The sky is pale blue now, with pink-edged clouds, and old men and women have come out to sit on the porches. Some speak to Furry, some do not. Cars are becoming more frequent along the street. Furry reaches out quickly with his broom to catch a windblown scrap of paper. When he gets to Calhoun, he swaps cans again and walks a block—past Tina's Beauty Shop, a tavern called the Section Playhouse, and another named Soul Heaven— to Fourth Street. He places his cart at the corner and starts pushing the trash toward it.

From a second-story window of a rooming-house covered with red brick-patterned tarpaper comes the sound of a blues harmonica. Two old men are sitting on the steps in front of the open door. Furry tells them good morning. "When you goin' make another record?" one of them asks. "Record?" the other man, in a straw hat, says. "That's right," says the first one. "He makes them big-time records. Used to."

Furry dumps a load into the cart, then leans against it, wiping his face and the back of his neck with a blue bandanna handkerchief.

Down the stairs and through the door (the old men on the steps leaning out of his way, for he does not slow down) comes the harmonica player. He stands in the middle of the sidewalk, eyes closed, head tilted to one side, the harmonica cupped in his hands. A man wearing dark glasses and carrying a white cane before him like a divining rod turns the corner, aims at the music, says cheerfully, "Get out the way! Get off the sidewalk!" and bumps into the harmonica player, who spins away, like a good quarterback, and goes on playing.

Furry puts the bandanna in his pocket and moves on, walking behind the cart. Past Mrs. Kelly's Home-made Hot Tamales stand, the air is filled with a strong odor. Over a shop door, a sign reads: FRESH FISH DAILY.

Now the sky is a hot, empty blue, and cars line the curb from Butler to Vance. Furry sweeps around them. Across the street, at the housing project, children are playing outside the great blocks of apartments. One little girl is lying face down on the grass, quite still. Furry watches her. She has not moved. Two dogs are barking nearby. One of them, a small black cocker spaniel, trots up to the little girl and sniffs at her head; she grabs its forelegs and together they roll over and over. Furry starts sweeping and does not stop or look up again until he has reached the corner. He piles the trash into the can and stands in the gutter, waiting for the light to change.

For the morning, his work is done. He rolls the cart down Fourth, across Pontotoc and Linden, to his own block, where he parks it at the curb, between two cars. Then he heads across the street toward Rothschild's grocery, to try to get some beer on credit. ✎

RECALLING BEALE STREET IN ITS GLORY

By Will Shade of the Memphis Jug Band
[As told to Paul Oliver, from
Conversation with the Blues, 1965]

Beale Street, Memphis: There used to be a red light district, so forth like that. Used to be wide open houses in them days. You could used to walk down the street in days of 1900 and like that and you could find a man wit' throat cut y'ear to ear. Also you could find people lyin' dead wit' not their throat cut, money took and everything in their pockets . . . and thrown outside the house.

. . . Sometimes you find them throwed out of winders and so forth, here on Beale Street. Sportin' class o' women runnin' up and down the street all night long . . . git knocked in the head with bricks and hatchets and hammers. Git cut with pocket knives and razors and so forth. Run off to the foot of Beale and some of them run into the river and drown.

⊕ ⊕ ⊕ ⊕ ⊕

Pee Wee's was the name of a—the name they used to call 'em was joints; some people used to call 'em honky-tonks—that's where I learned to play the blues, at the honky-tonks, which was originally called the joints. Some people called them saloons. Pee Wee's was wide open in there in them days, and they had crap games in there and runnin' policy games, bootleg whiskey, and everything like that. Come on down there used to be a place on Beale Street called the Monarch and that was a crap-shootin' joint.

There used to be a man there, they called him Bad Sam. He got into a shootin' duel there one time. Shot a man who was causin' bit of trouble, and the man fell downstairs. But he raised up enough to shoot back at Sam, so both of them fell; one went one way and the other went the other way and both of them died. I dunno, there was so much excitement down there on Beale Street it'd take me a year and a day to tell you about all that excitement. 🖝

Background:
Robert Crumb illustration
of the Memphis Jug Band

BOBBY "BLUE" BLAND: LOVE THROAT OF THE BLUES
BY ROBERT GORDON

Rolling into 1947 Memphis like a cotton boll loosed from the back of a field truck, Bobby "Blue" Bland was raw talent ready to be refined. Rural folk—black and white—had been tumbling into Memphis for generations. Some, like the crop they raised, were looking to be ginned; others, for gin.

In Rosemark, Tennessee, about thirty miles northeast of Memphis, Bobby Bland was raised on spirituals and field hollers. A family friend often drank hard lemonade on the Bland porch, strumming the guitar and singing Blind Lemon Jefferson, Big Boy Crudup, Walter Davis, and Big Joe Williams. The radio played country music—Roy Acuff, Eddie Arnold, Ernest Tubb's "Walking the Floor Over You," and Red Foley's hymns. Taking a Jew's harp and a tin can, Bobby sang at the country store. "My mother said, 'No, I'm not going to keep you out here; we're going to Memphis,'" Bobby remembered. "And that's why I got a chance."

Memphis was everything Rosemark was not. Bobby's mother worked behind the stove at the Sterling Grill, just off Beale Street. Bobby, seventeen and maturing into a quiet, simmering sexuality, learned every song on the jukebox there. "All the musicians coming through would stop at Mrs. Bland's place," Bobby said, his speaking voice mellow and silty, both in conversation and in song. B.B. King was a regular customer there. "I idolized him," Bobby continued, "and I still do. This was before B.B.'s first record came out. We were on Amateur Nights together on Beale Street." Beale's Amateur Night was dawning with stars—B.B., Rosco Gordon, Johnny Ace, and Bobby. Rufus

Thomas was the host. They were all learning their way around a stage.

In 1948, Memphis radio station WDIA began programming black music for a black audience, further energizing the African-American entertainment world. B.B. King was one of the earliest radio hosts, his growing popularity evident in the increasing crowds at clubs farther and farther from Memphis.

"I said, 'B., why don't you let me help you with your stuff?' to drive or whatever." Bobby smiled at the memory. "So he'd take me with him to small towns near Memphis if I didn't have anything to do—which was all the time. I learned a lot just standing around."

Bobby approached Rosco Gordon, and later Junior Parker. Bobby was chauffeur, valet, friend—the guy who liked to drive and didn't drink—and he continued to make the most of his opportunities. "Rosco, at all those juke joints, he'd come straight off the stage and head right to the gambling room in back. Do little tricks with the dice—roll them and they stay together, just like soldiers. It's dangerous if somebody catches you. I'd be over in the corner, out of the way of the dancing. The guy with the corn liquor would be back there if you needed a shot, and the houseman called all the bets and held the money. They had some big people to settle any argument that would happen. We all were hicks."

"I came out of the cotton field, too," said Rosco, who died in 2002. "Who do you think called the radio station and wanted to know who I was and if I would be back, eh? These were my fans from the cotton field." Rosco had built his audience through a stint on WDIA—recruited there from the Amateur Night. He and B.B. both cut their first records in the home of a local bandleader, Richard "Tuff" Green. Tuff Green hung blankets on the wall, counted off the beat for his Rocketeers, and cut "Three O'Clock Blues" behind B.B. and "No More Doggin'" with Rosco. Both became more than regional hits.

Rosco recounted one night when Bobby drove him to a gig in Arkansas. "Bobby started singing and said, 'I got the voice, but my timing's bad.' I said, 'All you got to do is say one, two, three, four, sing, two, three, four, shut up, two. . . ' So this night, I was dicing—if you didn't have money to shoot dice with me, I'd give you some—and I put Bobby on the stage. That night nobody came to get me because Bobby sang all night."

Bobby had once bragged to B.B. that he could sing everything his friend had recorded. "B.B. said, 'Good, Bob, I love that, but you got to get some identification of your own.' And so I would take that softness of Gene Ammons and Nat 'King' Cole and some things from Billy Eckstine and make one thing out of it. Out in the country there wasn't no music like that. In Memphis, I had the man put those records on my mother's jukebox. I listened to Tony Bennett; he had so much feeling it would remind you of a black person who's been hurt. And Perry Como, 'The Lord's Prayer'—nobody else phrases it like he does. I studied Nat 'King' Cole from front to back to upgrade my speaking ability and singing qualities. I'm not saying that it's perfect now, but it's a long way from Rosemark."

Ike Turner had already cut the landmark rock & roll single "Rocket 88" when Bobby met him in the 1950s. Turner was regularly finding and recording artists for Modern Records, a Los Angeles label with

"Beale Street was heaven for the black man. You'd come up from the Delta and go to Beale Street, don't owe nobody, no nothin'. I told a white fella on Beale Street one night, I said, 'If you were black for one Saturday night on Beale Street, you never would wanna be white anymore.'" —*Rufus Thomas*

a Southern presence. "Bobby 'Blue' Bland," Ike said. "His mother had a soul food restaurant and she told us her son could sing. We took him out to Tuff Green's house and recorded him." In 1952, Bland was signed to Memphis' Duke Records, run by WDIA's station manager. Before he could find his own style, he went into the army. Upon his discharge in 1955, he went to Houston, where Duke Records had relocated. There he met the trumpeter and musical arranger Joe Scott, who became his musical tailor. "Joe Scott guided me on how to approach a note and how you find the spots to enforce, the selling points in a song. The word has to be said exactly right. Joe Scott said, 'If you're going to get any kind of attention, you've got to let them know your feelings and have them feel it the same way you do.' He said, 'Everybody has a problem just like you do, and if you can conquer that particular thing in your singing, well then, it's all left up to the listener.'"

Invigorated, Bobby "Blue" Bland cut "Farther Up the Road" in 1957, "I'll Take Care of You" in 1959, and in 1961 both the album *Two Steps From the Blues* and the song "Turn On Your Love Light." A clean, cool ladies' man, he developed the signature love throat—a guttural squall of unequal parts groan, shout, and belch—that punctuates his songs. "I got the idea for the sound from Reverend C.L. Franklin, Aretha's father. I played a sermon that he had, 'The Eagle Stirreth Her Nest,' over and over and over. They build bigger cages for the eagle as it grows, but

I've been
All across the country
And I've played in every town
Cause I'm trying to find my baby
But no one has seen her around
Now you know which way I'm headed
If my baby can't be found.

I spoke
To the river
And the river
Spoke back to me
And it said, "You look so lonely
You look so full of misery
And if you can't find your baby
Come and make your home with me."

I don't
Want to leave her
Cause I know
She's still alive
And someday I'm gonna find her
Then I'll take her for a ride
Then we'll live our life forever
In a home among the tide.

when her wings hit the cage, they have to turn her loose." It's a powerful image, a climactic moment in an archetypal sermon. The story is a meditation on increasing power meeting the limits of the larger world it grows to inhabit. With each limit overcome, the world yields a new, larger vista. Franklin was preaching about the pain and the exhilaration of growth, about opportunities and obstacles.

Bobby zeroed in on the concussive sound of larger souls meeting larger cages. It is a vocal ejaculation, equally visceral and ethereal, both more and less than human. It is a common punctuation in African-American sermons—perhaps because American blacks have encountered that larger cage more often than most, and have soared.

Bobby Bland, like many blues musicians, takes from the church to give to the blues. For him, the love throat becomes an encounter with the sexual and the spiritual, the nexus between what is and what can be. From the tiny roost of Rosemark, Tennessee, he ascended the heights of blues mastery and stardom, conquering, with the help of mentors, all the bars his wings encountered. The love throat sings this ascension, but there is another, more pragmatic reason that he stayed with it: The strange sound drove the ladies wild. And where the wild ladies go, so too go the men. Bobby "Blue" Bland brings us all along. 🖐

RECOMMENDED LISTENING:
Bobby Bland, *The Duke Recordings, Volumes 1–3* (MCA, 1992, 1994, 1996). All of Bobby's greatest recordings, from 1952 to 1972.
B.B. King, *Classic Masters* (Capitol, 2002). Look for this—or any—collection of B.B.'s great early sides.
B.B. King and Bobby Bland, *Together for the First Time . . . Live* (MCA, 1974). Hear the lifelong friendship in their duets.
Rosco Gordon, *Rosco's Rhythm* (Charly, 1997). Includes most of his best Sun Records material.

Opposite: Bobby "Blue" Bland *(center),* circa 1957

ON THE ROAD WITH LOUIS ARMSTRONG BY DAVID HALBERSTAM

In the summer of '55, I took off from Cambridge, Massachusetts, in a 1946 Chevy to start my journalistic career in Mississippi. I took with me one suitcase of clothes and a new record player that, if memory serves, cost thirty-eight dollars and four long-playing records—the beginning of my music collection—and my devotion to a certain kind of jazz and blues (surely a hit back then, but hopelessly square today). To this day, for both musical and sentimental reasons, two of those albums remain particularly important to me: *Louis Armstrong Plays W.C. Handy* and a record with Sidney Bechet and Muggsy Spanier playing duets. In Mississippi, I ended up not on the metropolitan paper in Jackson, as I had expected, but as the only reporter on the smallest daily in the state, over in West Point, in the hill country in the northeast. There was not a lot of nightlife there, and after work I played my records incessantly. To this day I know which song follows which on my albums. I spent almost a year in Mississippi, drawn by my time there into an ever deeper appreciation of the roots of the

blues. Then I went on to a bigger and better paper in Nashville, where, with the help of the people at Zibart's book and record store, my Louis Armstrong collection expanded exponentially.

In those days I did a good deal of freelancing for *The Reporter* magazine, now deceased but back then a lively biweekly liberal publication of considerable independence, and a great show-case for independent young reporters like me—indeed some of the seeds of what would eventually come to be known as New Journalism were already being planted in *The Reporter*. (Actually it was a couple of freelance pieces on the racial crisis in Mississippi that had hastened my departure from West Point; my editor there, Henry Harris, had told me to either stop writing about race for the magazine or leave the paper, and, in time, because I refused his offer, he fired me.)

One day in March 1957, not long after I'd turned twenty-three and was working in Nashville, I noticed that Armstrong was coming to town for a one-night stand. I thought that hanging out

with Louis Armstrong and his band might make a good *Reporter* piece. I queried the magazine with the idea, got the green light, and arranged with Armstrong's people to meet him in Atlanta and travel with him to Nashville.

This was during the early part of the great civil rights confrontation that followed the Supreme Court's 1954 ruling that ended state-sanctioned segregation in schools. Martin Luther King Jr. was coming to power, helping to create what would become known as "the movement," and adding to the legal power of blacks (not yet known as blacks) their moral, economic, and spiritual powers. I was an aggressive civil rights reporter—to me race was the big story of the time—and in those days if *The Tennessean* did not assign me a story about race, then I would often assign it to myself for *The Reporter*, using my days off work for the reporting (as I had done earlier in Clinton, Tennessee, the first town to deal with integration in the state). But I did not see the Armstrong piece as a civil rights piece, and as such it was the one time when I was a young man that I missed an important part of the story. Not that I blew the piece entirely—I pulled it off, and *The Reporter* ran it in May 1957. It was okay, not one of my best articles; I was operating a bit on foreign turf, because I'm a sociopolitical reporter, not a music writer.

In 1957, it should be noted, Louis Armstrong was probably the most honored and beloved American outside our borders. He had traveled everywhere, playing to large and enthusiastic crowds wherever he went, and he always charmed his foreign audiences, much as he did his domestic ones—his talent and sheer pleasure in what he did were as palpable as his music was accessible. Memory tells me that there was even an album at the time called *Ambassador Satch,* depicting him in full diplomatic regalia. Yet on that day, on that six-hour, 250-mile trek from Atlanta to Nashville, because his bus did not have a bathroom, we had to stop by the wayside at one point, a place where the foliage was unusually thick, while this most distinguished and joyous American wandered into the bushes to take a leak. Then we continued on our way. And I did not mention that most painful moment in my article, even though in those days I was very

careful to look for the racial edge in everything I covered. I still do not know why I left this part out. Perhaps I thought it was in bad taste. Perhaps in some way I thought it was embarrassing to him, one more small but cruel humiliation thrust upon him by the country he loved, and therefore I pulled back from it in some misguided attempt to protect him.

But to this day when I think about that story and that trip, about my time with him and his band, it's the first thing I remember: Louis Armstrong getting off his bus to take that leak because there were no restaurants that black people could stop at along the roadside, and pulling in to a gas station was problematic—you could certainly buy the gas, but whether or not you could use the rest room was a very different question. Louis had certainly learned long before that it was rarely worth the ugly struggle that was sure to come with the request.

A young man's memories of a trip like that with one of his heroes are remarkably clear. I still remember how much fun it was talking to him: He was pushing Swiss Kriss to me, to keep me regular, as he did with everyone he met, and he kept telling me,

Louis Armstrong poses with two Tennessee fans, circa 1957.

in addition, that whenever you come home from a long trip, always call the lady you live with, never surprise her at home. I remember as well how generous his elegant trombone player, "Trummy" Young, was with me.

So this piece is by way of apology, some forty-six years later, and to note that when I hear him singing (on *Satch Plays Fats,* another of my favorite albums), "What did I do/to be so black and blue," I still ponder the meaning of those words, and the firsthand lesson I had in the blues that day, and the way he dealt with it all. And I remember as well the price and complexity of his joyousness. ✒

Sam Phillips *(right)* opened his Memphis Recording Service in January 1950 to provide an opportunity "for some of the great Negro artists of the mid-South." Rosco Gordon *(left)* and Ike Turner were the first of those artists to have Number One R&B hits. Phillips also recorded Howlin' Wolf, B.B. King, Rufus Thomas, and Bobby "Blue" Bland, among others, before a nineteen-year-old Elvis Presley cut his first single for Phillips' Sun label in July 1954.

"You know, I never had the feeling of categories of music as a whole being necessarily good or bad. Country, symphony, pop music were just fine—I didn't really care what it sounded like, or what category it might fall into. If you had something distinctive to say, it was up to you to go ahead and say it. But gutbucket blues—that was the kind of music I wanted to hear. And that was the kind of music I set out to record.

When I started, I had to pursue it singularly, because nobody was going to back me up in the idea that you're going to bring a bunch of black folks in here and record them. But that was what I was determined to do. And I was prepared to risk everything for it—my job, my family's future welfare, my own damn sanity—because it was an absolute inspiration that I carried with me. I *knew* the sound I had heard in the cotton fields, and I also knew that had I not tried to do it, I would have been the biggest damn coward that God ever put on this earth.

There's nothing that tells the truth like gutbucket blues. I mean, you got Jimmie Rodgers—you know I love Jimmie Rodgers—and Hank Williams, too, even if he didn't get down all the way like the Howlin' Wolf. But with the Wolf and some of those other great blues singers you have something that is so absolutely true, so close to the life that so many of our Southern people, black and white, have experienced, that how in the hell is the soul of man ever going to die when that is coming along to remind you of the most fundamental things— things that were so tough at the time, tough on the person that lived it, tough on the person that's singing about it? These things you can't buy in a book. You got to be there when it happens. And I guess I ought to know. It will always stay there. You won't forget it. You won't forget it." —*Sam Phillips*

WOLF LIVE IN '65 *By Robert Palmer*
[From *Deep Blues,* 1982]

I'll never forget a 1965 performance when Wolf played
Memphis on a blues package show. This was several
years before the blues revival made much headway
among local whites, and there were only three or four
of us, huddled right up front in the theater's most
expensive seats. . . . The MC announced Wolf, and the
curtains opened to reveal his band pumping out a
decidedly downhome shuffle. . . . Where was Wolf?
Suddenly he sprang out onto the stage from the wings.
He was a huge hulk of a man, but he advanced across
the stage in sudden bursts of speed, his head pivoting
from side to side, eyes huge and white, eyeballs
rotating wildly. He seemed to be having an epileptic
seizure, but no, he suddenly lunged for the microphone, blew a chorus of raw, heavily rhythmic
harmonica, and began moaning. He had the hugest
voice I have ever heard—it seemed to fill the hall and
get right inside your ears, and when he hummed and
moaned in falsetto, every hair on your neck crackled
with electricity. The thirty-minute set went by like an
express train, with Wolf switching from harp to guitar
(which he played while rolling around on his back and,
at one point, doing somersaults) and then leaping up
to prowl the lip of the stage. He was the Mighty Wolf,
no doubt about it. Finally, an impatient signal from the
wings let him know that his portion of the show was
over. Defiantly, Wolf counted off a bone-crushing
rocker, began singing rhythmically, feigned an exit,
and suddenly made a flying leap for the curtain at the
side of the stage. Holding the microphone under his
beefy right arm and singing into it all the while, he
began climbing up the curtain, going higher and higher
until he was perched far above the stage, the thick
curtain threatening to rip, the audience screaming

Howlin' Wolf, photographed two years after his
memorable Memphis performance

with delight. Then he loosened his grip and, in a single
easy motion, slid right back down the curtain, hit the
stage, cut off the tune, and stalked away, to the most
ecstatic cheers of the evening. He was then fifty-five
years old. 🖝

THE SOUL OF A MAN
Directed by Wim Wenders

Martin Scorsese had an idea for a series of several films made about the blues. There has never been a project like this, where seven directors actually worked on one subject and produced seven feature-length films. Each film has a very distinct point of view. Each director selected his territory in the history of blues himself. There were no stylistic or content limits. I think Marty really had a splendid idea when he started this thing.

I knew he was a blues fan, and he wasn't sure if I was one as well, so we started to talk about our favorite bluesmen first. I thought it was intriguing to be able to finally dedicate some time to my blues heroes. After all, I didn't know that much about them. Sure, I had every record I could ever find of Skip James, but I didn't know much about his life. And although I knew J.B. Lenoir's music for thirty years, I realized that if I had to tell anybody how he had lived, I wouldn't know what to say. I knew the music and just loved it. So the film was a great opportunity to really dive into the stories of these people and find out more about them myself.

I think my first memories of the blues are, rather, memories of spirituals. We didn't even have a record player at home when I was young, and the radio only played German music and classical music, but in school I once heard a record of so-called Negro spirituals. That was a sound I had never heard before, and its emotional honesty truly took me by surprise. I listened to it over and over again and soon knew some of the songs by heart, although I didn't speak English, so I didn't know what it all meant. I was just guessing. That was my first contact.

Later on, the first bluesman I actually knew by name was John Lee Hooker, and the first blues LPs I bought were John Lee Hooker's, because he had impressed me so much on the first hearing. Blind Lemon Jefferson, too, B.B. King . . . I soon started to know more about this music, but I only developed a better knowledge of the blues when the English bands in the sixties started to cover all the old bluesmen and play them electrically. I was guided by Van Morrison, the Pretty Things, the Animals, and the Rolling Stones and discovered the original versions of the songs that had inspired them.

The blues is utterly emotional music, with a very simple pattern inside which musicians can take enormous liberties. I liked that supposition of a structure that is simple, inside which a lot of freedom can play out. The blues really deals with all kinds of troubles, with all kinds of worries and sorrows, with hardship, so even a young white fellow like me could easily identify with its subject. It's the best music to hear when you're down and when you need comfort. It's very strong rhythmically, really at the roots of both jazz and rock & roll. I was a jazz fan when I was sixteen, eighteen. I played tenor saxophone, heavily influenced by John Coltrane, and only later got into rock & roll and the blues.

Music has played a paramount role in my enthusiasm for the craft of filmmaking. It all started when I made my very first short 16-mm silent film. I had no money to record any sound, so I had these silent images when I sat down for the first time in an editing room at film school to put these shots together. I had my tape recorder with me. I played some of my favorite tracks to these images of mine, and that was the greatest fun I've ever had. In terms of filmmaking, that was the greatest discovery for me: how to put images and music together! As soon as you start that, even if you think you know your images or that music, when you put them together, a third thing emerges that's more than the sum of both. And that precious moment when you first see your imagery and hear the music together with it, that for me, ever since that short film, is why I like to make movies—in order to get to that moment of joy. At times I think that's the whole reason I am in this moviemaking business to begin with. I just do not understand any director who'll have that taken away from him.

My musical taste is pretty wide: I love classical music, and I like Latin and African music. But when it comes down to it, my favorite music is really blues and rock & roll. That I'm so attached to American music, from early blues recordings of the late twenties up to the sixties, probably has a lot to do with the fact that I discovered this music for myself. It was something that belonged to me, a territory I found for myself that nobody had shown to me and that nobody had imposed on me. I had chosen it myself! Then these English kids came out of nowhere, when I was sixteen, seventeen years old. Bands like the Rolling Stones or the Beatles were quickly known, but the better ones, in my book, were the more unknown Them (with Van Morrison), or the Animals, the Pretty Things, or my all-time favorites, the Kinks. These kids, they were "my generation," just like the Who were saying it. They were just as old as I was, a couple of them maybe a year or two older, and most of them were art students who had invented that music from scratch. I identified with them—that was my own generation, and the music they made was really my music.

I once heard a song by Skip James on a compilation album sometime in the sixties, just one track, but it stood out. It was more haunting than anything else around it, and I knew I had to find out more about this singer of whom I just knew this one song. It took me awhile until I tracked down another album. His other songs all had that same quality, different from anybody else's voice. His guitar and piano playing, too, were very elaborate and didn't sound like anything else I knew. So I think he was

the first hero of mine. I felt here was the first guy who I picked myself, and I really got attached to him.

And then I remember in 1967, a new record came out by John Mayall, the godfather of the English blues movement. I had all of his LPs. Mayall's band was like a breeding ground of blues musicians in England. I loved this new album, *Crusade*, especially one song on it called "The Death of J.B. Lenoir." When I first heard it, I just had the shivers. That song was so moving and so personal, and there was such a great sense of loss. He was mourning the death of a friend, and I had never heard of this man his was singing about: J.B. Lenoir. So again I tried to find out everything I could, and I dug out a record of his. It actually had come out in Germany. It was acoustic blues, songs about the American South. Very powerful songs, very contemporary, dealing with the Vietnam War, for instance, and that was the first time I heard anybody sing about that war. Other songs were dealing with the fights of the black people in America for equality. When I originally heard the first notes of that first album of the real J.B. Lenoir, I thought I had been mistaken. This must be a woman, I thought at first, but it became clear after a while that this was not a woman. It was a man singing with the most unique high-pitched voice, but not really falsetto. Very emotional on top of that. By then my English was better, and I understood more of the words already. I understood that there was somebody who was singing about things that nobody else was singing about. Over the years, I found out that he had made music in Chicago in the fifties with a big band, using electric guitar and a big-band sound. I collected five, six, or seven obscure albums by this J.B. Lenoir, and in my heart he became my favorite blues musician of them all. Every now and then I would meet somebody who knew him. I remember, for instance, years later I was driving with Sam Shepard in his pickup truck across America; we were writing *Paris, Texas* together at the time and Sam had a few cassettes, and at one point he put in a new tape and said, "I bet you don't know this guy," and it was J.B. Lenoir. So he was one of the connoisseurs. All these J.B. fans had something in common: They were convinced that this was one of the greatest singers ever, yet he had remained strangely obscure. I found out that the first records I had bought in Germany had never come out in America. And that these songs about the Vietnam War, his song addressed to President Eisenhower from the fifties, his songs about Mississippi and Alabama, Americans simply didn't know them. No wonder he remained so obscure and unknown.

Musicians, like Jimi Hendrix, knew him; J.B.'s most famous song, "Mama Talk to Your Daughter," had been a moderate R&B hit. But nobody really knew so much about the man's life. So when Marty gave me the chance to select my territory in the story of the blues, I knew it had to be about J.B. Lenoir and Skip James. Later on, I figured it was a bit bizarre to just pick my two favorite musicians; I didn't even know how to link them, so I realized I needed more of a "theme." It hit me that the one topic in both of their lives was an overall issue in the blues anyway, which is that a lot of bluesmen are torn between the worldly side of their music and the spiritual side of it. It seemed like an important theme in the history of blues, this gap between the Sacred and the Profane. The tension between gospel and blues is a strange demarcation line that goes across the entire history of the blues. A lot of blues musicians travel between the two lives; others could only live inside one of them and then at one point in their lives would break with that life, like Skip James, who one day stepped out of the history of the blues and became a minister, never touching the blues again for thirty years. And that is not just him; a lot of blues musicians felt that they had to leave the devil's music behind to play God's music. So when it finally came time to write some sort of treatment for my film, I wrote that it was about the Sacred and the Profane. That might sound abstract, but it was really about two men.

And while I was preparing the film, I realized they both had a forerunner, and that there was a third musician I should really include: Blind Willie Johnson. I knew even less about him than the other two. There is not a single photograph of the man, just one rather graphic portrait that was an ad for a recording of his in the late 1920s. You can't really judge from that what he might have looked like. So Blind Willie was a total mystery, but he had written some great songs, one in particular, "Dark Was the Night," that I had at one point selected and used as temp music for *Paris, Texas* when I first showed the film to Ry Cooder. I had indicated to Ry that a bottleneck guitar style was what I would love to hear on the film somehow. Ry was very taken by the idea. He knew that song really well; actually, he had recorded it once himself. The theme of "Dark Was the Night" eventually became the main musical theme of *Paris, Texas*. Blind Willie Johnson only sang sacred music, never touched a single secular song, although his techniques, especially his bottleneck style, are among the finest in blues history, to quote somebody as competent as Eric Clapton. And of course as far as guitar playing, rhythm, or singing is concerned, it's the same music. Only later on, Blind Willie became the "narrator" of my film. That might sound weird, as he died in 1947. But Blind Willie really saved my film. I was at a loss as to which perspective I could tell our story from, until I remembered that Blind Willie's song "Dark Was the Night" had been picked as one of the handful of songs that represented contemporary twentieth-century music on the record that went out with the space probe *Voyager* into outer space.

The overall parameter of the entire series that Marty had discussed with the directors was to shoot these films digitally. We all more or less agreed that DV-Cam would be the ideal, very portable, very light equipment to shoot this. So I knew that most of the film (or at least anything that was contemporary) would be shot on DV-Cam, and I was fine with that. We had used similar equipment for some of *Buena Vista Social Club,* and I knew it was good enough to be blown up to film in the end. But my film's time period started in the late twenties, and the most glorious moment in the life of Skip James was a legendary recording session that took place in 1931. Of course, there is no filmed record of this whatsoever, only a few scratchy 78s on shellac. There is not even a single image of Skip James from the time when he did that recording. So I decided to reenact some of the lives of my heroes in order to show them: Blind Willie Johnson in 1927 and Skip James in 1931. And I figured to go back to the twenties or early thirties and shoot on DV-Cam was not a good solution. To reenact some of the lives of Skip James and Blind Willie Johnson, I needed to find a different medium. I chose to do that on a hand-cranked camera from the early twenties, a Debrie Parvo. I had shot on that camera once before and knew it worked really well. I love the effect of the irregularity of the hand-cranked camera movement. It is a really beautiful and authentic effect and transports you right back in time—so successfully, in fact, that when we showed a first cut of the film, most of the people who saw it believed we had found all this original archived material and didn't really understand that we had

The sole graphic of Blind Willie Johnson appears in this early Columbia ad.

produced it ourselves. The hand-cranked camera enables you to make this time jump and single-handedly, so to speak, produces the feeling of the era. And it's a lot of fun to work with such an old camera. It was also a challenge shooting with a hand-cranker: You're completely out of sync, because already the hand movement is never regular, and we shot on sixteen frames on top of that. Most of the scenes we were shooting involved playback! I first thought that playing in sync with these old recordings from 1927 or 1931 was a ludicrous idea and probably totally impossible, but we did a test and it actually seemed possible to sync up our hand-cranked material to the music. But it was not easy. Every second frame of our film, shot at more or less sixteen frames per second, would have to be doubled up to get to around twenty-four frames, and then you still had to manipulate it tremendously to achieve any synchronicity. Basically, you had to find sync moments for every word, or every stroke of the guitar, so you could advance second by second and extract or add frames, which you can only do now with digital technology. So our idea worked with a mix of the oldest possible technique and top-notch digital technology, thus enabling us to produce scenes that look as if they were filmed at the time.

The second half of the film concentrates on the life of J.B. Lenoir, in the fifties and sixties, when I felt the hand-cranked camera would no longer be appropriate. To get into the spirit of that period I decided we should shoot in 16 mm so it would look really different. And then we found this incredible material that nobody had ever seen, these two films actually shot of J.B. Lenoir in the early sixties. These two 16-mm films were shot by a couple of art students, Steve Seaberg and his wife, Rönnog, in Chicago. They had never made a movie before and didn't know much about filmmaking. But they had become friends with J.B. Lenoir, loved the music, and loved the man so much that they thought, We have to do something to get him known to other audiences. Rönnog was from Sweden, and Steve was American. And Rönnog had the fabulous idea that if they would shoot a little movie about J.B. and take it to Sweden with them, they could show it on Swedish television. So they went about it and made

the first film, actually shooting in a photographer's studio. They put J.B. in front of a backdrop, never moved the camera, and shot four songs in that one angle. Then they took these ten minutes or so to Swedish television. The Swedes looked at it and were horrified: It was uncut material that the Seabergs presented to them, and the sound was only on an optical track, which was not very good, so the Swedish television executives just flat-out said, "We can't show this, and also you should know that we don't have color here in Sweden, we only have black-and-white TV, so if you shoot something, it has to be black and white." So Rönnog and Steve went back home to Chicago a little disappointed and put their ten-minute color 16-mm film on the shelf.

But a year later, when they were going to Sweden again, they shot a second film. This time it was in black and white and much more elaborate. It was about twenty minutes long, was shot in J.B.'s living room, and had a lot of different setups, although every song is only one shot. They covered about twelve songs with J.B., and as they intended it for a Swedish audience, Rönnog and Steve were translating simultaneously whatever J.B. was saying—even what he was singing. Rönnog would translate in the middle of a song what the song was about. It was quite unique and extraordinary. Who at the time would do that—go to somebody's house and shoot a movie with him? Again they took it to Swedish television, and this time they were very sure of themselves, they had made these elaborate setups, the film was in black and white, and the sound was much better now, but Swedish television refused it again. By now they had color, and somebody had recently covered the Chicago blues scene for them, without J.B. Lenoir, of course. Rönnog and Steve sadly went back to Chicago again, put the second film on the shelf, and that was the end of their filmmaking career. Very disappointing. And nobody ever saw these two films again.

How did we find the Seabergs? Via the Internet and through research, we started to secure any photographs or footage that existed of J.B. Lenoir. Somebody knew that at some point these young art students had shot some footage, but nobody knew who they were, and finally we found somebody who knew their names. By now the Seabergs lived in Atlanta, Georgia, no longer in Chicago; forty years had passed. They were still artists, into acrobatic poetry, which sure is an elusive branch of the arts. They are no longer in filmmaking after the two disasters, but they still had the two films. And they had these memories of J.B.; they really had known him well and had become very good friends with him and also with his family. J.B. had died very early, and they had stayed in touch with his wife and his kids, so there was finally firsthand information on J.B. Lenoir. So the Seabergs and their two movies became the backbone of the second half of my film.

But as *The Soul of a Man* is really about the music and about the songs, and not so much a film that is dealing with the biographies of my heroes, I really wanted to have the music speak for itself. I wasn't so much interested in making a film with talking heads and people who remembered J.B. Originally I had shot lots of stuff, interviews both on Skip and on J.B., but in the editing process I decided not to use any of it. I used very sparse comments. Basically the only one who is commenting on Skip James is his manager Dick Waterman, who worked with him the last two years of his life and who was also a photographer. I felt it was better that people would hear about Skip and J.B. from one source only. It was more intimate that way, and you'd get to know these bluesmen more than if you'd hear lots of people talking about them. I have also shot extensive

stuff with J.B.'s wife and his kids, and I regret that none of it ended up in the cut, but it would have been such a different film. And I can still make a whole chapter for the DVD of these interviews and these witnesses about the lives of Skip and J.B. We have a great piece, for instance, of a very old lady in Bentonia, Mississippi, where Skip grew up. She was in her eighties, and she remembered that when she was a teenager, she had a crush on Skip. When we shot it, I was sure this was going to end up in the film, but even that is not in. I also found people who knew Skip in the fifties when he was working on a farm and didn't play the blues anymore. We found people who knew J.B. in the fifties and sixties in Chicago. But I finally just eliminated all these testimonies. There was no need for them.

With a documentary, even if you might have a clear view of the film while you're shooting your material, when you come to the editing room, you have to start from scratch. The film is still hidden in there, somehow, and you have to find the secret story inside. It took us almost a year to find that story in *The Soul of a Man*. Twice we went in the wrong direction. My editor, Mathilde Bonnefoy, and I basically finished two entire cuts before we managed to find the good one that we have now. Our problem from the very beginning was: There were these three bluesmen who had never met, who lived in different eras, and played very different music. They were basically only linked through the fact that I loved them more than any other blues musicians of the twenties and thirties up to the sixties. That wasn't such a solid link, as we had to find out painfully. The first version of the film we cut had me narrating it. We did that whole thing and recorded and arranged my voice-over, and then we looked at the film, and I just hated it. It was simply not the right thing to have this German fellow talk about his

Rönnog Seaberg (with camera) and Sunnyland Slim, Steve Seaberg, St. Louis Jimmy, and J.B. Lenoir.

three American blues heroes. Everything I wanted to achieve, everything I loved about them, was gone. The very fact that I was confessing it, so to speak, with my *own* voice, made it all strangely ineffective and pretentious. I wanted it to be a film just about the music, but had somehow destroyed my very aim. All of a sudden, my own experience had become the center of the film, which was the last thing I wanted.

So we threw that entire cut away and started from scratch. And now we were going to do the opposite; we were not going to have any narration, we were just telling it from inside the songs. Which we did, very elaborately. But that didn't work either. So we threw that away and started a third time. This time we were successful. I realized that the secret narrator of the film had always been there; we just

hadn't noticed him. It was the first of our three characters: Blind Willie Johnson. The fact that his voice was out there in space on *Voyager*—by now on the outskirts of the solar system—made him the perfect instrument to narrate our film. He had the necessary distance, so to speak; he had a beautiful "objective" point of view. Plus, there was a certain irony in the fact that a man who was long dead now became the commentator on the lives of his two colleagues who had lived after him. That narrative perspective really worked well for the overall film. It gave it a certain lightness that certainly my voice never had. I just knew I needed a good voice for that! My first idea for that was Laurence Fishburne. He sure has a gorgeous voice. I knew Laurence from long ago when he made *Apocalypse Now* in the late

Cassandra Wilson reinterprets the work of J.B. Lenoir.

seventies—he was a young man then. I didn't have to twist his arm. He accepted the invitation immediately. With his voice, talking from the impossible perspective of a man in outer space, everything fell into place, and all the problems we had before with the structure and how to find a story that would unify it all vanished into thin air. Everything I had ever hoped for was there. In documentaries, you often have to run into a dead-end street, make a U-turn, and come back in order to see the right passage for the film. You have to shape the story from inside the material, and it's not obvious right away what that might be.

Once Blind Willie emerged as the narrator, the film's title came by itself. Blind Willie wrote and recorded a song called "The Soul of a Man," and in a way that song summed up the entire journey—Skip's and J.B.'s, as well as his own. It defined the search that the blues is constantly on in very simple words. And it finally brought out the topic of the Sacred and the Profane that the film was still about, somehow. In short: It was the perfect song to come from heaven or from outer space. What is the soul of a man? How much can you tell about these people, how much can you try to know them, and what do you then know if you know their music and their

lives? Do you know the soul of these men? Have they expressed it in these songs? The blues is a very existential medium, as it goes to the core of things.

Wanting the music to be the center of the film, I soon realized that the best way to let the music speak for itself was to rerecord the old songs and to find contemporary musicians who would pick a song by Skip, J.B., or Blind Willie, and reinterpret it. This would also help to make my three blues heroes contemporary again and have an audience from 2003 listen to their songs and be attentive. I was hoping I could interest a number of musicians or bands to play some of these songs. I looked for those who had already expressed an interest in that work, maybe had already covered a song by Skip or J.B. But I also approached some of my friends like Nick Cave and Lou Reed, who I knew would be interested because they love the blues. In the end I think there are twelve old songs interpreted by singers and songwriters and bands who work today. They all recorded live, during the sessions when we shot the musicians, so it's not playback. One of the highlights was Beck, because he wouldn't play a song the same way twice. He covered two

Bonnie Raitt tackles Skip James' odd tuning.

songs by Skip James, "I'm So Glad" and "Cypress Grove," and each time he would start, he would play on a different guitar and in a different rhythm, and he would have a different approach. I think he played twelve variations of "I'm So Glad," but each one was different, and there was no way that you could intercut one with the other. That was exciting. And scary.

All these performances were fantastic, really. Over almost one year, we shot them in Los Angeles, New York, Chicago, and London. Bonnie Raitt was very generous—she gave us two songs. The one that she played on her own was extremely demanding. She actually played in Skip's tuning. And that really breaks your fingers, because Skip played in open D, which is very unusual and difficult to get your fingers around. So Bonnie was really heroic. I was also very taken by the performances that Cassandra Wilson gave. She actually sang three songs, two of which ended up in the film. "Vietnam Blues" is my favorite song of J.B.'s. Her version of it was just very, very moving, and strangely contemporary. Eagle-Eye Cherry put together the most unbelievable band of musicians, including James "Blood" Ulmer, an awesome guitar player and singer himself. T-Bone Burnett got together a big band with an amazing brass section, Jim Keltner on drums, plus two other percussionists. T-Bone sang in J.B.'s high tenor voice, with a woman singer doing the lower voice.

The most fun was probably the shoot we had with Lou Reed. He did a rare Skip tune and a twelve-minute version of "See That My Grave Is Kept Clean," during which he was smiling happily. The band did that entire song in a state of bliss. One take only! I don't know how often that happens in Lou's life, but I'm very proud and extremely lucky that I shot him for several moments laughing with joy!

A sad moment was our shoot in Chicago, because we just happened to arrive in time to witness the destruction of Maxwell Street. We were there to shoot when the bulldozers came in and tore it all down. None of it actually is in the film, because it didn't make sense to use it, but it was a really heartbreaking moment, to see this legendary place in the history of American jazz and blues just be obliterated—to be turned into offices, banks, and restaurants. In a sense this makes these films even more important to me, personally, because they show that the music itself is so vibrant that it will survive even the sort of callow indifference that would fail to preserve an institution like Maxwell Street. And my awareness of how the music is still alive in our culture today, still flourishing, really allows me to feel less blue about the loss of Maxwell Street—because no doubt the things that made Maxwell Street so remarkable at one time are happening right now, someplace else.

—Wim Wenders

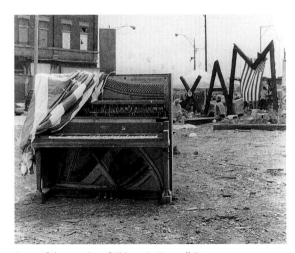

Some of the remains of Chicago's Maxwell Street, 2000

VISIONARY BLINDNESS: BLIND LEMON JEFFERSON AND OTHER VISION-IMPAIRED BLUESMEN BY CHRISTOPHER JOHN FARLEY

In the popular imagination, blindness and the blues seem to go together. When people are asked to envision a blues musician, many see in their mind's eye an old black man in a rumpled suit, probably wearing a brimmed hat and dark glasses and blowing on a harmonica or playing a guitar. For example, the 1986 movie *Crossroads,* a fictional story about the blues and its history, features a main character who's an old black man, who sometimes wears a rumpled suit and a brimmed hat and plays the harmonica and whose nickname is Blind Dog Fulton. He's not blind, but he sports large glasses and uses a wheelchair and just got out of a nursing home. In the 1980 movie *The Blues Brothers,* the title characters, symbolically, purchase instruments to restart their blues band from a store owner played by Ray Charles. And in Wim Wenders' documentary *The Soul of a Man,* the role of the film's narrator, and one of its three central subjects, is given to the great Texas bluesman Blind Willie Johnson, as portrayed by Chris Thomas King.

Music is often linked to cultural insurgency—slaves communicated through it, civil rights protesters in the fifties marched to it, and the socio-sexual upheavals of the sixties and seventies were set to it. To be a musician is to have power—over words, over rhythm, over the cultural history threaded through one's lyrics, and over the emotions of one's listeners. Imagining a blind black musician, perhaps, is a way of robbing a musician of a bit of his or her power, of letting a musician have his talent but making him culturally safe. Blindness

(wrongly and unfairly) is often associated with confusion and impotence in Western thought, and a long list of commonly used expressions underlines this attitude: blind alley, blind faith, blind rage, three blind mice, blind date, and so forth. On the other hand, love is blind, the personification of justice wears a blindfold, and time and time again politicians ask constituents to imagine a day when society is color-blind. For the sighted, blindness is both a disability and potential means of blocking out the world on the path to moral, social, and aesthetic harmony.

Blind Lemon Jefferson was one of history's most important blues figures—but he was far from the only significant sightless blues performer. In addition to Blind Willie Johnson, there were other greats: Blind Willie McTell, Reverend Blind Gary Davis, Blind Blake, Blind Boy Fuller, and Sonny Terry. Blind female performers also found a place in the music, including the blues gospel singer Arizona Dranes. As the blues became R&B, other blind performers emerged, including soulman Ray Charles and his heir, Stevie Wonder. Over the years, there has been a lot of speculation in blues circles about exactly why there seem to be so many blind blues performers. One answer, an unsatisfying one, is that it is all a strange coincidence and there is no reason or explanation behind it all. Another answer is that when one is blind, black, and living in the rural South, there are few options, professionally speaking, besides going into music. Another argument, perhaps the most persuasive of them all, holds that blind performers, whose focus, by nature, is on the senses they have remaining, are more suited to master an aural and oral discipline such as the blues.

Paramount Records, Jefferson's recording label, used his blindness as a marketing tool. His not at all politically correct biography in *The Paramount Book of Blues,* released around 1927, read, "Can anyone imagine a fate more horrible than to find that one is blind? To realize that the beautiful things one hears about—one will never see? Such was the heartrending fate of Lemon Jefferson, who was born blind and realized, as a small child, that life had withheld one glorious joy from him—sight. Then—environment began to play its important part in his destiny. He could hear; and he heard the sad-hearted, weary people of his homeland, Dallas, singing weird, sad melodies at their work and play, and unconsciously he began to imitate them—lamenting his fate in song. He learned to play a guitar, and for years he entertained his friends freely, moaning his weird songs as a means of forgetting his affliction. Some friends who saw great possibilities in him suggested he commercialize his talent, and as a result of following their advice he is now heard exclusively on Paramount."

Did Blind Lemon Jefferson have a special talent for the blues not in spite of but *because of* his visual impairment? Blindness and insight have also long been linked in popular lore. Egyptian tomb paintings often depict the image of potbellied, balding, blind harpists. Far from a negative image of the blind, the potbellies indicate that the musicians were well-fed and thus living well, and the bald heads indicated physical purity—such musicians were thought to be held in high social regard. In Norse mythology, the god Odin cast one of his eyes into the well of Mirmir in return for a sip of its

This anonymous blind street singer wandered Maxwell Street in Chicago in the 1960s.

waters and the accompanying gift of great wisdom. The Roman poet Ovid wrote of Tiresias, who, after resolving an argument between Jove and Juno in the former's favor, was struck blind by the latter. Jove, however, compensated Tiresias by opening his "inner eye."

Is there something specific about the blues, among all the arts, that either attracts blind artists or allows performers with visual impairments to excel?

"BLIND WILLIE McTELL"
By Bob Dylan
[1983]

Seen the arrow on the doorpost
Saying, "This land is condemned
All the way from New Orleans
   To Jerusalem."
I traveled through East Texas
Where many martyrs fell
And I know no one can
   sing the blues
Like Blind Willie McTell

Well, I heard the hoot
   owl singing
As they were taking down the tents
The stars above the barren trees
Were his only audience
Them charcoal gypsy maidens
Can strut their feathers well
But nobody can sing the blues
Like Blind Willie McTell

See them big plantations burning
Hear the cracking of the whips
Smell that sweet magnolia blooming
(And) see the ghosts of slavery ships
I can hear them tribes a-moaning
(I can) hear the undertaker's bell
(Yeah), nobody can sing the blues
Like Blind Willie McTell

There's a woman by the river
With some fine young handsome man
He's dressed up like a squire
Bootlegged whiskey in his hand
There's a chain gang on the highway
I can hear them rebels yell
And I know no one can sing the blues
Like Blind Willie McTell

Well, God is in heaven
And we all want what's his
But power and greed and corruptible seed
Seem to be all that there is
I'm gazing out the window
Of the St. James Hotel
And I know no one can sing the blues
Like Blind Willie McTell

Perhaps, but blind artists, of course, have also achieved prominence in other artistic endeavors. Homer, the poet who composed *The Iliad* and *The Odyssey,* was said to have been blind; some scholars believe he carried the entirety of his epic poems in his head, ready to be recited. A modern-day heir to Homer, James Joyce, author of *Ulysses,* also suffered from severe visual impairment, as did writers James Thurber and Aldous Huxley. Huxley, in fact, believed that will and imagination could improve impaired vision and wrote in his book *The Art of Seeing,* "For the person whose sight is subnormal, the correct mental attitude may be expressed in some words as these. 'I know theoretically that defective vision can be improved. I feel certain that, if I learn the art of seeing, I can improve my own defective vision.'"

⊕ ⊕ ⊕ ⊕ ⊕

Jefferson—whose given name was Lemmon, according to census records—was born on September 24, 1893, in Couchman, a small community about seventy miles south of Dallas. (His birth date is sometimes listed, less reliably, as July 11, 1897.) His parents, Alec and Classie Jefferson, worked as sharecroppers at a farm in town. Jefferson had six siblings; his brother John died around 1907 when he fell under the wheels of a slow-moving train. It is widely assumed that Jefferson was born without sight, but there are no medical records to support that. The only known official source that confirms his disability is the 1900 census, where he is registered as *BS,* which stands for "blind son." His family was active in the Shiloh Primitive Baptist Church. Locals recall that Jefferson's mother had a strong voice and would sing regularly at Shiloh and other churches in the region. Jefferson evidently mastered the guitar as a teenager and soon began

traveling into the nearby town of Wortham, playing in front of local businesses for shoppers and passersby. He would sit on a bench and place a tin cup nearby for tips (others say he used a hat) and play sometimes until 1 a.m. before walking back home to Couchman.

Jefferson was a solidly built man who stood five feet eight inches tall and, according to various sources, weighed somewhere between 180 and 250 pounds. At one point, in order to make ends meet, Jefferson briefly had a stint as a professional wrestler. Samuel Charters, who interviewed some of Jefferson's family members in the 1950s, wrote that Jefferson "wrestled for money in Dallas theatres. Since he was blind, he could be billed as a novelty wrestler. He weighed nearly 250 pounds, so he was never hurt, but it was a rough way to make a living. As soon as he started making a little money singing, he left the theatres."

Jefferson was usually nattily dressed, typically in a Stetson hat and a blue serge suit; he was also occasionally seen smoking cigars. He was tight with his money and, according to one report, wired his tin cup to the neck of his guitar. He would sing at Saturday night parties where revelers would dance the Black Bottom, the Charleston, the two-step, and the Buck Dance and drink corn whiskey, beer, and homemade wine. Although the parties often got wild, according to one observer, nobody ever saw Jefferson get drunk. When he played, he was known to sweat profusely; he would often crack jokes, and although he played the blues, he never seemed to get depressed or melancholic. When people shouted out requests, he would tell them, "Just wait awhile. Hold your cool."

A Wortham native, Arthur Carter, later recalled seeing Jefferson perform at a picnic near town. At the gathering, a dispute arose between Jefferson and a Holiness preacher who argued that singing the blues was a sinful act. Jefferson waited until the preacher's sermon had reached its climax and made his move. He started to play his guitar and sing. The crowd left the preacher and came to hear Jefferson. It was as if Jefferson was saying, through his music, that his work had to be touched by God because it clearly had a pull over the faithful.

Indeed, Jefferson's playing was something that was almost supernatural. Fellow bluesman Tom Shaw, who followed Jefferson around in the 1920s in the Dallas area, once said this about him, "Lemon was strictly a bluesman. . . . He was the king. Wherever he pull his guitar out, he was the king there. Wasn't no use for anybody else to come up talkin' about playin' against him, 'cause they couldn't even do what he was doin'—all they could do was look and wonder how in the hell he done it."

Jefferson's music found an audience, and he became perhaps the most popular bluesman of his era. His itinerant ways—he traveled to many of the small towns around East Texas, including Wortham, Kirvin, and Groesbeck—did much to popularize and romanticize the image of the blind blues musician. Later, when Jefferson moved to Chicago and began to record, he allowed himself one extravagance: He acquired a $725 Ford automobile for which he hired a chauffeur.

Jefferson brought the sound of the street corner to the whole world. Before him, blues players had mostly come from the musical theater. Jefferson made rich, variegated music that was made to be belted out over the sound of passing pedestrians, trotting horses, market conversation—it was music that could compete with life itself. He could play dance music, but the Jefferson songs that survive on record aren't party tunes. He would often break away from the main rhythm of a song with his guitar and contrast his vocal lines with spontaneous guitar riffs. He was perhaps the most adept guitarist of his time, and his instrument could sing, howl, keep time, whisper, or clang like a church bell. While other street singers were content to holler out songs about their poverty that aimed for cheap sympathy, Jefferson's songs were about a wide range of subjects and employed sly metaphors. "That Black Snake Moan" and "Hot Dogs Blues" were playfully sexual. "'Lectric Chair Blues," "Wartime Blues," and "One Dime Blues" could be read as early songs of social protest. "See That My Grave Is Kept Clean" captures something timeless and existential: the fear that all people have about what will be their posthumous legacy and the wish to have it preserved.

There are many questions about the circumstances of Blind Lemon Jefferson's death. When did he die? Most accounts put it in December 1929, but some say he may have perished as late as February 1930. How did he die? One account says he was mugged and left to freeze to death. Son House believed Jefferson was killed in a car crash. Another theory is that Jefferson died of a heart attack. One of his producers, Mayo Williams, said he heard that Jefferson collapsed in his car and was abandoned by his chauffeur. But many, if not most, chroniclers say Jefferson froze to death in a Chicago blizzard, unable to find his way to safety because of his blindness.

But Blind Lemon Jefferson, as it turns out, may not have been so blind. In one of only two known pictures of Jefferson, he is shown holding a guitar and wearing a suit jacket, a polka-dot tie, and a pair of wire-rimmed spectacles. His eyes are shut. It is not known why a man who was supposed to be blind was sporting a pair of glasses. In the other known photo of Jefferson, he is wearing a different pair of glasses. A number of musicians, including T-Bone Walker, Josh White, Lightnin' Hopkins, and Lead Belly, claimed to have helped lead Jefferson through the streets from place to place, but there are other accounts of Jefferson finding his way around by himself. He also seemed to have a way of identifying the denominations of bills: Once, when he was loaned a one-dollar bill, instead of the five-dollar bill he'd requested, he complained. He would often tell those who slipped money into his cup or hat, "Don't play me cheap." If they threw in a penny, he could tell, perhaps because of the sound, and he would toss the offending coin back out. Jefferson was also said to carry a loaded six-shooter—another suggestion that he at least had sight enough to see where to shoot.

Luigi Monge, a freelance teacher and translator in Genoa, Italy, analyzed all of Jefferson's known compositions and published the results in the spring 2000 edition of the *Black Music Research Journal*. Monge's research found that "no fewer than 241 direct or indirect visual references expressed in the first, second, or third person, or inferable from the context, are spread over Jefferson's currently available ninety-seven original recordings, alternate takes included. Only seven compositions have no visual references whatsoever." Examples include "She's a fine-looking fair brown" and "one train left the depot with a red and blue light behind/Well, the blue light's the blues, the red light's a worried mind." Others deal directly with vision: "We'll be seldom seen," "I've got your picture, and I'm going to put it in a frame," and "Some of the finest young women that a man most ever seen."

Do the visual references in Jefferson's songs suggest he had the ability to see, or were they simply figures of speech? Monge's research indicates that Jefferson not only has more visual references per

song than such visually impaired musicians as Blind Blake and Blind Boy Fuller (though a similar number to those in the songs of Blind Willie McTell) but he also has twice as many such references than sighted contemporaries like Charley Patton. Was Jefferson's blindness part of his act? Perhaps imagining vision in song was his way of compensating for what he lacked in reality. With his blues songs, Jefferson created a whole new world, one that could be envisioned but not seen, one with a rhythm but not necessarily a dance beat, one that was created to earn a living but that was bigger than life. In his music, Jefferson could see more clearly than even his fellow blues greats. He may have lost his way in the Windy City, but he never lost his way with his instrument. Legend has it that Jefferson was found dead with his hand frozen in place around the neck of his guitar.

RECOMMENDED LISTENING:

Blind Lemon Jefferson, *The Best of Blind Lemon Jefferson* (Yazoo, 2000). A fine survey of his best work.

Lightnin' Hopkins, *Texas Blues* (Arhoolie, 1990). Hopkins was a former escort of Jefferson's and was influenced by his work.

Bob Dylan, *Bob Dylan* (Columbia, 1962). Features perhaps the best cover of Jefferson's "See That My Grave Is Kept Clean."

The Beatles, *Past Masters, Vol. I* (Capitol, 1988). Early material from the Fab Four, including a rocking rendition of Carl Perkins' "Matchbox," which was his version of Jefferson's "Match Box Blues."

Nirvana, *MTV Unplugged in New York* (Geffen, 1994). Jefferson influenced Lead Belly, who inspired Kurt Cobain's take on "Where Did You Sleep Last Night?," a.k.a. "In the Pines."

LOCATING LIGHTNIN' *By Samuel Charters*
[From *The Country Blues*, 1959]

In a poor, shabby room in the colored section of Houston, a thin, worn man sat holding a guitar, playing a little on the strings, looking out of the window. It was a dull winter day, a heavy wind swirling the dust across the yard. There was a railroad behind the houses, and a few children were playing on the rails, shivering in their thin coats.

"There's a song my cousin learned when he was out on the farm." He was talking partly to me and partly to a friend of his, sitting in the shadows behind him. "Smokey Hogg got a little of it, but there hasn't been nobody done it right." Then he began singing:

> You ought to been on the
>   Brazos in 1910,
> Bud Russell drove pretty
>   women like he done ugly
>   men.

He was singing one of the most famous work songs of the Texas penitentiary farms, "Ain't No More Cane on This Brazos." His eyes were closed, he was singing quietly:

> My mama called me, I
>   answered, "Mam?"
> She said, "Son, you tired of
>   working?"
> I said, "Mama, I sure am."

He sat a moment, thinking of the hot, dusty summers on the flat cotton lands along the Brazos River, thinking of the convict gangs singing as they worked, the guards circling them slowly, a shotgun across the saddle.

> You ought to been on the Brazos
>   in 1904,
> You could find a dead man on
>   every turnin' row.

He shook his head; then he began to sing parts of the song again, playing his guitar a little. He stopped to drink some gin out of a bottle under the chair. He drank nearly a half pint of raw gin, using the metal cap of the bottle for a glass. His friend looked over and smiled, "He's getting it now." The singer went over two or three runs on the guitar; then he nodded and began singing:

> Uumh, big Brazos, here I come,
> Uumh, big Brazos, here I come.
> It' hard doing time for another
>   man
> When there ain't a thing poor
>   Lightnin' done. . . .
> Uumh, big Brazos, oh lord yes,
>   here I come.
> Figure on doing time for
>   someone else,
> When there ain't a thing poor
>   Lightnin' done.
> My mama called me, I
>   answered, "Mam?"

Lightnin' Hopkins, 1965

> She said, "Son, you tired of
>   workin'?"
> I said, "Mama, I sure am."
> My Pappa called me, I
>   answered, "Sir?"
> "If you're tired of workin'
> What the hell you going to stay
>   here for?"
> I couldn't . . . uumh . . .
> I just couldn't help myself.
> You know a man can't help but
>   feel bad,
> When he's doing time for
>   someone else.

The man was named Lightnin' Hopkins, from outside of Centerville, Texas. "Ain't No More Cane on This Brazos" was a song he had heard when he was a young man, working in the fields. His own song was a reshaping and reworking of the old work song into something intensely personal and expressive: He had changed it into a blues. 🖝

HENRY THOMAS: OUR DEEPEST LOOK AT THE ROOTS

By Mack McCormick

[From the notes to *Henry Thomas "Ragtime Texas": Complete Recorded Works 1927–1929,* 1974]

It was one of those bright winter afternoons in 1949. I was standing on a corner in downtown Houston, waiting for a signal light to change, when I noticed an old man with a guitar making his way along the opposite sidewalk. He was a formidable person, a bulky figure with a mashed hat who moved in a straight line through the crowd. People looked up at him, then gave him a quick second look and moved out of his path.

Whatever errand I was on was put aside and I set out after him, catching up to him at the corner of Crawford and Capitol. I had to call out to him twice to catch his attention. He stopped and swung around to face me, the guitar held tight across his chest, a dusty mountain of a man. He must have stood all of six feet three and the size of him was made all the greater by the enormous quantity of clothes in which he was wrapped. There were three overcoats, one on top of the other, all unbuttoned and flapping open in a chilly wind that gusted down the street. The outer coat was streaked with mud and grease. The inner garments were worn smooth with wear and brushing. Later, when a question sent him in search of some item, he roamed through all the different pockets like a man searching the closets and drawers of his house.

He was a street singer, perhaps a beggar, but there was nothing deferential about him. He first grumbled at me in a coarse voice and seemed about to brush on past. Then he paused and broke into a surprisingly bright smile. Many of his teeth were missing and it was difficult to understand what he said. Only here and there a few words came through gruffly. He did make me understand that he'd arrived in Houston on a train

that had pulled into Union Station only a few minutes earlier. He said he'd slept under a bridge in Palestine, Texas, the night before.

He agreed to play some music but what followed was a disappointment. His guitar strings were dead and terribly out of tune. He flailed away at them almost indifferently, as if he'd lost the ability to discriminate tones. His voice had a gay lilt but only occasionally could a phrase be made out. Nonetheless, there was a compelling vigor in his performance. He used a flat metal, kazoo-like instrument that he gripped in his mouth and blew, getting a curious buzzing sound from it—a sound with an energetic bite that carried up and down the sidewalk. He went through several pieces there on the street corner, at one point gathering a small crowd of pedestrians who tossed some coins in the mashed felt hat he'd set on the sidewalk.

I'd come across him a few years too late. He was far too old to be hoboing and sleeping under bridges. He was too old to be able to perform effectively. One could only wonder what he had sounded like before old age had worn him down.

Over the years a number of things have come along to suggest that the man on the street was in fact "Ragtime Texas" Henry Thomas. Harry Smith's somewhat madcap collection of old 78s, *Anthology of American Folk Music,* contained two items recorded in 1928 by a man named Henry Thomas, a fascinating performer who seemed to have a wealth of music at his command; an artist who offered a deep look at the black tradition that had taken shape in the nineteenth century. By the time these records came to my notice in the early 1950s, I'd forgotten the name of the man I'd heard on the street. I had some vague recollection that he'd claimed to have made some records and that I'd even found them listed in *Index to Jazz*. Much clearer is the memory of that gruff, towering man telling me he came from East Texas and bristling with pride when he said, "I left out from home when I was eleven years old and I been traveling ever since."

There are a striking number of similarities between the "Ragtime Texas" recordings and the man I'd stopped. Apart from the obvious Texas connections, there is the fact that both relied heavily on D-formation chords and made unusual use of the capo, pushing it three to seven frets up the neck of the guitar. They were unquestionably men of the same age and period, and there is a blunt heartiness in these records that is wholly consistent with and even suggests that dusty mountain of a man who'd played on the street corner that winter afternoon.

As more of those old recordings came to light, it became apparent that Henry Thomas was a singular and important figure. He left behind a total of twenty-three issued selections which represent one of the richest contributions to our musical culture. It's goodtime music reaching out from another era: reels, anthems, stomps, gospel songs, dance calls, ballads, blues, and fragments compressed in a blurring glimpse of black music as it existed five generations ago. As an old man among young recording artists, Ragtime Texas left behind a look at our roots like no one else's. It's the songs that came out of the shifting days when freedmen and their children were remaking their lives in a hostile nation.

Henry Thomas' guitar is rudimentary, but he plays with a thrusting drive that evokes a country dance. He uses one of the most ancient of all instruments, the panpipe (or quills or syrinx, as it is variously known) to punch out melodies. His songs continually underscore the lasting irony that much of our most expressive and satisfactory poetry has been composed by an illiterate and uneducated people. And, along the way, Henry Thomas sheds new half-light on a long-lingering mystery: the origin of the blues. He offers no quick solutions, but rather leaves us to our own devices after providing varied examples of the blues idiom at several early stages of development. He returns more than once to what is perhaps its most archaic form:

Look where the sun done gone
Look where the sun done gone
Look where the sun done gone, poor girl
Look where the sun done gone.

For me, the question of who it was that I stopped on the street that day in 1949 has never been answered to complete satisfaction. It cannot be settled, although the doubt has diminished—though not ended—since seeing copies of the original advertisements for his records "John Henry" and "Texas Easy Street Blues," which appeared in black newspapers when the records were first released. One of these advertisements contains a mottled photograph and the other a line drawing of a figure with the same physique and that egg-shaped head I first saw near Houston's Union Station.

In any case, through the happenstance of having made his twenty-three records in the late 1920s, Henry Thomas becomes a relic from the past, one of that flood of leftover things that we must come to treasure, or else discard because they clutter up our world. As with any relic, it's helpful to know the context and the role it placed in its own time, but ultimately the relic must stand on its own—holding our attention because it is a rich human testament that continues to please us. 🎸

"Growin' up in Texas, I heard a lot of blues singers—black cotton pickers singin' the blues. I always loved the blues and played a lot of blues. It's so close to country music—so many country songs are three-chord blues." —*Willie Nelson*

JANIE AND TEA CAKE *By Zora Neale Hurston*

[From *Their Eyes Were Watching God,* 1937]

Janie dozed off to sleep but she woke up in time to see the sun sending up spies ahead of him to mark out the road through the dark. He peeped up over the door sill of the world and made a little foolishness with red. But pretty soon, he laid all that aside and went about his business dressed all in white. But it was always going to be dark to Janie if Tea Cake didn't soon come back. She got out of the bed but a chair couldn't hold her. She dwindled down on the floor with her head in a rocking chair.

After a while there was somebody playing a guitar outside her door. Played right smart while. It sounded lovely too. But it was sad to hear it feeling blue like Janie was. Then whoever it was started to singing "Ring de bells of mercy. Call de sinner man home." Her heart all but smothered her.

"Tea Cake is dat you?"

"You know so well it's me, Janie. How come you don't open de door?"

But he never waited. He walked on in with a guitar and a grin. Guitar hanging round his neck with a red silk cord and a grin hanging from his ears.

"Don't need tuh ast me where Ah been all dis time, 'cause it's mah all day job tuh tell yuh."

"Tea Cake, Ah—"

"Good Lawd, Janie, whut you doin' settin' on de floor?"

He took her head in his hands and eased himself into the chair. She still didn't say anything. He sat stroking her head and looking down into her face.

"Ah see whut it is. You doubted me 'bout de money. Thought Ah had done took it and gone. Ah don't blame yuh but it wasn't lak you think. De girl baby ain't born and her mama is dead, dat can git me tuh spend our money on her. Ah told yo' before dat you got de keys tuh de kingdom. You can depend on dat."

"Still and all you went off and left me all day and all night."

"'Twasn't 'cause Ah wanted tuh stay off lak dat, and it sho Lawd, wuzn't no woman. If you didn't have de power tuh hold me and hold me tight, Ah wouldn't be callin' yuh Mis' Woods. Ah met plenty women before Ah knowed you tuh talk tuh. You'se de onliest woman in de world Ah ever even mentioned gitting married tuh. You bein' older don't make no difference. Don't never consider dat no mo'. If Ah ever gits tuh messin' round another woman it won't be on account of her age. It'll be because she got me in de same way you got me—so Ah can't help mahself."

He sat down on the floor beside her and kissed and playfully turned up the corner of her mouth until she smiled.

"Looka here, folks," he announced to an imaginary audience, "Sister Woods is 'bout tuh quit her husband!"

Janie laughed at that and let herself lean on him. Then she announced to the same audience, "Mis' Woods got herself uh new lil boy rooster, but he been off somewhere and won't tell her."

"First thing, though, us got tuh eat together, Janie. Then we can talk."

"One thing, Ah won't send you out after no fish."

He pinched her in the side and ignored what she said.

"'Tain't no need of neither one of us workin' dis mornin'. Call Mis' Samuels and let her fix whatever you want."

"Tea Cake, if you don't hurry up and tell me, Ah'll take and beat yo' head flat as uh dime."

Tea Cake stuck out till he had some breakfast, then he talked and acted out the story.

He spied the money while he was tying his tie. He took it up and looked at it out of curiosity and put it in his pocket to count it while he was out to find some fish to fry. When he found out how much it was, he was excited and felt like letting folks know who he was. Before he found the fish market he met a fellow he used to work with at the round house. One word brought on another one and pretty soon he made up his mind to spend some of it. He never had had his hand on so much money before in his life, so he made up his mind to see how it felt to be a millionaire. They went on out to Callahan round the railroad shops and he decided to give a big chicken and macaroni supper that night, free to all.

He bought up the stuff and they found somebody to pick the guitar so they could all dance some. So they sent the message all around for people to come. And come they did. A big table loaded down with fried chicken and biscuits and a wash-tub full of macaroni with plenty cheese in it. When the fellow began to pick the box the people begin to come from east, west, north, and Australia. And he stood in the door and paid all the ugly women two dollars *not* to come in. One big meriny colored woman was so ugly till it was worth five dollars for her not to come in, so he gave it to her.

They had a big time till one man come in who thought he was bad. He tried to pull and haul over all the chickens and pick out the livers and gizzards to eat. Nobody else couldn't pacify him so they called Tea Cake to come see if he could stop him. So Tea Cake walked up and asked him, "Say, whut's de matter wid you, nohow?"

"Ah don't want nobody handin' me nothin'. Specially don't issue me out no rations. Ah always chooses mah rations." He kept right on plowing through the pile uh chicken. So Tea Cake got mad.

"You got mo' nerve than uh brass monkey. Tell me, what post office did *you* ever pee in? Ah craves tuh know."

"Whut you mean by dat now?" the fellow asked.

"Ah means dis—it takes jus' as much nerve tuh cut caper lak dat in uh United States Government Post Office as it do tuh comes pullin' and haulin' over any chicken Ah pay for. Hit de

ground. Damned if Ah ain't gointuh try you dis night."

So they all went outside to see if Tea Cake could handle the boogerboo. Tea Cake knocked out two of his teeth, so that man went on off from there. Then two men tried to pick a fight with one another, so Tea Cake said they had to kiss and make up. They didn't want to do it. They'd rather go to jail, but everybody else liked the idea, so they made 'em do it. Afterwards, both of them spit and gagged and wiped their mouths with the back of their hands. One went outside and chewed a little grass like a sick dog, he said to keep it from killing him.

Then everybody began to holler at the music because the man couldn't play but three pieces. So Tea Cake took the guitar and played himself. He was glad of the chance because he hadn't had his hand on a box since he put his in the pawn shop to get some money to hire a car for Janie soon after he met her. He missed his music. So that put him in the notion he ought to have one. He bought the guitar on the spot and paid fifteen dollars cash. It was really worth sixty-five any day.

Just before day the party wore out. So Tea Cake hurried on back to his new wife. He had done found out how rich people feel and he had a fine guitar and twelve dollars left in his pocket and all he needed now was a great big old hug and kiss from Janie.

"You musta thought yo' wife was powerful ugly. Dem ugly women dat you paid two dollars not to come in, could git tuh de door. You never even

'lowed me tuh git dat close." She pouted.

"Janie, Ah would have give Jacksonville wid Tampa for a jump-back for you to be dere wid me. Ah started to come git yuh two three times."

"Well, how come yuh didn't come git me?"

"Janie, would you have come if Ah did?"

"Sho Ah would. Ah laks fun just as good as you do."

"Janie, Ah wanted tuh, mighty much, but Ah was skeered. Too skeered Ah might lose yuh."

"Why?"

"Dem wuzn't no high muckty mucks. Dem wuz railroad hands and dey womenfolks. You ain't usetuh folks lak dat and Ah wuz skeered you might git all mad and quit me for takin' you 'mongst 'em. But Ah wanted yuh wid me jus' de same. Befo' us got married Ah made up mah mind not tuh let you see no commonness in me. When Ah git mad habits on, Ah'd go off and keep it out yo' sight. 'Tain't mah notion tuh drag *you* down wid me."

"Looka heah, Tea Cake, if you ever go off from me and have a good time lak dat and then come back heah tellin' me how nice Ah is, Ah specks tuh kill yuh dead. You heah me?"

"So you aims to partake wid everything, hunh?"

"Yeah, Tea Cake, don't keer what it is."

"Dat's all Ah wants tuh know. From now on you'se mah wife and mah woman and everything else in de world Ah needs." ⌐

PHOTOGRAPHER PETER AMFT ON J.B. LENOIR

Photographer Peter Amft got turned on to music during the early-sixties folk revival in his native Chicago. Around the same time, he began shooting album covers for Mercury Records, as well as the Chicago blues label Delmark. He became close friends with Michael Bloomfield, whom he photographed many times, in addition to Howlin' Wolf, Muddy Waters, B.B. King, Big Joe Williams, Willie Dixon, and other blues artists.

Back in '63, there were hootenannies all over Chicago. That's when I first saw Steve Seaberg, at the No Exit Café. He would get down on one knee and sing and play ukulele. It was all very vaudeville—a mixture that included flamenco and blues, anything wacky. I was working full time as a commercial photographer's assistant at the time. We did everything from naked ladies for *Playboy* to Hormel Ham billboards, often on the same day. We worked seven days a week, day and night, but it was a great learning experience for me. There was so much work to do, the photographer would let me do a lot of it, and I had free run of the studio.

Steve and his wife, Rönnog, knew I was a photographer. They asked me to make a little film with them of J.B. Lenoir. They could only afford to rent a 16-mm Auricon—just a cigar box with a lens. The sound recorder was a little suitcase with a handle, like a kid's toy that only had an on-off button—very simple, primitive, probably from the fifties.

I hadn't seen J.B. before. He showed up with a zebra-skin tuxedo and a funky guitar. We just stuck the Auricon on a stationary tripod, put J.B. in front of a white background with a chair, and turned him loose. There wasn't a lot of preplanning or produc-tion. J.B. showed up with Sunnyland Slim and St. Louis Jimmy as an audience, we took our coats off, did the movie, and it was done. Like that.

We sent the film out and got it processed, and when I went to pick it up, there were two rolls and I had them spliced together. Then I borrowed my uncle's big clunky projector, an old Bell & Howell. I was twenty-two, and my wife and I were living on Michigan Avenue in a big loft. J.B. brought his whole family over for the screening, and they *loved* the movie. It was in color, with sound. That was totally unheard of—that you would go to some white people's house and they would have a color and sound movie of your uncle or son—J.B.—where he was playing. It was so startling.

We had a duplex, and J.B. and I went upstairs while the others watched the film over and over again. He told me he had written a song almost every day of his life, and he showed me a notebook of his songs. He had a poignant look on his face, talking about his friends who had died in the Korean War. He had written songs like "Eisenhower Blues" about his experiences.

We went downstairs, and I had him sit by the window light. I had my Rolleiflex camera on a tripod, and I took a deliberate double exposure of him looking happy—like he always did—and sad. J.B. had this very angelic quality, an innocence, to him. He was like an old-fashioned black guy you'd find waiting on you if you were taking the New York Central train and you were the stupid white person and the guy waiting on you had more dignity than you. He had an old-fashioned look about him. He sang in a real high falsetto, which was kind of strange. He was a special person. 🖎

J.B. Lenoir, photographed
by Peter Amft the night of
the screening of the
Seabergs' film

DRIVING MR. JAMES BY JOHN SZWED

September 1967: The bombing of North Vietnam had just begun; the Marines were still occupying the Dominican Republic; cities were still smoldering from a summer of riots; sit-ins were spreading across campuses; "Alice's Restaurant" was on the radio; Lenny Bruce was dead; and me? I was in the fall of my discontent, teaching at Lehigh University, in Allentown, Pennsylvania, and desperate to connect with the outside world. Somehow I convinced the university to let me stage a modest folk festival. The name act was the New Lost City Ramblers, but to me the secret star was the almost legendary bluesman Skip James, recently returned from the dead and living in North Philadelphia, fifty miles away. I heard him for the first time on a new album for Melodeon, a record whose antique-looking cover made it appear recorded in the 1920s. His voice was high and faint, his guitar precise and classical. To me it was as strange and beautiful as anything on Harry Smith's *Anthology of American Folk Music,* a kind of chamber music from the Mississippi Delta.

The morning of the festival, I headed south in a VW van to pick him up at his house, where I found him waiting on the front porch, neatly dressed in hat and suit, the top button of his pants left stylishly unbuttoned. Driving out of the city, Skip said very little, and what he did say was whispered. His wife, Lorenzo (the niece of Mississippi John Hurt), did the talking for both of them.

Once we were at Lehigh, I introduced Mr. James to a small group of students seated under some pine trees on the side of a hill. He casually pulled out his guitar, lowered his head, and drifted into the strange muted cry of "Illinois Blues." One song flowed into the next, as he played on, motionless and unamplified, in that dappled afternoon light of what someone later told me was the summer solstice.

Afterward, he and his wife sat by themselves, sharing fried chicken and jars of iced tea from a basket they'd brought, until it was time for the evening concert. When his turn came on the stage, Skip was a different man, sitting on a kitchen chair in the spotlight, chatting briefly between songs, explaining his arcane tunings, while the students—most of whom had never heard of him—cheered him on, especially after they realized that Cream's "I'm So Glad" was his own tune. So it went for an hour, then two hours, as he plowed though his

"**As** a listener, I tend to go for the odd-metered performances: the weirder Muddy Waters and Sonny Boy Williamson tracks ('Too Young to Know' and 'Your Funeral and My Trial'), all of Jimmy Reed, the unhinged Cobra sides by Otis Rush (particularly 'Three Times a Fool' and 'It Takes Time'), and the best of the Delta masters: Tommy and Robert Johnson, Charley Patton, and Skip James. I've never been tempted to try and sing any of these songs (apart from the occasional stab at Sonny Boy's 'Help Me' and a few Little Willie John titles). I wouldn't know where to begin. Looking at a James Ensor painting doesn't make me want to pick up a brush. I am just in wonder. I just don't know how to get inside. Or is it 'outside'? Skip James sounds like music from Venus most of the time." —*Elvis Costello*

Skip James at the Newport Folk Festival, 1964

whole repertoire, the students with him all the way. As it drew close to midnight, the New Lost City Ramblers became restless backstage and let me know that somebody was going to have to get him off. They ignored my suggestion that they just walk onstage, reminding me that it was I, the chauffeur, who was going to have to cut that old man off and take the boos that were about to be showered on me. Backstage, I tried to apologize to Skip James, paying him in cash, counting it out slowly—but Skip took some care to let me know that it was all right, and his wife added that I should have told him to get off a long time before then.

A year or so later, I heard that Skip had found Jesus, hung his guitar on the wall, and was preaching somewhere. I also read in a book that he was a murderer—a cold psychopath of a man who still carried a pistol everywhere. Maybe it was all true, maybe none of it, but for those few moments in the Lehigh Valley, time had stopped in the presence of a transparently beautiful music in the hands of a pure artist. 🎸

CLIFFORD ANTONE ON LIVIN' AND LOVIN' THE BLUES

Clifford Antone founded one of America's preeminent blues clubs, Antone's, in Austin, Texas, during a time when the blues had been cast aside in the public consciousness. Antone's zeal helped to create a Texas blues scene that produced national sensations the Fabulous Thunderbirds and Stevie Ray Vaughan—who cut their teeth at the club playing with such heroes as Albert King and Muddy Waters during the great bluesmen's residencies at Antone's.

Seeing Bobby "Blue" Bland and James Brown at the National Guard Armory as a teenager in Beaumont, Texas, changed my life. You'd hear all this music where I lived: Louisiana blues, like Slim Harpo, Lightnin' Slim, Katie Webster, Lazy Lester, Guitar Slim; and the Texas blues—Junior Parker, Bobby Bland, Johnny Ace. But I didn't hear the Chicago blues till I was in my later teens. When I heard that, that was it—that became my thing.

During the hippie days, when I was listenin' to Fleetwood Mac when it was a straight blues band with blues guitarists Peter Green and Jeremy Spencer, a guy at the record store said, "I just got this weird import thing, *Fleetwood Mac in Chicago,* a double record. Here, take it." I put this record on, and it was Fleetwood Mac with Willie Dixon and Otis Spann, and I said, I'm gonna find out who these guys are, so I went to the record store. There was a record on, Otis Spann, and an Elmore James record. I heard Otis Spann playing the piano, and Elmore James. That's the first time I really knew myself. I said, *"This is how my mind is!"* I could never explain it to anyone. This music is me—that's how I think. The other stuff on the radio was just music. The whole thing was good; there was no bad

music. But this was my own thing! When I heard those guys' voices—Otis Spann and Elmore James—it was like, That's what I been trying to explain to people, teachers at school. I can't explain myself: "Why're you not listenin' in class?" "I dunno." The music always had a hold on me, but when I listened to that, those voices, that was mine. It still is. The only thing I listen to is the blues. No jazz, no rock. I always wonder, Why me?

Back then, there was still a twelve o'clock drinking law. In 1975, they made two o'clock the drinking cutoff. Soon as they did that, I knew that opening a blues club was what I wanted to do. The first Antone's opened on July 15, 1975. It was on Sixth Street, then a completely dark, deserted street. It was a six thousand-square-foot building, six hundred dollars a month. It'd be ten thousand dollars today. I been blessed to do this. We were kids, opening this club with no money. People started coming and bringing us stuff: A plumber comes in, says, "Lemme do this for you." Air-conditioning man with big ol' units says, "Lemme put this in for you, pay me later." Turns out his partner bought an old church in the country with this old wood. Came in and designed the back wall with wood and mirrors. Just brought it to us, let us use it.

The first week we opened, we had Clifton Chenier and the Red Hot Louisiana Band—Clifton and his brother Cleveland, the best scrub board player ever, and Blind John Hart on sax. Unbelievable band. Got us off to a good start. Then we had Percy Mayfield and Ray Charles for a week. We had pianist Sunnyland Slim and harmonica player Big Walter Horton the third week we were open. Then Sunnyland went back to Chicago and told everyone about us. Jimmy Rogers, Eddie Taylor, Muddy Waters, Buddy Guy—everyone started calling me and came down to play. Sunnyland turned everyone on to us. He was like your grandfather and godfather rolled into one.

Also in '75, the Thunderbirds started. Harmonica player Kim Wilson came down, and vocalist Lou Ann Barton was an original Thunderbird. Jimmie Vaughan and Stevie Ray Vaughan were two guitar players. Stevie didn't sing at all then. Thirty percent of what Stevie played, he owed to Albert King. He was as good as you get, but he borrowed everything from Albert King—in a great way.

The Texas blues sound is different from the Chicago blues sound. You can't get Buddy Guy and Albert Collins in a jam together. It doesn't work. The Texas shuffle is hard to explain—these Texas blues drummers can't back up the Chicago guys, generally speaking. An exception is Memphis harmonica player Junior Parker: He's a guy who plays Texas style, Memphis style—on Sun Records as Little Junior and the Blue Flames—and Chicago style. He did all three styles. That's rare. Not a lotta guys like that.

One time I had guitarists Buddy Guy, Otis Rush, and Albert Collins all together. They had a jam and [Texan] Albert couldn't fit in with them. He would play, but he wasn't comfortable. That's when I first realized how different the Chicago and Texas styles are—especially the drumming. Chicago drummers like S.P. Leary just play a different kind of feel than the Texas shuffle.

Seeing Muddy onstage was so exhilarating—like a religious experience, like seeing God. I was so young and so totally dedicated to the blues. That was the only thing in my life. Muddy would come to my house, my mother would cook for him. Albert King, too, was so nice. They were just like family. Our

Some of the great bluesmen from the state of Texas

shows were for five days, Tuesday through Saturday. So I got to know the musicians, and the local guys got to hang out with the old-timers. You can't imagine in '75: Jimmie and Stevie playing a gig together couldn't draw a hundred dollars. But Stevie got to play with Albert King, his hero. Jimmie and Kim [Wilson] got to be onstage with Muddy Waters. To me it was like, we gotta make it happen. This has got to be recorded. Where we gonna get the money? These guys are dying! We never had the funds to record this stuff the way we wanted to, still don't. I ain't got nothin'. I threw everything I had away. But that's okay. I've got their friendship. I can tell you this: Muddy Waters is with me wherever I go. 🎸

JIMMIE VAUGHAN ON BEING BORN INTO THE BLUES

Guitarist Jimmie Vaughan left home to play the blues when he was fifteen. His brother, Stevie Ray, joined him in Austin, which the two turned into a new blues capital.

My mom and dad moved us around a lot when we were kids, going from town to town all over Texas. My little brother, Stevie, and I were in the backseat watching the world go by. We'd stop for a Dr. Pepper, and there'd be a black man with a guitar, playing his heart out. I'd wander over and just watch. I was mesmerized. I wanted to know how he made that thing talk. It sounded so personal, like he was revealing all his secrets.

"How does he do that?" I asked my mom.

"He's blessed," she said, "with talent."

"What's he singing?" I asked Dad.

"I got to work with Lightnin' Hopkins in Los Angeles. Warner Bros. set that up. They knew he was a big hero to me. I had 'Polk Salad Annie' out at the time. I played acoustic guitar on his *L.A. Mudslide* LP. He came in the studio with his wife, and I was already there by the microphone. He had a paper sack with a big jug of wine in it. Gave the sack to his wife, walked by me, and said, 'You playin' wit' me, boy?' I said, 'Yeah,' and I played a couple of his licks, and he said, 'Hey, all right, all right.' He just looked up at the engineer and said, 'Turn it on.' And he played twelve songs and didn't hardly stop between songs, except for a sip of wine. He wouldn't even look at me. I just *felt* what to play. If you didn't feel it, you'd be quiet till you did feel it. Then he got up, shook my hand, said, 'I sure like the way you play, man.' Went in there in the studio, held out his hand, a guy in a suit put ten one-hundred-dollar bills in his hand. He put the thousand dollars in the paper sack, and him and his wife walked out. No royalties, no paperwork— pay me now, bye-bye." *—Tony Joe White*

"The blues, son. The man's singing the blues."

That's when I understood that the blues are a blessing. Later, I also understood that growing up in Dallas, where the blues are so strong, was an added blessing. Blessings were all around me. Dallas was home to Blind Lemon Jefferson and Lil' Son Jackson. T-Bone Walker, who invented big-city electric-blues guitar, led Blind Lemon around town and was called Oak Cliff T-Bone. Oak Cliff is the section of Dallas where I was raised—guitar country.

I'd lie in bed every night listening to Jim Lowe's Kat's Karavan, a local radio show that played Jimmy Reed. In Dallas, Jimmy Reed was God. The sound of his harmonica, the sound of his voice, the sound of Eddie Taylor's guitar—those were the sounds that shaped my childhood. Jimmy Reed encompassed everything—he was low-down, he was simple, he was sensuous, he was easy to copy, and he was popular.

Lightnin' Hopkins is another towering influence. Lightnin' is beautifully simple and deceptively sly. I felt the elegance of his touch. Lightnin' penetrated my soul and helped form my musical character. So did Freddie King. In Dallas, radio played Freddie's "Hide Away" more than the Beatles. I bought tons of records—every B.B. King record in the store. I'd take those suckers home and wear 'em out. I studied them until I knew them. Every last lick.

Stevie was sitting up in the bed next to me, watching my every move. Like all little brothers, he was dying to do everything Big Brother did. The minute I brought home a Lonnie Mack or Jimi Hendrix record, Stevie was right there with me, studying me as I studied the music. That's how we both learned to play. Off the records. No reading, no writing, no training. All by ear.

SOMETHIN' THAT REACH BACK IN YOUR LIFE *By John Lee Hooker*

[As told to Paul Oliver, from *Conversation with the Blues,* 1965]

John Lee Hooker, circa 1965

Way back before you and everybody else and all the peoples was born, spirituals was the thing. Nobody can reach way back and find out just when it was born. But when spirituals was born it was born on the blues side. You can compare spirituals and blues almost along together because both of them got a very, very sad touch. Because that's why you could take some spirituals and some blues and compare them together and you get a sad feelin' out of each one. So that's why I sing the blues. I used to be a spiritual singer. But I get just as deep a feelin' from the blues as I would from the spirituals, because I do it sad and I do it to satisfaction until the whole thing reaches me, what happened to other people, and I get that real deep down sad feelin'.

⊕ ⊕ ⊕ ⊕ ⊕

There's a lot of things that give you the blues, that give me the blues, that give any man the blues: It's somewhere down the line that you have been hurt someplace. I mean, it's no certain type of hurtin', but you have been hurt someplace and you get to playin' the blues that reaches. And so that's why when I sing the blues I sing it with the big feelin'. I really means it. It's not the manner that I had the hardships that a lot of people had throughout the South and other cities throughout the country, but I do know what they went through. My mother, my daddy, and my stepfather, they told me these things and I know that they must have went through those things themselves. And so when you gets the feelin' it's not only what happened to you—it's what happened to your foreparents and other people. And that's what makes the blues.

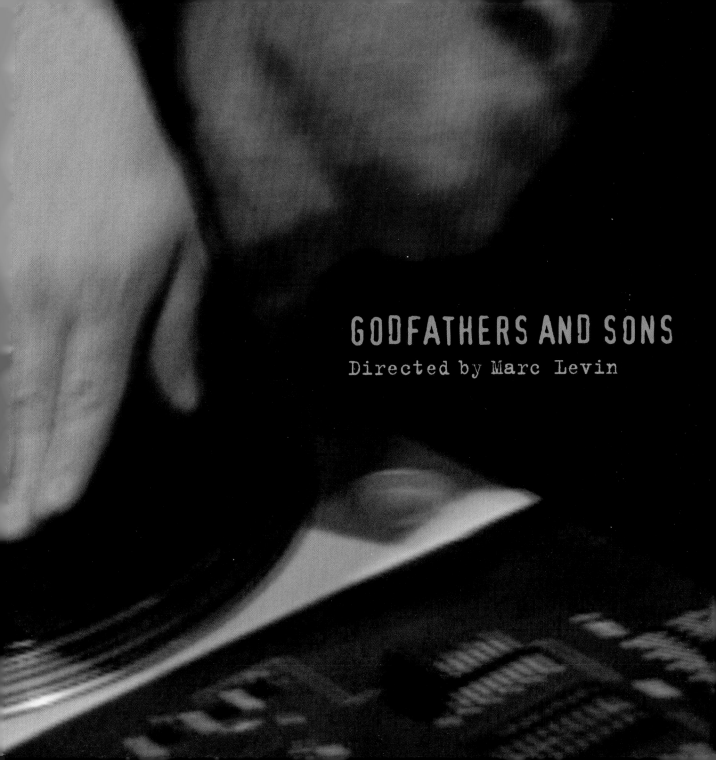

GODFATHERS AND SONS

Directed by Marc Levin

Chuck D (*right*) and Common

What's unique about this documentary series is that there's an overall historic narrative on the blues, but unlike the more traditional approach, here we have all these directors picking a part of that story and that chronology and then diving in and somehow personalizing it.

Chicago blues and Chess Records have always been my love, since I was a kid. The first Paul Butterfield Blues Band album originally got me into the Chicago blues during the summer of '65. We used to look at that album cover that showed one of the first interracial bands. Sam Lay, the black drummer, was the coolest—it was like, "That's what we want to be like." So with this film, I got to come full circle and go back to where it all started.

For me, rock & roll comes out of the Chess Records sound—Muddy Waters, Howlin' Wolf, Little Walter, Koko Taylor, Chuck Berry, Bo Diddley. That whole world was a revelation to me. I was thirteen, fourteen years old and listening to rock & roll, but I didn't realize where it came from. Rock & roll had an element of danger, and it was sex, it was liberated, it was bohemian, but I didn't realize it came out of Chicago.

Marshall Chess, the son of Chess Records cofounder Leonard Chess, has obviously been radioactively supercharged by being exposed at a young age to all these great blues artists. He had to calm down by being the Rolling Stones' manager for ten years. This story of Chess we tell in the film is his personal story—his family's story. We decided to take his personal story, which encompasses all this

great music, and hook it up with today's younger generation. We wanted this music to come alive—not come across as a thing of the past. This music is now; you feel the beat, you feel it in your gut.

Marshall called me one day and said, "You're not going to believe this, but I just got an e-mail from Chuck D. He read *Spinning Blues Into Gold,* the book on the Chess family that Nadine Cohodas wrote, which is a great book. Chuck D said, 'It was *Electric Mud*'—Muddy Waters' blues-rock album produced in 1968 by Marshall—'that got me into this. I hear you're going to do this film trying to connect the blues and hip-hop, and I'm down.'" This was literally an act of fate, and it became the inciting incident in *Godfathers and Sons.* What personalized the film was the idea that not only is the story intergenerational, but it's a family story, it's black and white, it's blacks and Jews, it's all these connections, but it's done in a very real, natural way, and it just happened. We didn't write it. We were searching for it, wondering what it would be. But Chuck D just sat down one day at his keyboard and sent that message into cyberspace, and that's what started it.

When we began talking about the film, we wondered about the connection between blues and hip-hop. Rock & roll and the blues is easy, and there have been many films and books about that connection. The bluesmen were the fathers and the rock & rollers were the sons. But somehow the grandkids got lost, because hip-hop was a whole new thing, and it wasn't built around an electric guitar. It was built around turntables and beats. It was built around digital technology, not the amplified technology of the electric guitar, which was what blues and rhythm & blues were, so, I wondered, looking at the twelve-bar structure, What is really the connection? But then, in the film, there's that scene at the Blues and Jazz Record Mart, where hip-hop artist Juice is checking out the old album covers, and you start looking at the personalities, you start looking at the stories that are being told, and the whole vibe. And you see it's the same as rap music today. When Louis Satterfield says, "My grandmother didn't want me to play music because she didn't want me to play them blues." It was the devil's music, and it was sex, and it was all that stuff that your parents didn't want you to do, just like hip-hop and rap. You start seeing the similarities between the different kinds of music, and you see that every generation has got to find it on its own sound. In the world we live in today, which is so instantaneous, there are kids out there who don't even know who Chuck D is, who think that Eminem is the man who invented rap. We move so fast, you can lose that sense of history.

I hadn't realized that Chuck D is a musicologist and historian, and that he also has a tremendous interest in finding these parallels. There was also the indie record-label connection: Chess was an indie record label, and hip-hop and rap were born out of a new generation of indie record labels, which were also built on a new technology, a digital technology. So the basic similarity is that every generation tries to find what you would call that street, raw, real sound. That's what the Chicago blues had. That's what lit the imagination of my generation, and every generation has to find its way to turn on and light the fire—that's the source. "This world may put you down, but no, you don't have me down. Not tonight, you don't!" Koko Taylor said that, which is interesting because we shot a good part of this at her club, and I thought that was an interesting comment. She said, "People say *the blues,* and you think it's about the sorrows in your life and the difficulties and the troubles—obviously, a lot of

music is that. But my blues inspire you. My blues makes you want to get up and dance." And I think that is the common bond, and that you want to make that connection. The album *Fathers and Sons* that Marshall produced back in 1968, which had members of the Paul Butterfield Blues Band—Paul Butterfield, Mike Bloomfield, and Sam Lay, playing with Muddy Waters and Otis Spann—it was those guys doing it, connecting it. And this generation is just beginning, it's kind of worked its way back, it's gotten to funk and soul, and now it is about to discover the blues, the source.

Another level of this whole thing is that great art, great culture, great music are created sometimes in the craziest ways, in the most spontaneous ways, in the most insane ways. I've always believed that blues and jazz have that aesthetic, which is: You find the continuity in chaos, you find the inspiration, and you let go. That influenced me deeply as a filmmaker. It's what makes it authentic. Meeting a lot of these characters with Marshall and Chuck just reinforced that belief. In other words, that's what everybody wants to try to get: What is real? As Chuck says, "What was the Chess sound?" It was the raw, real sound. Why did the Rolling Stones want to record in Chess studios? It had that authenticity, that sense that this is really it. And that kind of feeling just can't ever be truly programmed. In the end there is something spontaneous and alive that moves you. As Willie Dixon says, "The blues are the roots and everything else is the fruits."

—Marc Levin

"It's no doubt that there's a connection [between the blues and hip-hop]. Hip-hop is definitely a child of the blues. And I think you gotta know the roots to really grow. It's [like] knowing your parents, it's like knowing your culture, so you could be proud of that culture and take it to the world." —*Common*

MUDDY, WOLF, AND ME: ADVENTURES IN THE BLUES TRADE
BY PETER WOLF

This all happened many years ago when I was a student at the Boston Museum School of Fine Arts looking to become a painter somewhat in the German Expressionist manner. But then I was sidetracked by the blues.

I got my induction at a very early age. At twelve, through a series of the usual preadolescent alienations and personal dislocations, I started going to the legendary Fifty-second Street jazz club Birdland. You could do that back in those days if you were accompanied by an adult, which was anyone eighteen years or older, and I heard Art Blakey and the Jazz Messengers, Dinah Washington doing *very* double-entendre songs, Cannonball Adderley, and a host of others. It was just a natural progression to start going up to the Apollo Theatre in Harlem for the Wednesday night show (which included Amateur Night in addition to the entire bill), and that was what I did all through high school.

That was where I first heard Muddy Waters. It was on a show called the Blues Cavalcade, with Jimmy Reed, Bobby "Blue" Bland, Jimmy Witherspoon, Muddy, and B.B. King, and it was a time when young black people were reacting against the blues. "We don't pick cotton no more," someone yelled out in the middle of B.B.'s rap, and feelings were definitely running high when Muddy took the stage. Except he didn't just take it, he *commanded* it. And when he went into that jitterbug dance that you would never see in later years but that you can catch on film from the 1960 Newport Jazz Festival, the crowd went wild. Even though his music was the most downhome thing on the bill, Muddy wasn't

talking about picking cotton—he was saying, "Don't jive with me, I'm gonna get respect," not in so many words, and with the suggestion that it could be taken as all in good fun, but with an undercurrent that broke the spell and brought that whole audience back to the blues. That was the power of Muddy's music.

By the next time I saw him I had hitchhiked around the country a bit, begun art school in Boston, and started fooling around with a bunch of like-minded fellow art students, trying to put together a little blues band that became the Hallucinations and would eventually metamorphose into the J. Geils Band. I was trying to learn how to play the harp, and we went to see Muddy at the Jazz Workshop, kind of a sharp upscale place where it was more common to see Thelonious Monk or Charles Mingus, two of my other heroes.

Muddy was, as always, impeccably dressed, wearing an elegant gray suit with an off-color white shirt, slim, perfectly knotted tie, manicured fingernails, and beautifully shined shoes—it was impossible to take your eyes off him as he approached the stage with that slow regal walk. But even before he took the stand, his band had set the stage for him with several instrumentals and a vocal number or two that showed off *their* virtuosity. There was James Cotton on harp, sounding like a cross between Little Walter and Sonny Boy Williamson, and Otis Spann playing some of the most intricate, *deepest* piano fills you ever heard while puffing on a cigarette and sipping a glass of gin even as he was turning around to talk to some pretty young lady sitting up next to him. There were guitarists Sammy Lawhorn, Pee Wee Madison, and Luther "Georgia Boy Snake" Johnson, bass player Calvin "Fuzzy" Jones, and drummer Francis Clay, each with a distinct and individual style, musical and sartorial, of his own. But then it was Show Time, the band would segue into its introductory theme, and Cotton introduced Muddy as the Star of the Show. Which is exactly what he was from the moment he took the stage.

He raised his hand, and as he slowly brought it down, the band stopped on a dime. It was as if he possessed some master switch with which just by the slightest gesture—a nod, a wink, the raising or lowering of his hand—he could control all that power, all the dynamics and all the musicality of that remarkable band. Muddy smiled then, raised his hand, and by the time it came down, the music had already started, at a very, very slow tempo at first, almost like a slow crawl that pulled you into the story he was about to tell. That story seemed to come from somewhere deep within, and when Muddy closed his eyes to sing, it was as if he were going somewhere far away and mysterious, and you were going there with him. The band's gaze never wavered; even though it was clear that this was all as intricately arranged as an Ellington tone poem, they never took their eyes off him, as if they were all playing the song for the very first time—except, of course, for Spann, who was still talking to that pretty lady by his side.

In between sets, a friend of mine and I wanted to try to figure out how James Cotton got such a unique sound. We were both Little Walter fanatics, and this was the first time either of us had sat close enough to anyone with anything resembling the Little Walter sound to try to figure out where that sound might come from. We could see it wasn't the

Muddy Waters and a young Peter Wolf, 1964

microphone, which was just your standard-issue Radio Shack bullet mike, so we figured it must be some secret device in Cotton's amplifier that helped him create all those swoops and bends and soaring special effects. We waited till the band had left the stage, and then we decided to go up and look behind that beat-up old red amp. We weren't really aware that we were trespassing on someone's private domain, and it never crossed our minds that we might be taken for thieves, musical or otherwise, but then all of a sudden we sensed this looming presence behind us, along with the strong smell of Scotch and a kind of heat all around.

"What the hell are you doin' up here?" demanded a large, angry James Cotton, just staring down at us with unforgiving eyes. "We were just looking at your amp," I replied, unable to think of anything else to say. "And what the hell are you looking at my amp for?" he said, getting even angrier. "Well just to see how you—you know—

Muddy Waters celebrating Father's Day with his extended family, Chicago, 1973

you make that sound. How you get it. What kind of machine you got back there." "It's got nothing to do with the damned amp," he said, more exasperated now than really angry, but in a manner that made it very clear that my friend and I should get the hell off the stage—*now*. I'm not sure that we altogether believed him—we knew there still had to be some magic involved—but we didn't raise any more questions, we just got out while the getting was good.

The next time I saw Cotton it was under less trying circumstances, and it was to become the basis for a lifelong friendship with Muddy and the band. Muddy had been booked into a folk club in Cambridge for the better part of a week, and the manager had alerted me that they would be arriving in the late afternoon. I had started playing around town a little with my own band by now, but that just made me even more of a fan, so I got to the club by midafternoon and sat on the steps waiting for their arrival. Finally, after several hours, this big long Cadillac pulled up, followed by a station wagon

crammed with musicians and equipment. Muddy's driver, Bo, a huge man with a hard look and a suspicion of anyone who might take advantage of his employer, got out, came around to the passenger side, and opened up the door for these two perfectly shined shoes to plant themselves on the pavement. I rushed over and said, "Hello, Mr. Waters. I saw you not too long ago at the Jazz Workshop, and I'm a huge fan." He nodded graciously, almost as if he might have remembered, then introduced me to the rest of the band and allowed me to help them carry in their equipment, including, of course, that beat-up red amp that I still believed had to contain the secret of James Cotton's sound. The band proceeded to set up while Muddy went to the small dressing room, and I walked into the bathroom, where I overheard a conversation between James Cotton and Otis Spann. They were counting their money, and Spann said to Cotton, "Man, you know they're calling this place a coffeehouse." And Cotton said, "Does that mean they only serve coffee?" "I don't know," Otis said, "but I just found out they ain't got no booze." "No booze?" said Cotton. "Man, we better find some place to get a bottle." Well, that for me was just the sound of opportunity knocking. "I'll get a bottle," I said, ignoring the fact that I was two years underage and looked it. So I rushed down to the liquor store to buy my heroes some whiskey, after first finding someone who would go into the store and buy it for me.

That was how I became a kind of impromptu valet to the band. All of a sudden everyone was coming up to me like I was their best friend, and I was scurrying to and fro buying whiskey, running errands, just trying to make things right. Later that night in between sets, the band stepped outside for a drink, since Muddy occupied the one tiny dressing room and the bathroom had become too crowded. I told them I had an apartment just a couple of blocks away, so Spann, Cotton, and Sammy Lawhorn all followed me to my place, a cramped, one-room, almost furnitureless space with a mattress on the floor, a piece of foam rubber on a board that served as a couch, and several large stacks of 45s. "We should let Muddy know about this place," Otis said, and the next night Muddy showed up, preceded by Bo, and they all sat around smoking and drinking, just kicking back, and all of a sudden my apartment felt like the Taj Mahal.

Within a couple of nights, James Cotton had moved in and, in a pattern that would be repeated in various configurations over the next ten or twelve years whenever Muddy or his band members came to town, we quickly worked out a routine, where I would take Cotton to the market to buy food for the band's dinner, then Bo would bring Muddy around in the late afternoon and Cotton would start preparing a huge downhome feast. I'd leave them alone then so they could have their privacy, but when I'd come back there would always be a card game going on amid gales of laughter, loud discussion about every subject under the sun, and if the drinking got out of hand, the kind of occasional disagreement that could lead to the drawing of pocketknives but which was always quelled by a look or a nod from Muddy. I could never get over the unlikely sight of Muddy in my own apartment, shoes off, shirt and suit jacket neatly hung up, wearing a T-shirt and a do-rag (to preserve his carefully straightened and sculpted hair) on his head. Sometimes I would play him some of his early singles, he would ask for certain ones that he hadn't heard in years, and we would sit and talk about the music and the early recording sessions. I would read to him from the blues books and magazines I had around the house—he was fascinated by all the newfound

interest in the blues, and there was an unspoken understanding between us that it was up to me to communicate whatever I thought might be of particular interest by reading it aloud to him. But most of all, what made me feel good was that he clearly felt at home. We could sit without talking sometimes. We could talk about nothing. Muddy might bring up the baseball standings. Or he might describe a woman he knew. It just felt right.

I got to know James Cotton really well, too, but in a different kind of way. He had come up under Sonny Boy Williamson II in West Memphis and recorded as a teenager for Sun Records, but he had never played in the more urban, big-band-oriented Little Walter style until he replaced Junior Wells in Muddy's band, after Walter had gone out on his own. He told me how nervous he was about filling such big shoes, but most of all about trying to re-create the pioneering sound that Little Walter had established with the band. One time he had even approached Walter at a club to try to get some advice, but Walter just took the harmonica from him, turned his back, played some of his typically swinging Lester Young–styled riffs, and then turned back around and said to James, "See? It's that easy." Which, of course, just made his young replacement all the more insecure.

Then one night, after James had been working with Muddy for only a few months, Little Walter came into the club where they were playing, took the mike and harmonica from him, and just blew the place away. James retreated to the back of the room practically in tears. He thought he might just as well quit the band right then and there, but just at that moment Sonny Boy Williamson happened to walk in and, seeing how upset his young protégé was, asked him what was wrong. "They all so crazy about Walter," James said. "I just can't get that sound."

Sonny Boy, a proud, irascible, somewhat inscrutable older man with the look of a grand vizier, drew himself up to his full height and said, "I taught you my style, and if you was doing what I taught you, you wouldn't be having no problem." Then, after telling Cotton, "I'm going to teach you something I want you always to remember," he got up onstage and, without even using the microphone, started playing in what he called his "country style." By the time he was done, as James recalled, he had three harmonicas going at once, two out of the side of his mouth and one that he was blowing through his nose. The club went stone crazy, and Walter stomped out in a huff. Then Sonny Boy came back to Cotton and said, "Don't you *ever* doubt yourself again." It was a story, I realized, that James was telling me as much because he knew I was having a hard time trying to find a harp style of my own as to tell me about his own youthful difficulties. And I thought to myself, Well, you know, at one time James was searching for that secret machine, too, same as me!

Howlin' Wolf came in right behind Muddy, and Muddy tried to warn me off him. "That Wolf, he's crazy," he told me. "You stay away from him." But, of course, I knew there was a long-standing rivalry between them, and there was no way anyone could have warned me off someone whose music was so powerful and had exerted so huge an influence on me anyway. Mudddy was right in one way, though: Wolf *was* different. And as much as I tried to assume the same role with him as I had with Muddy, and as often as he came by my apartment with various band members, it was never quite the same.

You just didn't get that close to Wolf. He maintained at all times an air of intentional inscrutability that was almost impenetrable. I remember one time at the club, this kid said, "Isn't it great we've got two Wolfs in the same city?" And even though it wasn't me saying it, Wolf just gave me that icy stare that could go right through you and said, "As far as I know there's just one Wolf," glaring at me with a look that I didn't even want to *try* to comprehend.

Where Muddy was cool and elegant, with all the glamour of a Hollywood movie star, Wolf sent out a signal that said to all onlookers, "Look out! Proceed with caution." Muddy's music was always insinuating that there was something going on behind closed doors, but Wolf's performance was about something else—it was almost like, "Hey, baby, break down the doors, bust open the windows, you're going deep into the heart of darkness with me tonight." I remember one time there was a young college girl sitting at the front table with two of her friends, and Wolf just stalked toward her, put his face right up next to hers, dangled the microphone between his legs, and waggled it around not suggestively—altogether explicitly. Then he strutted back and forth across the stage, his eyes rolling back in his head, until suddenly he stopped dead, gave his band members a strange hypnotic stare, waved his hands once in the air, and then from his great height fell with a thud to his knees. I think everyone in the room was tilting as far back in their chairs as they could possibly go—I don't know if I can ever recall a moment quite like it, when an audience was as enchanted as it was petrified. But that was Wolf, on and off the stage.

With the J. Geils Band I got to play and travel with Muddy. But whenever he came to town I was still his Boston valet. He had a bad automobile accident in 1969, and after that he couldn't make the long drives with the band anymore, so he would fly in, and after the gig I would take him to get something to eat and then we'd go out to the airport and wait for whenever his plane was scheduled to depart in the morning. We would talk, and sometimes he would nap under the cold fluorescent light, and I would find myself looking at him in some wonderment not just that I was sitting in a lonesome air terminal next to the great Muddy Waters but that it was all so *ordinary* somehow, that all of the grandeur of his music, the nobility of his character, could be contained within such sad, humdrum surroundings.

Sometimes I thought about the journey he had traveled, how he had known the young Robert Johnson and Son House, seen Louis Jordan and all the great jump bands, absorbed a tradition that went back more than a century. He had come out of another world but found his own voice, a voice that transcended time and space and was just as up to date and contemporary, just as *vital* at the end as it had been when he made his first recordings on the Stovall Plantation. The last time I saw him, we sat together all night at Logan Airport, and in the morning I walked him to the gate. He was limping badly by that time, and it was almost as if he knew we might never see each other again. "Little Wolf," he said, in that familiar form of address that the Howlin' Wolf would have instantly rejected, "Peter the Wolf," he said, "thank you, thank you, thank you, my friend." He repeated it once or twice more, and then, with that regal bearing that never let you forget you were in the presence of a *king*, he walked down the jetway to the plane, turning just once to wave before he disappeared from sight. 🖎

Otis Spann, Willie Mae "Big Mama" Thornton, Muddy Waters, James Cotton, Luther "Georgia Boy Snake" Johnson Jr., Francis Clay, and Samuel Lawhorn *(counterclockwise from bottom left),* San Francisco, 1965

CHICAGO PEP *By Robert Palmer*
[From *Deep Blues,* 1982]

One humid night in May 1978, I drove to Morgen's Liquors, at Sixty-first and Calumet on the South Side, to hear Sunnyland [Slim] play. Morgen's was in the shadow of an El stop, and when one walked in, it seemed to be a perfectly ordinary ghetto liquor store. But behind a curtain in the back, where you'd expect to find a stockroom, there was a long, crowded, dimly lit bar, and in back of that, behind a heavy door, was a plain, square music room, with cheap plywood wall paneling, bare bulbs, and a few paper streamers. Sunnyland Slim, long, lanky, and weathered, was sitting on the tiny bandstand behind a battered red Wurlitzer electric piano, flanked by guitarist Louis Myers, from Byhalia, Mississippi, and a much younger rhythm section. He flexed his arms, grimaced, and downed a shot of booze—he was stabbed in both arms in a 1968 South Side robbery and says he has trouble limbering up—and then Myers counted off a crisp shuffle rhythm and stepped to the microphone. "Woke up this mornin', lookin' 'round for my shoes/ You know I had them mean old walkin' blues." It was "the theme," as Muddy calls it, the Delta anthem, and the crowd, all black except for my friend and me, was a middle-aged Mississippi crowd. The beat was different— a trace of funk from the bassist, snappy fills from the drummer—but Louis and Sunnyland were playing "Walkin' Blues" pretty much the way they played it in the thirties.

Slim sounded magnificent, rapping out tone clusters in the treble and walking the basses with all the authority of someone who's been playing the blues for sixty-odd years. "I don't like to play in these kind of places no more," he said during a break, pushing his face up close to be heard over the buzz of conversation and the B.B. King record on the jukebox. "I'll be seventy-two soon. I just been out to California, playin' in Europe. . . . I'm just down here helping Louis out on his gig." Muddy's name came up. "Me and Muddy started out together at the same time," he said. "I brought him in to play guitar for me when I got the call to make a record, 1947. We did a couple of my numbers, and then the man asked me, 'Say, what about your boy there? Can he sing?' Talkin' about Muddy, you know. And I said, 'Like a bird.' "

Sunnyland met Muddy Waters at the Flame Club on Chicago's South Side sometime in the mid-forties. It was Muddy's first really decent musical job, fifty-two dollars a week as guitar accompanist to his old friend Eddie Boyd. He was still holding down a day job as well. His musical engagements in Chicago up to that point, had included house parties with guitarists Jimmy Rogers and Lee Brown, occasional out-of-town gigs with John Lee "Sonny Boy" Williamson (who was drinking more and more and seems to have appreciated the fact that Muddy owned a car and was willing to drive to nearby towns like Gary and back to Chicago overnight), and a few informal tavern engagements in West Side joints that paid five dollars a night, if that, with Rogers on harmonica and Blue Smitty (Claude Smith, from Marianna, in the Arkansas Delta) on second guitar. During the course of these jobs Muddy picked up, largely from Smitty, a rudimentary but adequate knowledge of guitar styles that were at the time considered "modern." When he came to Chicago, he was limited to Delta-style bottleneck playing, while Smitty's more urban style has been described . . . as "an awkward compendium of such diverse influences as [Big Boy] Crudup, Yank Rachell, and [the jazz guitarist] Charlie Christian." It was a single-string lead guitar style, a more basic version of the kind of melodic runs and fill-ins a jazz guitarist might play behind a singer.

The sophisticated jump blues of performers like Louis Jordan and smooth blues ballads, as sung by Charles Brown, Nat "King" Cole, and other California-based artists, were the latest trends in black popular music, and these were the sounds Eddie Boyd was purveying at the Flame Club. Despite the coaching he'd had from Smitty, Muddy just didn't fit in. "Eddie wanted me to play like Johnny Moore," he says, referring to the fluent, jazzy guitarist who picked tastefully behind Charles Brown. "He wanted it to be a sweet kind of blues." But then Sonny Boy Williamson offered Boyd a better-paying job playing for steel mill workers in Gary, and he left the Blue Flame; Sunnyland Slim replaced him. With Sunnyland and Muddy playing strong Delta bass patterns, Blue Smitty filling in modern-style leads, and all three singing, they had a jumping little combo. But Smitty kept sweet-talking various women and disappearing into a nearby hotel when he was supposed to be on the bandstand, and one evening he drank too much and made the mistake of picking a fight with Sunnyland. As a result, the band lost their job, and their next gig at the Cotton Club as well.

By that time, Sunnyland had had enough of Smitty, but he liked Muddy. They were both from the Delta, both old enough to be serious and professional about their music (Muddy was in his early thirties, Sunnyland almost forty), both proud, dignified men who showed up for work well dressed and sober—even if they didn't always stay that way all night. "I got drunk and got in a fight once on that job with Eddie Boyd," Muddy admits. "I was foolin' around with one of them little ol' girls. She made

good money and was paying the note on a car, and she started it all. I throwed all the whiskey bottles they had on the table, and when I got through, I went behind the bar and started throwing *them* whiskey bottles. They put me in jail overnight. But mostly, you know, I didn't do that. I wanted to be nationally known, and I worked on it." Sunnyland stayed in touch.

In September 1946, Lester Melrose arranged a session for Columbia Records featuring three unknown blues vocalists. Sunnyland, who was asked to play piano on the session, made sure one of them was Muddy. (The other two, Homer Harris and James "Beale Street" Clark, rapidly dropped from sight.) Muddy and Harris played guitars, Sunnyland filled in the sound with his rolling upper register tremolos, and an unidentified bassist and drummer carried the rhythm. Muddy tried his best to sound modern. He picked simple single-string lead figures and heavy boogie basses on his three vocal selections, and his bottleneck was nowhere in evidence. His singing was strong but restrained. The result was a set of recordings that were slick and shallow compared to what Muddy could do but too downhome, it seems, for Columbia. The company released nothing from the session, and Lester Melrose, the kingpin of Chicago blues recording for more than a decade, let the city's next and eventually its biggest blues star slip through his fingers.

By this time Muddy was working days at "the best job I ever had in my life," driving a delivery truck for a company that manufactured venetian blinds. "After I learned all the calls in the city," he says, "I'd take my

"For me, to be able to make a record with Muddy Waters [*The Muddy Waters Woodstock Album*], that was the pinnacle of success. And after the playing was over, of course, I'd get to go out and eat supper with him. *Man!*" —Levon Helm

load out at eight-thirty, and by one in the afternoon I'd be back at my house—in the bed. Around four-thirty I'd get up and carry the mail to the post office—boom!—I'm through. I had to sleep 'cause I was playing five nights a week."

Sometime in 1947 Sunnyland arranged to record a session for Aristocrat, a company that had been started earlier that year by two Polish-born Jews, Leonard and Phil Chess, along with a woman named Evelyn Aron. The Chess brothers, who arrived in the United States in 1928, had worked hard; by 1947 they owned several bars and clubs on the South Side, including the Macomba, where popular jazz and rhythm & blues artists performed. Their first Aristocrat releases were strictly jazz and city R&B, but Sammy Goldstein, the company's talent scout, thought Aristocrat might do well in the blues field and called Sunnyland to arrange a session. It was going to be a duo, with Big Crawford on bass, but late in the game someone, probably Goldstein, suggested the addition of a guitarist, and Sunnyland thought of Muddy. "I caught the streetcar up there to Muddy's house," the pianist recalls, "and [his live-in girlfriend] Annie Mae told me he was out with the truck. The session was for two o'clock." A friend of Muddy's, Antra Bolton, was there visiting and offered to track Muddy down, and since his delivery routine rarely varied, it didn't take long. Muddy had been disheartened by the Columbia experience and wasn't about to let another opportunity to get on records pass him by. He called his boss, explained in a voice shaking with emotion that his cousin had been murdered in a ghetto alley, turned the truck over to Bolton, who finished the run, hurried home to get his guitar, and made it on time to Universal Studios, on North Wacker Drive in downtown Chicago, for the session.

First Sunnyland recorded two numbers, including one of his best, "Johnson Machine Gun," a violent urban fantasy with a touch of sinister humor. "I'm gonna buy me a Johnson machine gun," he sang, with a high, slightly pinched sound that was more than a little reminiscent of Dr. Clayton, "and a carload of explosion balls/I'm gonna be a walkin' cyclone, from Saginaw to the Niagara Falls." The song began as a boast and ended as a threat: "Now, little girl, the undertaker's been here, girl, and I gave him your height and size/Now if you don't be makin' whoopee with the Devil tomorrow this time, baby, God knows you'll be surprised." After he recorded the more conventional "Fly Right, Little Girl," someone, again probably Goldstein, asked him if Muddy could sing. Characteristically, Muddy was ready, this time with two tightly composed original blues that were much better than the mostly traditional material he'd recorded for Columbia. "Little Anna Mae," the second number he recorded, was a personal account of trouble with his live-in girlfriend; "Gypsy Woman" was more intriguing: " . . . Well now you know I went to a gypsy woman to have my fortune told/Say you better go back home, son, and peek through your, your keyhole/You know the gypsy woman told me that you your mother's bad luck child/Well you're havin' a good time now, but that'll be trouble after while. . . ."

Muddy still thought people wanted to hear modern guitar playing, not his Delta bottleneck blues, and once again he played single-string lead lines. But his work was much improved—he sounded something like Joe Willie Wilkins or perhaps Willie Johnson, two Delta guitarists with backgrounds similar to his who began recording in Memphis a few years later. And he was singing strongly, letting his Delta pronunciations of words like "gypsaay" come out naturally, varying his timbre and playing with pitches to suggest subtle shadings of emotion and meaning. The lyrics were probably inspired by the gypsy fortune-telling salons of Chicago's Maxwell Street area and should have been perfect for the black blues audience of the period. But Leonard Chess didn't think much of the record. He let it sit on the shelf for several months before he released it and apparently didn't push it even then.

Then, early in 1948, Aristocrat called Muddy in to do another session. . . . At the rehearsal that immediately preceded it, Muddy ran through his repertoire. This time, having failed twice in his attempts at contemporary urban blues, he brought his bottleneck and tried some of his old Delta numbers, including several he'd recorded for the Library of Congress. "What's he singing? I can't understand what he's singing," Chess reportedly protested. . . .

Despite Chess' skepticism, Muddy recorded "I Can't Be Satisfied" and "I Feel Like Going Home." On a Saturday morning in April 1948, copies of the record went out to Aristocrat's South Side outlets, which included barber and beauty shops, variety stores, and other "mom and dad" businesses, as well as a few record shops. A little more than twelve hours later, the initial pressing was sold out.

The next morning Muddy got up early and went right over to the Maxwell Radio Record Company. The crowded, chaotic little shop was run by one-eyed Bernard Abrams, another of Maxwell Street's Eastern European Jewish immigrants. Abrams had primitive recording equipment in the back and had made acetates for a number of Maxwell Street blues performers. Muddy had played in front of the store in 1947 to help advertise the release of one of two discs Abrams put out in a brief and discouraging attempt to enter the record business, "I Just Keep Loving Her" and "Ora Nelle Blues" by harmonica player Little Walter Jacobs and guitarist Othum Brown. Muddy had been playing with Little Walter off and on for a few years but says he "kind of bypassed around Walter for a while 'cause he had a bad, mean temper, always stayed in fights." He didn't hang around Maxwell Street much, either, but this Sunday morning he wanted a couple of copies of a certain record—*his* record. The crafty Abrams had stockpiled a

few and was selling them for $1.10 each, one to a customer (list price was 79 cents). Muddy complained that it was his name on the label, but Abrams adamantly refused to sell him more than one copy or lower the price. Disgusted, Muddy took the one record, went home, and sent Annie Mae over for another one.

Leonard Chess was caught off guard by the success of "I Can't Be Satisfied"/"I Feel Like Going Home," but, like any good businessman, he knew a good thing when he saw it. More copies were rapidly pressed, and soon the disc was selling steadily in Chicago and throughout the South. "I had a hot blues out, man," Muddy says, still feeling cocky about it after all these years. "I'd be driving my truck, and whenever I'd see a neon beer sign, I'd stop, go in, look at the jukebox, and see is my record on there. I might buy me a beer and play the record and then leave. Don't tell nobody nothing. Before long, every blues joint there was, that record was on the jukebox. And if you come in and sat there for a little while, if anybody was in there, they gonna punch it. Pretty soon I'd hear it walking along the street. I'd hear it *driving* along the street. About June or July that record was getting *really* hot. I would be driving home from playing, two or three o'clock in the morning, and I had a convertible, with the top back 'cause it was warm. I could hear people all upstairs playing that record. It would be *rolling* up there, man. I heard it all over. One time I heard it coming from way upstairs somewhere, and it scared me. I thought I had died." 🎸

"Man, I'm Jewish, you know, I've been Jewish for years. Hell, man, I'm no Son House. I have not been pissed on, stepped on, shit on. But [Paul] Butterfield's something else. There's no white bullshit with him. It wouldn't matter if he was green. If he was a planaria, a tuna fish sandwich, Butterfield would still be into the blues." —*Michael Bloomfield*

MEMPHIS MINNIE AND THE CUTTING CONTEST
BY CHRISTOPHER JOHN FARLEY

Before *It's Showtime at the Apollo,* before *American Idol,* and long before Eminem faced off against rival rappers in Detroit, blues musicians used to battle each other in what were called "cutting contests." The way Big Bill Broonzy tells it in his autobiography, June 26, 1933—his fortieth birthday—marked the day that he and Memphis Minnie, who'd moved to Chicago in 1930, engaged in what he described as "the first contest between blues singers that was ever given in the U.S.A." The night Big Bill took on Memphis Minnie may have been the most celebrated cutting contest of them all.

The tale begins in a Chicago club. It was a good night for the blues: The hall was packed with blues fans, there was lots of booze on hand, and there were plenty of musicians in attendance to drink that booze, including Big Bill and Memphis Minnie. Bill and Minnie had a long history together: They had played many of the same joints, they knew many of the same people. For a while, according to Big Bill, there was some other woman going around Chicago calling herself Memphis Minnie. When Big Bill ran into the imposter, he let her have it, saying, "Hell, no, that's not Memphis Minnie, because the real Memphis Minnie can pick a guitar and sing as good as any man I've ever heard. This woman plays like a woman guitar player."

Big Bill had plenty of respect for Minnie. So, on that June night in that Chicago club, when a cutting contest was proposed, Big Bill got a little worried about squaring off against Memphis Minnie. The prize: a bottle of whiskey and a bottle of gin. The crowd began to buzz: a woman versus a man? Of course Big Bill was going to win! One patron came up to the bluesman and told him that he was sure he was going to come out on top. "I don't know about that," Big Bill told the man. "But I'm gonna try to win those two bottles so I can get in a corner and drink until I get enough."

The judges were picked: Sleepy John Estes, Tampa Red, and Richard Jones. The bottle of gin and the bottle of whiskey were ready. Other musicians wrapped up their sets, and at 1:30 a.m. the cutting contest was set to start.

⊕ ⊕ ⊕ ⊕ ⊕

A couple things people should know about Memphis Minnie: She wasn't born in Memphis, and her real name wasn't Minnie. Her given name was Lizzie Douglas, and she was born in Algiers, Louisiana, just outside of New Orleans, on June 3, 1897. She was the eldest of thirteen children, but from an early age she was a standout. When she was eight, her father bought her a guitar for Christmas, and she quickly learned how to play it. The rest of the Douglas family worked the fields as share-croppers, but young Lizzie—everyone called her Kid at that time—didn't much care for that sort of labor so, when she was thirteen years old, she left home, taking the guitar with her. And of course, she headed straight to Memphis. Beale Street, to be exact.

People nowadays tend to think of the blues as something tragic, something downbeat, a kind of music that drapes around you and weighs you down like a wet overcoat. Those weren't the kind of blues that Memphis Minnie played and those weren't the

Memphis Minnie, circa 1946

instrument. She had three husbands during her lifetime, and each of them was a musician. In 1929, a talent scout spotted her and her second husband, Joe McCoy, playing for dimes on Beale Street and invited them to record. The record company renamed them Kansas Joe and Memphis Minnie, and she began churning out the hits, including such songs as "When the Levee Breaks" and "Bumble Bee." Her voice was full of fun, loaded with sex, and charged with smarts; her guitar playing was adept and vibrant and seemed to make melodies jump around in the ear. Lots of folks played the guitar, but Memphis Minnie could make you believe that her instrument was at play, that it was a living thing, and that it was having as good a time as you were. Said Big Bill, "Memphis Minnie can make a guitar speak words, she can make a guitar cry, moan, talk, and whistle the blues."

⊕ ⊕ ⊕ ⊕ ⊕

So Big Bill knew what he was up against when it came to a cutting contest with Memphis Minnie. But the challenge had been made, so he had to do his best to face up to it. At 1:30 a.m., one of the judges, Tampa Red, called Big Bill to the stand. He was expected to go first. It was a good crowd—when they caught sight of Big Bill, they cheered for ten minutes before he even started his first song. Then he got into it: He played one of his best numbers, one of his signature tunes, a song called "Just a Dream." Then he followed up with "Make My Getaway." After that, he was done. He had taken his best shot; now it was Memphis Minnie's turn.

Tampa Red called out for Memphis Minnie to come up and play her two selections. A hush settled over the audience as she began. The first song she played was "Me and My Chauffeur Blues," a rollicking number that chugs along steadily like a

kind of blues that she lived. Memphis Minnie's blues were red hot. Around 1916, she hooked up with the Ringling Brothers circus and toured the South. When she would play her guitar for the crowds, she would stand up on a chair, lay her guitar across her head, and play her music any which way she could to get a response. Men who knew her also understood she was just as rambunctious in her personal life. In the biography *Woman With Guitar: Memphis Minnie's Blues* by Paul and Beth Garon, one musician, Johnny Shines, recalled, "Any men that would fool with her she'd go for them right away. She didn't take no foolishness off them. Guitar, pocketknife, pistol, anything she'd get her hand on she'd use it." Her friend Homesick James had this to say about her: "That woman was tougher than a man. No man was strong enough to mess around with her."

Any man who wanted to spend time with Memphis Minnie had to know how to play an

car on a sunny Saturday afternoon drive. It was the perfect song to get a rise out of the crowd; the lyrics are wittily bawdy (in the song, she sings of wanting her chauffeur to "drive me downtown") with just a hint of violence (she also sings of shooting her chauffeur down if he drives any other girls). After she finished, Big Bill reported later, the crowd cheered for twenty minutes. Memphis Minnie's second song was another winner: "Looking the World Over." With its cries of *"whoo-hoo!"* and the affable guitar solo at the song's center, it was another crowd pleaser.

People connected to Memphis Minnie's blues because, although her music was rooted in her own life, her concerns and experiences were so broad and universal that her songs became about everything. Indeed, on her song "Looking the World Over," she even makes the boast that she's seen everything "but the bottom of the sea." In a way, Memphis Minnie was everybody, only a little bit bolder, a little bit stronger, and a little bit sexier than everybody else. Her lyrics documented a personal history and people's history that you couldn't find in school books. "When the Levee Breaks" was based on the famous flood that hit Mississippi two years before the tune was recorded; "Frankie Jean (That Trottin' Fool)," a song about a horse, was based on a mule Minnie had as a kid; "He's in the Ring" and "Joe Louis Strut" were her tributes to the heavyweight champ; and "Ma Rainey" was her elegy to the pioneering blueswoman.

So Memphis Minnie won the contest, just as Big Bill had feared and kind of expected from the start. She was a bard of the people, and the people responded. Two of the judges, Estes and Jones, went over to Minnie, picked her up and carried her around on their shoulders. But Big Bill ended up with at least some of the winnings. As the crowd celebrated, Big Bill grabbed the whiskey and drank it. It was his birthday, after all.

Now, it should be said that at least some of this tale could be apocryphal. Big Bill's memory, according to many blues experts, wasn't always accurate, and he was known to take artistic license with the telling of his tales. But other blues musicians who were contemporaries of Memphis Minnie testify to her prowess at cutting contests. James Watt, a singer with the group the Blues Rockers, recalls Minnie going toe to toe with the great Muddy Waters. Said Watt, "They used to have these contests, the one who win the contest, they would get the fifth of whiskey. And Memphis Minnie would tell Muddy, 'I'm getting this fifth of whiskey.' She'd get it every time, though. She would get it *every time*. Muddy just couldn't do nothing with Memphis, no, uh-uh, not back then. . . . I saw her beat ten different artists one night."

Female vocalists such as Ma Rainey, Bessie Smith, and Billie Holiday helped create and perfect the blues. But Memphis Minnie helped women take full possession of the form. Vocalists—wrongly—are often seen as mere interpreters, and not true creators. Oftentimes, it's true, they are not songwriters, but artists who find new art in the work of others. Instrumentalists—guitarists, pianists, horn players, and the like—are seen by some as true creators because they carry tools in their hands and use them to beat ideas and inspiration into new forms. Memphis Minnie was one of the tool carriers. She was a creator any way you looked at it. She proved, if anybody doubted it, that women could sing songs and play them, too.

Although she began her musical life playing an acoustic guitar, later in her career she also employed an electric guitar, becoming a pioneer with that instrument as well. Her performances, judging from the reports of those who saw them, seem to have been precursors to the guitar heroics of the rock & roll era. Sadly, there are no known recordings of Memphis Minnie on electric guitar, and we are left to wonder just what her guitar, charged with lightning and played with abandon, might have sounded like.

In the 1950s, Memphis Minnie began a slow decline. In 1960, she suffered her first stroke and, after residing in Chicago for thirty years, moved back to Memphis to live with her sister Daisy. In 1961, her third husband, Son Joe (with whom she recorded "Me and My Chauffeur Blues," among other songs), died, and his passing so upset Minnie that she suffered another stroke and had to move into a nursing home. In her final days she was very poor and was forced to sell her guitar and accept welfare and contributions from a local church. When she was in her mid-seventies, a small blues magazine appealed to the public for charity: "Everyone enjoys her music, but real appreciation should be shown by way of small gifts or just letters to cheer her. We just can't forget the poor woman because she can't perform anymore, so please help."

Memphis Minnie isn't a name that most of today's rock, rap, and pop fans know; the ripples of her fame, in the twenty-first century, have barely moved beyond the circle of the blues. Because of the health problems she experienced in her sixties, she was unable to hit the road or reenter the recording studio for any significant amount of time to take advantage of the blues boom of the 1960s, when many of her colleagues were rediscovered by the music industry and the general public. So, as many of the men Memphis Minnie had bested in cutting contests reentered the spotlight, and as some of the blues musicians she had played with toured Europe accompanied by the screams of delighted audiences, Minnie remained shuttered away, mostly forgotten, in the shadows of her nursing home.

If a musician isn't heard, does she make a sound? We all have childhood experiences, before the age of five or six perhaps, that have been entirely forgotten. Those episodes, however, forgotten or not, may still form the basis for our personalities, for our choices and predilections, for our failures and our successes. More than a few people have spent more than a few dollars in therapy trying to remember things they had forgotten but that still rule their lives. Memphis Minnie is kind of a formative musical memory. Whether remembered or not, her impact is, and will be, felt. Her lifestyle and her guitar playing have entered the bloodstream of American popular music. Led Zeppelin turned her song "When the Levee Breaks" into a hard-driving rock song; Lucinda Williams rerecorded "Nothin' in Rambling" and "Me and My Chauffeur Blues," and any number of female rockers owe her a debt, whether they know it or not. Other musicians may be enjoying the whiskey of success. But Memphis Minnie is still the champion. 🎸

RECOMMENDED LISTENING:
Memphis Minnie, *Queen of the Blues* (Columbia, 1997). Includes such classic tracks as "When the Levee Breaks."
Memphis Minnie, *The Essential* (Classic Blues, 2001). Featured numbers include "Ma Rainey" and "In My Girlish Days."
Sister Rosetta Tharpe, *Precious Memories* (Savoy, 1997). A great album by the fabled singer/guitarist and mistress of gospel and blues.
Various Artists, *The Roots of Rap: Classic Recordings From the 1920s and '30s* (Yazoo, 1996). Interesting compilation that includes a Memphis Minnie talking-blues hit, "Frankie Jean (That Trottin' Fool)."

HAPPY NEW YEAR! WITH MEMPHIS MINNIE *By Langston Hughes*
[From the *Chicago Defender,* January 9, 1943]

Memphis Minnie sits on top of the icebox at the 230 Club in Chicago and beats out blues on an electric guitar. A little dung-colored drummer who chews gum in tempo accompanies her, as the year's end—1942—flickers to nothing, and goes out like a melted candle.

Midnight. The electric guitar is very loud, science having magnified all its softness away. Memphis Minnie sings through a microphone and her voice—hard and strong anyhow for a little woman's—is made harder and stronger by scientific sound. The singing, the electric guitar, and the drums are so hard and so loud, amplified as they are by General Electric on top of the icebox, that sometimes the voice, the words, and the melody get lost under their noise, leaving only the rhythm to come through clear. The rhythm fills the 230 Club with a deep and dusky heartbeat that overrides all modern amplification. The rhythm is as old as Memphis Minnie's most remote ancestor.

Memphis Minnie's feet in her high-heeled shoes keep time to the music of her electric guitar. Her thin legs move like musical pistons. She is a slender, light-brown woman who looks like an old-maid school teacher with a sly sense of humor. She wears glasses that fail to hide her bright bird-like eyes. She dresses neatly and sits straight in her chair perched on top of the refrigerator where the beer is kept. Before she plays, she cocks her head on one side like a bird, glances from her place on the box to the crowded bar below, frowns quizzically, and looks more than ever like a colored lady teacher in a neat Southern school about to say, "Children, the lesson is on page fourteen today, paragraph two."

But Memphis Minnie says nothing of the sort. Instead, she grabs the microphone and yells, "Hey, now!" Then she hits a few deep chords at random, leans forward ever so slightly over her guitar, bows her head, and begins to beat out a good old steady downhome rhythm on the strings—a rhythm so contagious that often it makes the crowd holler out loud.

Then Minnie smiles. Her gold teeth flash for a split second. Her earrings tremble. Her left hand with dark red nails moves up and down the strings of the guitar's neck. Her right hand with the dice ring on it picks out the tune, throbs out the rhythm, beats out the blues.

Then, through the smoke and racket of the noisy Chicago bar float Louisiana bayous, muddy old swamps, Mississippi dust and sun, cotton fields, lonesome roads, train whistles in the night, mosquitoes at dawn, and the Rural Free Delivery that never brings the right letter. All these things cry through the strings on Memphis Minnie's electric guitar, amplified to machine proportions—a musical version of electric welders plus a rolling mill.

Big rough old Delta cities float in the smoke, too. Also border cities, Northern cities, Relief, W.P.A., Muscle Shoals, the jukes. "Has Anybody Seen My Pigmeat on the Line," "C.C. Rider," St. Louis, Antoine Street, Willow Run, folks on the move who leave and don't care. The hand with the dice ring picks out music like this. Music with so much in it folks remember that sometimes it makes them holler out loud.

It was last year, 1941, that the war broke out, wasn't it? Before that there wasn't no defense work much. And the President hadn't told the factory bosses that they had to hire colored. Before that, it was W.P.A. and Relief. It was 1939 and 1935 and 1932 and 1928 and years that you don't remember when your clothes got shabby and the insurance lapsed. Now, it's 1942—and different.

Memphis Minnie and Kansas Joe McCoy, 1929

Folks have jobs. Money's circulating again. Relatives are in the army with big insurance if they die.

Memphis Minnie, at year's end, picks up those nuances and tunes them into the strings of her guitar, weaves them into runs and trills and deep steady chords that come through the amplifiers like Negro heartbeats mixed with iron and steel. The way Memphis Minnie swings, it sometimes makes folks snap their fingers, women get up and move their bodies, men holler, "Yes!" When they do, Minnie smiles.

But the men who run the place—they are not Negroes—never smile. They never snap their fingers, clap their hands, or move in time to the music. They just stand at the licker [sic] counter and ring up sales on the cash register. At this year's end, the sales are better than they used to be. But Memphis Minnie's music is harder than the coins that roll across the counter. Does that mean she understands? Or is it just science that makes the guitar strings so hard and so loud? ☞

BIG BILL AND STUDS: A FRIENDSHIP FOR THE AGES
BY STUDS TERKEL AND JEFF SCHEFTEL

Jeff Scheftel recently interviewed Studs Terkel about his old friend Big Bill Broonzy. Studs Terkel is a legend in his own right. A Pulitzer-prize winning author, popular radio and TV show host, and raconteur extraordinaire, he roamed the back streets of Chicago and sought out music that touched his soul. Studs, who befriended and championed numerous musicians, says Big Bill Broonzy was the greatest country-blues singer of all time.

I heard Big Bill Broonzy one day when I used to buy records, ten cents apiece, in the Black Belt of Chicago. I'd stop off there on my way to work to Chicago Law School on the streetcar. In the black community you heard music coming from inside the doors and I never heard such music in my life. There were blues, country blues, Big Bill, Tampa Red, Memphis Minnie, Roosevelt Sykes, and more, but Big Bill had a special voice and a guitar that was even more special. A virtuoso if ever there was one.

Big Bill was a mentor to Muddy Waters. He was the teacher. Bill was one of the earliest bluesmen to arrive from the South. He came from Mississippi and Arkansas, where he was a sharecropper at the age of eight. When other young singers came along to Chicago, he would see they didn't get cheated on their contracts. He served as a father figure for a lot of them: Muddy Waters, Memphis Minnie, Sonny Boy Williamson, Roosevelt Sykes, and you could name many others.

I played Big Bill on my radio program, and then I was part of a group that traveled together for a while when the folk music revival was beginning.

We had this program called "I Come for to Sing," which was also the name of an old ballad. We would tour colleges. We performed all over the Midwest at any college that would have us. Big Bill would sing the country blues, mostly his own, but some of his buddies' too. Bill had no shortage of great songs—he wrote hundreds. Win Stracke, who sang bass, would sing American frontier songs, and Larry Lane offered up Elizabethan ballads. They'd perform about the same things, three different epics of mankind; it might be fickle love, and so the Elizabethan singer would do "Greensleeves," and Win would sing "The Frozen Martyr," a summer song about an old martyr and a mighty faithful love. And Big Bill would sing "Willie Mae" to tremendous applause. I was the narrator and general cheerleader.

In 1948, four of us were in an old jalopy going through an almost desolate Indiana town headed for Purdue University. It'd been about ten days we'd been traveling those roads. And they weren't the freeways we're used to now. We were three white guys and a black guy. Bill and Win were about six feet two, six feet three each. Win looked like a biker. Larry was short, but I was the shortest. And so we're two hours early and reach Lafayette, a blue collar town near Purdue. We're hungry and we see this big tavern. It's a warm day, and the doors are open, and we see these great liverwurst-sausage sandwiches with onions. So Win says, "Let's the four of us go in there and get some of that liverwurst and onions and a shot and a beer." And Bill says, "Why don't you three go in and get me the stuff and bring it out to me." Of course, Win and I go, "No, four or nothing." Bill goes, "Well, okay, if you insist." As soon as we hit that door and they saw Bill's black face: *Bang!* Dead silence. And they stare at us, and you could sense hostility that you could cut with a knife, and we're walking toward the bar and we're like Gary Cooper in *High Noon*: these three white guys and a black guy. And Win's talking, "We'd love those liver and onions and sausage sandwiches and of course a beer and a shot." The bartender is very genial and says, "Well, I'll serve three of ya," and Win says, "How dare you?" Meantime, I'm thinking, These guys are gonna kill us. And I'm leaning in, all five feet six of me, and I say, "How dare you," and all of a sudden Bill starts to chuckle very softly. "I'll go outside," he says, and so all four of us shuffle out to beat it.

But the important thing is Bill's chuckle. And I found out often when you hear a black person describe a moment of humiliation, he chuckles, because it's a safety valve. It's like the blues lyric: "laughin' to keep from cryin'." So that was it, laughing to keep from raging, you'd say today. I once asked Bill why is it that that laugh comes at a moment of humiliation, and he said, "Without laughter we wouldn't last. Laughter is remedy." Oh, he had a certain kind of wisdom about him. He died before the civil rights movement came into being, and that's the tragedy. He'd have been lionized and recognized as Bill the Great Artist.

We often appeared as a group with Memphis Minnie and Roosevelt Sykes. We even played at a jazz club in Chicago, the Blue Note. On dark nights the owner of the Blue Note, Frank Holzfiend, would have these great artists there: Billie Holiday, the Louis Armstrong Quintet, Duke Ellington with a small group. We'd be there, and he'd feature us, and we developed a cult following, the four of us. And

Big Bill Broonzy

that's where the country blues was heard. The first time country blues was heard in a big-time jazz place was Monday nights when we did "I Come for to Sing."

Bill had been to Europe a number of times. He was there with Alan Lomax. Bill had quite a stature as a blues artist in England—one that grew beyond the confines of Chicago. It was the first time Brits ever heard blues, sung by a blues artist. Bill introduced Muddy Waters to England, persuaded English audiences to like Muddy because they didn't like the electric guitar in the beginning.

Bill had a lot of wisdom. One night we were playing a club back in the early fifties. I was the MC, and Bill was singing "Plough Hand Blues"—I'll never forget that—and when he sang that and you heard him play the guitar, you could just feel the fields and you could just feel the sharecroppers. It's about the mule dying on him.

In the middle of the song, a couple of hipsters rudely walked out. One was a white kid, one was a black kid, and I was furious because I was caught unaware, otherwise I'd have chopped them up as you have to do as an MC. I'd have done a job on them, but they walked out. As we're sitting at the bar during intermission, I was furious. Bill says, "Why you sore?" and I says, "Those kids walking out on that song." And Bill says, "Why, it's not their fault. Don't blame them—it's about a mule, what do they know about a mule?" That's the Big Bill Broonzy I knew and loved. ✒

CHICAGO BLUES, SIXTIES STYLE

By Samuel Charters

[From the liner notes to *Chicago/The Blues/Today!, Vol. 1,* 1966]

To get down to the South Side, you get the Elevated somewhere in the Loop, or walk down one of the entrances on State Street where it's still a subway. The lines fan out across the flattened hand that's Chicago—like the veins close to the skin. Over the rooftops, you can see the trains, on their rusted metal trestles, moving above the streets. The buildings have been dredged out of the ground for twenty blocks below the business district for an urban renewal project, but after the Elevated gets south of this you begin to see the slums, Chicago's sprawling Negro ghetto. The backs of the buildings line the tracks, rows of wooden porches, spindly and weathered, painted a dull gray-blue. The patches of yard between the porches and the tracks are black with coal dust and littered with loose trash and garbage. Toward the lake you can see the stone apartment buildings along South Parkway and Prairie Avenue. After a spring rain, or on a slow, fading sunset afternoon, there is a dim elegance to the South Side. The bricks and stones have a soft warmth, and since the buildings are low you can see the sky hanging over your head. But when you get off the train and walk down the painted iron stairway to the street you can see the worn paint on the windowsills and doorways, the cracking pavement of the sidewalks, the worn ground in front of the buildings, which always means too many children and no place for them to play.

But you go down to the South Side for the blues, not for its dirty streets or shabby apartment buildings. The South Side is the last place left in the country where a living music is still played in local bars and neighborhood clubs. It's what New Orleans used to be like in the thirties, what Memphis was like in the twenties. In Chicago, on the South Side, it's still today for the blues.

You can get off the train at two or three stops if you want to find the music. Turner's Blue Lounge is just below the tracks at Fortieth and South Indiana, a one-story building with a few tables inside, a bar along one wall, a jukebox, and a small bandstand. The music at Turner's is like the place, rough and direct, and everybody's played there at one time or another. One night there was a noise around the neighborhood because there was a new musician just up from Mississippi, a young intent singer who was playing an electrified slide guitar. He had to tune it two or three times for the crowd, and then they watched his fingers while he played: "When I get to Chicago nowhere for me to go/When I get to Chicago nowhere for me to go/Left my hometown, everyone I know."

If you get off at Forty-third Street it's only a few blocks down the street to Pepper's Lounge. There's still a window mural painted on the outside of the club, a large drawing of one of the bluesmen, "The Boss, Pepper's," "Otis Rush . . . The Great Muddy Waters . . ." usually a sign over the door listing who's going to be playing for the week. Beer's 35 cents a bottle, and there's usually a chair empty at a table near the bandstand; so you sit until the night's half over listening to the blues.

It's only a block to Theresa's from the El stop at Forty-seventh Street—an old basement apartment in a brick building at the corner of Forty-eighth and Indiana. You go down a short flight of steps to get to the door, past a signboard fastened to a wire fence beside the steps. "Beer to go at popular prices . . . featuring live music . . . free gifts to the ladies." A tattered notice, "Every Fri. Sat. & Sun. Jr. Wells." A narrow, dark room, the bandstand at the far end with a little space left cleared between the tables for anybody who wants to use the concrete floor for dancing. And from Theresa's, it isn't too far down Forty-seventh Street to the J and C Lounge, with its painted strip of cartoons that slowly revolves above the bar and its suspicious doorman who holds the door shut with a length of chain until you can prove that you're old enough to drink. Inside it's crowded and the music clamors against the narrow walls over the heads of the dancers milling in front of the bandstand. The guitar player and the drummer stay on the stand, but a harp player from the neighborhood pulls the microphone cord as far as it will go and sits at a table beside his girl, blowing the blues for her over the din. You keep your coat on for a set or two; then you finish the bottle of beer and get back out to the street. The blues is still the South Side's music, and the stares get hostile if you stay too long. But the music stays with you as you ride the El back to the Loop, rubbing against your skin with its hard strength. 🖝

Junior Wells *(right)* in a late-night harmonica duet—or duel—with James Cotton at Theresa's, 1976, ten years after Sam Charters first visited the Chicago club.

GETTING A HIT BLUES RECORD
By Willie Dixon [with Don Snowdon]
[From *I Am the Blues,* 1989]

Chess gave me a contract and this contract didn't have too much of a stipulation on it. They insisted that I assist them in everything they'd do. At that time, the Chess company was on the northwest corner at Forty-ninth and Cottage Grove. Then they moved down to a bigger place at Forty-eighth and Cottage Grove.

When I first met the Chess brothers, I thought this was going to be a beautiful thing for me to execute some of what I thought I knew. They let me have a free run with just about everything because Leonard used to admit that he didn't know as much about it as he thought I did. He treated me with respect, about as much as the average black folks was getting, and that wasn't too much anywhere.

My job was to assist. I did everything from packing records to sweeping the floor to answering the telephone to making out orders, but they weren't giving me much of a pay thing. They promised to give me so much a week against my royalties, and then every week, I'd have to damn near fight or beg for the money. . . .

I had told Leonard Chess I had quite a few songs, but he never wanted too many of them at first. A couple of years after I started working there, I told him about this particular song, "Hoochie Coochie Man."

"Man, Muddy can do this number," I said.

"Well, if Muddy likes it, give it to him," he said, and told me where Muddy was working. Muddy and I had talked about the song on a couple of occasions. I had sung "Hoochie Coochie Man" out there where we used to go out and meet him and play on the South Side when I had the Big Three Trio.

I went over there to the Club Zanzibar at Fourteenth Street and Ashland. At intermission, I had Muddy come off the stage and I was telling him, "Man, this song is a natural for you."

"Well, it'll take me a little while to learn it," Muddy said.

"No, this is right down your alley. I got an idea for a little riff that anybody can play."

You know how it is, a lot of guys feel like if you made a song complicated, it would do more. I always tried to explain that the simpler a thing is, the easier it can get across with the public.

He and I talked about it and I said, "Get your guitar." We went and stood right in the front of the bathroom by the door. People were walking by us all the time and I said, "Now, here's your riff: 'Da-da-da-da-Da.'"

"Oh, Dixon, ain't nothing to that."

"Now remember this: The gypsy woman told my mother/Da-da-da-da-Da/Before I was born/Da-da-da-da-Da/You got a boy child coming/Da-da-da-da-Da/He's gonna be a sonuvagun."

He could remember those words because they were the type of words anybody can remember easily. All through the history of mankind, there have been people who were supposed to be able to tell the future before it came to pass. People always felt it would be great to be one of these people: "This guy is a hoodoo man, this lady is a witch, this other guy's a hoochie coochie man, she's some kind of voodoo person."

In the South, the gypsies would come around and tell fortunes. When I was a little boy, you'd see a covered wagon coming along and these women with their great big dresses—doggone knows how many dresses they'd have on—and all of them would have pockets up under them. I didn't know some of them would steal, you know. Nobody's paying attention to a little kid like me walking around there, and these gypsies would take little gadgets from rooms.

Naturally, if somebody who wants your money and wants to use you is going to tell you a story, they have to tell you something you want to hear. If the gypsies come up to some lady's house and she's pregnant, the first thing they'd say is, "Ooh, you're going to have a fine fat boy. He's gonna be able to tell the future before it comes to pass."

The average person wants to brag about themselves because it makes that individual feel big. "The gypsy woman told my mother/Before I was born"—that shows I was smart from the beginning. "Got a boy child coming/ Gonna be a sonuvagun"—now I'm here. These songs make people want to feel like that because they feel like that at heart, anyway. They just haven't said it, so you say it for them.

Like the song "I Just Wanna Make Love to You," a lot of times people say this in their minds or think it. You don't have to say it but everybody knows that's the way you feel anyway because that's how the other fella feels. You know how you feel so you figure the other fella feels the same way because his life is just like yours.

To know the blues is to know a feeling and understanding within people that puts you in the position of other people by feeling and understanding the plight that they're involved in. You don't always get the experience in the blues from the life you live because sometimes these things are built into a certain individual.

A man don't have to be starving to know how it feels to starve. All he's got to do is know how it feels to miss one or two meals and he knows that other fella is in

Willie Dixon in Chicago, 1989

much worse shape. But if a person don't have no feeling, no imagination or understanding, you can't create a feeling with him because he doesn't hear what you say.

We fooled around with "Hoochie Coochie Man" there in the washroom for fifteen or twenty minutes. Muddy said, "I'm going to do this song first so I don't forget it." He went right up onstage that first night and taught the band the little riff I showed him. He did it first shot and, sure enough, the people went wild over it. He was doing that song until the day he died. . . .

I really wasn't well known as a songwriter until "Hoochie Coochie Man." I must have had 150 songs, a whole bagful, when I went there but I couldn't get 'em out. . . .

[Then] "Hoochie Coochie Man" was selling so good Leonard wanted me to come up with another one right away. We did this "Make Love to Me" ("I Just Want to Make Love to You") and then I told him about "I'm Ready" so we went with that and it got to going pretty good. . . .

I've been real lucky about writing people songs but a lot of times, if I picked the song, the guy didn't want the song for himself. Muddy didn't want the ones I was giving him and Howlin' Wolf didn't want the ones I was givin' him. The one Wolf hated most of all was "Wang Dang Doodle." He hated that "Tell Automatic Slim and Razor-Toting Jim." He'd say, "Man, that's too old-timey, sound like some old levee camp number."

I wrote several songs for Muddy but after that first one, I didn't have to convince him very much about a song. I had been trying to give Little Walter "My Babe" because of his style of doing things, but it took damn near two years for him to record it.

Whenever I work with an artist or group, I like to hear them and get a feeling about the style that people like to hear them sing. I could make a song on the spot sometimes that would fit the individual just by watching his action. There are certain ways people act and music just fits what they're doing.

The average blues song must have a feeling or the world won't accept it. You have to have a lot of inspiration and you have to be able to sell that inspiration to the other fellow. If the artist can express the song with inspiration, it inspires the public because music has that generating thing. If it touches you and you can feel it, you can inspire someone else. It's just like electricity going from one to the other.

Feeling has a lot to do with it all the time. If some guy calls you a dirty name, you know when the guy means it and when he's just kidding. Dusty Fletcher was a comedian who used to do the "Open the door, Richard" routine onstage everywhere. He would come on at the Regal Theater in Chicago and cuss and raise hell and talk more bad talk onstage and everybody would be crying they laughed so much. Somebody else says "damn" onstage and everybody's insulted.

I felt Little Walter had the feeling for this "My Babe" song. He was the type of fellow who wanted to brag about some chick, somebody he loved, something he was doing or getting away with. He fought it for two long years and I wasn't going to give the song to nobody but him.

He said many times he just didn't like it but, by 1955, the Chess people had gained confidence enough in me that they felt if I wanted him to do it, it must be his type of thing. The minute he did it, BOOM! she went right to the top of the charts. ☛

"I feel like the blues is actually some kind of documentary of the past and the present—and something to give people inspiration for the future." —Willie Dixon

AND IT'S DEEP, TOO BY TOURÉ

There is no collective organ south of the brain that can claim a greater impact on American history than the black penis. Only a foot fetishist would argue otherwise. The black penis, with its perpetual promise of gargantuan size and guaranteed satisfaction, is an icon as integral to this country's fabric as baseball and apple pie.

In the Old South during slavery, as another way of dehumanizing them, black men—and women too—were portrayed as animalistic and in touch with raw, wild sexuality. But the implicit sexual power of the black man was a challenge to the paternalism of the day. Many lynchings, sparked by a black man's actual or fictional approach to a white woman, concluded with the lynched man's organ in his mouth. During the summer of 1955, fourteen-year-old Chicago boy Emmett Till was murdered in Mississippi for supposedly whistling at a white woman. The fear of black male sexuality had led to de facto laws separating black men from white women, which were enforced no matter how puny the transgressor.

One might think an iconography so littered with blood and death would die away by itself, but in the years since slavery the myth of the Big Black Dick has been embraced by black men, remaining central to how we relate to America. The oversexed, ultracool, impossibly cocksure black superstud who walks like there's a loaded weapon in his pocket and is self-reported to be fabulously endowed is alive on our streets and in our cultural self-expression—from the original Shaft, to the career personas of Prince, Barry White, Samuel L. Jackson, and 2Pac, to the phallocentric swagger that pervades hip-hop. Richard Pryor loved to tell a joke that was quite

obviously older than him, in which two black men stop by the side of the river to take a piss. One says to the other, "Water sure is cold." The other says, "Yeah. And it's deep, too." The joke was so seminal to Pryor's oeuvre that his nine-disc retrospective was named *And It's Deep, Too!*

One of the greatest characters in the long line of legendary black cocksmen is the Hoochie Coochie Man as painted by Muddy Waters in his epic pair of songs "Hoochie Coochie Man" and "Mannish Boy."

In 1954, when Emmett Till was thirteen and still living with his mother in Chicago, McKinley Morganfield, known to all as Muddy Waters, also resided in Chicago and was about to record the biggest hit of his career. Willie Dixon wrote "Hoochie Coochie Man," and in January of 1954 Muddy recorded it with Dixon on bass. The song was an immediate success. Muddy's record sold four thousand copies in a week, reaching Number Eight on the *Billboard* R&B chart, and enabling him to buy a house on Chicago's South Side. A year later, just months before the Till murder rocked the nation, Muddy wrote "Mannish Boy," which is basically a second draft of "Hoochie Coochie," using the same rhythm and, more, telling the same story. Both songs are constructed like short stories, and when the stories are laid together they tell the tale of one of the greatest cocksmen who ever lived.

The story of the Hoochie Coochie Man, as told by Muddy Waters, begins before he's born when a gypsy woman tells his mother she's going to have a boy child and he's going to be something else. "He's gonna make pretty womens jump and shout," Muddy tells us of the unborn child. When the Hoochie Coochie Man gets to age five (in "Mannish

Boy"), his mother tells him he's going to grow up to be the greatest man alive. In both songs, Muddy's vocal attack is so aggressive that he's growling almost as if to suggest a sexual monster, thus he needs to give no proof that these epic prophecies will come true.

In "Mannish Boy," a harem-chorus screams with just-ravished delight behind Muddy's swaggering boasts in a wonderful bit of music theater.

In both songs, most of the verses are not about sex but about fixing the Hoochie Coochie Man's voodoo credentials, because now the lyrics are racing to catch up with the promises inherent in Muddy's growling bluesy voice. We learn that he was born on the seventh hour of the seventh day in the seventh month with seven doctors, and that he's got a black cat bone and a John the Conqueror root. We get voodoo credentials (instead of, say, the description of his technique) because this enhances his sexual mystique and highlights the magic realism and gross exaggeration that a storyteller relies on to tell this sort of a tale accurately.

The key verse of "Mannish Boy," for me, comes when Muddy paints a succinct little scene showing us exactly how powerful the Hoochie Coochie Man has become:

Sittin' on the outside
Just me and my mate
I made the moon
Come up two hours late
Well, isn't that a man?

He's so sexually powerful and theatrical and astounding that if he's outdoors with his woman, this will have an effect on everyone and everything, including the moon. Was the moon late because it was too bashful to watch his masculine prowess, or

because it was so enthralled in watching him it forgot to rise? Either reading is fine.

I love the Hoochie Coochie Man because he embraces the idea that sexual prowess is a black man's birthright. But that birthright is not passed on through the genes. The black male collective cocksureness begins at home with the men in the house or the men on the street corner. My own father has always been unabashedly sexual (though also doggedly faithful to my mother). He is the shortest man in his family but has a broad chest and golden skin and exudes such an immense sexual confidence that any thoughts of an Oedipal conflict were crushed before I could walk. Just looking at the way he struts (like many black men), you would think he was quite large. I learned sexual confidence by osmosis.

But therein lies the untold secret behind the legend of the Big Black Dick. Of course, every single black man is large enough to live up to the stereotype. But the reason why black men, like the Hoochie Coochie Man, stride cocksurely through the American zeitgeist as its sexual lions is because of the symbolic dick black men have in our minds, what a psychologist might call the sexual ego, the psychic armor that helps us wade through the mud called American white supremacy. In a world that constantly tells us we're nothing, we tell ourselves we're great, especially in that most crucial arena, the bed. Whether or not we have the anatomical advantage, the sexual ego gives us the advantage. These are not idle boasts: When we walk down the street like there's a loaded weapon in our crotch, that's part of a mental survival strategy to give us armor in a world that seems constructed to destroy us. Armor built from the scraps of racist stereotype. Once again we done made something from nothin'. *Now ain't that the blues?* 🖝

BETWEEN MUDDY AND THE WOLF: GUITARIST HUBERT SUMLIN

By Paul Trynka

[From *Portrait of the Blues*, 1996]

Hubert Sumlin would become Howlin' Wolf's greatest collaborator. A young pup who [Wolf] regarded as practically an adopted son, Sumlin had been hanging out in Memphis with James Cotton and Pat Hare before he got the call from Wolf.

Nowadays Hubert is more or less retired and has moved away from the noise and crime of Chicago up to a peaceful suburban street in Milwaukee. Hubert and Bee Sumlin's house is brightly painted and looks as if it's made of gingerbread, with little garden gnomes outside, and an interior filled with cuddly toys and lace. Hubert himself has the friendly, guileless demeanor of a teddy bear and threads his stories with self-deprecating jokes and sneaky metaphors, all of which remind you of his eccentric, mercurial guitar playing. He greets you like an old friend and, after Bee has plied you with coffee and cakes, takes you down to his inner sanctum, where he plays guitar and listens to records late into the night, accompanied only by Lucky, his laid-back and ludicrously fluffy cat. It's years since he's had a good talk about Wolf, and he enjoys telling the story, slapping you on the knee to emphasize the good points.

"I was just a little bitty old boy, and I come by this old warped record in this old garbage pile, and I put this record on and it was so warped, really *wooh waaah,* I said, 'Oh, shoot,' and then it sounded all right. I asked my daddy who it was, and he said, 'This is a guy died before you was born—Charley Patton.' Later on, Wolf told me that was how he started out, too, as a little old boy listening to Charley Patton.

"I played with James Cotton; he had this little band in West Memphis, Arkansas. Wolf was already established, and I was just this little old boy checking him out. Scared me to death, he did. Then one day I'm staying with Cotton at this old hotel, and I get this call from Wolf. He said, 'Hubert, I'm putting this band down, and I'm going to Chicago and forming me a new group, 'cos these guys, they think they're too good, they don't wanna play, and this and that.' I said, 'Okay.' Like that. I didn't believe him. I really didn't. So Cotton said, 'Hey man, you know he meant what he said?' I said, 'Hey, I sure hope so.'

"Sure enough, two weeks later he calls up the hotel, tells me the train leaves at so-and-so time, and you are going to be met by Otis Spann, Muddy Waters' piano player. And that's what happened. I packed my little suitcase, gets on the train, and finally arrives at the big ol' Illinois Station on Twelfth Street. Otis Spann met me, man, I got to see all these big lights, and I got scared, so we went straight back to Leonard Chess' daddy's apartment building. Wolf had his own apartment there, he got me an apartment there and had done got my union card and everything. So the second day, me and Wolf we done had lunch and he starts to telling me how this worked, how that worked, and we're sitting around the apartment going over the numbers, and hey, I got to like that old man. I was kind of scared of him at first, he was so big and huge, you know what I'm talking about, but that didn't last long—he was just like a little baby if anybody knowed him, man."

Wolf ran his band like a machine, dictating what clothes they should wear, paying their union dues, finding them accommodation, and, in Sumlin's case, organizing guitar lessons: "I had just started playing with him, man, and I wasn't seasoned good enough, and Wolf said, 'Hey, Hubert, tomorrow I want you to go with me. I'm gonna show you something I think you are going to like.' Sure enough, he took me downtown to the Chicago Conservatory of Music, where Wolf took lessons, and then he paid for two years' lessons for me. It was some opera guitar player, name was Gowalski, he was playing symphonies over in Europe, and now he's teaching me scales and stuff! 'Cept I only took six months' lessons 'cos the guy dropped dead right in front of me of a heart attack. But hey, with what he taught me and what I knew, I made out."

Although Wolf had a reputation in Chicago for whupping any musicians who didn't toe his line, most musicians who worked with him considered him the best bandleader in the city. Jimmy Rogers, Muddy Waters' long-term guitarist, remembers: "Wolf was better at managing a bunch of people than Muddy or anybody else. Muddy would go along with the Chess company, Wolf would speak up for himself—and when you speak up for yourself you're automatically gonna speak up for the band." As Billy Boy Arnold, a regular on the Chicago club circuit, puts it: "The difference with Wolf was, if you played in Wolf's band and got fired or quit, you could draw unemployment compensation. If you walked up to Muddy and said something like

unemployment compensation, they'd think you were crazy—'What the hell's that?' Wolf would be sitting in the corner with his spectacles on in intermission, studying his book; he went to night school, he took music lessons, he was always trying to advance.

"He was a guy stayed on top of things. When you went to see Wolf he would be on that stage kicking ass all night long. I used to play in clubs with Muddy in the late fifties, and Muddy used to let Cotton run his show—he would only come on for the last few numbers. Muddy was a great artist, but he became less of a draw in the Chicago clubs than Wolf, until the white audiences came along and rescued him."

As the two leading bandleaders in a city famed for cut-throat musical competition, it was inevitable that Waters' and Wolf's rivalry would develop into open enmity. Waters had originally welcomed Wolf, but by the mid-fifties, the King of Chicago Blues was becoming increasingly fearful that Wolf would steal his crown. "Muddy and Wolf, they really had a feud going," says Sumlin. "Those two were just like the McCoys, man!" The rivalry extended to arguments over who got the best songs from the Chess house songwriter, Willie Dixon, and constant attempts to poach the other's best musicians. In 1956 Waters pulled off a particularly satisfying coup. "We were playing the Zanzibar," says Sumlin, "and Muddy sent his chauffeur over in his Cadillac, the chauffeur had on diamonds and everything, and I am looking at this big roll of money. I ain't saw so much in all my days. Muddy done sent him over there to bribe me, man! He's telling me, 'Muddy say he'll triple the money that Wolf paying you, what do you want to do?'

" 'Course when you're young you think money's everything, so I say all right, and I'm wondering how am I gonna tell Wolf. I got this money, four hundred and something dollars, and it is ten minutes before we get ready to go back on the bandstand. The place is full of folk, jammed, so I goes in the bathroom to count my

"I could never explain really what seeing Wolf was like. I had his records, 78s, then I walked into a club and find this big man crawling around on his knees, draggin' his tail and howling like a wolf! Then you hold a conversation with him, and this guy's not faking this tone of voice, it's natural, and I'm saying, 'Oh my God—who am I?' 'Cause I knew who he was, and who am I to be talking to him? It's like, I'm in heaven and I don't even know it." —*Buddy Guy*

money and to think about what I am going to tell him. Shoot, man, Wolf comes straight in there, and he done change colors, man—he got blacker! This guy got a ton of color I ain't never seen a man turn. I say, 'Oh shit, he is gonna kill me, man!' I didn't have to tell him 'bout how I was going with Mud, the guy knew already. He says to me, 'Get out of my sight, get your stuff off the bandstand now.' In the middle of the show! I takes my shit down, scared, trembling, just knowing I'm gonna get bopped any minute, and get out of there quick as I can. Mud's chauffeur must have had an idea what was going on, he's waiting on me outside, helps me put my amplifier in the trunk, and drives me over to Sylvio's, where Muddy is at. Man, I cried a-a-a-all the way over there."

From the moment he joined the Waters camp, Sumlin started to miss Wolf's comparatively well-organized outfit, not least when the Waters band set out on an arduous tour of the South: "Mud told me we were leaving town, we're fixing to leave and he asked me did I have enough clothes. I said, Sure. I had me one suit. He said, 'Is that all you got, just that one suit? You know we gonna be away about forty days?' I'm going, 'What the . . . This man ain't told me nothing about no forty days.' Man, that forty days like to kill me. Some of them jobs was one thousand miles apart, man, nothing under five hundred miles, twenty days out of the forty didn't nobody get a chance to take a bath, 'cos by the time we arrive in the next town, it's time to play. Man, we did so much driving, I got the hemorrhoids so bad I couldn't sit down! They brought me feather pillows that I had to sit on!

"We drove about fourteen hundred miles back to Chicago, and the moment I got back in town, I called Wolf; I said, 'I got the hemorrhoids, this guy done work me forty days and forty nights. I am quitting Mud, and I wanna go back with you.' He said, 'You say you're comin' back?' I said, 'I'll be there in three minutes, man.'" 🎸

CLUB PARADISE
645 EAST GEORGIA AVENUE · MEMPHIS, TENNESSEE
Sat., Oct. 24, 1964 8:00pm Until
★ ★ ★ BATTLE OF THE BLUES ★ ★ ★
The HOWLING WOLF
"TAKE IT FOR ME", "SPOONFUL", "EVILS"

vs. MUDDY WATERS
"I GOT MY MOJO WORKING", "HOOTCHIE COOTCHIE MAN"
ADMISSION: ADVANCE $3.50 - DOOR $4.00

ME AND BIG JOE

By Michael Bloomfield [with S. Summerville]

[An excerpt from *Me and Big Joe,* 1980]

It was the early sixties at a Chicago nightclub called the Blind Pig that I first met Joe Lee Williams. He was a short and stout and heavy-chested man, and he was old even then. He wore cowboy boots and cowboy hat and pleated pants pulled way up high, almost to his armpits. Just visible above the pants was a clean white shirt, and a tiny blue bow tie decorated his bullish neck. He played a nine-string Silvertone guitar and to keep others from copying his style he'd put it up in a very strange tuning. I was familiar with all stringed instruments and eventually worked that guitar every way possible, but I never learned to play it and to this day don't know the tuning he used.

Big Joe, as he was often called, had been a well-known artist in the thirties and forties and wrote one of the real standards in the blues field, "(Baby) Please Don't Go," a song later cut by, among others, Mose Allison and Muddy Waters. At the time I met Joe Lee I was trying to meet as many blues artists as were alive in America, because music was the field I most wanted to pursue, and blues was the music I most wanted to learn. So between sets that night I talked with Joe, or at least I tried to—he lacked teeth and had a thick piney-woods accent, and at first I found him nearly indecipherable. I had to ask him to repeat himself over and over, but he didn't seem to mind and after a while I caught on somewhat to his speech. He told me Crawford, Mississippi, was his birthplace, and that since the early thirties he'd done nothing but hobo around the country with his guitar. Now, most bluesmen I'd met had two jobs—they'd play and sing nighttimes, but during the day they kept up a straight gig of one kind or another. But Joe never did that—he traveled and he played, and that was it.

Joe and I got along well that night, and as he packed his guitar away after his last set he invited me to visit him sometime.

⊕ ⊕ ⊕ ⊕ ⊕

"Drive me down by Gary," Joe said one day, "and I'll carry you to see Lightnin' Hopkins—him an' me is old, old friends." So Joe and I and [harmonica player] Charlie Musselwhite and Roy Ruby, who for a time played bass with Barry Goldberg and Steve Miller, climbed into Roy's car and headed east to Indiana. Actually, we had to go out beyond Gary, into the countryside, where eventually we came to a barbeque pit, or roadhouse. This kind of place was also known as a barrelhouse or chockhouse, and seems to have pretty much disappeared from the North, and maybe the South, too. The roadhouse was run by an older black couple and consisted of a barbeque pit in front and a large bare room in back. This back room was heated only by body heat—when there were enough people in the room, the place got warm. And that night it was hot.

Joe had gotten himself a center seat and was buying drinks and ordering people around when the opening act, J.B. Lenoir and His Big Band, came on. J.B. was a short man in a zebra-striped coat that hung down low behind him. He had straight hair, but it wasn't up in a high process, it was slicked down flat against his head. He looked a little like a seal. The band he had backing him featured three horn players of such advanced stages of age and inebriation that they had to lean against one another to avoid collapse. J.B. played guitar and sang through a microphone on a rack around his neck. He had a high, almost feminine voice and was a fine singer. He danced through the crowd as he played and sang, and Joe sat nodding his approval—he liked J.B. quite a bit. Then old Lightnin' came on, and he was as sly and slick and devilish as a man could be. He had a real high black conk on his head and wore black, wraparound shades. He had only a drummer behind him, and when the blue lights hit that conk—man, that was all she wrote. Lightnin' ran his numbers and everything was cool.

When the set ended, Joe went over to Lightnin' to say hello, but before he could get a word out, Lightnin' said, "What are you doing down here? I'm the star of this show, you know." "I know you're the star," Joe replied, "and we don't mean no trouble. I carried these white boys down here tonight to see you, and I just wanted to pay my respects." So Lightnin' mellowed and bought Joe a drink, but that was a mistake, because Joe didn't need it. Sure enough, Joe got rummed out and quarreled with Lightnin', and we were turned out of the place. When we got to the car, Charlie hustled into the back seat and pretended to fall asleep. I rode shotgun and feigned sleep, too. Roy was driving and Joe was between us, trying to direct Roy where to carry him. Joe was hard enough to understand sober, but drunk you had no chance at all—it was just syllabic noise.

What Joe had a penchant for doing when he was drunk was to look up distant relatives of his, sisters-in-law or whatever, and see if their husbands were working a nightshift so he could screw their women. So he had us driving through all the ghetto areas of Gary, Hammond, and East Chicago, ranting and roaring at Roy, who was unable to understand a word of what he was saying—he might well have been speaking Tagalog. And Roy would look over and say, "Michael! I know you're not asleep—you've got to tell me how to get home!" And

Big Joe Williams posed for this photo in 1967, around the time that he held Bloomfield and his pals "captive."

Michael Bloomfield loved playing—and writing about—blues.

when I wouldn't respond he'd turn to Charlie and say, "Charlie, goddammit, wake up—you gotta show us how to get out of here!" But Charlie'd just lie low, too. Joe's eyes were tiny, squinchy red slits, and we weren't about to go up against that moaning, cursing, grousing, heaving, indecipherable angriness. If Joe wasn't ready to return to Chicago, that was it—we weren't going. And we didn't—not that night, anyway. But as dawn finally broke over the smokestacks and railyards and cracking towers of northern Indiana, Joe directed Roy home.

Around the Fourth of July, Joe took it into his head to visit some people of his down in St. Louis. The owner of the record store [where Joe lived in the basement] thought it was a good idea. "Yeah, Joe," he said, "you go down there and be a talent scout. Take a tape recorder along and say you represent my company. Record some people, see what kind of deal we can make, and bring back some tapes."

Joe needed a ride, as usual, and asked if I wanted to go along. Well, I'd begun to have doubts and trepidations about taking these field trips with Joe, because once outside Chicago my friends and I were pretty much at his mercy, and you could get into some strange situations with the guy. But St. Louis was new territory for me, and I knew there were supposed to be some famous old bluesmen living down there, so I said okay. I called up another pal of mine, George Mitchell, and asked him to join us. George was a college student, originally from Atlanta, and had once worked at the record store [where Joe lived]. He wore those Kingston Trio–type button-down shirts and had a real neat Ivy League haircut. He really dug blues, and while in his teens had gotten to know many artists in the South. He got along well with older black people, and especially well with Big Joe, so I thought he'd be an ideal guy to have along.

The drive to St. Louis was real nice. Wonderful, in fact. Joe talked to George and me about things from thirty years ago as though they'd happened that morning. He reminisced about Robert Johnson and Willie McTell and Blind Boy Fuller, he told how Sunnyland Slim had helped Muddy Waters get a record contract, and explained how Big Bill [Broonzy] had gotten rich. Being with Joe was being with a history of the blues—you could see him as a man and you could see him as a legend. He couldn't read a word of English and he couldn't write a word, but he had America memorized. He was a wise man in so many ways—from forty years of hiking roads and riding rails he was wise to every highway and byway and roadbed in the country, and wise to every city and country and township they led to. Joe was part of a rare and vanished breed—he was a wanderer and a hobo and a blues singer, and he was an awesome man.

It was nightfall when we got to St. Louis. It was a Fourth of July weekend and it was hot. . . . I couldn't imagine what the days would be like. The first place we stopped was the home of Joe's sister, or sister-in-law, or stepsister, or something. When we walked in, there were little kids sleeping on every available surface, so we all sat down in the kitchen and Joe said to his relative, "Now, you know I play the guitar, and this boy Michael do too, so we'll play some while we visit." He brought out his guitar and, with it, a bottle of schnapps. I took George aside and said, "Man, we better not let this guy start drinking. It's a long weekend, and if he starts now his brains'll fly right out the window—we'll have a lunatic on our hands the whole time!" But Joe was set on drinking, and when he said, "Michael, why don't you have a little taste?" I went ahead and put some down. I figured if Joe was going to get drunk and go crazy, I was going to get drunk and be crazy right along with him. So I drank as much gin and schnapps and beer and wine as I could get in me that night, and I sat with Joe and played the blues. And man, I got sick. For the first time in my life I got king-hill, shit-faced, tore-up drunk. I puked all over that house. I puked in the kitchen, I puked in the hall, I puked on the sofa, and I puked on the wall. I was just rolling in puke—I was sick, sick, sick.

I woke up on a bed the next morning to find Joe standing over me. He had stayed up all night drinking and he was more than drunk—he was on a bender. His nostrils were flared and his eyes were red and runny. A barbeque fork was in his hand and on it was a pig nose, and hot grease from the nose was dripping on my chest. He opened his mouth and his schnapps breath hit me in a wave. "Snoots, snoots," he shouted, "I promised you fine barbeque, an' snoots is what we got!" My head was throbbing and my stomach still queasy, and when I looked up and saw this horribly fat and greasy pig nose an inch from my face, I lurched out of bed and threw up again. Joe began to curse me. "Man, you done puked all the damn night and into the mornin' an' now you pukin' up again! Can't you hold that stomach down?!" And I slunk out of the house with George, who wasn't on top of the world himself, to try to find something to settle my stomach. Joe stood roaring at us as we left. "Where do you think you is, you home in Chicago now? You *ain't* home in Chicago now, an' those niggers out there'll kill ya!" But my head and stomach were already killing me, so I took my chances on the street. And it was the funkiest street I'd ever seen. . . . But we found a drugstore with no trouble and got some aspirin and bicarbonate and Coca-Cola, and they seemed to help a little, but they sure didn't help a lot.

When George and I got back to the house, Joe was on the porch with his relatives and their friends, strumming his guitar. And he was crazy. Every woman who came by he clawed at, and every man who passed he argued with. If there was a woman in the street he'd shout, "Say sweet mama—come on over sweet mama, an' set down your daddy's knee!" And she'd look around and see a seventy-year-old, three-hundred-pound man yelling at her, and she'd get a funny look on her face and keep on walking, maybe a little faster than before. Finally, I said, "Joe, I thought we came down here to do some scouting and find us some singers. Let's do it!" But Joe just said, "Now, don't you rush me—it's the Fourth of July and I want to spend some time with my people!"

But his people got put out by his rowdy behavior, and an older woman, a church woman, finally threw him away. "You can't act this way around here," she said. "Just where do you think you is? You nothing but a damn crazy animal what ought to be in a cage! Now, why don't you up an' leave an' let us right folks be?!" 🖝

PHOTOGRAPHER PETER AMFT
ON CHICAGO BLUESMEN

I knew Big Joe Williams when he was sleeping in his car—a beat-up vintage Buick Terraplane. The guy I worked for, Joel Harlib, was Michael Bloomfield's manager and also managed the Fickle Pickle; he got the idea to make Wednesday nights "blues night," and he let Bloomfield run that as a very enthusiastic and hyper MC. Michael was the house guitarist, and he would feature Big Joe, who would sleep in the club's basement after the gig. I photographed Big Joe for the poster for the show.

When B.B. King first played *The Tonight Show*—around 1969—Johnny Carson was talking to him, and B.B. said, "You all wouldn't know about me if it wasn't for a white boy in Chicago named Michael Bloomfield." One day, Michael wanted me to go with him to Maxwell Street so that he could buy a little leather bag with a black cat bone in it. Back then, supposedly, on Maxwell Street you could buy those little charms, like a John the Conqueror root. Then we went to see Muddy at his auntie's house. We went into the kitchen and there was this big pot of steaming red beans and rice—it was really sweltering in there. Mike goes over and grabs Muddy's Telecaster. Muddy was sitting very regal-like there in his undershirt. He'd just had his hair unconked and he had this long black waterfall of glistening pompadour, and he looked like an Egyptian prince, muscular and wearing a pencil-thin mustache. He had a Benevolent Highness look to him. He looked at Mike, and *blang*, Mike breaks the big E string, and Muddy just smiles. They were friends. Mike was a liaison between the white and black worlds.

So much wouldn't have happened without Chess Records, too. But when the blues musicians made records, they didn't make much money from them. They made them in small numbers, and by the skin of their teeth. When Bruce Iglauer started Alligator Records, he put out Hound Dog Taylor's very first release. Bruce had been working for Delmark as a shipping clerk because he loved the music. He'd come down from Wisconsin, and he loved Hound Dog, but Bob Koester, who owned Delmark Records, wasn't interested in recording Hound Dog. When one of Bruce's aunts died and left him five thousand bucks, Bruce said, "I'll record him myself." Around '71, Bruce asked me to shoot that first Hound Dog Taylor jacket cover. Hound Dog was born with six fingers on each hand, but one night at Theresa's nightclub, he was drunk and he was like, "That thing is getting caught in the strings!" So he cut the sixth finger off his right hand with a razor blade and damn near bled to death. When I met him, he was very shy and didn't want me to do a photograph of his six fingers, but I told him I wouldn't publish it till he died. Now, all these years later, it's on a T-shirt with his hand in the background, and over it, it says, WHEN I DIE, THEY'LL SAY HE COULDN'T PLAY SHIT, BUT HE SURE MADE IT SOUND GOOD!

Hound Dog Taylor, 1971

BUDDY GUY ARRIVES IN CHICAGO
[From *Portrait of the Blues,* by Paul Trynka, 1996]

When I was a kid I would listen to the music on the radio station, Rambling Records, out of Memphis, Tennessee, and they'd be playing John Lee Hooker, Muddy Waters, and early Howlin' Wolf—and it seemed like all of that stuff was coming out of Chicago. It seemed like there was nowhere else you could go if you wanted to play music.

I was a sharecropper's son in Louisiana, and those were bad days. We couldn't afford any air conditioning or anything like that, but my mother had a screen on one door to keep the insects out, and that's what I made my guitar strings out of. I'd take a kerosene can, nail a stick in and stretch the wires across there. You couldn't finger it, but I'd just bang away on it. Now my daddy and his friends would see me play this thing and they'd say to themselves, Well, if that boy had a guitar, I'm sure he would learn to play. Then when I was about sixteen my daddy saw a relative who sold him a guitar that only had two strings on it, for around a couple of dollars. . . .

After that I would play with a lot of guys who would come to Louisiana, Lazy Lester, Slim Harpo, and some more, but I knew I had to do something better. So I explained to my mom and dad, I'm gonna take off and go to Chicago. Seems to me it's better there.

So I took off on the train, and when I got off the train I just had my guitar and two suits of clothes. I didn't know anybody there. So I would walk around, didn't have nothing to eat, and stayed hungry into my third day, so hungry I was about to cry when . . . this stranger came up to me and said, "You got a guitar there—can you play that thing?" I said yeah, and he said, "Well, if you play me a song we'll get some drinking done." I said, "If you buy me a hamburger or something to eat I'll play all night for you." And he said, "I don't buy no food, man—I don't know where you from but we're just gonna drink now!"

So I tote my bag and I'm trying not to cry, and I knew my mother was going to worry if she knew what shape I was in. But I'd seen those old Western movies and thought, Well, if I take this drink of whiskey at least I'll have some strength, something to keep me going for another day. So I took the first drink of whiskey I ever had, and man, my eyes flipped around four or five times, and every song I ever knew, and some I didn't, I could play. So we're at this man's house, and we's just jammin', and this guy says, "Jesus Christ, man, we got to go where someone can hear us." So we walked to this club about four or five blocks away. This particular night was Otis Rush night, and evidently this guy knew Otis. Now, the guy who owned the club was in to pick up the take, and on his way out I played him "The Things I Used to Do" by Guitar Slim, and this guy turned around and said to the manager, "Whoever that guy is, hire him." So the manager says, "You can come in Tuesday, Wednesday, and Thursday—have you got a band?" I said, "Sure," I was that desperate to play. I had to go back the next night and say to the manager, "Look, I'm just new from Louisiana, and I ain't got a band." He told me, "We'll get a band, you just be here," and he came over with Fred Below, a drummer. I didn't have a bass player or nothing.

Then the second night I was playing there I looks out in the audience, and there is Muddy Waters, and Little Walter, and I thought, Oh Jesus, what am I going to do now? But I knew I had to do something good, 'cause now that I'd seen these guys, I was never going to go back to Louisiana. 🖛

THE GIFT BY PAUL OSCHER

When I was a kid in Brooklyn in the late fifties, I worked in a grocery store. I would hang around after school, waiting to make a delivery. My uncle had given me a Marine Band harmonica, and one day, outside the store, I was trying to play "Red River Valley" from the directions that came with the harmonica. Jimmy Johnson worked in the store as a stockboy. He wasn't a boy—he was about twenty-eight years old, a stocky, dark-skinned man from Georgia with a processed hairdo. I was twelve. He said to me, "Let me see that whistle you got, son." I said, "It's a harmonica." He took the harp from me and tried to play it. Not much was coming out. He was jiving, making believe he couldn't play. Then he turned the harp around with the numbers of the holes reading backwards and played it, *Wah! Wah! Wah!,* some cool blues lick. I couldn't believe the sounds coming out of that harp. The tone was so loud and strong you could almost touch it. He could play all that country stuff like "The Fox Chase" and "The Train" but with a huge sound. He'd do this little dance while he played, and he had a trick where he'd be blowing two different licks at the same time, playing out of each side of his mouth. He was a pro. It turned out he used to play in medicine shows down South.

I had heard harmonica on records, but this was the first time I really heard it in person. I just fell in love with the sound of a blues harmonica. I had to learn how to play it. Jimmy showed me a lot, and he also hipped me to a lot of blues records. I've always said that the gift of talent is the fact that you fell in love with the music; that mad love you have for the music is what makes you learn. That's what takes you over the hurdles. Love—that's the real gift. For me, it was the gift of a lifetime.

There were two black clubs in Brooklyn I used to walk past all the time, the Seville and the Nite Cap. The Seville was the fancier place, had a round bar with a fountain in the middle with colored lights. The Seville served food, had a real stage, and a real show. Charlie Lucas and the Thrillers were the house band. They had a horn section, all the guys in the band wore gold jackets, and when they played, the whole band would be rockin' back and forth in time with the music.

The Nite Cap was a little bit rundown. No fountain—Pabst Blue Ribbon beer. Christmas decorations stayed on the wall all year. The Nite Cap didn't serve any food unless it was someone's birthday party and they brought in their own food: homemade potato salad, pigs feet, collard greens, cornbread, fried chicken, black-eyed peas. The Nite Cap had a band but they didn't all dress alike. The leader of the band was guitarist/singer Little Jimmy May. These guys played more blues than at the Seville, and when the band quit at about three or four o'clock in the morning they would head out to an after-hours joint and play some more. Smilin' Pretty Eddie was the MC and host in the club. This is the club where I got my start playing for a live audience. Pretty Eddie was standing outside the club one night, and I asked him if I could blow my harp for the people. He brought me right in and put me on the stage: "Ladies and gentlemen, put your hands together for our little blue-eyed soul brother." Then I played a blues—the band backed me up and the people loved it.

There was a shake dancer working there that night, Little Egypt, and she asked me to help her to press on her pasties. Man, I was hooked on this place, the people, and the scene. I got tight with Little Jimmy May and we used to go out to different clubs and sit in on the shows for tips. Jimmy knew all the blues clubs and local musicians: Little Buster, Elmore Parker, Bo Diddley Jr. Jimmy May was the guy who introduced me to Muddy Waters at the Apollo in 1965, at a great blues show: Jimmy Reed, Lightnin' Hopkins, John Lee Hooker, Bobby "Blue" Bland, T-Bone Walker, and Muddy Waters.

Me and Jimmy had seats in the balcony. I think I was the only white person in the house. T-Bone stole the show. He had a big band, and he came out dressed in a white suit. He played a couple of licks on the guitar, then started singing "Stormy Monday." He held the guitar out with one hand and played it one-handed. The people went nuts. T-Bone was a real entertainer. He did splits and played the guitar behind his back too. After the show, me and Jimmy went backstage. Jimmy knew Otis Spann, who invited us back to the Theresa Hotel, where the band was staying. We hung out with the guys, drank, and shot dice. That's when I met Muddy. I had played a little for him in the stairwell at the Apollo. He told me he liked my sound.

One day I got a phone call that really changed my life. Luther "Georgia Boy Snake" Johnson, one of Muddy's guitar players, called me in New York and told me to come down to this gig where Muddy needed a harp player. Big Walter was supposed to be on the gig, but he never showed up at Muddy's house in Chicago when they were leaving town. I sat in, played two numbers, and Muddy asked me, "Can you travel?" I said, "Yeah," and Muddy said, "Then you got a job!"

Soon after that, I took the train to Chicago, then got a cab from the train station to the South Side. When I got out at Muddy's house, the cab driver told me I'd better watch myself. I opened the gate to his house, 4339 South Lake Park Avenue, and saw the name MUDDY WATERS on the screen door. I rang the bell. Muddy's granddaughter Cookie answered the door. I told her who I was, and she shouted to the back, "Daddy, one of your band members here." Muddy came to the door wearing a robe. His head was tied up in a do-rag. He told me to come in and introduced me to his wife Geneva. "This is my wife, we call her Grandma." We all went in the kitchen. Muddy's stepson Charles had been drinkin', and Muddy and Charles had been arguing. When I walked in, the argument stopped. Muddy pointed to me and told everybody, "This is my white son." Then he pointed to Charles and told me, "That's your brother." I sat down, and Grandma fixed me a plate of chicken and dumplings from a big pot on the stove. Grandma then reached up over the sink and took a pint of J&B out of the cupboard and poured herself a little drink, then told Charles that he had to go to the store to get some more.

Muddy went into the bedroom and laid down. I spent the rest of the day sitting on his porch hanging out with Cookie and Charles, checking out the neighborhood and people that passed by, and they were checking me out.

Snake lived across the street from Muddy at 4340 South Lake Park Avenue on the second floor. He had a room and shared a bathroom in the hall with four other people on that floor. When you visited Snake, you rang bell number two, twice. Snake always answered the door with a pistol in his right hand. Snake had big bones but was skinny as hell. He had long arms and big hands, and his overall look was gangly. He wore sharkskin suits, and when he didn't have to play, he always had a do-rag on his head. He always wore shades, and he liked to look at you under-eyed over his glasses—the whites of his eyes were always bloodshot and yellow. He drank 100-proof Old Granddad or Wild Irish Rose wine and always kept a pint of wine or a half-pint of whiskey. He'd wash it down with anything—Coke, orange pop, grape Nehi. Snake usually started his day off with a Bromo seltzer and a drink of whiskey. You couldn't get too close to him because his breath stank like a garbage can.

Snake had a tough, mean, and raw sound on his guitar and his voice was just as raw. His blues were low-down and lonesome. There was an urgency in his playing; it was clear that this was all that mattered. He was a bluesman from his heart. Muddy liked him for his low-down ways. Muddy had a lot of respect for the underdog and for cats who were on the edge. He didn't pay them too much, but it kept them from sleepin' in cars and things. They had the blues.

Otis Spann came out of Muddy's basement, where he lived, and greeted me as "Brother Paul." Spann told me we were going to St. Louis for the weekend and asked if I had any clothes to wear for the gig. He told me he would loan me some money to get sharp. Spann took me over to Forty-third Street and bought me a pair of rust-orange-colored sharkskin-type pants, a fedora hat, and a black shirt. He also handed me an African carved-head necklace and told me, "This'll keep the wolves off your back."

When we got back to Muddy's house, guitarist Pee Wee Madison and Snake were there, both with garment bags for their clothes. They greeted me and said, "We're leaving out soon." Later bassist Sonny Wimberly pulled up in a gypsy cab. He lived in the projects over on State Street. Drummer S.P. Leary was walkin' down the street, carrying his cymbal and a garment bag. He had taken the El train from the West Side. We were all ready to go. We went down to Muddy's basement to get the equipment. Bo, Muddy's driver and valet, lived in the front room of the basement, and Spann stayed in the back with his wife Lucille.

Bo pulled up in a Volkswagen bus, and we loaded up and headed out for St. Louis. The ride was about six hours, during which time we all drank and told stories. S.P. had been workin' with Howlin' Wolf for a while and told a story about Howlin' Wolf and Sonny Boy II. They were working together in this club down South where they were playing for tips. Sonny Boy collected the tips in his hat, walked out the door, and never came back—left Wolf stranded. Wolf never forgave him. Spann said, "Sonny Boy was somethin' else. We used to call him 'Ol' Bigfoot.' His feets were so big he had to cut his shoes open around the toes." Spann got to talking about all the great harp players: Little Walter, Forest City Joe Pugh, Pots Henry Strong, James Cotton, and Big Walter. S.P. called Cotton "Big Red." Spann called Big Walter "Ol' Shakey Head Walter" because of the way Walter would shake his head like he was shaking water out of his ear after he played a hot lick. Spann said to me, "All y'all harp players are crazy, that harp does somethin' to your brains." I laughed. He said, "One time Little Walter made the band stop by some watermelon patch just so Walter could steal him some watermelons. We didn't do nothin' but break 'em open and eat out they hearts."

When we arrived in St. Louis, the sun was setting. We pulled up to the hotel, and prostitutes, standing on the corner, hiked up their dresses and shouted out greetings: "The Muddy Waters Band is here!" The band got rooms at this little hotel on Enright Street. There was a rib-tip place in the hotel, and we bought bags of rib-tips and went to the lounge, drank some more, then we left and went to

Miss Herb's Moonlight Lounge on Goode. There was a big sign in the window advertising the gig: MUDDY WATERS AND HIS HOOCHIE COOCHIE BOYS. On the way to Miss Herb's place, S.P. pointed out the Club Caravan and told me, "That's where the Wolf plays."

The Moonlight Lounge was a pretty good-sized room with a circle bar and tables on either side of the room. There were pictures of flamingoes on the walls. The area for the band was in the rear of the room, roped off with a chain. We set up the equipment and Spann tuned the piano; he always carried a tuning wrench for that purpose. We went back to the hotel and got ready for the gig. Snake made a deal with one of the prostitutes that she could use his room to turn tricks, in exchange for a piece of the action.

The band opened the set with "Chicken Shack" and some other instrumental numbers. Snake sang. Spann sang. Albert King sat in. Muddy didn't play the first set, just sat at a table nearby entertaining some female companions. When Muddy played the second set, the place went wild. He sang "Long Distance Call," "Hoochie Coochie Man," and "I Just Want to Make Love to You." When I played my harmonica solo on that number, I dropped down on my knees. A woman in the audience shouted with a big, gold-toothed grin, "Don't stop now, baby, my drawers are wet." We played "Mannish Boy" for our last number, and Muddy had a longneck Budweiser bottle concealed in his pants before the song. He really worked the crowd on that song, shouting like a preacher possessed, and when he got the crowd hot enough, he'd shout out, "I'm gonna show you a man," then he'd move that bottle in his pants like he had a huge hard-on. The audience screamed.

The next night the band played even more intensely. Muddy walked the bar and sang, "Got My Mojo Workin'." The crowd went nuts. I couldn't believe what was happening to me. These were my heroes. I was living out my dreams. 🎸

HOW I MET MY HUSBAND BY SUZAN-LORI PARKS

The first time ever I saw Paul Oscher's face, it was on the cover of his CD: *Knocking on Heaven's Door.* A good-looking guy. A good-looking white guy— and me a blues lover who'd been learning the harmonica. My harp teacher hipped me to the Oscher album, just handing it to me one day. "Is this another one of those white guys lost in the blues?" I ask.

"Hell no, this dude's the real deal," my harp teacher, Jasper, tells me. Jasper's black. Jasper also knows the blues. I listen to the album and love it.

A few years pass. I'm between harmonica teachers. Out of the blue, I get a phone call.

"You want a harp lesson?" the man asks, his voice rough and sexy from too many beers and cigarettes. It was Paul Oscher himself calling me. A friend had given Paul my number saying, "There's a cute chick who wants harp lessons." So it's around 11 p.m. and he's calling me.

"Is this really Paul Oscher?" I ask.

"Yeah," he says. "The guy who got his start with Muddy and all that?" I say.

"Yeah," he says. "I heard you were looking for a harp teacher."

I want to say yes but I play cool. "Maybe I'll call you next week," I say.

About a week later he calls again, closer to midnight this time. This guy's got a good rhythm, I'm thinking. He asks me what I can play on the harp and starts teaching me for free over the phone. Then we get to talking about all kinds of stuff. Six or seven hours later we're still talking.

"I'm playing at Frank's Lounge tomorrow night," he says. "You can hear me play and decide if you want lessons. I'll put you on the guest list."

I show up at Frank's with two girlfriends. Frank's Lounge is this hole-in-the-wall bar in downtown Brooklyn, on Fulton Street. Frank and Ruby are owners and hosts. They've got Christmas lights up year-round with photographs of blues and jazz legends on the walls. The place, with its Southern roots, has the snugness of an alley, neat and close—friendly and a little dangerous at the same time. The feeling of the place can pull you in off the street and keep you sitting at the bar for longer than might be good for you. It's got a black clientele for the most part. A hangout for old-school hustler types.

I stand in the doorway. There's this guy on the bandstand tuning his guitar. It's Paul. His vibe is strong. And he hasn't even started playing yet.

"That's my guy," I tell my friends, hoping he isn't married or engaged already. From my spot in the doorway, I wave. We meet in the middle of the room. He guides us to a table, covered with a red checkered oilcloth, and we sit down. He orders us some drinks and tells his band to start playing without him 'cause he has to talk to me. He puts his arm around me, touching the small of my back.

He's really checking out my butt, but he says, "Nice back."

The man in Parks' life: Paul Oscher (*right*) onstage with Muddy Waters at Miss Herb's Moonlight Lounge, 1967

"I washed it just for you," I say.

He joins the band onstage for the second set. Paul sings "Tin Pan Alley," "Dirty Dealing Mama," and other songs from his records. During "Dirty Dealing Mama," a guy jumps up shouting, "Man, that sounds like my woman! Tell it like it is!" When he plays "Tin Pan Alley," he walks out in the audience, falls to his knees, and plays his harp solo in a girl's lap. The crowd goes wild. I'm hooked.

We schedule a harmonica lesson for the next afternoon. I show up at his room. He lives in downtown Brooklyn in a rooming house that looks like a skid-row hotel. I never did get the harmonica lesson, but we've been together ever since.

Paul tells me that Otis Spann once told him, "Every baby child born into this world is gonna have a touch of the blues someday. I don't care what color they are—red, yellow, orange, green, or purple—everybody gets the blues."

Paul Oscher's a bluesman. He lives the life. He's taught me lots of things—from how to play the guitar to the tricks of three-card monte—but I'm still waiting on that harp lesson. 🎵

RED, WHITE AND
BLUES

Directed by Mike Figgis

My dad was crazy about jazz and blues. Growing up, my first memories are of albums, actually of 78s, because my dad inherited this very concise, catholic collection of blues and jazz records: Louis Armstrong, Jelly Roll Morton, Billie Holiday, Bessie Smith. I learned everything I know about music from listening to albums. In the case of my dad, he'd put on, say, an Eddie Condon record, sort of white Chicago blues from the thirties and forties, and say, "Just listen to the drummer. He is maybe the greatest drummer you'll ever hear, because you can't hear him. But if you really listen carefully, you'll hear what he was doing and it's miraculous." And so through my dad, I developed the skill of just listening to what bass players did, and what drummers did, and understanding rhythm sections and things like that. Talking to all these musicians whom I had the good fortune to meet while making *Red, White and Blues,* it emerges that they all had the same experience. It was all about listening to albums—whether it was in London or Birmingham or Newcastle or Manchester. They all got together in a house, smoked some dope, or drank some beer or whatever, and listened to albums all night.

My dad played the piano, so I started playing drums when I was ten, trumpet when I was eleven, took up the guitar when I was about fourteen, and eventually took up the piano, as well. I understood the structure of the blues, in terms of the music, pretty early on. And as I then expanded into free jazz, classical music, and things like that, I always retained the sense that musicians whom I loved, like Charlie Parker or John Coltrane, remained grounded in blues. I never went for music that didn't contain some element of blues. So it was always something that was, I guess from birth, ingrained. If you listen to Bessie Smith, you understand what blues is.

One of the first things that my dad made me do when I got a trumpet was put a Louis Armstrong record on, and he said, "Play along with it," to develop my ear by listening and playing along.

My ambition was to be a jazz trumpet player like Armstrong or Bix Beiderbecke. Then I started listening to bebop, Miles Davis, and Dizzy Gillespie when I was sixteen, seventeen. Then, about the mid-sixties, there was an explosion of pop music, even up in the north of England where we lived. I found a pop band looking for a trumpet player; the band played covers of Del Shannon, the Shadows, the Beatles, and stuff like that. So I started to play and discovered I really enjoyed public performance, being in a pop band. And then in the local university, at Newcastle, there was a blues band called the Red, White and Blues Band. The lead singer was Bryan Ferry, and the guitarist was John Porter. They were looking for a brass section, because they were just getting into Otis Redding and Bobby Bland. I found myself very popular because there weren't that many trumpet players around who understood that kind of stuff. So I found myself in a blues band, and I really got into it, started playing guitar a bit more, singing a little bit. Interestingly enough—much as the documentary charts some of this—you go into a band and do covers of Otis Redding and Bobby Bland, then you start listening to Dylan and more way-out stuff from the Beatles, or the Byrds: You start fusing those ideas and what's happening culturally. I didn't see that expansion as being detrimental to what the blues was.

What characterized that period, which is the middle and late sixties, early seventies, was a very open attitude toward music and culture, and toward race, as well. So the idea that, for example, in a place like Britain, which was far enough removed from the problems of race as it was experienced in

America and the problems with blues musicians there, you could listen to a very eclectic range of music, from, say, Ray Charles, to a guitarist like Steve Cropper, or to the Beatles, and think of them as coming from the same idea. There wasn't a wall between those cultures.

I've always felt that a kind of certain selective amnesia takes place, and also a selective viewpoint takes place when people talk about the period of the sixties, and it's just fallen into its cliché compartment. Having been through it myself, and being, in a limited way, part of it, and certainly as an observer very passionately a part of it, I've always felt the story wasn't really told properly. I still have some bands' albums; I still listen to them, and they are stronger than ever. A classic example would be Steve Winwood, a young guy who could sing "Georgia on My Mind," play the piano like a cross between Ray Charles and Oscar Peterson, play the guitar really well, and sing like a dream. In talking to Steve, I've realized he had a very similar background to my own. You realize that there is a very interesting viewpoint and story to be told about that aspect of the blues and the reinterpretation of it.

What we talk about in terms of the evolution of black music has entirely to do with the invention and development of recording. Really, this is as much a documentary about that phenomenon, about recorded music. Eric Dolphy once said that music shouldn't be recorded, it should be heard and kept in the memory. Well, great if you were at Woodstock, great if you were at that famous Ellington concert at Newport, great if you were at the Ray Charles gig; but what a terrible loss that would be if it hadn't been recorded.

What I didn't want was to put together a jam session to film at Abbey Road studios that was self-indulgent, where musicians are having a great time and there are great moments, but the self-indulgence is what comes across and it cuts people out. The great temptation with fantastic musicians is for them to become florid, and I didn't want that to happen. I made a rule that it should be acoustic; that there were to be no headphones; the amplified guitar could only be as loud to the point where it wasn't overwhelming; string bass; brushes on the percussion; and the piano would be an acoustic piano and not amplified; to get a great room with great acoustics; and to make everyone sing live. I felt if that were the discipline, it would not allow people to get indulgent. Indulgence comes when there are two electric guitars and they keep turning up the volume, and it keeps getting louder and louder, and at a certain point you can't hear the rhythm section anymore unless they use sticks. I just felt that set of rules would be repressive enough to make people listen to each other. Every time I felt it was getting a little indulgent, I would say, "I'd like it to be more minimal. I'd like you all to cut back a little bit."

As to why I chose the musicians who participated in the film: Over the years, watching Tom Jones and occasionally catching him doing something on TV or listening to an album or something—the guy's got a great voice! And I know when he was with the Squires in the sixties, he was a good blues singer; you don't lose the ability to be a blues singer. I also once did a gig with Lulu where I was in the backing band, and she was with the Lovers. She was a tough little cookie! She was eighteen years old—a great singer. And I always knew she had the chops. Van Morrison, no one questions. Jeff Beck, really since the Yardbird days and the stuff he did with Stevie Wonder, has always been someone who clearly is a phenomenal musician.

During one of the first conversations I had with Tom Jones, we were talking about Sinatra and Harry "Sweets" Edison playing with Sinatra, and Tom was saying the great thing about those sessions was that the accompanying musicians who were playing loose and free never ever cut across a vocal line. That was the genesis of the idea for an Abbey Road studio to be a great venue, because it has history and the room has great acoustics. The idea of using brushes and string bass meant that everyone had to listen and play quietly. And then the singers came in, and I just did my best to make sure that everything stayed tight and down in that way, so that the singers had all of the room to express themselves and were never having to fight, in terms of volume, with anyone else.

I brought saxophonist Peter King in because I think he's a phenomenal musician, a phenomenal blues player, and he can play anything. He's one of the most respected British jazz musicians alive. I'd been a fan for years and finally got to play with him and also just to feature him. I felt that bringing in someone from a jazz background but who is a blues player would temper Jeff Beck in a way that would make them both listen to each other because they weren't familiar with each other's styles. They'd never played together. I think Peter had played with Van Morrison once, but Van and Peter weren't particularly familiar with each other. I know Van has a very jazz ear, so he likes jazz blues, that sort of Jimmy Witherspoon, jump-and-shout-and-jive blues. When

Van came in, everyone said, "Van is very eccentric. He could come in and decide he doesn't like this and leave." I said, "Well, that's entirely his prerogative. What I'm going to do is just rehearse the band for an hour." So we played the blues for an hour and got it down, and it's sounding gorgeous. Van walked in during the middle of one of the takes and said, "What key is this in? Is there a guitar?" He just wanted to get straight in and play. He was only there for a couple of hours. He went straight in, did those numbers, did the interview for the film, and left. He liked the vibe.

I personally have always loved listening to musicians working and discussing music together. The way to identify great musicians is if you put an album on, they'll all respond at the same moment to something that someone who doesn't understand won't even hear; it'll just be some little turnaround, and they all go, "Ahhh!" And they'll do it together, it will be an entirely collective move. And this was like putting those musicians together who would all make the same collective response. It was a joy.

I operated one camera during the jam session. I'm sometimes tough on other cameramen who don't have the nerve, or actually, really don't have the authority, to get that close to Van Morrison or Tom Jones. Because I'm in there and I'm directing it, I think they tolerate me more, so I can get right in their face. Sometimes the only way to film musicians is to get that close. I do feel that sometimes, cameramen or camerawomen are polite, and they want to stay back, and you get a polite wide shot. But sometimes you just want to get right in. I want to see exactly what their hands are doing and not necessarily with a telephoto lens. I want to get the sense of being somehow part of what's going on.

I make big-budget films, and I make very small independent films. I make documentaries, I take

"We were taken into the depths of Chicago, and we went to record at the Chess studios—J.T. Brown, Willie Dixon, Buddy Guy, Shakey Horton were there. It was like living out the wildest fantasies you could possibly want—we were all thrilled. To play their music in the studios where they recorded those songs . . . It could have gone horribly wrong [but] truly didn't. There was a moment where there was a testing—the [Chess artists] were blown away by how this little bunch of English kids could sound so . . . it was so heartfelt by us bunch. J.T. Brown turned around and said, 'That was good.' " —Mick Fleetwood

photographs, I make recordings, and I am obsessed with recording and documenting and capturing moments that I think are special. After all this time, I think that my eye has developed in a way that is individual enough for me to trust it now. If I see something, I don't need someone else to endorse it; I kind of go, Let's get that. I follow my own instinct. When I first started, I often got talked out of certain things, and I regret many instances of that.

Doing this documentary made me realize that there is so much music out there. I wanted to go to New York and just sit with Elvin Jones for a weekend and watch him play the drums and talk about drumming and how he changed the world as a drummer. Years ago I made a list of people whom I wanted to interview—and it included people who have now departed, like Dizzy Gillespie, but there are still a lot of them on that list—and just have them play music in that kind of environment where you are not forcing it and it does not have to be an event; it's an intimate thing, pretty much like Wim Wenders did with *Buena Vista Social Club*.

It surprised me how touching this documentary turned out to be. Because I was in postproduction on one film and preproduction on another, and so I was running to these venues to film interviews without any notes—but the notes were already in my head. I knew what I wanted, so each time it was like a one- to two-hour conversation, in and out. I knew the questions I wanted to ask, and I knew—not the answers, because that would have been presumptuous—but I knew enough about the musicians and I felt enough of an intimate knowledge of them to lead them into the area where I thought they would be most interesting. In my head, I had this sort of sense of how this patchwork would cut together. What I was not prepared for was just how very incredibly proud I felt of this group

Tom Jones and Jeff Beck jamming at Abbey Road studios

of British guys who had a ball and loved what they were doing. It was summed up in a way by what Eric Clapton said: It was almost like his mission to respect this music, not to adulterate it, not to convert it into heavy metal or something like that, but to really play it in an original way, at the same time retaining a deep respect for where it came from, and also talking about where it came from and giving the credit straight back to the source, which was what we consider to be a sacred group of black musicians who we felt were unsung heroes. And there is a kind of unselfishness and a dedication about that, when I saw the whole thing cut together for the first time, I was actually deeply moved by it. And it was very gratifying having someone of iconic status, like B.B. King, saying, "Thank you, because if it hadn't been for you guys, I don't think I would have been here talking to you today," or words to that effect. I found that so moving. And therefore I think the film is very worthwhile. I am really proud of it. It was worth making. I think it was valid to make it, and I am glad I did it.

—Mike Figgis

A CONVERSATION WITH ERIC CLAPTON [1990] BY PETER GURALNICK

I don't think I'd even heard of Robert Johnson when I found the record; it was probably just fresh out. I was around fifteen or sixteen, and it was a real shock that there was something that powerful. A friend of mine gave it to me, a very dear friend who was at school with me, and we were both avid blues collectors. This guy always seemed to be—I don't know why—one step ahead. You know, it was almost like something he did to spite me, as if whatever I was into, he would come up with something sharper. And he came up to me and gave me this record and said, "See if you can learn some of *this*." You know? I played it, and it really shook me up, because it had—it didn't seem to be concerned with appeal at all. It was like all the music I'd heard up until that time seemed to be structured in a way for recording. What struck me about Robert Johnson's record was it seemed as if he wasn't playing for an audience. It didn't obey the rules of time or harmony or anything. It all led me to believe that here was a guy who really didn't want to play for people at all, that his thing was so unbearable for him to have to live with that he was almost, like, ashamed of it, you know. This was an image, really, that I was very, very keen to hang on to.

What was it about Robert Johnson that initially drew you in? Was it the lyrics, the music . . . ?

I was very much of a working-class kid when that [Robert Johnson] record was around. But it was as if there was some kind of radar that . . . It's far too magical to be put down as pure chance somehow. Why would it mean so much to me, or for someone like Keith Richards, to hear that in England of all places? Why didn't we grow up listening to European music or English music?

Why did black American blues get through to me? I don't know. . . .

Tell me about the first time you met the blues.

I think it was Sonny Boy Williamson at this blues festival they had once a year in England, around '63. Or Memphis Slim. The first guy I saw play that way live was Matt "Guitar" Murphy when he was with Memphis Slim. I ventured to talk to him after the show. This was at the Marquee Club. And he disappointed me, because he said that he didn't care about the blues, he was just doing this for the bread. He really considered himself a jazz musician. What a kind of wake-up that was! But, you see, I'd already selected my heroes at that point, and the guys that were coming over weren't necessarily my heroes. My heroes were Muddy and Little Walter. The first person I saw who was my hero was Little Walter. Somehow or another he'd got himself into a tour of England on his own. I don't know how the hell that happened, because he was pretty hard to deal with, but I loved him. I mean, I saw him play with a pickup band at the Marquee Club, and every number he would start and stop and tell them it was all wrong, and he'd start it again. It was sheer chaos. And the promoter of the club was saying, "Ahhh, what did I get involved in here? This guy is drunk. He's drinking two bottles of rum a day." To me it was pure magic, just the sound that came out—I mean, he could not *not* play. You know what I mean? He was very reticent to get into anything for very long, but whenever it happened, even if it was just, like, for thirty seconds that he'd blow, it was heaven for me. And I just thought, Well, these guys can't—they don't understand. This is what it is; you take the rough with the smooth. You're lucky to have this guy here. You're lucky he's alive and that he condescends to play for you. *No* way I could complain about that. No way. I thought it was magic.

What was the blues scene like in London at that time?

I was a student in Kingston, which is just on the outskirts of London, so I would go into London and bum around a lot when I was in my late teens. There was Alexis Korner and Cyril Davies and, of course, later the Stones. I found it very, very exciting. Except that Alexis was a little jazz-oriented, he was into a Cannonball Adderley kind of thing now and then instrumentally, and he wasn't a great singer, but he would do great material. You see, the thing to me, it was like the simplicity of the blues was almost impossible for anyone to master. So they would—even if they were playing [the] blues, they would lean toward the jazz side of things to give it some respectability. The only person on the scene then who was playing blues fairly straight, and even then with a little jazz, was John Mayall. Which is what attracted me to John, you know. He was strictly a bluesman.

What about yourself? As you started playing professionally, did you have any doubts about the authenticity of your own playing, about your own ability to play the music?

Not at all. In fact, because of the isolationist point of view of it being in England, I was actually very dogmatic, and I considered myself a kind of bearer of the flame, you know. I was very proud of what I was doing. I didn't have any self-doubts at all.

What about the racial issue?

I think my ego made me regard it as being all right in my case, but not all right in anybody else's. Do you know what I mean? So that I didn't really like any other white guy's playing. Except for mine.

For some reason, I believed that I had the kind of hidden key.

And you had no hesitation about playing a song by Otis Rush, say, one of your idols?

No, I would just play it. We were playing "All Your Loving" then. What I was doing, even at that stage, was taking the bare bones of what Otis Rush was doing, or Buddy Guy was doing, or B.B. King or Freddie King, and then playing my way. For instance, "Hideaway" isn't anything like Freddie King's version, really. I had the confidence to play my version even then, and when I did, and when I got a reaction, I knew I was doing the right thing.

Was this challenged at all when you played with guys like Sonny Boy Williamson?

Yeah, of course. I mean, then you had to kind of own up. *Especially* with Sonny Boy. I was with the Yardbirds, and we were becoming more of a pop band at the time that he came along. And you could see that he didn't think much of us at all. He made us very aware of the fact of our shortcomings.

How did you respond to that?

I did my best and tried to play the way that I thought he would like. And on certain occasions he did seem to sort of approve. You know, begrudgingly. I found out later that he wasn't really one to give encouragement. He got the best out of you by being pretty aggressive.

Did this at all challenge your romance with the blues?

Not at all. No. Because I considered him to be right. And us wrong. You see, I knew his songs, I had *heard* them, but at that point in time it hadn't occurred to me that to know a song was different to being familiar with it. I thought it would be in a key, and it would have a tempo—I didn't realize that the detail was important. It didn't occur to me that there would be strict adherence to a guitar line, to an intro, to a solo. And that's what I learnt very quickly

Eric Clapton and Howlin' Wolf recording 1971's
The London Sessions

with him. Because he didn't just want to count it off. That's what really shook me up—because I thought we could get away with just busking it, and he wasn't at all happy with that. We would rehearse, but still, even then, we were nowhere near getting it right to his satisfaction. And it was a little bit panic-making, but at the end of the day, when we got onstage, it was different. In rehearsals he'd be really mean, and no matter what you did, you could never please him. But onstage, then he would forget, because he was dealing with the audience and he wouldn't be so concerned with what you were playing. Given the situation that I was in—a band of musicians who were less well equipped to deal with it—I felt that it was my responsibility to bridge the gap between him and the band. I was the liaison. And what it did, in a way, was to strengthen my belief

that that's where my root was. Which happened later with Muddy and all the other great bluesmen I played along with. They rekindled my fire.

It was an education in the blues.

Very rapid. The one other time that really shook me up was playing with Howlin' Wolf. But I could see that I was better equipped than anyone else, in that sense again. And it gave me a sense of pride in myself, and in my knowledge of the genre, that I could deal with it better than, say, Ringo, who decided on the first night he was never going back in the studio with anybody *like* Howlin' Wolf. Because Howlin' Wolf, on the first night he was just so miserable and so scathing to everyone—because we were going to approach it from a fairly ad-lib point of view. His attitude was the same as Sonny Boy's. You know, like, We're going to do "Little Red Rooster," and it goes like *this*. And it doesn't go like anything *you* think it goes like. And he was tough and very aggressive, and a certain number of the guys in the studio were just too shook up to come back the next day. And I was pretty shook up, too. It scared me. You see, I was already going along a different path. I was a rock musician. And it's not that I'd left my blues roots behind; it's just that I'd forgotten a lot of the ways things went. And to get it all back in the space of an evening is no easy job. But I spoke to the [album's] producer from Chicago [Norman Dayron], and he said, "Well, come back tomorrow. It'll be all right." And I did, and it was better. But Ringo didn't come back. He didn't see the point. It wasn't that much of an issue for him. But I wanted to get it right. I really did. You see, it introduced me to the reality of playing. Because up until then, it had always been a bit of a fantasy, you know, listening to the records and harboring a sense of belonging to it. Which no one else could really shake until I met the real guys, and then I felt a bit of a stranger. But it fortified my urge to get it right. Because once you got the reward, it made you realize that there was something there. That I did have something there. That I could make these guys smile.

Did you have a sense of anything else going on? That there were others like you out there?

I had the first Butterfield album right after it came out. It was just by word of mouth; I can't remember how I found out about it. But I thought it was great. Especially Butterfield's playing. I thought Bloomfield played too much. It wasn't until I met him that I realized it was his character to be that way. He couldn't hold himself in rein. He was just one of those ebullient characters. But I loved it all the same.

Did you see that as offering you . . .

A chance? Yeah. 'Cause they came to England, and they came looking for John Mayall, and we hung out and played together, and I realized then that if I wanted to go to America and play that it was going to be acceptable.

Did this help resolve the whole issue of actually singing the blues? Because you really hadn't sung much up till then.

Yeah, I thought Butterfield was the first one I heard who could come anywhere near it. John Hammond I thought too much "characterized" it. It didn't seem like it was coming from him. More that he was . . . imitating. I mean, I wasn't convinced as much as I was with Butterfield. My singing doesn't stand up to the test, 'cause I don't consider myself a singer. I still consider myself a guitar player, and I always did.

Was it a huge leap for you to do your first vocal [on the Robert Johnson song "Ramblin' on My Mind"] on that John Mayall album?

Well, I'd been singing and playing in that style for so long it was really just a question of turning

the tape machines on. The leap came in accepting that this thing was going to go onto plastic and would be recorded. Accepting that took a lot of convincing from John, who really kept having to tell me that it was worth it.

You said that Muddy Waters acted as a kind of mentor to you, that he served almost as a kind of salvation. Personally?

When we worked together [on an extensive 1979 tour], yeah, he was doing a lot of character building for me. 'Cause I was losing my identity at the time. I didn't know where I was going. I lured myself off the path of being a blues player and was trying to . . . I even got into country music. I was very heavily influenced by J.J. Cale in those days and wanted to find a different way to play. We talked about that a lot, and Muddy would say, in a very simple way, "Well, I love listening to your band, but my favorite song you do is 'Worried Life Blues.' That's really where you're at, and you should realize that. You should realize it and be proud of it." And he helped to instill that feeling in me again. Because at the end of the day, I got something out of his company, and his music, that I could get from no one else. And it was only by getting back with Muddy, and then occasionally seeing Buddy Guy and people like that, that knocked on the door again. The knock that reminded me where I was really from.

But getting back to your interpretation, the way you've always approached what could be regarded as classic blues.

The way that I've always looked upon any interpretation of a great blues musician's material was to take the most obvious things and simplify them. Like my way of doing "Crossroads" was to take that one musical figure and make that the point, the focal point. Just trying to focus on what the essence of the song was—keeping it simple.

You mean you simplify to reach a broader audience?

No, no, just to make it . . . playable for me. I am very limited in my technique, really, so what matters in my playing is the simplicity of it and that it gets to the point. Rather than playing around everything.

But very few of the bluesmen are virtuosos.

No, nor am I. That's how I identified with them. It's not what is said but how it's said. Not how much is said, but the way it's said. And that's what I would try to draw out of anything that was a great influence on me, try to draw out of Robert [Johnson] what was the spirit of what was being said as much as the way or the form or the technique.

Where would you draw that spirit from?

From what I heard.

When you started out, you tried to envision the car the person was driving, the smell of the car, the specific locale or milieu . . .

Yeah, the outward sensations that would echo what was going on inside.

Was it almost like method acting? Was it a specific discipline you put yourself through to try to get to the core of the thing?

Yeah, it would be. It would be a discipline you would introduce to make that possible. On the surface of things, the sound of the music kind of overwhelms you. And then all these pictures come into your head. Say if I've got a gig tonight with Buddy [Guy], I've really got to kind of call up all this stuff that goes right back to when I first heard Robert Johnson, or Little Walter "live." They're all in there. All this stuff is inside me. It's just a matter of tapping it.

Do you tap into your own reserve of emotional experience, memories of your grandparents, your mother . . . ?

That's all I've got to refer to. . . . It isn't labeled. It's a bag of emotions that have been untapped by—

I mean, even when I was in psychotherapy for a while, I would reserve . . . Even in deep psychotherapy there was a certain place that no one . . . that I wouldn't let him go. Because that is meant to be used for my music.

That's what maintains its spontaneity? Otherwise it would become formulaic for you?

Yeah, I think so. It's always fresh. And that kind of, like, leads me to a troubled life, in a way. My personal life really suffers from that. Suffers from a lot of . . . kind of inability to deal with relationships, things like that. Because, you know, I keep a lot of this stuff inside.

It disallows total unburdening?

Total intimacy with other people. Yeah.

Do you feel this is true for all artists?

I think so. To a greater or lesser degree. There's a place that you won't let anyone else go. . . . I don't think it's a question of being frightened of losing their creativity or anything like that. It's deeper than that.

You've often said that you felt the best of Buddy Guy has never gotten onto record, that the spirit of the music, the almost total freedom of his blues, isn't really transferable to record. Do you feel that's true of your own music as well?

To a certain extent, yes. I still think my best playing exists separately from the songs. It's just something that is of its own. To get that onto a record is difficult, because you kind of become much more studied.

Have you thought about taking a mobile recording unit and attempting to capture moments like those?

No, because I kind of like it the way it is. You know, there's something very true, in a way, that some music belongs to the concert hall and the audience and should remain that way. And for the gods. ✒

BIG BILL BROONZY: KEY TO THE HIGHWAY
BY CHRISTOPHER JOHN FARLEY

*I got the key to the highway, yes, and I'm billed
out and bound to go
I'm gonna leave, leave here runnin', because
walkin' is most too slow*
— Big Bill Broonzy, "Key to the Highway"

Even when Big Bill was small, he was on the move.

His father, Frank, and mother, Nettie, were sharecroppers and former slaves. When Big Bill was born on a June day in Scott, Mississippi, in 1893, Frank, a Baptist and a deacon in the church, cursed for the first and only time in his life. He had left for several days to get food for the family and arrived home to find that his wife had given birth to twins, Bill and his sister, Lanie. Bill was one of sixteen children in the family, and that added up to more mouths than Frank had expected he'd have to feed.

The family, looking for a better sharecropping situation, relocated to Langdale, Arkansas, when Bill was eight years old. Then, when Bill was twelve, they moved to Scotts Crossing. By that time, Bill had taken up the fiddle—he fashioned his first one out of a cigar box. In his early years he was a devout Christian, but he eventually left the church to earn a living doing odd jobs and playing music. "Christian's one thing, and money's another," he said. "I had to quit church because they wouldn't pay me no money to preach." He was caught up in the draft in 1917 and was sent off to Europe. It was a confusing period for the youngster, who went quickly and without training or schooling from plantation life to World War I's international conflict. He did what he was told but didn't really know what he was doing. "I don't know

the names of all the places where we went, but it was in France," Bill said.

When Broonzy returned from the war back to Arkansas in 1919, a white man he had known before he left confronted him. "Those clothes you got there," the man said. "You can take 'em off and get you some overalls. Because there's no nigger gonna walk around here with no Uncle Sam's uniform on, see, up and down these streets." Broonzy was a big guy—over six feet tall and solidly built. War had changed him, made him tougher, less willing to follow orders. The new Bill was not easily pushed around. Something in him had grown bolder; he now laughed in the face of conflict. He wanted to follow his own path and not the roads that others laid down for him. This particularly postwar confrontation, however, got to him, and he remembered it long afterwards. He grew to dislike the South and its oppressive ways. Even when he was home, Bill didn't feel at home. From then on, he'd only feel at home on the road.

*I'm goin' down on the border . . . where I'm
better known
'Cause you haven't done nothin', woman, but
drive a good man away from home*

In 1920, Big Bill Broonzy left Arkansas and went to Chicago. "The main reason I left home was

Big Bill Broonzy died a few months after this photo was taken in 1958.

because I couldn't stand eating out of the back trough all the time," Broonzy said. "In the army, I had been used to being considered a man irregardless." He wasn't alone in his journey. Many thousands of blacks at that time were making the great migration, leaving the South and heading to what they hoped would be better prospects in the North. "Sweet Home Chicago," as Robert Johnson once put it, was the new gathering place for a wave of itinerant blues and jazz musicians, including Papa Charlie Jackson, Blind Lemon Jefferson, Blind Blake, and Memphis Minnie. All hailed, originally, from places in the South. All came to the Windy City in search of better jobs, better venues in which to play music, and better recording opportunities. Broonzy was in the center of the blues world.

After moving to Chicago, Broonzy worked as a molder in a foundry, and also as a cook, a grocery packer, a piano mover, and a Pullman porter. He

took the work as it came. "None of us would ever make enough money just playing music," Broonzy said. Along the way, he kept playing his music, in taverns and nightclubs, at parties and on street corners, and eventually he recorded some of his songs. Soon enough, Broonzy was considered by many to be the most popular blues star around. He made his first record under his own name in Chicago in 1927; it was a recording of "House Rent Stomp" for Paramount Records. He went on to lay down tracks for a number of different companies over the course of his career, including such labels as Bluebird, Columbia, OKeh, Champion, Melotone, and Oriole. In 1938, Broonzy (filling in for the late Robert Johnson) was a performer at the "Spirituals to Swing Concert" at Carnegie Hall.

Through all of the acclaim, Broonzy kept his day jobs. He once calculated that, out of 260 of his compositions, he made perhaps two thousand dollars. He also said he never saw even a penny of royalty money until 1939, well into his recording career. "I made more playing in taverns and nightclubs than I ever did out of records," he said. "A lousy guy that lets you work your head off and then gets on easy street and leaves you still where you were? I don't understand people like that. It's just outrageous to me."

Broonzy was known, but he wasn't really famous, and he sure wasn't rich. Other performers rerecorded his songs without giving him any credit or money. His records sold, but the traditional blues audience was still a niche market. White performers singing blues-based music seemed to be the ones making the real profits. Broonzy once said of Elvis Presley, "He's singing the same thing I'm singing now. And he knows it. 'Cause really, the melody and the tune and the way we used to call it 'rocking the blues' years ago when I was a kid . . . that's what he's doing now. . . . Rock & roll is a steal from the old, original blues."

So Broonzy kept on the road and kept playing concerts, trying to steal back a little of his own thunder. Life on the road could be chaotic, filled with the temptations of women and alcohol, and sometimes Broonzy happily gave in to both. Big Bill liked to tell the story of a gig he once landed in New York City. He had been in the habit of taking two or three drinks before he performed; he felt it dulled his fear and helped him remember his songs. But for his new singing job, his bosses told him he couldn't drink. One night, Broonzy, after spending the evening carousing with friends, showed up at his new gig loaded. "I'm drunk," he admitted to his new boss. "Please forgive me. It'll never happen again." Broonzy went on to play two shows that night. Afterward, his boss gave him his pay, which included five more dollars than usual. "Take this," said the boss, "and be drunk tomorrow night. You played better tonight than ever."

Still, Broonzy came to long for some stability. He had been running all his life, from Arkansas and back, to war and back, from the South to the Midwest to the North. Near the end of his career, Broonzy played a summer gig at Iowa State College at Ames. When the college offered him a job as a janitor there, he took the offer and stayed. He considered the position a dream job. Big Bill Broonzy, master of the blues, now spent more time with a mop than with a guitar.

> Now when the moon creeps over the mountain,
> I'll be on my way
> Now I'm gonna walk this old highway, until the
> break of day

In the 1950s, Studs Terkel asked the British actor John Neville if he had ever heard Big Bill Broonzy.

Neville famously replied, "Everybody in England knows Big Bill. Who doesn't?"

Terkel, a native of Chicago who was, frankly, shocked that a bluesman who was little-known in his home country and even his hometown could be so famous abroad, replied, "Ninety-nine out of a hundred of his countrymen have never heard of him."

Now it was Neville's turn to be stunned. Why wouldn't such a talent, so beloved by Europeans, be embraced by his fellow Americans?

Broonzy's conquest of Europe began with his first tour there. Friends in Chicago and admirers abroad helped set up a European sojourn for Broonzy in 1951, as well as a subsequent visit. Broonzy wasn't worried whether his very American music would translate. "A cry's a cry in any language," he said. "A shout's a shout, too, in any language." Indeed, his concerts in Europe were a smash and he achieved a fame there that he never enjoyed in the States. Years later, Max Jones wrote in *Melody Maker* about Broonzy's first concert in London, held at Kingsway Hall in 1951: "He found there an audience receptive to the best songs in his extensive repertoire and to his finest feats of guitarmanship, an audience that regarded him as a combination of creative artist and living legend." Broonzy created a new musical iconography for a generation of young British musicians. His songs were rich and varied, from hollers of pain to sly social commentaries. He had, over the course of his career, experimented with the electric guitar and played with a drummer; he had performed with a variety of backing bands. But late in his career, he presented himself as the last of a dying line, a true bluesman from the South, standing alone, summoning old ghosts, single-handedly repre-senting an old, grand culture. British kids, desperate for some culture to grab hold of in the shattered post–World War II world, saw in his music a kind of escape. Not an escape to some carefree place but an escape to a place where things mattered, where instrumental prowess was prized, where social protest was savored, where blue pain could be transmuted into musical joy.

The blues, in America, are black-and-white. It's difficult to listen to the blues, in an American context, without also hearing the echo of slavery, of segregation, of field hands communicating to each other in the secret rhythms of their own music. That's why when white men first took up the blues it was seen as some sort of cultural breakthrough, as if some invisible line had been crossed. Many Europeans had no such guilt; they recognized no such lines. They could listen to the blues without hearing some conflict of cultures and colors. For them, there was no discord in the music, there were no cultural barriers, there was only art. The Europeans who adopted the blues was, arguably, better able than some of their American counterparts to see the artistic possibilities in the form and to speak in their own tongues rather than in voices that seemed crude parodies of the music's originators. Blues, as a music, traveled. The cultural baggage stayed home.

Broonzy's journeys had an effect on him, too, especially a trip that he took to Senegal. "I look at those people an' I felt I must've been here before, my people, I mean," Broonzy said. "All my family is tall. And I looked at all these seven-footers, I felt like a midget. I run into a family named Broonzie. They spelt it IE instead of Y, but it was the same name. Yeah, I think my ancestors came from there."

In the last year of his life, Broonzy suffered from lung and throat cancer. Many of his contemporaries were dead or long forgotten. Rock & roll was all the rage, and the blues was out of fashion. Broonzy's own voice was being eaten away by his ailments. He began to think about his legacy. Broonzy said, "I don't want the old blues to die because if they do I'll be dead, too, because that's the only kind I can play and sing and I love the old style. I have traveled all over the U.S.A., in every state and also in Mexico, Spain, Germany, England, Holland, Switzerland, Italy, Africa, Belgium, France, trying to keep the old-time blues alive, and I'm going to keep on as long as Big Bill is still living."

Broonzy died of cancer on August 15, 1958. Services were held at Chicago's Metropolitan Funeral Parlor. A tape was played of Big Bill singing "Swing Low, Sweet Chariot." Messages of condolence came in from London, Paris, Rome, and Brussels. In the years and decades afterward, British performers whom Broonzy influenced, such as the Rolling Stones and Eric Clapton, brought his music back to America, inspiring new generations of blues fans. The blues would never be as hot as they had been once upon a time in the South, but the art form was still on the move, just like Bill was when he was alive, traveling from city to city, from continent to continent, from decade to decade. Big Bill was dead, but the blues sure weren't.

RECOMMENDED LISTENING:

Big Bill Broonzy, *Trouble in Mind* (Smithsonian/Folkways, 2000). A fair sampling of his work.

Big Bill Broonzy, *The Young Big Bill Broonzy 1928–1935* (Yazoo, 1991). A look at the early years.

Keith Richards, *Talk Is Cheap* (Virgin, 1998). His best solo album.

Derek and the Dominos, *Layla and Other Assorted Love Songs* (RSO, 1970) Eric Clapton and sidemen, including Duane Allman, cover "Key to the Highway."

THE FIRST TIME I MET THE BLUES *By Val Wilmer*
[Excerpt from a longer reminiscence, first published in *Mojo,* 1995]

The first time I met the blues he was wearing a large charcoal overcoat, pegged navy pants and a hand-painted tie. A soft brown trilby was pushed to the back of his head, the tartan muffler around his neck unknotted despite the chill of the February night and the wind that came whistling off the Thames. Dwarfing an entourage of critics, collectors, and other musicians, guitarist Big Bill Broonzy was a powerful presence as he emerged from the backstage depths of the Royal Festival Hall, accompanied by fellow Mississippian Brother John Sellers and smelling of whiskey. To a fifteen-year-old who barely knew where the South Bank was—let alone Chicago's South Side—he was a conquering hero, the legend made flesh. In 1957, he certainly had the edge on Lonnie Donegan and "Rock Island Line."

My memory of him is of a big man who seemed pleasantly full of himself and laughing, but he allowed himself to be waylaid for a moment by the teenager who waved an autograph book under his nose. With a quip to his companions, he leant on his guitar case as he struggled to see in the half dark and write his name. Clearly penmanship wasn't his forte, but the bold scrawl he made in my book and "Best wishes to Valerie" across his photo in the program were sufficient reward for the long wait outside the stage door and the knowledge that I had to get up early for school in the morning. They remain a cherished reminder for me of one of the most exciting nights of my life. . . .

The excitement that greeted the arrival of Big Bill and Muddy, and the fascination with the fabric of their lives, is impossible for the present generation of blues fanciers to imagine—just as the idea that this music would enjoy a second revival would have been inconceivable to those of us who were there the first time around. The adulation was intense, the kind pop idols got—although most of the purists would not have admitted that.

The little knowledge we'd gleaned from those pioneering writers who had actually been to the Deep South and heard people like Elmore James in the Northern ghettos set us apart from people who bought the songs in what was still known as the Hit Parade. Because we could brag that we'd heard records by Ma Rainey, Blind Lemon Jefferson, and Sleepy John Estes, we thought it was safe to listen to the blues as an art form removed from commercial considerations—never stopping to think that our idols earned their living this way. We had no idea of the reality of the lives of the people who played the music. All that began to change around the start of the sixties when some of us had the chance to sit down and actually talk to the bluesmen.

Center of everything for a while was Airways Mansions, a tiny hotel just off Piccadilly Circus. If we wanted to listen to the music we could go along to a place like the 100 Club or the Marquee, then also on Oxford Street, but it was after-hours that the musicians began to tell us their stories. Beginning with Champion Jack Dupree, who arrived in 1959, London hosted a steady stream of honky-tonk piano players who had learned their craft in the barrelhouses and sporting houses of New Orleans and the turpentine and lumber camps of the Deep South. All of them were a long way from home, all of them ready to welcome people with a genuine interest.

Airways Mansions was home to other musicians as well. Virtuoso instrumentalists who had played with Count Basie and jazz players here to accompany Ella

Jesse "Lone Cat" Fuller in the Wilmers' kitchen

Fitzgerald enjoyed its relative freedom, and occasionally paths would cross and there would be an interesting breaking-down of barriers. Unlike the larger hotels with their racist hall porters who objected to their guests having "company," whether female or male, the desk clerk at Airways Mansions virtually encouraged it. On occasion he'd come up to someone's room for a drink, leaving the desk unmanned and the telephones ringing. The hotel became a kind of twenty-four-hour center of learning and many were the afternoon hangovers as glazed fans staggered back to work following a late lunchtime session. . . .

It's hard to remember now just how the various piano players came and went, for their visits crisscrossed with several others who came here to play with Chris Barber. Chris, who was largely responsible for launching me on to an unsuspecting world as a writer, was a key figure in bringing over a number of important artists. Touring the States with his band during the Trad boom, he would seek out bluesmen in tough joints white people seldom, if ever, visited. In Harlem, Chris stocked up on gospel 78s at the legendary Rainbow Records on 125th Street, and imported the sensational gospel guitarist Sister Rosetta Tharpe to tour with his band— another gig I caught when I was fifteen. His chart successes enabled him to subsidize the roots music that was his first love; credit where due, it was mainly through his tenacity that audiences had the chance to hear Louis Jordan and Jimmy Cotton as well as Muddy and Otis and the perennial folk favorites, guitar/ harmonica duo Brownie McGhee and Sonny Terry.

One person who didn't stay at Airways Mansions was the one-man-band folk "songster" Jesse Fuller. My relationship with Jesse was special. I was still at school when I wrote to him and asked him to tell me his life story. Amazingly, my extraordinary cheek succeeded. Over a number of months a series of pencil-written letters arrived, which I then worked up into a magazine article. This marked my beginning as a published writer and fired my ambition. Jesse, who composed the folk standard "San Francisco Bay Blues," played guitar and harmonica or kazoo simultaneously (the harmonica harness he designed was copied by Dylan). He also played the fotdella, an instrument of his own creation, with one of his feet. I was looking forward to our meeting, but I found him a difficult individual, permanently dissatisfied with his lot. Following a short trip to Germany, he returned to London to find there was no more work in the offing. I took him back to my mother's house and he stayed with us for a few awkward days. There, at least, he could cook himself something resembling a hamburger, but it was strange to discover that I could not get along with the one person I'd expected to like. 🖋

THE ROLLING STONES COME TOGETHER

[From *The True Adventures of the Rolling Stones,* by Stanley Booth, 1984]

"Technical school was completely the wrong thing for me," Keith [Richards] said. "Working with the hands, metalwork. I can't even measure an inch properly, so they're forcing me to make a set of drills or something, to a thousandth-of-an-inch accuracy. I did my best to get thrown out of that place. Took me four years, but I made it."

"You tried to get yourself thrown out how? By not showing up?"

"Not so much that, because they do too many things to you for doing that. It makes life difficult for you. I was trying to make it easier for me. . . .

"But in kicking me out, they as a final show of benevolence fixed up this place for me in art school. Actually, that was the best thing they could have done for me, because the art schools in England are very freaky. Half the staff anyway are in advertising agencies, and to keep up the art bit and make a bit of extra bread they teach school, like, one day a week. Freaks, drunks, potheads. Also, there's a lot of kids. I was fifteen and there are kids there nineteen, in their last year.

"A lot of music goes on at art schools. That's where I got hung up on guitar, because there were a lot of guitar players around then, playing anything from Big Bill Broonzy to Woody Guthrie. I also got hung up on Chuck Berry, though what I was playing was the art school stuff, the Guthrie sound and blues. Not really blues, mostly ballads and Jesse Fuller stuff. In art school I met Dick Taylor, a guitar player. He was the first cat I played with. We were playing a bit of blues,

Chuck Berry stuff on acoustic guitars, and I think I'd just about now got an amplifier like a little beat-up radio. There was another cat at art school called Michael Ross. He decided to form a country & western band—this is *real* amateur—Sanford Clark songs and a few Johnny Cash songs, 'Blue Moon of Kentucky.' The first time I got onstage and played was with this C&W band. One gig I remember was a sports dance at Eltham, which is near Sidcup, where the art school I went to was.

"I left technical school when I was fifteen. I did three years of art school. I was just starting the last year when Mick and I happened to meet up on the train at Dartford Station. Between the ages of eleven and seventeen you go through a lot of changes. So I didn't know what he was like. It was like seeing an old friend, but it was also like meeting a new person. He'd left grammar school and he was going to the London School of Economics, very heavily into a university student number. He had some records with him, and I said, Wotcha got? Turned out to be Chuck Berry, *Rocking at the Hop.*

"He was into singin' in the bath sort of stuff, he had been singin' with a rock group a few years previous, couple of years. Buddy Holly stuff and 'Sweet Little Sixteen,' Eddie Cochran stuff, at youth clubs and things in Dartford, but he hadn't done that for a while when I met him. I told him I was messin' around with Dick Taylor. It turned out that Mick knew Dick Taylor because they'd been to grammar school together, so, fine, why don't we all get together? I think one night we all went 'round to Dick's place and had a rehearsal, just a jam. That was the first time we got into playing. Just backroom stuff, just for ourselves. So we started gettin' it together in front rooms and back rooms, at Dick Taylor's home,

Charlie Watts and Keith Richards *(from left)* backstage at the Odeon Theatre in Manchester on their first national tour of England, 1965

"There was a [racial] boundary line which no one thought could be crossed, but the Rolling Stones broke it by getting Wolf on *[Shindig!]*. That was something that we never would even have thought of, the hairs were just standing on my head. [Wolf] and I talked about it later, he said about how the man next door don't know who I am, and here's some British kids from thousands of miles away. . . . 'Cause as far as the record companies or the news media or anything, we were all ignored until those English kids came in." —*Buddy Guy*

particularly. We started doing things like Billy Boy Arnold stuff, 'Ride an Eldorado Cadillac,' Eddie Taylor, Jimmy Reed, didn't attempt any Muddy Waters yet, or Bo Diddley, I don't think, in that period. Mick laid a lot of sounds on me that I hadn't heard. He'd imported records from Ernie's Record Mart.

"At this time the big music among the kids was traditional jazz, some of it very funky, some of it very wet, most of it very, *very* wet. Rock & roll had already drifted into pop like it has already done again here because the mass media have to cater to everybody. They don't have it broken down into segments so that kids can listen to one station. It's all put together, so eventually it boils down to what the average person wants to hear, which is average rubbish. Anyway, that was the scene then, no good music coming out of the radio, no good music coming out of the so-called rock & roll stars. No good nothing.

"Just about the time Mick and I are getting the scene together with Dick Taylor, trying to find out what it's all about, who's playing what and how they're playing it, Alexis Korner starts a band at a club in the west of London, in Ealing, with a harmonica player called Cyril Davies, a car-panel beater at a junkyard and body shop. Cyril had been to Chicago and sat in with Muddy at Smitty's Corner and was therefore a very big deal. He was a good harp player and a good night man; he used to drink bourbon like a fucking fish. Alexis and Cyril got this band together and who happens to be on drums, none other than Charlie Watts. We went down about the second week it opened. It was the only club in England where they were playing anything funky, as far as any-body knew. The first person we see sitting in—Alexis gets up and says, 'And now, folks, a very fine bottleneck guitar player who has come all the way from Cheltenham to play here tonight'—and suddenly there's fucking Elmore James up there, 'Dust My Broom,' beautifully played, and it's Brian [Jones]." 🎸

MY BLUES BAND: THE ROLLING STONES
BY RICHARD HELL

"A swift, too-pretty grackle swarming over a plate of noodles." —Brian Jones on the Stones[1]

When I was fifteen, I had three music albums: *The Rolling Stones Now!*, *Bringing It All Back Home* by Bob Dylan, and *Kinks-Size* (featuring "All Day and All of the Night" and "Tired of Waiting for You") by the Kinks. I really liked all three, though I didn't think about it. (I remember I was suspended from school for a week in the ninth grade, and my mother made me paint the house. I ran a cord to a little portable record player in the yard and had those records repeat while I painted. The Stones one started to melt and warp in the sun, so that night I put it between two frying pans in the oven, and the next day it sounded even better.)

At that time I didn't know what the music classification "the blues" meant. I had the vague idea of it being the sad folk music of African-American slaves and their oppressed sharecropper descendants. But you'd hear jazz people and TV singers claim it, too. Anyway, I thought of it as dated and corny, and the oppressed black people weren't listening to it much then, either; they'd more likely be listening to Otis Redding or Mary Wells or Marvin Gaye.

I've done some research, and I know what people mean by blues music now. And the Rolling Stones, back then, in the mid-sixties, were a blues band who also did some R&B, and they were good. They were my blues band, and I will defend them.

Muddy Waters himself admitted to writer Robert Palmer in the seventies, "They got all these white

Keith Richards, Mick Jagger, Brian Jones *(from left)*, 1965

kids now. Some of them can play *good* blues. They play so much, run a ring around you playin' guitar." He added, "But they cannot vocal like the black man," and I grant there's not much denying that, but I'd propose Dylan as an exception,[2] and also, with some caveats, Mick Jagger.

Of course, the teenage Rolling Stones, unlike thirties Delta farmhands, learned most of what they played from records—but that was often true of black blues musicians, too, by the mid-fifties—and it was the music of the R&B and Chicago blues players of that time that the Stones grew up loving and imitating when it was current: Muddy Waters, Chuck Berry ("rock & roll" but who was brought to Chess Records by Waters), Howlin' Wolf, Bo Diddley, Jimmy Reed, Arthur Alexander. Keith Richards is always saying there's only one song. That's a stretch, but in a few real ways there is only one blues song—

almost anything that can be called a blues follows a I–IV–V chord progression, and there are thirty or forty lines of lyrics that show up in half the songs that count as blues. The original country-blues players shuffled those lines continuously, depending on circumstances, not only among songs but within a given song. Players would habitually take credit for composing songs they recorded that were only a few words separated from their preexisting sources. The composition was really in the delivery.

The Rolling Stones were scrupulous about crediting their models, but they did carry on in this spirit of the blues recombinant dreamlike history. For instance, Muddy Waters' first commercial recording, in Chicago, in 1948, was "I Can't Be Satisfied," and it was a huge regional hit. The Stones covered this song on their second album, *The Rolling Stones No. 2* (British Decca, 1964), and then a year or two later, their original international smash was "(I Can't Get No) Satisfaction." "Satisfaction" is a rock & roll song, and it's only related nominally and in spirit to that earlier blues, but it's consistent with blues history and is an extension of the tradition. Of course, the Stones took their very band name from a Waters tune.

It's a progression, and all one thing that evolved from the earliest turn-of-the-twentieth-century, first-person, country-blues prototypes that were never recorded—with their repetitions, calls and responses, African rhythms, and African musical value of roughness (Palmer cites, for instance, early New Orleans jazz horn players pressing their necks between frying pans[3])—to the ramblin' showmen, buskers, and Saturday-night dance entertainers like Charley Patton, Son House, and Robert Johnson, whose music we have some direct record of and whose recordings during their lifetimes were only popular among blacks and primarily in the South; to

the Delta-drawn Chicago electric bands of Waters and Wolf and Reed, boogie of John Lee Hooker, and Texas-rooted style of Lightnin' Hopkins, who made nationwide hit records that were still half-hidden from white listeners as "race" records; to the Rolling Stones, who had worldwide megahits (their 1964 British Number One version of Howlin' Wolf's "Little Red Rooster" was the first and only full-fledged blues song to ever top the pop charts there or here). The progression took place over a span of only about sixty years, and though at each stage the music became a little less local and eccentric, it's all blues, until it disperses into a kind of loamy "pop" that the blues (and other folk music) made possible, like the Stones, Dylan, and Prince. (I'd figured that this dispersion was where the tradition became so diluted as to necessarily be thought of as played out and finished, but check the White Stripes now.)

I was amazed when I heard the original versions of those records of fifties electric blues that I'd first heard in the Stones' renditions. The thing that amazed me then was how ludicrously blatant the rip-off was: how the Stones would imitate the originals not only in arrangement and guitar tone, for instance, but also in the vocals, which imitated the accents of those Southern black men and the twists of the styles of their singing, line by line. By comparison, Elvis Presley's covers of early R&B songs were awesomely creative. At the same time you could make a case that the Stones' versions of Muddy Waters songs were to him as he was to, say, Son House. It's true that the homogenization of the sound at the Stones' level is mostly in the singing. What Robert Johnson and Howlin' Wolf and Muddy Waters did with their voices has not been touched by a white rock & roll singer (except, I'd maintain, for Bob Dylan). The way those great blues singers cut loose, playing their voices like something they're beating on with sticks, while also whistling through like horns, and somehow at the same time talking in words like possessed confessors, interspersed with yelps and moans in seeming spontaneity of excitement or anger or pain, is barely hinted at by Jagger. Jagger is good, though, and in ways other than mimicry. That fresh-voiced, snotty-kid defiance of his, mixed up with, of all things, a lisping femininity—his outrageous, girlish, threatening contempt—is completely "rock & roll," completely weird blues. It works, and ultimately it's probably the biggest contribution to the "canon" the Stones make as a blues band.

But the Stones aren't legitimate as a blues band just because of their musical ability anyway. There are qualities of blues—as well as its extension, rock & roll—that get expressed by means other than through the music: namely, that weirdness, that insolence and snottiness, as well as miscegenation—sacred profanity, say, heartfelt entertainment, loving cruelty, say, black whiteness, happy sadness, say, rhythmic blues—a swaggering, freak, mutant thing of self-involved promiscuity and slick show-off duds, and the Rolling Stones were there by their ordinary nature. They were these ugly, skinny, all-jawed, girly-haired, British working-class kids dressing like romantic dandies, singing the folk music of another race, of another country, in obscene sibilant taunts and come-ons. Like Tommy Johnson and Robert Johnson, they sold their souls to play the way they did. You can only play that music if you don't give a fuck. What could selling your soul mean but never worrying about restraining your evil impulses anymore? And any way you look at it, they're corrupt. It cuts in the most mundane and pathetic ways, too—the Stones immediately dropped their old friend and original band member, pianist Ian Stewart, from the group because their first manager

thought his looks didn't fit in with what could be popular at the time. Chuck Berry was maybe the most corrupt of all: His songs were written specifically to appeal to white high school kids. Charley Patton himself was looked down upon by many in his time and place for being too much of a showman, pandering to the crowd. Nothing is pure in this world.

"Nothing is pure in this world." There are those who revel in that perception and take it as a license. I am not among them. But I did get a lot from the Rolling Stones when they were new, and I think what I got was pretty much the same as what Saturday-night dancers to Robert Johnson got on the plantations and in the roadhouses in the thirties: some raw emotion, strong pride, sharp attitude, ideas about what clothes would attract sexy women, and a kind of dance music that physically felt good and made you want to jump around and take off. The Rolling Stones had that effect on me, because they were a real good blues band. ☛

---

1. In a dream I had.

2. Exhibit A being the famous 1966 Royal Albert Hall live date, where, incidentally, of fourteen original compositions Dylan performs, three happen to be pure blues constructions: "She Belongs to Me," "Just Like Tom Thumb's Blues," and "Leopard-Skin Pill-Box Hat."

3. Palmer didn't really say that thing about horn players pressing their necks between frying pans. He did say they'd use handfuls of kazoos as mutes. And then regarding blues "history," there's also a lot to the point made by Robert Gordon in *It Came From Memphis*, paraphrasing his friend Jim Dickinson, "The best songs don't get recorded, the best recordings don't get released, and the best releases don't get played."

PIANO BLUES AND BEYOND
Directed by Clint Eastwood

Fats Domino came to the plains of the Grand Tetons in Wyoming when we were making *Any Which Way You Can*. He started playing one of his songs, "I Want to Walk You Home" on a grand piano. All of a sudden everyone stopped and looked over the side of the hill and there were about ten elk. They were all standing there with their heads tilted to where the sounds were coming from—and as soon as Fats stopped playing, they left. They were fascinated. Everybody likes the blues.

I think music plays a very important part in a movie by punctuating the drama, and it is important that it enhances the drama and not intrudes upon it. There are moments when silence in a film can play a very important part as well. To me the complications of the theme are dictated according to what the story calls for. I've done a lot of movies where I have been lucky enough to incorporate jazz and the blues—two of America's great art forms.

When I was a kid music was a constant. After Fats Waller died, my mother brought home a whole collection of his records, saying that they would be the last of his music to be available. I learned to play the piano by listening to his records and trying to imitate other jazz and blues artists of that era. I taught myself to play a little stride piano and a three-chord eight-beat thing. I became interested in boogie-woogie, jazz, and bebop. I was telling stories on the piano long before I ever directed a movie. In my movies, I like the image of the piano player: The piano player sits down, plays, tells his story, and then gets up and leaves, letting the music speak for itself.

My love for the blues continued while growing up in Oakland, California. On the radio and on records, I heard great piano players, like Art Tatum, George Shearing, Dave Brubeck, Oscar Peterson, and Erroll Garner, as well as the boogie-woogie piano players, such as Clarence "Pine Top" Smith, Albert Ammons,

Jay McShann *(left)* and Pinetop Perkins, 2003

Pete Johnson, Meade "Lux" Lewis, and Jay McShann. There was a musical scene that allowed all kinds of styles to flourish, including gospel, which is where I think much of the blues started in the churches of the South.

A few years ago, I had the pleasure of being on a program with Jay McShann at Carnegie Hall. I was playing "After Hours" by Avery Parrish on the piano, and I hadn't played this song in many years. The deal was Jay was going to come in and take over. I had said, "I don't know if I know all of it . . . be sure and make certain McShann comes in and takes over." So, there I am playing on stage at Carnegie Hall and all of a sudden I am coming to the end of my repertoire and Jay wasn't there. Afterward, Jay said, "Well, you seem to be doing OK, I just thought I'd let you go."

Recently I asked Jay McShann, "Would you describe yourself as happy?" He told me, "Pretty much, but sometimes you can't see from lookin'." In doing the movie about piano blues I want the camera to look but not get in the way of seeing.

—Clint Eastwood

OUR LADIES OF THE KEYS: BLUES AND GONE
BY CHRISTOPHER JOHN FARLEY

In 1975 Marcia Ball gave birth to her own blues.

She was a Louisiana gal, born in 1949 in Orange, Texas, right on the state line, but raised in Vinton, Louisiana, close to the border and a four-hour drive from New Orleans. In the mid-1970s, she was married, fooling around with a band or two, and living in Austin, Texas. She was pregnant and realized she had to make some big decisions. Was she gonna be in the blues or out of it? Was she gonna lead a band or be led by one? She had been involved in music since she was a kid; all the female members of her family—her mother, her grandmother, her aunt, her cousins—played piano. She had worked with other musicians, and she had worked alone. She understood now, by experience and by sweat, that if she was going to have a baby—and she was planning on it—she would have to call the shots in her musical life if it was going to work; otherwise, she wasn't going to be able to work at all. So she started her band, the Marcia Ball Band, and she's been running it ever since. She kept right on playing almost until she gave birth to her son, Luke; and a few days after she had him, she was back onstage, playing locally. She was a child of the blues now, and nothing was gonna stop her. Maybe she was never going to make much money doing what she was doing, maybe she was never going to make it out of Austin, but that's love. That's life. That's the blues.

⊕ ⊕ ⊕ ⊕ ⊕

Women—all those unrelated Smith gals: Bessie, Mamie, Trixie, and Clara, as well as Ma Rainey, Alberta Hunter, Ethel Waters, Billie Holiday, and others—gave birth to the blues. In the early part of the twentieth century, women were the first to record the blues (Mamie Smith's 1920 rendition of "Crazy Blues" was the first blues record ever made), and they were the first to make it really sell. In the early part of the twenty-first century, it might be argued that women are the driving force behind the rebirth of the blues. While female vocalists such as Bessie Smith helped launch the form nearly a century ago, today the genre is being championed by a generation or two of female instrumentalists, many of them keyboard players, some of them guitarists, most of them singer/songwriters. And while a fair number of these female players are perhaps more pop-y than rootsy, the blues—the same blues that Ma had, that Bessie had, that Billie had—informs their music or colors it in a significant way.

Female instrumentalists—women with their fingers flickering across keys, with their hands on guitars, with their arms raised, leading big bands—have been a key part of the development of the blues, jazz, and rock, though their contributions are often undercelebrated. Lil Hardin Armstrong, Louis Armstrong's second wife, was a brilliant pianist and singer, and after convincing the young Louis to quit King Oliver's band and strike out on his own, she played and sang on some of his seminal Hot Five and Hot Seven recordings. Galveston, Texas–born blues-and-boogie pianist Camille Howard, with her strong, sexy, two-fisted keyboard attack, helped, along with other performers, to engineer the

Katie Webster

cultural and musical shift between jump blues and rock & roll. Trinidad-born performer Hazel Scott (at one time the wife of Congressman Adam Clayton Powell Jr.) was the first black woman in the United States to have her own TV show, appeared in several movies, and perfected a sophisticated blend of blues, jazz, and classical music. The list of accomplished female piano heroes in blues and jazz—such a rundown would have to include the trailblazing Mary Lou Williams; the swamp-boogie queen Katie Webster; Toshiko Akiyoshi, who cross-pollinated traditional Japanese music with bebop; and many others—is long and continues to grow, even if the general public, and most musicians, haven't committed its entries to memory.

And of course, there are also female blues guitar heroes, from the great, bold gospel queen Sister Rosetta Tharpe, who matched sacred lyrics with secular rhythms, to, more recently, Bonnie Raitt, Rory Block, Susan Tedeschi, Sue Foley, and the much-heralded young, Austin, Texas–based guitarist Eve Monsees.

Members of the newer generation have shown both a deep respect for tradition and a willingness to remake it to suit their needs. The guitarist and singer/songwriter Deborah Coleman, for example, performs Koko Taylor's rewrite of Muddy Waters and Bo Diddley's "Mannish Boy," renamed "I'm a Woman" and transformed into a declaration of musical and sexual independence. The virtuoso jazz vocalist Cassandra Wilson, who has covered Son House and Robert Johnson in her recordings, has increasingly turned to playing acoustic guitar in concert and writing her own songs. And Madeleine Peyroux, an exceptional young jazz-and-blues singer, has taken to infusing her concert performances with folksy blues songs, accompanying herself on acoustic guitar.

But around the turn of the century from the twentieth to the twenty-first, it was female pianists who were making the biggest commercial impact among blues-based performers. Canadian jazz pianist Diana Krall's 1999 album, *When I Look in Your Eyes,* was the first jazz release to be nominated for an Album of the Year Grammy in more than twenty years. Marcia Ball staged a musical breakout in 2003, shooting a segment for NBC's *Today* show. And while music critics debate whether Norah Jones is a jazz performer or something more mainstream, it's clear to anyone who has listened to her music closely that she has the blues in her soul. On her Web site, she has posted a live version of her rendition of "Bessie Smith," a bluesy, meditative track from Bob Dylan and the Band's classic album *The Basement Tapes.* To hear Jones sing that song, her voice sliding down the notes, sliding back into the late 1960s, when the song was first recorded, back into the 1920s when the blues was still young, is to hear the jazz and blues and roots music transmogrified, perhaps not into what they once were, but maybe into what they should or must be.

"You've taken my blues and gone," Langston Hughes once lamented. Certainly the blues is not what it once was. The days of Ma Rainey and Bessie Smith, of Son House and Robert Johnson, of Muddy Waters and John Lee Hooker, are long gone. Even the blues pioneers who continue to perform, while still great, and while certainly worth seeing and celebrating, are not the entertainers they were when they were young and vital, and to believe anything else is to fool oneself and to dishonor the past. Even Mick Jagger, the man who learned from the blues masters, who took the music to the next generation of rock listeners, while an entertaining showman, is not the dramatic sexual presence he was in the green of his youth.

In one sense, of course, the blues can never die. Just as some dinosaurs, instead of becoming extinct, sprouted feathers and evolved into birds, blues—in the form of Jimi Hendrix and Bob Dylan, Janis Joplin and Eric Clapton, Nirvana singing a Lead Belly classic and the White Stripes tearing into "Death Letter Blues"—took wing back in the forties, fifties, and sixties. It evolved into folk, electric blues, rock & roll, blues rock, and hip-hop, invigorating and playing a role in the gestation of all the popular music forms that followed.

The question is, however: Does real blues still exist? While it's fun to listen to Chris Thomas King meld hip-hop and the blues, and while it may be intriguing and profitable for a techno artist like Moby to sample old blues field recordings and remix them into something modern and danceable, true blues lovers will always want to hear blues that adheres, at least somewhat closely, to the classic contours of the form.

After all, the blues is a power source, and so people turn to it, as naturally as campers crowd around a fire for warmth. The blues and its related musical forms not only changed the way people heard the world; the blues changed the way the world was visualized, processed, and interpreted. Rockers, rappers, poets, DJs, movie stars, painters, and even computer hackers have all adopted parts of the image. Outlaw-rebel cool, a quintessentially American pose, has its roots in the blues. Mondrian drew from the music in such paintings as his 1942–43 *Broadway Boogie Woogie* (in his take, New York City streets became jazzy bright blocks of red and yellow and blue), and his philosophy of art was intimately connected with his love of jazz (he wrote an essay on the subject in 1927 titled "Jazz and Neo-Plastic"). Jackson Pollock's wife, Lee Krasner, once said that her painter husband would spend days at a time listening nonstop to records by Duke Ellington, Billie Holiday, and Louis Armstrong. Said Krasner,

Marcia Ball performing at the W.C. Handy Blues Awards, Memphis, 1994

"Jazz? He thought it was the only other really creative thing happening in this country." T.S. Eliot borrowed rhythms from ragtime for the meter of his poem "The Waste Land"; F. Scott Fitzgerald infused *The Great Gatsby* with the spirit of the Jazz Age; Ralph Ellison, Langston Hughes, and Zora Neale Hurston funneled the blues into the written word. When James Baldwin went to Switzerland to start writing *Nobody Knows My Name,* he took three things with him: a typewriter and two Bessie Smith records. He wrote that it was Bessie, "through her tone and her cadence," who helped him "remember the things I had heard and seen and felt" in order to find his writing muse.

Listening to the blues helps us remember America—not as it was but as it should be. The cultural critic Albert Murray, in his book *The Hero and the Blues,* located in the music the country's most heroic self. "Improvisation is the ultimate human (e.g., heroic) endowment," he wrote, going on to argue that "the ability to swing (or to perform with grace under pressure) is the key to that unique competence which generates the self-reliance and thus the charisma of the hero . . . " In other words, the blues is always green, it always finds a way to overcome obstacles and adversity and perhaps even obsolescence. Even when the form was new, it was old and embattled; the heroes who created the music, the Bessies and the Billies, all, almost to a person, died poor and out of favor. That's the blues. It is the music of the outside looking in. To love the blues is to wrap your arms around the outside, to go against prevailing trends. Because the blues is never trendy, loving it is to go against the times. It means romancing something that may never romance you back. That's love. That's life. That's the blues. ☛

RECOMMENDED LISTENING:

Lil Hardin Armstrong, *Chicago: The Living Legends* (Original Jazz Classics, 1961). Blues and jazz from an innovator on the keyboard.

Hazel Scott, *Relaxed Piano Moods* (Debut Records, 1955, 1985). An elegant, thoughtful recording.

Marcia Ball, *So Many Rivers* (Alligator, 2003). Rollicking good tunes from a master entertainer.

Cassandra Wilson, *Blue Skies* (Verve, 1988). America's finest vocalist deconstructs jazz standards.

Cassandra Wilson, *Blue Light 'Til Dawn* (Blue Note, 1993). Features majestic, groundbreaking covers of Robert Johnson's "Come On in My Kitchen" and "Hellhound on My Trail."

Norah Jones, *Come Away With Me* (Blue Note, 2002). An elegant, jazzy album for lovers and those looking for a peaceful, easy feeling.

Various Artists, *Dealin' With the Devil: Songs of Robert Johnson* (Cannonball, 2000). A new generation of blues artists tackles the songs of the master.

Rory Block, *Best Blues and Originals* (Rounder, 1987). A solid collection of blues numbers.

Deborah Coleman, *Soul Be It!* (Blind Pig, 2002). Hard-driving electric blues performed live.

Lucinda Williams, *World Without Tears* (Lost Highway, 2003). A timeless brew of blues, folk, and rock.

One evenin' my dad said to me, "You wants to be a blues player?" Because he knew how I bin tryin' to play like Friday Ford. Friday Ford was a great man and a wonderful player, matter-fact I think he was genius. And down to the present time before he died he taught me all I know. I have a real strong feelin' in my heart for him. He was in Belzoni, Mississippi, and he used to take me and put me across his knee and tell me, he says, "The reason you right here at the piano 'cause I'm tryin' to make you play." But I couldn't because I was too young and my fingers wasn't develop. After they got develop it were too late because he were dead and gone, but I didn't forget what he taught me . . . I had it in my head. So that's how I picked it up and played it behind him. So my daddy said, "You want to be a blues player? You want to be a blues singer?" I told him, "Yes." He said,

"Well, I buy you a piano." So he bought me a piano and brought it to the house. It was on a Friday, which my mother didn't know because my mother was a Christian woman, she didn't like blues. That Sat'dy mornin' my mother and daddy went to town from the country and that was the only time they'd go to town. Well, I locked the house up—I wanted no one but myself in the house, and I started to playin' the blues. But my mother forgot her pocketbook and she had to come back and get her pocketbook before she got to town. And when she come back to the house, well she unlocked the door and I was playin' the blues. She went out and told [my] father, say, "You know what! You know Otis is playing the blues!" My father say, "Well that's so, he's playin' the blues, let him play the blues." And my father kept me up for three nights playin' the blues! 🖝

"Blues has been borrowed from and stolen from, and altered and changed over the years in many ways, but when you hear that real thing, it stands out. Everyone can tell what blues is and isn't. Blues is something that will not go away, no matter how little airplay it gets or how little acknowledgment it gets. It's the fundamental roots of American music." —*John Hammond*

POWERHOUSE *By Eudora Welty*

[From *A Curtain of Green and Other Stories*, 1941]

Powerhouse is playing!

He's here on tour from the city—
"Powerhouse and His Keyboard"—
"Powerhouse and His Tasmanians"—
think of the things he calls himself!
There's no one in the world like him.
You can't tell what he is. "Nigger
man"?—he looks more Asiatic,
monkey, Jewish, Babylonian, Peruvian,
fanatic, devil. He has pale gray eyes,
heavy lids, maybe horny like a lizard's,
but big glowing eyes when they're
open. He has African feet of the
greatest size, stomping, both together,
on each side of the pedals. He's not
coal black—beverage colored—looks
like a preacher when his mouth is
shut, but then it opens—vast and
obscene. And his mouth is going every
minute: like a monkey's when it looks
for something. Improvising, coming on
a light and childish melody—*smooch*—
he loves it with his mouth.

Is it possible that he could be this!
When you have him there performing
for you, that's what you feel. You know
people on a stage—and people of a
darker race—so likely to be marvelous,
frightening.

This is a white dance. Powerhouse is
not a show-off like the Harlem boys, not
drunk, not crazy—he's in a trance; he's
a person of joy, a fanatic. He listens as
much as he performs, a look of hideous,

powerful rapture on his face. Big arched
eyebrows that never stop traveling, like
a Jew's—wandering-Jew eyebrows. When
he plays he beats down piano and seat
and wears them away. He is in motion
every moment—what could be more
obscene? There he is with his great
head, fat stomach, and little round
piston legs, and long yellow-sectioned
strong big fingers, at rest about the size
of bananas. Of course you know how he
sounds—you've heard him on records—
but still you need to see him. He's going
all the time, like skating around the
skating rink or rowing a boat. It makes
everybody crowd around, here in this
shadowless steel-trussed hall with the
rose-like posters of Nelson Eddy and the
testimonial for the mind-reading horse
in handwriting magnified five hundred
times. Then all quietly he lays his finger
on a key with the promise and serenity
of a sibyl touching the book.

Powerhouse is so monstrous he
sends everybody into oblivion. When
any group, any performers, come to
town, don't people always come out
and hover near, leaning inward about
them, to learn what it is? What is it?
Listen. Remember how it was with the
acrobats. Watch them carefully, hear
the least word, especially what they say
to one another, in another language—
don't let them escape you; it's the only

time for hallucination, the last time.
They can't stay. They'll be somewhere
else this time tomorrow.

❋ ❋ ❋ ❋ ❋

Powerhouse has as much as possible
done by signals. Everybody, laughing
as if to hide a weakness, will sooner or
later hand him up a written request.
Powerhouse reads each one, studying
with a secret face: That is the face which
looks like a mask—anybody's; there is a
moment when he makes a decision. Then
a light slides under his eyelids, and he
says, "92!" or some combination of
figures—never a name. Before a number
the band is all frantic, misbehaving,
pushing, like children in a schoolroom,
and he is the teacher getting silence. His
hands over the keys, he says sternly,
"You-all ready? You-all ready to do some
serious walking?"—waits—then, STAMP.
Quiet. STAMP, for the second time. This is
absolute. Then a set of rhythmic kicks
against the floor to communicate the
tempo. Then, O Lord! say the distended
eyes from beyond the boundary of the
trumpets, Hello and good-bye, and they
are all down the first note like a waterfall.

This note marks the end of any known
discipline. Powerhouse seems to
abandon them all—he himself seems
lost—down in the song, yelling up like
somebody in a whirlpool—not guiding

them—hailing them only. But he knows, really. He cries out, but he must know exactly. "Mercy! . . . What I say! . . . Yeah!" And then drifting, listening— "Where that skin beater?"—wanting drums, and starting up and pouring it out in the greatest delight and brutality. On the sweet pieces such a leer for everybody! He looks down so benevolently upon all our faces and whispers the lyrics to us. And if you could hear him at this moment on "Marie, the Dawn Is Breaking"! He's going up the keyboard with a few fingers in some very derogatory triplet-routine, he gets higher and higher, and then he looks over the end of the piano, as if over a cliff. But not in a show-off way—the song makes him do it.

He loves the way they all play, too— all those next to him. The far section of the band is all studious, wearing glasses, every one—they don't count. Only those playing around Powerhouse are the real ones. He has a bass fiddler from Vicksburg, black as pitch, named Valentine, who plays with his eyes shut and talking to himself, very young: Powerhouse has to keep encouraging him. "Go on, go on, give it up, bring it on out there!" When you heard him like that on records, did you know he was really pleading?

He calls Valentine out to take a solo.

"What you going to play?" Powerhouse looks out kindly from behind the piano; he opens his mouth and shows his tongue, listening.

Valentine looks down, drawing against his instrument, and says without a lip movement, " 'Honeysuckle Rose.' "

He has a clarinet player named Little Brother, and loves to listen to anything he does. He'll smile and say, "Beautiful!" Little Brother takes a step forward when he plays and stands at the very front, with the whites of his eyes like fishes swimming. Once when he played a low note, Powerhouse muttered in dirty praise, "He went clear downstairs to get that one!"

After a long time, he holds up the number of fingers to tell the band how many choruses still to go—usually five. He keeps his directions down to signals.

It's a bad night outside. It's a white dance, and nobody dances, except a few straggling jitterbugs and two elderly couples. Everybody just stands around the band and watches Powerhouse. Sometimes they steal a glance at one another, as if to say, Of course, you know how it is with *them*—Negroes— band leaders—they would play the same way, giving all they've got, for an audience of one. . . . When somebody, no matter who, gives everything, it makes people feel ashamed for him. . . .

⊛　⊛　⊛　⊛　⊛

They play "San" (99). The jitterbugs start up like windmills stationed over the floor, and in their orbits—one circle, another, a long stretch, and a zigzag— dance the elderly couples with old smoothness, undisturbed and stately.

When Powerhouse first came back from intermission, no doubt full of beer, they said, he got the band tuned up again in his own way. He didn't strike the piano keys for pitch—he simply opened his mouth and gave falsetto howls—in A, D, and so on—they tuned by him. Then he took hold of the piano, as if he saw it for the first time in his life, and tested it for strength, hit it down in the bass, played an octave with his elbow, lifted the top, looked inside, and leaned against it with all his might. He sat down and played it for a few minutes with outrageous force and got it under his power—a bass deep and coarse as a sea net—then produced something glimmering and fragile, and smiled. And who could ever remember any of the things he says? They are just inspired remarks that roll out of his mouth like smoke.

They've requested "Somebody Loves Me," and he's already done twelve or fourteen choruses, piling them up nobody knows how, and it will be a wonder if he ever gets through. Now and then he calls and shouts, "Somebody loves me! Somebody loves me, I wonder who!" His mouth gets to be nothing but a volcano. "I wonder who!"

"Maybe . . ." He uses all his right hand on a trill.

"Maybe . . ." He pulls back his spread fingers, and looks out upon the place where he is. A vast, impersonal and yet furious grimace transfigures his wet face.

". . . Maybe it's you!" 🎸

RAY CHARLES DISCOVERS THE PIANO *By Michael Lydon*
[From *Ray Charles: Man and Music,* 1998]

West of Greenville, Florida, North Grand Street soon wore down to a double wagon track, and songbirds and buzzing bugs drowned out the sawmills. Wild morning glories wrapped green vines and blue trumpets over sagging fence posts. Rickety shacks perched on tiny lots squeezed between forests and farms. Across from the big wooden New Zion Baptist Church, a nameless smaller road turned south across the railroad tracks and past a second wooden church, the modest New Shiloh Missionary Baptist. A half-mile farther a cluster of small houses and shacks stood under tall pines and oaks, a black quarter everybody called Jellyroll.

The name, rightly, had a raffish air. Colored folk who had lived in Greenville for years lived in Blackbottom, the black quarter in town watched over by the white folks on top of the hill. Jellyroll was out from under white eyes, a sandy clearing in the woods where transient workers had thrown up tar-paper shacks when work held through more than one season. Nobody had lived in Jellyroll long, nobody knew where the others had come from or might go next. The men and women of Jellyroll were by and large greenhorns from the plantations, drawn by the promise of cash for menial labor. Living close to Greenville felt more like town than the sharecropper cabins they had left, but Jellyroll was still country. On Sunday the people prayed hard, all week they worked hard, and Saturday night they found a bit of the free and easy at Mr. Pit's Red Wing Cafe.

Wiley Pitman was a jovial brown-skinned man, fat, with a wide grin, and known far beyond Jellyroll as a fine piano player. With his wife, Miz Georgia, he owned the Red Wing, a wooden plank building facing the road from North Grand. The cafe doubled as a small general store where Miz Georgia sold kerosene and matches, flour and salt, cold beer and pig's-foot sandwiches. A few tables filled the middle of the floor, and against one wall stood a jukebox and a piano. Out back stood a boardinghouse where Mr. Pit had rooms for the watermelon pickers who overflowed the place in summertime, and rooms, as one longtime resident put it, "for husbands going with other men's wives." Behind the boardinghouse stood several shacks.

[This is where the young Ray Charles Robinson ("RC," as everyone called him) grew up.]

"Either RC was playing the piano or he was listening to the jukebox"—that is Greenville's universal memory of the young Ray Charles, and the grown man's memory fully agrees. "I was a normal kid, mischievous and into everything," Charles recalled years later, "but I loved music, it was the only thing that could really get my attention." One day when he was about three, RC was playing by the shacks when he heard Mr. Pit break into a driving boogie-woogie on the Red Wing's battered old upright. Magnetized by the clanging chords and rocking beat, RC ran up the alley past the boardinghouse, pushed open the battered screen door, and stared amazed at Mr. Pit's flying fingers. Seeing him, Mr. Pit laughed, swept the boy onto his lap, and let him reach out his hands to the keys, run his fingers up and down over their warm ebony and ivory textures.

From then on whenever RC heard Mr. Pit playing, he'd race into the cafe and, as he remembered years

Ray Charles recording for Atlantic Records, New York City, 1962

later with gratitude, "the man *always* let me play." Wiley Pitman was no amateur, as Ray Charles recalled him, but a stride pianist who, had he not chosen the simple life in Greenville, could have duked it out with giants like Pete Johnson and Willie "the Lion" Smith. That may be a student's exaggeration, but Mr. Pit did prove to be a superb teacher, showing RC first how to pick out a melody with one finger."Oh no, son, you don't play like that," he said when RC banged too hard on the keys, but when out of awkward fumblings the boy got a beat going on his own, Mr. Pit encouraged him with noisy shouts of "That's it, sonny, that's it."

Near the piano stood the cafe jukebox, a marvel of flashing lights and moving metal. For a nickel, a mechanical arm would lift a black platter from a drum of records and set it spinning, the steel needle falling into the groove with a scratchy hiss, filling the room with electric sounds magically recorded long ago and far away. RC soon had a special place on a bench beside the jukebox where he sat for hours, his ear pressed up against the speaker. Sometimes when he was given a few coins for candy, they'd end up in the jukebox instead. More often RC didn't have the money to pick his own songs, so he listened to everything anybody played: boogie-woogie piano by Albert Ammons, gutbucket blues by Tampa Red, the big bands of Fletcher Henderson and Duke Ellington. Work and music, running in the woods, church on Sunday—life flowed on for RC. 🖎

FINDING PROFESSOR LONGHAIR *By Jerry Wexler*
[From *Rhythm and the Blues: A Life in American Music,* 1993]

Ahmet Ertegun had eyes to make records. He also had ears and tremendous taste. His taste led him to a suite at the Ritz-Carlton when he came up to New York to see about getting into the business. His taste also drained his meager finances. Counter to what many believed, he did not have an inheritance of any consequence. What he did have were his instincts, and they led him into a friendship with Herb and Miriam Abramson. I also knew Herb and Miriam and respected them both; they were a culturally evolved couple with a righteous feeling for hip music and left-wing politics. Herb was a blues expert, especially well versed in the Delta school. He'd also gone to dental school and worked for National Records, producing great sides with Joe Turner, Pete Johnson, and the Ravens. He'd begun his own gospel label, Jubilee, and jazz label, Quality. Though short-lived, they gave Herb experience. He was someone Ahmet admired, and in 1947 they formed a partnership. They were advised by record store owner Waxie Maxie and Jerry Blaine, a record promoter and close friend to Ahmet. With financing from Dr. Vahdi Sabit, a Turkish dentist, they started Atlantic.

I'd started noticing Atlantic's early releases with Professor Longhair's "Hey Now Baby," "Hey Little Girl," and "Mardi Gras in New Orleans." Fess—as the Professor was called—was a revelation for me, my first taste of the music being served up in Louisiana in the late forties. There were traces of Jelly Roll Morton's habanera–Cuban tango influence in his piano style, but the overall effect was startlingly original, a jambalaya Caribbean Creole rumba with a solid blues bottom. In a foreshadowing of trips I myself would later take to New Orleans, Ahmet described the first of his many ethnomusicological expeditions.

Henry Roeland Byrd, a.k.a. Professor Longhair

"Herb and I went down there to see our distributor and look for talent. Someone mentioned Professor Longhair, a musical shaman who played in a style all his own. We asked around and finally found ourselves taking a ferry boat to the other side of the Mississippi, to Algiers, where a white taxi driver would deliver us only as far as an open field. 'You're on your own,' he said, pointing to the lights of a distant village. 'I ain't going into that niggertown.' Abandoned, we trudged across the field, lit only by the light of a crescent moon. The closer we came, the more distinct the sound of distant music—some big rocking band, the rhythm exciting us and pushing us on. Finally we came upon a nightclub—or, rather, a shack—which, like an animated cartoon, appeared to be expanding and deflating with the pulsation of the beat. The man at the door was skeptical. What did these two white men want? 'We're from *Life* magazine,' I lied. Inside, people scattered, thinking we were police. And instead of a full band, I saw only a single musician— Professor Longhair—playing these weird, wide harmonies, using the piano as both keyboard and bass drum, pounding a kick plate to keep time and singing in the open-throated style of the blues shouters of old.

"'My God,' I said to Herb, 'we've discovered a primitive genius.'

"Afterwards, I introduced myself. 'You won't believe this,' I said to the Professor, 'but I want to record you.'

"'You won't believe *this*,' he answered, 'but I just signed with Mercury.'"

DR. JOHN AND JOEL DORN ON NEW ORLEANS PIANO STYLES

Born Malcolm John Rebennack, in 1942, Dr. John—or "Mac" to his friends—is one of the best-known musicians New Orleans has produced. He started his career as a teenager, playing guitar and piano on recording sessions. When Rebennack began combining his interest in voodoo and psychedelia with his funky rhythms, he created the persona Dr. John the Night Tripper. His first hits, "Right Place, Wrong Time" and "Such a Night" (both 1973), and over-the-top costumes and stage presence brought him national notoriety. Longtime producer Joel Dorn first met Dr. John in the late 1960s, when Rebennack was signed to Atlantic, where Dorn was a staff producer. A Philadelphia native, Dorn began his music career as a disc jockey on a jazz station in that city. In addition to working with roots artists like Dr. John and numerous jazz musicians, Dorn signed Roberta Flack (producing her first hits), among many other popular artists. Dorn and Dr. John got together one icy December day in 2002 to talk about New Orleans' post–Jelly Roll Morton piano sound combining Delta blues, ragtime, jazz, zydeco, and boogie-woogie, pioneered by Professor Longhair, Huey "Piano" Smith, Fats Domino, Allen Touissant, James Booker, and others Dr. John has known and played with over the years.

JOEL DORN: When did you start to play piano?
DR. JOHN: I was real little. My uncle Joe and aunt Andre used to come by the pad and play boogies. And my aunt taught me how to play "The Texas Boogie." I learned how to play with two hands as a little bitty kid. I could do the left-hand part with two hands. All of a sudden, I figured out how to do it with one hand. Then she showed me the other part with the other hand, but she had to modify it so I could play both hands at once. She taught me a right-hand part that was different notes but the same rhythm, and then one day I figured out how to do something she did without her showing me, and that's when she took an interest in me. From that, I learned how to play a Fats Domino song. The guy that was my hero was Pete Johnson, the piano player from Kansas City—I had dreams of being like him. I used to listen to his record with Big Joe Turner. I had all them old records my dad [who owned a record store] used to play—I'd get the old 78s.

JD: The first time I heard New Orleans piano was on *American Bandstand* in 1955. Dick Clark was playing a record called "Happy Times." Remember the first album Allen [Toussaint] made on RCA? *The Wild Sounds of New Orleans by Tousan?* The first time I heard that, I went nuts. That was the warmest piano I ever heard in my life. I was about fourteen. And then the first place I heard "Rockin' Pneumonia"— with that great piano figure—was also on *Bandstand* again. Then I would hear other records by guys and I could tell that they'd been to New Orleans or that they'd recorded in New Orleans, or they were thinking about New Orleans. Like you'd hear Ray [Charles] and you knew he went through there. You'd hear it on [Little] Richard's records.

DJ: Huey Smith played piano on some of the first New Orleans R&B sessions. And after that it was [Little] Richard. And he played the shit.

JD: To me there's three kinds of piano that make me nuts: gospel, New Orleans piano, and real boogie-woogie like when Albert Ammons and Meade Lux Lewis got together and they were both chuggin'. You can listen to [jazz players] Bud Powell, Tatum, it's all spectacular. But it doesn't make you feel the same way boogie-woogie makes you feel, the same way

New Orleans piano makes you feel. When I first heard that Huey Smith stuff—[1959's] "High Blood Pressure" and "Don't You Know Yockomo"—that piano stayed in my brain. Where does New Orleans piano start for you?

DJ: Professor Longhair was an institution.

JD: Did anybody do that shit before him?

DJ: His shit came out of a lot of them guys. He always told me about guys I never heard of. He used to tell me about a guy named Kid Stormy Monday. They were all known for playing "Junker's Blues" and Fess' eight-bar blues, New Orleans style. There was a million guys who played eight-bar blues, and they all had these piano players' cuttin' contests.

JD: I know what Jelly Roll Morton sounds like, and then there's Fess. There had to be a lotta cats in between, with a trick here and a trick there, that eventually became Fess'.

DJ: My aunt Andre who taught me to play used to play a style that was called the "butterfly stride." James Booker played that stuff. That style with Booker's left hand. It's a trick where you bend certain notes with the stride. Not just a straight stride. All of them piano players had something coming up in them days. The butterfly stride came after Jelly Roll. Edward Franks played piano on a lot of New Orleans sessions. There was a record that me and Allen Toussaint and Edward did as three piano players with [saxophonist] Red Tyler, [saxophonist] Lee Allen, [drummer] Earl Palmer— all of the old fifties studio band that we could roust up for something. Edward Franks had had a stroke and played only with his right hand. Edward played rings around us all with one fuckin' hand.

What Fess did—and I guarantee you this is where he shifted the gears—was he envisioned stuff. Fess looked at the piano and heard other things in his head. He heard Caribbean; one day he said, "I just

Dr. John in the dressing room of San Francisco's Boarding House, 1983

did a record, 'Mardi Gras in New Orleans,' and they're gonna play it every year at Mardi Gras," and he says, "Man, I wanna produce it next. I wanna cut this record and I want four banjos, but I don't want 'em to play the strings, I just want to use it like a snare drum. And just a bass drum." And he says, "I want three trombones like elephant calls on this song."

All of my favorite piano players—Art Neville, Allen Toussaint, Huey Smith, Edward Franks— they were all ridiculously different, but all had in common a certain respect for Professor Longhair's funky thing. In a recording session, we'd say, "Let's play this shit a little more funky butt," and somebody'd play a little Professor Longhair lick, and we'd come back and play a tune, funky style. That was why most of the record labels came [to New Orleans]: the Bihari brothers [from Modern Records], all of them [label] people from California, Art Rupe, and all of them people. Lew Chudd had producer Dave Bartholomew, and that was his whole company [Imperial], with Fats [Domino] and all of that . . . they started the whole New Orleans R&B scene almost single-handed. Their studio band was basically Red Tyler, Lee Allen, various piano players, whether it was Edward Franks and later Allen Toussaint or Huey Smith, various guitar players.

I used to hear Smiley Lewis' band with Tuts Washington—they called him Papa Yellow then. They could play locked-in together in a way I've never heard any other piano player and guitar player play. They could play different chords to the same tune in between each other, where both chords worked. It was like a magical thing that those two guys did.

JD: You've been playing for fifty-some years and you heard 1,005 different guys, not only in New Orleans but all over the world, so you pick shit up that you don't even know you picked up . . .

DJ: If you play a gig with a guy, all of them guys leave that little chunk of something on you. Once Professor Longhair needed a band for a gig, so we got a steady gig, and I wound up doing a record with Fess. That guy left a huge stain. Watching Papa Yellow left a huge stain. Watching Allen Toussaint on a million sessions. Watching [James] Booker, watching Huey Smith—between him and Allen Toussaint, I worked more dates with those two guys than any other piano player.

JD: Talk to me about Fats Domino as a piano player.

DJ: If you listen, Fats was a band piano player: "Lawdy Miss Clawdy" with Lloyd Price, that great piano intro. Fats is old school, comes out of Albert Ammons. If you ever listen to any of his old records, he actually recorded a lot of Albert Ammons songs way back in the fifties on Imperial Records.

JD: What do New Orleans guys think of him as a piano player?

DJ: Dave Bartholomew made him into a huge act. Dave and him wrote a lot of great fuckin' songs.

More than anybody but the Beatles. I dig Fats 'cause Fats, to me, covers that corner that certain real blues guys had that makes 'em stick out in left field. They're country—and when I say country, I mean hillbilly country. 'Cause the Ninth Ward where Fats was from when he came up was in the sticks. It was part of the city of New Orleans, but there was no streets. No streetlights. Fats has that in him. He could sing. When I hear Fats, I'm hearing Jimmie Rodgers, the old hillbilly. He sang that song "Waitin' for a Train." He knew that shit. Fats has a country side to him, he played the blues, he had Champion Jack Dupree's shit mixed up with Albert Ammons. He had a little bit of a lot of all of what I grew up hearing. Champion Jack Dupree did make the original record of "The Junker's Blues," but Fats made the first real hit record on it called "The Fat Man" [in 1949]. But Fats played the shit out of "The Junker's Blues" on "The Fat Man." Fats could play.

JD: When I heard him I heard the hits. "Blueberry Hill," "I'm in Love Again." The commercial shit.

DJ: "Going Home." These were the songs. [Sings] "Every Night About This Time." [Sings] "Please Don't Leave Me." That sounds like a hillbilly song. But it's blues. And the way he played it: Some of them songs was gutbucket blues, some of 'em was that country shit, but it's all this little weird mixture. They were big R&B records. They wasn't on no Dick Clark then. Might have been in *Cash Box* or *Billboard*. They were probably only played where race records were played. But they wasn't pop records until about the time he cut [sings] "Ain't That a Shame." All of a sudden Fats is big, and it just kept going from there. But prior to that, I think he had "My Blue Heaven."

I'd go hear Fats' band, and I tried to always get there 'cause his guitar player was my teacher. So I'd go to watch him. And he'd sing some Little Willie John songs. I watched him in rehearsal in Local 496. I knew everything—their Latin songs they played. The band was really special. They wasn't what it sounded like from the record dates.

New Orleans is a small area where everything overlaps. That's the good thing, and it's the problem with it. I don't care what culture winds up in New Orleans, they become part of New Orleans.

JD: In schoolyard basketball, the one thing you know is you gotta play with guys who are better than you. You're gonna get your ass kicked, but you're gonna end up bein' a better player than when you started. It's the only way to learn.

DJ: I understand the principle to that, but these guys was all up on so many things that I wasn't. I'd hear a little piece of something, but I didn't know the fundamental shit about any of it. I absorbed little pieces of this and that. But I missed the boat.

JD: I don't think those guys would've even given you the chance to fuck up unless they thought you had somethin'.

DJ: Them guys threw me out more times . . . and it was okay. I liked hanging out with these guys. I didn't give a fuck. At the time I was living at Cosimo [Matassa]'s studio [where many early R&B and rock & roll hits were recorded]—my old lady had kicked me out of the pad. I'm homeless before it's fashionable, I'm living in a studio, my whole life was a disaster. When Cosimo locks me out of the studio, I'm staying in a condemned part of a building with rats and maybe a wino for company every now and then.

JD: That'll motivate ya.

DJ: I'd have to wait till Cosimo would come open the studio, sneak in and try to look presentable, go in his little bathroom, clean up, and cop my little hit, then come back over and try to look legit.

JD: Good judgment comes from experience, experience comes from bad judgment. When I first heard you play the *Gris Gris* record at Atlantic, I couldn't believe how young you were. I knew you musta done a million things, and been a jillion places to get that shit to filter through.

DJ: I've been through some weird shit, just to survive, but you love something about the music and there's something that . . . it don't matter where the music's coming from sometimes. Whatever that thing is. It's like watching Professor Longhair when he used to do this one gig and he'd place the chicken on the piano and he'd wear these white gloves and a turtleneck shirt with a necklace with a watch on it. And a full tux. He'd eat the chicken, take the gloves off, and play. And it was like—I'd never seen anybody do that before. Sit down and eat and play a gig. He would talk more trash with the people. Give everybody a drink *on the house!* Between every song. Real old school. But his version, his take on life—there's no amount of money, no amount of schooling that would give me whatever that was.

Dave Bartholomew's band used to work at a joint, and Fess used to live by there, and there'd be times I'd see Fess and he'd be talking, and we'd walk for a long time and he'd tell me these fuckin' killer stories. He's your hero—you wanna hang by the guy. He'd tell me this shit, and he'd take me and he'd say, "That's where I'm playing," and I was like, Oh, my God. Back then it wasn't safe. Now it's crack dealers with pieces.

JD: You still listen to a lot of music?

DJ: Anything I get my hands on, I listen. New, old. I don't like a lot of it. I'll listen anyway. I'm gonna check it out, whatever I got, and if I don't like it I skip through it. They got a button, you skip to the next track. Sometimes I skip right off to the next record. 🖝

MARCIA BALL ON BIG EASY BLUES

I grew up in blues country. And I had piano players in my family. First, my grandmother, who played ragtime piano, was an influence on me. She had a pile of Tin Pan Alley sheet music. So I got to hear a lot of that. My aunt played beautiful piano and played a certain amount of boogie-woogie. I can remember trying to stretch my little hands, so I could boogie. So that started it. But then in my part of south Louisiana, southeast Texas, there was Cajun, zydeco, rhythm & blues, and blues, and it was all mixed up. And we got the New Orleans stuff. We got Fats Domino. Of course, everyone had Jerry Lee Lewis, Little Richard, and Fats Domino. I remember when the record "Corinna Corinna" was popular. I was ten, eleven, twelve years old, and I had an aunt in New Orleans who liked blues, and she would buy records that other people didn't have. When I was about thirteen, I saw Irma Thomas play in New Orleans on a big package show. That was the first time I ever saw a woman get onstage and lead the band, be the star of the show. Blew my mind.

New Orleans is a blues town, a piano town. Pianos and horns are big in New Orleans, as opposed to guitars and harmonicas in Chicago. I love the Chicago players, Pinetop Perkins and Sunnyland Slim and Otis Spann—who is the king of all that to me. But New Orleans stuff is *rhythm* & blues, and the accent is on the rhythm. Professor Longhair and Tuts Washington before him, Roosevelt Sykes, Big Maceo, and all those guys who played early New Orleans piano—all the way back to Jelly Roll Morton—there's been a wonderful tradition of syncopation in the blues, and that's a New Orleans thing.

Musically, Professor Longhair was a huge influence on me, along with the people he influenced, James Booker and Dr. John. I love the syncopation; I love the rumba beat and the Latin influence he brought to the music.

Another big influence would be Fats Domino. I don't think anybody who plays music today wasn't moved in that direction by Fats Domino. What he does with that 6/8 thing—which is the hallmark of his music—is still enormous in my music.

A lot of women went before me and opened all these doors for me that I've been able to walk through without having to think about it. Old blues women like Bessie Smith: They paid hard, hard dues. Etta James. I had a real mentor—someone who was important to me as a piano player and as a performer, and who is from the Gulf Coast as well. Her name is Katie Webster, and she passed away in 2001. She was born in Houston and spent most of her young years along the Gulf Coast. She was a great piano player. She played with Otis Redding; she opened a show for him one time, and he just snagged her, and she became his piano player, his bandleader. Really, she is one of the important women piano players of the style and really of the blues in general.

There are other women, too, who gained respect for their music—not just as a novelty act but as a musician, a singer—who have inspired me: Koko Taylor, Janis Joplin, Bonnie Raitt. All the way up the line, they've opened doors for me, and I've been able to walk right through because of them. ☛

CHRIS THOMAS KING'S TWENTY-FIRST-CENTURY BLUES
BY JOHN SWENSON

Chris Thomas King as Blind Willie Johnson in Wim Wenders' *The Soul of a Man*

The blues tent at New Orleans' 2002 Jazz and Heritage Festival was packed with sweaty, expectant fans, many of whom knew Chris Thomas King for his role as Delta blues giant Tommy Johnson in *O Brother, Where Art Thou?* Over the course of his set, those fans got what they wanted, but not without a healthy dose of what King wanted them to hear— what he calls his "twenty-first-century blues." To the driving sound of an electronic beat, Thomas insisted on making hip-hop an integral part of the show: "This is the blues of the twenty-first century," he rapped, as if throwing down a gauntlet, "and I don't give a damn if you're not down wit' me."

Some fans left the tent, muttering imprecations against hip-hop. Those who stayed saw the future of the blues performed by its most daring practitioner.

❊ ❊ ❊ ❊ ❊

King grew up as a child-prodigy guitarist learning the blues at the feet of some of the music's masters at the Baton Rouge, Louisiana, club Tabby's Blues Box, owned by his father, Ernest Joseph "Tabby" Thomas. For the past decade, King has been trying to forge a new concept of music yet meeting tremendous resistance at every turn. Ironically, it's his performance as an acoustic bluesman that has given him the status required to play his futuristic music on his own terms. King followed his success in *O Brother* by playing the lead role and acting as musical director for the New Orleans stage production *Goodnight Irene: The Legacy of Lead Belly,* and he was cast as Blind Willie Johnson in Wim Wenders' *The Soul of a Man.* King's portrayal of Johnson is central to his concept of merging traditional blues with the ethos of hip-hop. He feels they are essentially the same music.

"Hip-hop came from the same neighborhood as the blues," argues King. "What Cash Money and Juvenile are doing is coming from the same neighborhood where Blind Willie Johnson recorded in 1925 in New Orleans. A couple of blocks away, in that same neighborhood. A lot has changed, a lot hasn't changed. The underground, the hard-core hip-hop, was coming from the same place as the blues came before. It was the grandkid of the blues, with new instruments. Just like blues was acoustic at one time, then Muddy Waters plugged in and went electric, I sampled it, I digitized it. So my thing is, where Muddy Waters electrified it, I digitized it.

Bring the blues to the twenty-first century, that's my approach to it."

King's dad, Tabby Thomas, is best known as one of Louisiana's greatest blues figures, the King of Swamp Blues. His 1961 national hit, "Hoodoo Party," is a treasure of Louisiana blues history. Chris Thomas King, then, was literally born to the blues. Born Chris Thomas on October 14, 1964, he grew up surrounded by music. Thomas started out on trumpet in sixth grade but was fascinated by his father's guitar and tried to play it when he wasn't home. At his dad's club, the young Thomas learned from such bluesmen as Guitar Kelly, Silas Hogan, and Henry Gray. But even as he soaked up the classic blues influences, the guitarist was listening to more contemporary influences, such as Jimi Hendrix, funk, and early hip-hop. "I wanted to play music that reflected the world I was living in," he says. "I couldn't really relate to the older blues themes at the time."

What opened his eyes to the possibilities of the blues was a European tour with his father, on which he saw blues musicians treated with the respect that was denied them at home. He returned to Louisiana, recorded a demo tape, and was discovered by Arhoolie Records. His first album, *The Beginning*, came out in 1986. After moving to Austin, Texas, Thomas signed with Hightone, releasing the well-received 1990 album *Cry of the Prophets*. He wanted to follow that record with a more contemporary vision of the blues, but the album was turned down by the label.

Frustrated with the American record industry, King moved to Europe, first living in England, then finally finding a refuge for his music and artistic conception in Copenhagen, Denmark. When he returned to the United States, Chris Thomas changed his name to Chris Thomas King, and his musical vision of contemporary blues was justified on the groundbreaking *21st Century Blues,* which finally came out in 1995. In recent years, he has been releasing albums on his own 21st Century Blues label. *Dirty South Hip-Hop Blues* (2002) is the fullest realization of his vision, an absolute triumph that incorporates his roots with the music of his father, who sings on "Da Thrill Is Gone From Here," a reworking of B.B. King's "The Thrill Is Gone." It also features King's traditional acoustic-blues work on "Hard Time Killing Floor Blues" and "Southern Chicks"; showcases his hard hip-hop–blues fusion on tracks such as "Welcome to Da Jungle," "Mississippi KKKrossroads," and "N Word Rap"; and demonstrates his ability to write softer, inspirational blues material including "Gonna Take a Miracle," which follows the instrumental "9/11 Interlude."

"Blues come from such a deep place of sorrow, a deep place of a miserable existence—where you question how could God let this happen, where you don't really understand exactly what's going on, but there's this little glimmer of hope that it isn't always gonna be this way, in time it's gonna get better," says King. "There's always that glimmer of hope. A lot of hip-hop, hard-core music, that glimmer of hope isn't there most times. . . . What's beautiful about the blues is that there's that touch of spirituality to it that says, I'm not in this alone. It's not always gonna be this way. If I can just endure, if I can just make it another day, it just might be a little bit better. Sometimes people need that glimmer of hope. 'It's Gonna Take a Miracle' is a ballad. The lyrics are 'What the world needs now is some kind of miracle, some kind of sign to light the way.' The world needs a hero in these unsure times."

When it comes to the blues, Chris Thomas King certainly qualifies as that hero. ✒

SHEMEKIA COPELAND ON HER MELTING-POT BLUES

The twenty-four-year-old daughter of the late Texas bluesman Johnny Copeland, vocalist Shemekia Copeland has been performing since she was a teenager. Having spent time on the road with her father and absorbed a panoply of sounds since childhood, she makes powerful blues recordings that reflect her wide range of influences. While respecting the blues of the past, she's put her own stamp on the sound—leading the way for the music's future.

My earliest musical memories are of my dad, just sitting around playing acoustic guitar around the house. I was singing when I was three, around the house with my dad, and listening to him play records. He used to listen to everything—he was never limited: gospel, soul music, African music. I got to listen to all of that. Now it's just a part of me, because that's what I did my whole life.

I grew up in the hip-hop era. All those rappers who were big back then were coming up in my neighborhood in Harlem; in the late seventies, early eighties, it was huge. That was what was going on around me. I got a chance to listen to everything.

My daddy took me to see lady blues singers when I was young, too. I used to go see a Chicago lady named Big Time Sarah. I saw Koko Taylor and Ruth Brown. My dad was good friends with all those ladies.

My dad was a really great singer, but he was never interested in singing. That was a much later thing. He was more interested in playing guitar. He talked about teaching yourself, not having any kind of training—and when I think about it, I never had any vocal training. The stuff comes so natural to me.

Shemekia Copeland belts it out at the Salute to the Blues Concert, New York City, February 7, 2003.

I think I've got a melting pot of everything in my style. I've got all my daddy's guitars and videos and all sorts of things to remember him by. His music keeps me really close to him. I feel like he's around all the time. 🎸

MY JOURNEY TO THE BLUES BY ANTHONY DECURTIS

Recently, as I sat in Madison Square Garden waiting for the Rolling Stones to take the stage, I listened with more than usual care to the preshow music the band had chosen to be played through the arena's sound system. It was all blues—Slim Harpo, Elmore James, John Lee Hooker, Jimmy Reed, Howlin' Wolf, and Muddy Waters were among the artists I recognized, but I didn't recognize all of them. And if it wasn't just the usual suspects, it also wasn't just their most familiar material. I couldn't identify a number of the songs I heard.

People who don't like the blues complain that the music "all sounds the same," but what struck me as I listened that night was how individual and idiosyncratic each performance was. Every vocal, guitar part, and arrangement had its own distinctive element—it was as if nobody else would have, or could have, done that song in exactly that way. At a time when even much good music is highly formulaic, in which all the tricks seem not only to have been learned but memorized, digitized, and sonically exploited in every conceivable way, the ease and originality of the songs I heard that night were striking.

I was reminded of how even the best versions of Robert Johnson's songs—for example, the Stones' "Love in Vain" and "Stop Breaking Down," or the weary version of "Ramblin' on My Mind" Eric Clapton sang with John Mayall's Bluesbreakers—never quite get everything that he put into them. His performances are at once complex and irreducible, immediately accessible and absolutely elusive. Other artists' renditions often focus Johnson's power, lift the choruses, embellish the verses, and, ultimately,

simplify his mastery. As with all the greatest music, listening to his songs is an endless process of discovery.

I know it's easy to romanticize the blues. With radio still a local medium and travel an infinitely more complicated endeavor than it is today—not to mention the isolating effects of segregation—it was nearly unavoidable that musicians would create a deeply personal sound. The price they paid for that privilege was high, which, of course, only enhances their achievement.

That night at the Stones show made me think about my own blues journey. I can't recall the first time I realized that there was a specific style of music called the blues. During my childhood in New York in the fifties, I may well have heard the term while listening to the standards programs—focusing on Frank Sinatra, Tony Bennett, Rosemary Clooney, and the like—that my father always played on the radio. That would have been a far more stylized version of the music than anything that would ever interest me, but it might still have brought something called "the blues" into my ken.

Like so many people my age, I really began to engage the blues at the time of the British Invasion. I was twelve when the Beatles arrived in the United States in February 1964—and when they mentioned Bo Diddley and Muddy Waters at their airport press conference. But the real breakthrough occurred a few months later with the release of the first Stones album. I had heard Marvin Gaye's "Can I Get a Witness" and Rufus Thomas' "Walking the Dog," both of which the Stones covered on that album, but I had never made a distinction between those songs and any other pop music. Now I began to understand that they were related to something called rhythm & blues that the Stones professed to be interested in. The notes on the album's back cover by the band's manager/producer, Andrew Loog Oldham, expressly trumpeted the Stones' "raw, exciting basic approach to Rhythm and Blues."

There were other wonders on that album, as well—versions of Muddy Waters' "I Just Want to Make Love to You," Slim Harpo's "I'm a King Bee," Jimmy Reed's "Honest I Do," among them. I had no idea who any of those artists were, and nothing on the album even hinted at their existence. But, again, right on the back cover there were writing credits—Dixon, Moore—that would eventually lead me to Willie Dixon and James Moore, which was Slim Harpo's given name.

Along with the information and terminology, needless to say, came the music itself, which was more demanding than anything I'd heard to that point. It had elements that flat-out confused me. I'd never associated harmonicas with anything cool, but the first time I ever saw the Stones perform— on *Hollywood Palace,* a Saturday-night variety show hosted by Dean Martin—there was Brian Jones playing harmonica on "I Just Want to Make Love to You." Martin's now-infamous drunken insults to the band didn't faze me—he was part of the musical world my father loved and, therefore, an

embarrassment by definition. But Brian Jones— Brian Jones! The coolest guy in the band—playing *harmonica.* What could that possibly mean? I decided to suspend judgment until I knew enough to decide how I felt about that. And I just won't tell you how long it took me to figure out that a harp wasn't necessarily a large stringed instrument.

The Stones, happily, were not my only guide into the underworld of the blues. Others, like the Yardbirds, the Animals, the Blues Project, and the Paul Butterfield Blues Band, emerged, and each in their own way provided more clues to the secrets of this music. A cool record store opened on the north side of Bleecker Street between Jones and Cornelia Streets in Greenwich Village, four or five blocks from where I lived. Even though I rarely had the money to buy albums there, I could at least see what John Lee Hooker, Bo Diddley, and Sonny Boy Williamson (whose very identity presented another

"If it wasn't for the British musicians, a lot of us black musicians in America would still be catchin' the hell that we caught long before. So thanks to them, thanks to all you guys. You opened doors that I don't think would have been opened in my lifetime. When white America started paying attention to the blues—it started opening a lot of doors that had been closed to us."—*B.B. King*

set of vexing problems) looked like and learn which songs were on which records.

But less obvious sources also proved a treasure trove. Along with a version of "Hoochie Coochie Man," *The Manfred Mann Album,* which came out in 1964, provided my introduction to Howlin' Wolf by way of a gripping rendition of "Smokestack Lightnin'." While no match for the incomparable original, Manfred Mann still managed to channel the bizarre, abstract terror of that eminently strange song. When I saw Manfred Mann perform live that year at the old Academy of Music on Fourteenth Street, Paul Jones, the group's lead singer, delivered a performance that, like Mick Jagger's at the time, combined the sexual bravado of the blues with the androgynous teasing just beginning to become prevalent in the still not fully formed counterculture.

So, it seemed for a time, the blues were liable to pop up anywhere. Peter and Gordon, one of the opening acts at the Manfred Mann show, performed Little Walter's "My Babe." The Zombies, of all bands, did "I've Got My Mojo Working" on their American debut album. And, most incredibly, Herman's Hermits played that same song in a matinee show I saw them do one Saturday at the Academy of Music. Even at thirteen, I was flabbergasted to hear that tune alongside "Mrs. Brown You've Got a Lovely Daughter" and "I'm Henry the VIII, I Am." Sorting out which group was a blues band and which wasn't could be trickier than it might seem.

Needless to say, I didn't have the slightest idea what a mojo was. So that became my other pressing blues project—unraveling the folklore and culture behind the music. Black-cat bones and special riders, diving ducks and backdoor men, gypsy women and High John the Conqueror, red roosters lording it over the barnyard and mules kicking in their stalls—all of that couldn't have been more

"The time when I was with John Mayall, I was asked to play with Muddy and Otis Spann when they came into London—that was unbelievable—they were in their heyday and they had these big silk suits on. I was just gobsmacked—I could hardly move." —Eric Clapton

foreign to a working-class, Italian kid who had rarely ventured beyond the confines of New York City's five boroughs. It helped that the Catholic faith in which I was raised was itself a hotbed of fetishes and superstition, that my mother would tell me stories that her mother had told her about the gypsy fortune-tellers in Italy, and that the English poetry I was beginning to read in school was as dense with rural imagery as any blues lyric. Words could mean exactly what they said and also mean far more—that lesson, as important as any I've learned in my life, was coming to me from a variety of directions.

The next phase of my blues journey was hearing the music performed live by the legendary artists themselves, not their white translators. A passing comment by Eric Clapton in a *Rolling Stone* interview led me to B.B. King, whom I saw at a free concert in Central Park. Those beautiful round notes dripped from his guitar like wax from a burning candle. I saw a flashy and stylish Buddy Guy prowl the aisles of Fillmore East, firing off explosive lead lines. I saw Albert King stand dignified in the dark in that same hall, crooning a promise that also sounded like a fated life sentence, "I'll Play the Blues for You."

Most unforgettably, I saw Muddy Waters at the Schaefer Music Festival in Central Park on June 6, 1968. Three times in my life I've seen opening acts who made it impossible for me to sit through the headliner: Jimi Hendrix opening for the Young Rascals, Led Zeppelin opening for Iron Butterfly, and, on this date, the Muddy Waters Band, featuring Otis Spann, opening for Moby Grape.

It was an outdoor show in the daytime, and it may well have been free or only a dollar or two. Muddy was indomitable, simultaneously fierce and rigorously disciplined. His band's taut playing mesmerized the crowd as if the venue were a smoky late-night club, not an ice-skating rink with rows of portable chairs set up. The show's MC was Jonathan Schwartz, an eminent New York disc jockey, and the performance clearly blew him away. "McKinley Morganfield!" he exuded, using Muddy Waters' given name. "Wasn't that something?" He could barely muster the energy to introduce Moby Grape, and, after the majesty of Muddy's set, the band, through no fault of its own, just sounded silly.

As time went on, my understanding of the blues deepened, and my appreciation for the heroism of its greatest practitioners became a point that I felt I had to communicate whenever I wrote about the music. To produce art as monumental as those musicians did would be a wonder, even if they had grown up in privileged circumstances. That they overcame the direst poverty and racist brutality of segregation is an accomplishment so extraordinary that it is almost impossible to convey. I also found blues outside the Delta-Chicago tradition, like the scarifying trance music of Junior Kimbrough from the north Mississippi hill country, that moved me as powerfully as any music ever has.

Eventually I got to meet and interview John Lee Hooker, B.B. King, and Willie Dixon, and to speak with Albert King, Buddy Guy, Junior Wells, and Bo Diddley. Keith Richards once mentioned to me how impressed he always was by what gentlemen the blues giants were, and I found my encounters with them to be similar—surprising modesty, good humor, and little bitterness.

I can still recall my joy at going to interview Willie Dixon and finding him in a plush suite at the Parker Meridien hotel in midtown Manhattan. "Finally," I thought, "somebody in one of these places who deserves to be there." I actually got to ask the man who wrote "I ain't superstitious/ But a black cat crossed my trail" about those mojos and black-cat bones. "You see, all those things have been superstitions for people through generations," he told me. "Even back in Biblical days, even in astrology.

"My mother might have believed in some of that," he continued, "but my old man wouldn't let none of it go on around him. He'd have a fit, man: 'Didn't you learn no better sense than that?' He'd go into raising hell, man, and nobody could rest for a month. If somebody started talking to him about bad luck, he'd say, 'The only bad luck you had was when your poor parents got off the boat here. They took your country, they took your language, they took your religion, they took your culture, they took your god—and they turned you against yourself.'"

Asked for a definition of the blues, Buddy Guy once told me, "We write according to the facts of life, everyday life. If you live and die here, you got a part of the blues in you. Something you have to get up to do, it don't work, that's what blues is all about. I think a person will have the blues as long as he lives, but some people just don't want to bring it out like we do."

That ability to articulate and address life's deepest traumas is ultimately what has sustained the music's hold on me. I remember when I was in graduate school and had separated from my wife because I was having an affair with another woman. Both relationships were unraveling. I was living in a boarding house, and I had been diagnosed with walking pneumonia. I had to get up to teach an

8 a.m. remedial writing class every morning during one of the coldest winters in Indiana history.

One dark morning, the clock radio came on, and as I lay in bed, I heard, "Woke up this morning/ And the blues, they walked like a man/Woke up this morning/And the blues, they walked like a man/ I said, Good morning blues/Let me shake your right hand." That notion of your troubles as a kind of companion floored me, and to this day, every time I wake up with that feeling of dread in the pit of my stomach, I think, "Good morning, blues."

Even more profoundly, when a friend of mine was dying from leukemia a few years back, I'm ashamed to say that I found myself avoiding her because I simply didn't know what to say when we spoke. One day I was listening to Skip James, and I heard "Sick Bed Blues" in a way I never had before. Chronicling his own battle with cancer, James sings in one climactic verse, "*Mmm, mmm,* I ain't gonna cry no more/Because down this road every traveler got to go." That simple statement about our common mortality made me realize that I had been experiencing my friend's condition as somehow different from my own, when it really wasn't. We were both heading down the same road to the same place, it just seemed like she was going to get there a little sooner than I would. Once I understood that, it seemed that I had plenty I could say to her. We spoke regularly about the most meaningful and the most trivial things in the weeks before she died.

Now Congress has declared 2003 the Year of the Blues, and at a "Salute to the Blues" concert at Radio City Music Hall in New York, the music achieved something approaching the recognition it deserves. In a head-spinning collaboration on Jimi Hendrix's "Red House," Buddy Guy and Vernon Reid transported the blues to outer space and back to the Delta. The peerless Mavis Staples found all the modesty and

Willie Dixon, smiling through the tears

spiritual desire in Blind Lemon Jefferson's "See That My Grave Is Kept Clean." And Chuck D of Public Enemy transformed John Lee Hooker's "Boom Boom" into a blistering, anti-war rant.

The show movingly dramatized the resilience of a music whose origins in the grimmest oppression could not have been less auspicious. But the reality of the music of "everyday life," as Buddy Guy put it, is that its triumphs occur at all times in the hidden moments of millions of private lives. Every year, then, is the year of the blues, and every day is the day you meet that music and all it means. My journey was no doubt different from yours, but, finally, down that road every traveler must go, always getting closer, always just two steps from the blues. 🗡

THE BLUES IS THE BLOOD BY DAVID RITZ

The deeper the wisdom, the deeper the paradox. And what music is more paradoxical and deeper than the blues? What form is simpler, what content more complex, what message more mysterious? Sometimes cloudy, sometimes clear, the blues brews up a concoction of feelings, a stew of hurt and healing that excites our imagination even as it relaxes our heart. Happy, sad, fast, slow, up, down, mellow, and manic, the blues expand and contract in all directions.

That sense of contradiction was revealed early in my career of pursuing blues people with blues stories. I was a college kid in Austin, Texas, when I met Lightnin' Hopkins and followed him home to Houston. "The blues don't lie," he told me in a Dowling Street barbershop. "The blues is wise."

"What's its wisdom?" I wanted to know. He winked, took a drink, and played a song about a boy like me, a stutterer who stopped stuttering when he started singing. My question was never answered, or maybe it was.

That summer in Dallas I went to see Jimmy Reed, whose string of Top Ten R&B hits convinced my analytical mind that he couldn't be singing blues. Besides, the structure of his songs defied the traditional twelve-bar form that music books insisted defined blues. Yet his howling harmonica and plaintive voice were bluer than any blues I'd ever heard. After the show, speeding down the Fort Worth Turnpike in the back of his limo with him and his girlfriend, I felt like Superman's sidekick, Jimmy Olsen, mild-mannered reporter. "What are the blues, Mr. Reed?" I asked. Busy fighting with his lady, he never heard the question. She accused him of having a wandering eye. He accused her of squandering his money. She cursed him. He flashed his razor and slashed her arm. The driver sped to a hospital, where I sat with the great bluesman while, in the next room, a doctor attended to the wound. I stayed stone silent.

A lifetime later—it was the seventies, and I was in my thirties—I had two long years to ask Ray Charles every question imaginable about the blues. I was ghostwriting his autobiography, *Brother Ray*. We met at his midcity L.A. studio in the midnight hour. The lights of his recording console flickered as he ran his fingers over the controls. A huge ring of keys hung from his belt. To Ray, control was everything— control of his money, his women, his music. He saw the blues the same way.

"The blues was the first link in letting me control my musical life," he said. "I was brought up in the backwoods, so I heard country blues early on—Tampa Red, Washboard Sam. Man, I related. I felt what they were feeling. Later I liked Charles Brown, whose keyboard technique was tremendous, and saw that Charles, under all his sophistication, was a bluesman. You could say the same thing for Charlie Parker. Bebop is built on blues. It all is. My own style changed, and I went from imitating Nat Cole into my own thing. That's when I heard how the blues gave my voice the edge that let you know it was me. I also saw I didn't have to sing blues. Singing Hank Snow's 'I'm Movin' On' or Hoagy Carmichael's 'Georgia on My Mind,' it was all blues. Billie Holiday could be singing Gershwin, or Oscar Peterson playing Cole Porter, but it's still blues. Once the blues is in your blood, it stays. Fact of the matter, the blues is the blood."

Marvin Gaye, who never sang traditional blues, was as touched by blues as anyone in the history of American music. His sources of blues wisdom were the dreamy doo-wop of Clyde McPhatter and the blues ballads of Little Jimmy Scott. "The flexibility of the blues is something incredible," he mused while I was interviewing him for *Divided Soul,* my biography that came out a year after he was murdered by his father. "It's a primitive form that shaped every aspect of our music. Bluesmen like Robert Johnson and Muddy Waters led to rhythm & blues that led to rock & roll. Count Basie and Duke Ellington created fabulous swing bands based on the blues. Soul music of the sixties—my contemporaries like Otis Redding, Wilson Pickett, David Ruffin, and Bobby Womack—are really reinvented blues singers. Even the gospel singers, who might reject the blues, are influenced by the blues. The truth is, Thomas A. Dorsey invented modern gospel behind blues feelings. His 'Precious Lord' is full of blues."

Aretha Franklin, whose gospel roots shape every note she sings, agreed with Marvin. While we were collaborating on her memoir, *From These Roots,* she lovingly described the appreciation that her famous father, the Reverend C.L. Franklin, a brilliant student of African-American culture, expressed for blues. He not only frequented nightclubs to hear bluesmen Jimmy Witherspoon and B.B. King; he invited them into his Detroit home, where they played in his living room. "My dad revered these men as poets," said Aretha. "He understood how they laid the foundation. He never saw blues as the 'devil's music.' His vision was bigger than that. He saw the grand plan of our culture that began with the blues."

"The only difference between a gospel career and a blues career," explained B.B. King when we wrote his life story, *Blues All Around Me,* "was money. When I sang gospel on the street corners of those little towns in the Mississippi Delta, I got a pat on the head. When I sang blues, I got a dime. The blues represented economic progress, pure and simple. It meant getting off the farm into the city. Modern blues also meant the electric guitar of T-Bone Walker. I thought of myself as a modern bluesman until, sometime in the sixties, I was opening a show for Jackie Wilson when the audience—a black audience—booed me for being a relic of the past. I hurt so bad I cried. Then I played my heart out until the boos turned to cheers. I won them over that night, but I've never gotten over the fact that bluesmen like Muddy Waters and myself were championed by Englishmen like John Lennon and Eric Clapton. They're the reason we crossed over to the real money. The black audience can be fickle. They're looking for the new thing. They don't want to look at the past. The past is pain. Well, the blues is pain, but it's pain that brings joy."

B.B.'s blues philosophy embraced the essential paradox of his life as an artist. "The blues are a simple music," he said, "and I'm a simple man. But the blues aren't a science, the blues can't be broken down like mathematics. The blues are a mystery, and mysteries are never as simple as they look."

"I didn't want to look like a blues singer," Etta James told me when we began on her book, *Rage to Survive.* "I wanted to look like all the ultracool jazz divas. Funny, though, but when I got out and started touring as a kid, the biggest influence on my singing was a cat called Johnny "Guitar" Watson. Johnny was a genius—genius guitarist, genius writer, genius singer. The source of his genius, he showed me, was the blues. He'd take the corniest ballad and paint it the prettiest shade of blue you can imagine. So I copied Johnny. I didn't set out to sing blues, but Johnny showed me how to use the blues to improve every song I sang."

Aretha Franklin shares an intimate moment with her father, Reverend C.L. Franklin in 1968.

Art Neville, eldest of the Neville Brothers of New Orleans, is a fountainhead of Louisiana music. When I began researching his family's biography, I was overwhelmed by the complexity of Crescent City culture. The confluence of Caribbean, European, African, and Native American sounds had my head spinning. A hellacious keyboardist, Art set me straight. "The professors of piano," he explained, "took whatever was in the air—rumbas and boogies, mambos and waltzes, ragtime and calypso—and wove them together with the same fabric. Sounds crazy, sounds like it shouldn't make sense, but it does. The blues makes sense of it all. Smiley Lewis, Fats Domino, James Booker, Professor Longhair, Earl King—these were the deans schooled in blues.

Blues, you see, is the magic fabric. It never tears. It stretches. The more you stretch it, the further it goes. The more you wear it, the better it feels. The older it gets, the newer it looks."

Listening to the blues people, I learned that blues paradoxes lead to blues lives. Blues lives, like the music they reflect, are wholly spontaneous and wildly unpredictable, floating above and below a continuum of ecstasy and pain. They survive as testimonies to the transformational nature of the blues. The life that has moved me most is that of Little Jimmy Scott, the seventy-eight-year-old jazz vocalist afflicted with Kallmann's Syndrome, a hormonal deficiency that left him with grave physical and emotional challenges. With abnormally small genitalia and an unnaturally high voice, Scott moved through the blues world with both uncertainty and grace. That world embraced him. His friends and supporters were Dinah Washington, Billie Holiday, Charlie Parker—artists who were viewed as oddities themselves. Bedeviled by drink, motivated by love, blessed with uncanny talent, Jimmy has led the blues life since he was a teenager. Time and again, the world has shot him down. Time and again, he has shot himself down. Time and again, he has risen from the ashes of humiliating defeat. His signature song—"Everybody's Somebody's Fool"—is a heartbreaking metaphor that, at once, confirms and denies that defeat.

"The blues," said Jimmy, "has lasted because the blues is about reality. Life is blue. Life ends. Sorrow is certain. Pain can't be avoided. The blues lays it out. But as you sing the blues, and as you listen to the blues, something happens to you. In the middle of songs that have some of the saddest stories ever told, you feel more alive than ever. That's the strength of the blues. That's the miracle—watching the blues chase the blues away."

Blues: The Footprint of Popular Music By Chuck D

Being a so-called veteran of the genre labeled hip-hop and rap music, you can't help being a musicologist, or at least a student of music, by default. Quite simply put, the basis of rap music from its humble beginnings happens to be the application of the rap vocal on top of records. It's no secret by now that today's rock cats are still doing steroid-laden blues-guitar riffs spawned from the Mississippi Delta, but what might still be tucked away, what people don't realize, is that much of the timing and rhythm of rap harkens back to those elements as well.

As original American musics, both blues and rap are laced with attitude and coded double entendre. One can easily find comparisons in the lives of both Tupac Shakur and Little Walter; a turntablist like DJ Babu of the Dilated Peoples and the behind-the-head playing style of Texas great T-Bone Walker; the throaty rawness of DMX and Howlin' Wolf—even in the way record companies then and now hustle the sounds *from* "the hood" back *to* the hood, and even abroad. Labels like Chess, Sun, Cobra to Sugarhill, Tommy Boy and Def Jam. The similarities are baffling.

The fact that most of today's MTV crowd cannot draw the comparisons because they don't even know the legendary artists' and labels' names—eventually this affects all music today and tomorrow. The seemingly mass rejection of the blues by the black community in the 1960s came on top of an academic and media agenda that detached blacks from their contributions in the past and in the present. It was no surprise that in a music so connected to that "cat" Jim Crow, folks looked ahead to the future of music, called R&B, and its more favored cousin, rock & roll. Still, the British, in their quest for world culture to fill in the gaps left by the collapse of their dominant, one-sided monarch drill, became some of the best record collectors on the planet. (This is still the case today.) This foundation is parallel to the original beat digger DJs of hip-hop: It was imperative for the Brit bands of the late fifties and early sixties to lace their skiffle and americopied rock & roll riffs with the pure elements of the great bluesmiths.

Artillery for the now-famous British Invasion set precedent for those U.K. artists who questionably became more legendary than the root of their muse. The real story of the blues carried the history of black people alongside it by default. Their migration into northern cities offered this soundtrack of life to the world played through these musicians. Brothers carried their guitars and riffs with them, sketching a picture of the roads traveled up and down the land. Some cats claimed it was the antithesis of the black gospel movement—god and the devil squaring off.

A look back tells us it was just a difference of some words, ideologies, and the opinions of the time, running on the same tracks—one dealing with getting to the heaven of the unknown, the other dealing with the hell of now. Still, some brothers continued the tradition of taking the music alongside the road of a troubled and traveled past. Jimi Hendrix was that aberration, mixing religion in his lyrics and putting his blues on a modern primal scream path to heavy metal.

The blues is as much a story about the meshing of people as it is a tale of their mass movement. Marshall Chess has often said that the immigrants from Europe (like his father and uncle, who founded Chess Records) and the migrants from the South (like many Chess recording artists) were of similar breed, servicing each others' needs by arranging and adapting culture to the recorded twentieth century: to escape the brutal hard-working conditions of before by aligning new duties alongside new stories sung, played, and spoken on new technology. This was major, and it rang volumes, transmitting new blues across the world as the first massive doses did in the 1920s. The creation of the transistor radio helped jump the blues into faster tempos, ushering in the era of rhythm & blues as named by Atlantic Records mogul Jerry Wexler—and thus ushering in rock & roll in the process.

All to say that everything has its starting point, and we must find ways to draw that line to its origins. I was sparked about the blues as a beat digger coming across an album of immense layers and well-played sounds. This record was *Electric Mud* by Muddy Waters, recorded in 1968 and produced by Marshall Chess. Myself and my co-producer Gary G-Whiz fell in love with the record, a psychedelic trip replaying and singing Muddy's classics of the past. Who knew he'd recorded these songs before? Not me. This record made me understand the concept of the blues. It was no surprise why I couldn't find a decent review of the album. It wasn't meant for the purists who panned it; it was for the people who got turned on by being introduced to a whole new world. Thus the line leading to the blues was drawn for a cat like me, showing there's ways that it can be drawn to and from the oft-sampled and riff duped sounds of blues recordings.

The great blues writer and producer Willie Dixon was an ambassador for all of us to follow. He helped us to explain whatever music we might be a part of, simply by making understanding the blues so easy.

Chuck D performing his version of "Boom Boom" at the Salute to the Blues concert, 2003

By understanding the blues, you're understanding life. You are spitting everything that's been built up in your soul and mind out into the world for ears and souls to attach themselves to, as simple as that. That's the essence of making records for yourself and the people as opposed to merely a contractual agreement to a company, sponsored and co-signed by "the hood" as a reminder of where we came from. The seed sprouted into the modern financial backbone of corporate entities overseeing various music styles presently bought and downloaded. One could've never guessed that a porch riff strummed on a sleepy Mississippi fall afternoon would be America's main signature to the world of music as we know it today. The footprint of where sound walks tomorrow. 🎸

Acknowledgments

An extraordinary team composed of numerous chefs hailing from various culinary backgrounds created this feast of ideas entitled *Martin Scorsese Presents the Blues: A Musical Journey*. And what a journey the making of this book has been! It was nearly two years ago when, in July 2001, Alex Gibney, Bob Santelli, and I had our first phone meeting (connecting New York, Seattle, and Roanoke Rapids, North Carolina) regarding the notion of an illustrated book to accompany a forthcoming documentary series on the blues. Since that day, two entire films were added to the original concept; our "notion" translated into a book deal with the prestigious publisher HarperCollins; and several other important people became contributors to dozens of brainstorming sessions. There were energizing discourses on literature and music and impassioned debates about which gardens our vegetables should come from, which bakeries our bread, whether to serve red, or white, or both. . . . In the end we were in agreement that our seven-course meal required, above all else, variety and the finest of ingredients. We're sure there's something here to suit every palate.

Throughout the process our chefs had one thing in common: We'd all been "gobsmacked" by the blues (to paraphrase Eric Clapton). Our love for the music and our wanting to do it justice through the written word fueled the passions that went into the making of this book. I'd like to personally thank my fellow editors, from whom I learned so much: Bob Santelli, Peter Guralnick, and Christopher John Farley. The exchange of ideas and their masterful abilities to put them into words were truly gratifying to me as an editor. Our fearless leader, Alex Gibney, kept us all running around and looking for exotic new (and old) spices to add to our stew, and he, of course, provided plenty of his own. Ellen Nygaard Ford, Dan Conaway, Mikaela Beardsley, Nina Pearlman, Margaret Bodde, Shawn Dahl, and Moira Haney are the uncredited editors of this book; their amazing ideas, unflagging creativity, and tireless dedication to our project made it what it is today. Others who helped tremendously in this regard include Andrea Odintz, Dan Luskin, Agnes Chu, Salimah El-Amin, Susan Motamed, Richard Hutton, Bonnie Benjamin-Phariss, Jill Schwartzman, John Jusino, Betty Lew, Rockelle Henderson, Dianne Pinkowitz, Nita Friedman, Brigitte Engler, Andrew Simon, Robin Aigner, and Ruthie Epstein. Our gratitude also goes to literary agents Sarah Lazin and Luke Janklow for their publishing expertise and counsel.

In addition, the following folks helped in various ways to make this book happen: Inah Lee, Bruce Ricker, Anya Sacharow, Robert Legault, Amy Blankstein, Michele Garner Brown, Andrea Rotondo, Ann Abel, Tom Di Nome, Ashley Kahn, Laura Draper, Rachel X. Weissman, Heather Tierney, Richard Skanse, David Gahr, Jim Marshall, Peter Amft, Frank Driggs, David Ritz, Andrew Bottomley, Kent Jones, Don Fleming, David Tedeschi, Charles Sawyer, Tony Decaneas, Jonathan Hyams, Helen Ashford, Geary Chansley, John Sutton-Smith, Michael Singh, Mikal Gilmore, Susannah McCormick Nix, Michael Hall, Clifford Antone, Mark Jordan, Alexandra Guralnick, the staff at the Carnegie Public Library, Robert Birdsong of Travel House in Clarksdale, Mississippi, Jim Dickinson, Joel Dorn, Leslie Rondin, Andy Schwartz, Hannah Palmer, Jeff Scheftel, James Austin, Kandia Crazy Horse, Richard Meltzer, Mark Lipkin, Jeff and Ben Cohen, Robert Gordon, Banning Eyre, Jeff Peisch, Steve Weitzman, Howard Mandel, Mitch Myers, Bernard Furnival, Aliza Rabinoff, John Swenson, Elvis Costello, Michael Ochs, and Walter Leaphart. I'm also grateful to all the writers and musicians (and their staffs) for their contributions to this book.

Just like Muddy had his Hoochie Coochie Boys to rock the party, I had my Bitchin' Bay Ridge Blues Babes who gave their all through those many endless nights and days in the editorial trenches. Without them—and our incredibly patient, supportive, and techie-expert love objects, Robert Warren, Jack Warren, and Joe Ford— you would not be reading page 282 right now.

So enough givin' props: Put on Memphis Minnie, Robert Johnson, or Howlin' Wolf, turn back to this book, and let the blues take hold of you.

Holly George-Warren
New York City, May 2003

Attributions and Sources

A CENTURY OF THE BLUES: **"Stones in My Passway"** written by Robert Johnson © 1990 Lehsem II, LLC/Claud L. Johnson; **"Dream Boogie"** from *The Collected Poems of Langston Hughes* by Langston Hughes © by the Estate of Langston Hughes. Used by permission of Alfred A. Knopf, a division of Random House, Inc.; **"You Know I Love You"** by Lou Willie Turner Administered by Warner Chappell. Used by permission. All rights reserved. **"Prisoner's Talking Blues"** written by Robert Pete Williams © 1971 (re: 1999) Tradition Music (BMI)/Administered by BUG. All rights reserved. Used by permission.

FEEL LIKE GOING HOME: **Farley/Son House:** the *Atlanta Journal Constitution*, July 10, 1994; *Ethnomusicology*, January 1975, pages 149–54; *The Blues Makers* by Samuel Charters, (Da Capo); *Rochester Times-Union*, "I Swear to God, I've Got to Sing These Gospel Blues" by Steve Dollar, February 24, 1987; *Rochester Democrat and Chronicle*, "Still a Great Delta Blues Singer" by Lawrence Cohn, October 6, 1968; *Rochester Democrat and Chronicle*, "Son House: Travelin' Blues" by Rich Gardner, August 30, 1981; *Rochester Times-Union*, "Let It Shine..." by Mary Anne Pikrone, March 26, 1968; *Rochester Times-Union*, "Son House Records Blues Again" May 29, 1965; *Guitar Player*, "Deep Down in the Delta" by Jas Obrecht, August 1992; *Guitar Player*, "Requiem for Son House" by Jas Obrecht, January 1989; *Sing Out!* "I Can Make My Own Songs" by Son House, July 1965; *Living Blues*, "Living Blues Interview: Son House" by Jeff Titon, March-April 1977; *New York Post*, "The Rhythm Section: The Blues Eldest Statesman" by Ralph J. Gleason, December 10, 1969; *Nothing But the Blues: An Illustrated Documentary*, edited by Mike Leadbitter (Hanover Books, 1971); *Son House, The Original Delta Blues* (Columbia/Legacy, 1998), CD liner notes; *Son House & Bukka White–Masters of the Country Blues* (Yazoo video, 1960); *Searching for Robert Johnson* by Peter Guralnick (Plume, 1998); *Robert Johnson: The Complete Recordings* (Columbia, 1990), CD liner notes; *King of the Delta Blues* (Columbia/Legacy, 1997), CD liner notes; *The Big Book of Blues* by Robert Santelli, (Penguin, 1994); **August Wilson:** *Romare Bearden: His Life and Art* by Myron Schwartzman Harry N. Abrams, 1990; **"Hellhound on My Trail"** written by Robert Johnson © 1990 Lehsem II, LLC/Claud L. Johnson; **Lomax:** copyright © 2002 *The Land Where the Blues Began* by Alan Lomax. Reprinted by permission of the New Press. (800-233-4830); **Gordon:** from

Can't Be Satisfied: The Life and Times of Muddy Waters by Robert Gordon. Copyright © 2002 by Gordon. By permission of Little, Brown and Company (Inc.); **Palmer:** reprinted by permission of the Estate of Robert Palmer; **Farley/Toure:** *Jali Kunda: Griots of West Africa and Beyond* (Ellipsis Arts, 1996), CD liner notes; *Ali Farka Toure, Radio Mali* (World Circuit/Nonesuch, 1999), CD liner notes; *World Music: the Rough Guide* (The Rough Guide/Penguin, 1994); *Ancient West African Kingdoms: Ghana, Mali and Songhai* by Mary Quigley (Heinemann, 2002); AP Worldstream, March 8, 2001; *Boston Globe*, July 28, 2000; *In Griot Time: An American Guitarist in Mali* by Banning Eyre (Temple, 2000); *The Independent* (London), June 18, 1999; *Chicago Tribune*, August 6, 2000; *Mali Blues* by Lieve Joris (Lonely Planet, 1998); *Waiting for Rain: Life and Development in Mali, West Africa* by Lewis W. Lucke (The Christopher Publishing House, 1998); *World Music: the Rough Guide–Africa, Europe and the Middle East* (Rough Guide/Penguin, 1999); *Ali Farka Toure, The Source* (World Circuit, 1992), CD liner notes; *Rhythm Planet: The Great World Music Makers* by Tom Schnabel (Universe, 1998); *Various Artists, Mali to Memphis: An African-American Odyssey,* (Putumayo, 1999), CD liner notes; *Various Artists, Mali & Guinea: Kora Kings and Griot Minstrels,* (World Music Network, 2000), CD liner notes; *Various Artists, The Music of Mali* (Nascente, 2001), CD liner notes.

WARMING BY THE DEVIL'S FIRE: **Farley:** *BackWaterBlues: In Search of Bessie Smith* by Sara Grime (Rose Island Publishing Co./Sara Grimes, 2000); *Baltimore Afro-American*, April 10, 1926; *The Essential Bessie Smith* (Columbia, 1997), CD liner notes; *Bessie Smith–The Collection* (Columbia, 1989), CD liner notes; *Bessie Smith, Volume I* (Frog, 2001), CD liner notes; *Bessie Smith: The Complete Recordings Vol. 1,* Columbia/ Legacy, 1991), CD liner notes; *Bessie Smith, The Final Chapter, The Complete Recordings Vol. 5* (Columbia/ Legacy, 1996), CD liner notes; *The Jazz Makers*, edited by Neil Shapiro and Nat Hentoff (Rinehart & Company); DownBeat.com; *Nothing but the Blues: An Illustrated Documentary*, edited by Mike Leadbitter (Hanover Books, 1971); *Personal Politics: The Roots of Women's Liberation in the Civil Rights Movement and the New Left* by Sara Evans (Random House, 1979); *A Shining Thread of Hope: The History of Black Women in America* by Darlene Clark Hine and Kathleen Thompson (Broadway Books, 1998); *Black Pearls: Blues Queens of the 1920s* by

Daphne Duval Harrison (Rutgers University Press, 1990); *Blues Legacies and Black Feminism: Gertrude "Ma" Rainey, Bessie Smith, and Billie Holiday* by Angela Davis (Pantheon, 1998); *Women, Race and Class* by Angela Davis (Vintage, 1983); *Bessie Smith* by Jackie Kay (Absolute Press, 1997); *Blues Traveling: The Holy Sites of Delta Blues* by Steve Cheseborough (Mississippi, 2001); *Bessie* by Chris Albertson (Stein and Day, 1982); *Nobody Knows My Name* by James Baldwin (Vintage, 1960); *The American Dream, The Death of Bessie Smith, Fam and Yam,* by Edward Albee (Dramatist Play Service); *Bessie Smith–Empress of the Blues,* by Chris Albertson and Gunther Schuller, (Schirmer, 1975); *Brown Sugar: Eighty Years of America's Black Female Superstars* by Donald Bogle (Harmony, 1980); *Jazz Masters of the Twenties* by Richard Hadlock (MacMillan, 1974); *Pittsburgh Courier,* October 9, 1937; *Clarksdale Press Register,* ibid, September 26, 1957, ibid October 3, 1957, ibid, September 27, 1937; *Chicago Defender,* October 2, 1937; ibid, October 9, 1937; *Baltimore Afro-American,* March 7, 1926; *Down Beat,* October 1937; ibid, November 1937; ibid, December 1937; *Hollywood Rhythm Vol.1: The Best of Jazz and Blues* (King Video, 2001); *Stomping the Blues* by Albert Murray (Da Capo, 1976); *Somebody's Angel Child: The Story of Bessie Smith,* by Carman Moore (Dell, 1969); *The Big Book of Blues,* Santelli. **Brown:** all lines from "Ma Rainey" from *The Collected Poems of Sterling A. Brown,* edited by Michael S. Harper. Copyright © 1932 by Harcourt Brace & Co. Copyright renewed 1960 by Sterling A. Brown. Reprinted by permission of HarperCollins Publishers, Inc.; Marshall: **"Shave 'em Dry"** by Lucille Bogan (n/a) Solome Bey Matthews (SOCAN), reprinted by permission of Hot Usama Music; **Titon:** *Early Downhome Blues: A Musical and Cultural Analysis,* second edition, by Jeff Todd Titon, Copyright © 1995 by the University of North Carolina Press. Used by permission of the publisher. **Shines:** "Remembering Robert Johnson" by Johnny Shines, from *American Folk Music Occasional,* 1970, reprinted with permission of Chris Strachwitz; **Ellison:** from *Invisible Man* by Ralph Ellison, copyright © 1947, 1948, 1952 by Ralph Ellison. Copyright renewed 1975, 1976, 1980 by Ralph Ellison. Used by permission of Random House. **Edwards:** from *The World Don't Owe Me Nothing: The Life and Times of Delta Bluesman Honeyboy Edwards,* by David "Honeyboy" Edwards as told to Janis Martinson and Michael Robert Frank. Reprinted with permission of Chicago Review Press, Inc. **Faulkner:** from *Soldiers' Pay* by William Faulkner. Copyright 1954 by William Faulkner. Copyright 1926 by Boni & Liveright, Inc. Used by permission of Liveright Publishing Corporation. **Baldwin:** excerpted from "Down at the Cross: Letter From a Region in My Mind" by James Baldwin, originally published in *The New Yorker.* Collected in *The Fire Next Time* © 1962, 1963. Copyright renewed. Reprinted by arrangement with the James Baldwin Estate; **Bond:** reprinted with permission of the author.

THE ROAD TO MEMPHIS: **Booth:** "Furry Blues" by Stanley Booth. Reprinted by permission of the author. **Shade:** from *Conversation With the Blues* by Paul Oliver. Cambridge University Press, 1965. Reprinted by permission of the author; **"The River's Invitation"** by Percy Mayfield. © 1952 (renewed) Sony/ATV Songs LLC. All rights administered by Sony/ATV Music Publishing, 8 Music Square West, Nashville, TN 37203. All rights reserved. Used by permission. **Palmer:** from *Deep Blues* by Robert Palmer. Published by Viking Press, 1982. Reprinted by permission of the Estate of Robert Palmer.

THE SOUL OF A MAN: **Farley:** *Nothing But the Blues: The Music and the Musicians* by Lawrence Cohn (Abbeville Press, 1993); *The Land Where the Blues Began* by Alan Lomax (Pantheon, 1993); *A Natural History of the Senses* by Diane Ackerman (Vintage, 1990); *Blind Lemon Jefferson: His Life, His Death, His Legacy* by Robert Uzzel (Eakin, 2002); *Blindness: The History of a Mental Image in Western Thought* by Moshe Barasch (Routledge, 2001); *Twilight: Losing Sight, Gaining Insight* by Henry Grunwald (Knopf, 2000); *Aldous Huxley, The Art of Seeing* (Creative Arts Book Company, 1982); *Tales From Ovid,* translated by Ted Hughes (Farrar, Straus and Giroux, 1997); "Music Rooted in the Texas Soil" by Robert L. Uzzelm , *Living Blues,* November/December 1988; *The Blues Makers* by Samuel Charters; "Blind Lemon Jefferson: the Myth and the Man" by Alan Govenar, *Black Music Research Journal,* Spring 2000, "The Language of Blind Lemon Jefferson: The Covert Theme of Blindness" by Luigi Monge, *Black Music Research Journal,* Spring 2000, "Musical Innovation in the Blues of Blind Lemon Jefferson," by David Evans, *Bluesland,* edited by Pete Welding and Toby Byron (1991); *Arizona Dranes, Complete Recorded Works in Chronological Order 1926–1929* (Document, 1993), CD liner notes; *Sight Unseen* by Georgina Kleege (Yale University Press, 1999); *The Best of Blind Lemon Jefferson* (Yazoo, 2000), CD liner notes; "Moanin' All Over," (Tradition Records, 1996), CD liner notes; *The Big Book of Blues* by Robert

Santelli; **"Blind Willie McTell"** by Bob Dylan, Copyright © 1983 Special Rider Music; **Charters:** reprinted with permission of the author; **McCormick:** reprinted by permission of the author; **Hurston:** pages 142–47 from *Their Eyes Were Watching God* by Zora Neale Hurston, copyright 1937 by Harper & Row, Publishers, Inc.; renewed © 1965 by John C. Hurston and Joel Hurston. Reprinted by permission of HarperCollins Publishers, Inc.; **Amft:** interview with Holly George-Warren, 2003; **Antone:** interview with George-Warren, 2003; **Vaughan:** interviews with David Ritz, 2002–03; **White:** interview with George-Warren, 2003. **Hooker:** from *Conversation with the Blues* by Paul Oliver, Cambridge University Press. Reprinted by permission of the author; **Nelson:** interview with George-Warren, 2003.

GODFATHERS AND SONS: **Palmer:** from *Deep Blues*, by Robert Palmer, reprinted by permission of the Estate of Robert Palmer; **Hughes:** "Happy New Year! With Memphis Minnie" by Langston Hughes, from the *Chicago Defender*, January 9, 1943. Reprinted by permission of the *Chicago Defender*; **Farley:** *Woman with Guitar: Memphis Minnie's Blues* by Paul and Beth Garon (Da Capo, 1992); *How Sweet the Sound: The Golden Age of Gospel* by Horace Clarence Boyer (Elliot and Clark, 1995); *Sister Rosetta Tharpe: Original Soul Sister* (Proper, 2002), CD liner notes; *Big Bill Blues: William Broonzy's Story As Told to Yannick Bruynoghe* by Big Bill Broonzy (Cassell, 1955); *Memphis Minnie: Queen of the Blues"* (Columbia, 1997), CD liner notes; *Memphis Minnie: The Essential* (Classic Blues, 2001), CD liner notes; *Chicago Defender*, January 9, 1943; "My Girlish Days" *Blues Unlimited*, December 1970; "Memphis Minnie" by Steve LaVere and Paul Garon; *Living Blues*, Autumn 1973; *The Blues Makers* by Samuel Charters; *Nothing But the Blues: The Music and the Musicians* by Lawrence Cohn; *The Story of the Blues* by Francis Davis (Hyperion, 1995). **Charters:** reprinted by permission of the author. **Dixon:** from *I Am the Blues*, 1989 by Willie Dixon with Don Snowdon, Da Capo, reprinted with the permission of the Estate of Willie Dixon; **Trynka:** from *Mojo*, February 1996, reprinted by permission of the author; **Bloomfield:** from the book *Me and Big Joe* by Michael Bloomfield with Scott Summerville. © 1980 Re/Search Publications, San Francisco (www.researchpubs.com); **Amft:** interview with George-Warren, 2003.

RED, WHITE AND BLUES: **Farley:** *Big Bill Blues: William Broonzy's Story As Told To Yannick Bruynoghe* by Big Bill Broonzy; *The Land Where the Blues Began* by Alan Lomax;

Big Bill Broonzy, Trouble in Mind (Smithsonian Folkways, 2000), CD liner notes; *The Young Big Bill Broonzy* (Yazoo, 1928), CD liner notes; *Nothing But the Blues: The Music and the Musicians* by Lawrence Cohn; *Chasin' That Devil Music: Searching for the Blues* by Gayle Dean Wardlow (Backbeat, 1998); *Deep Blues* by Robert Palmer (Penguin, 1981); *Blues Masters: The Essential History of the Blues* (Rhino Home Video, 1993); *The Big Book of Blues* by Robert Santelli. **Wilmer:** from *Mojo*, 1995, reprinted by permission of the author; **Booth:** from *The True Adventures of the Rolling Stones*, 1984, reprinted by permission of the author.

PIANO BLUES AND BEYOND: **Farley:** Firmly Rooted," by Matthew Socey, *Down Beat*, November 2002; "Marcia Ball: Pounding the 88s Across 50 States," by Ernie Rideout, *Keyboard*, October 2001. "Marcia Ball: Of Crawfish and Edna St. Vincent Millay," by Mindy Giles, July 2001. ABC News: Nightline, "Satchmo's Blues: Louis Armstrong in his own words," by Dave Mrash, August 17, 2001; The Gold Coast Bulletin, "Norah on the Rise," by Barry Ralph, January 4, 2003. Sojourner: the Women's Forum "A Century of Jazzwomen," by Cathy Lee, September 30, 1984; *Stormy Weather: The Music and Lives of a Century of Jazzwomen,* by Linda Dahl (Pantheon, 1984); The Washington Post, "Women Sing the Blues" by Mike Joyce, May 13, 1998; The Dallas Morning News, "All Through Singing the Blues," by Thor Christensen, September 20, 1998; The Times Union (Albany, New York), "True to Blues: Women Crossing Genre's Racial Divide," by Dana Jennings, August 17, 2000; The Washington Post, "Hazel Scott, Jazz Pianist, Singer, Dies; Once Wed to Congressman," October 4, 1981; The Washington Post Magazine, "Power and Love," by Wil Haygood, January 17, 1993; Albert Murray, "The Hero and the Blues," (Vintage, 1973); Ralph Ellison, "Living with Music: Ralph Ellison's Jazz Writings" (Modern Library); **Peterson:** interview with George-Warren, 2003; **Hammond:** interview with George-Warren, 2003; **Welty:** reprinted by the permission of Russell and Volkening as agents for the author © 1941 by Eudora Welty renewed in 1969 Eudora Welty; **Spann:** from *Conversation with the Blues* by Paul Oliver, Cambridge University Press. Reprinted by permission of the author; **Lydon:** from *Ray Charles: The Man and His Music* by Michael Lydon, reprinted with permission of the author. **Wexler:** from *Rhythm and the Blues: A Life in American Music* by Jerry Wexler and David Ritz, reprinted with permission of the authors; **Ball:** interview with Richard Skanse, 2003.

Contributors

HILTON ALS is a staff writer for *The New Yorker*. His work has also appeared in *The New York Review of Books*.

STANLEY BOOTH, author of *Till I Roll Over Dead*, *Rythm Oil*, and *The True Adventures of the Rolling Stones*, met Furry Lewis in 1966. They were friends till Furry died in 1981.

SAMUEL CHARTERS has written and produced numerous books and albums on the blues since writing *The Country Blues* in 1959. He has also published novels and books of poetry.

ANTHONY DECURTIS is a contributing editor at *Rolling Stone* and the author of *Rocking My Life Away: Writing About Music and Other Matters*. He holds a Ph.D. in American literature and teaches in the creative writing program at the University of Pennsylvania.

CHRISTOPHER JOHN FARLEY, born in Jamaica and raised in New York, is author of the novel *My Favorite War* and the biography *Aaliyah: More Than a Woman*. As the chief music critic for *Time* in the 1990s, Farley interviewed Bob Dylan, John Lee Hooker, U2, Radiohead, and Aretha Franklin, among other artists. Farley is currently a senior editor of *Time* and a contributor to CNN Headline News, where he hosts the weekly music report *Christopher John Farley's Jukebox*.

HOLLY GEORGE-WARREN is coeditor of *American Roots Music* and *The Rolling Stone Encyclopedia of Rock & Roll*, and author of *Cowboy: How Hollywood Invented the Wild West* and *Shake, Rattle & Roll: The Founders of Rock & Roll*, among many other books.

ALEX GIBNEY, series producer of *The Blues*, is an Emmy Award–winning writer, director, and producer. His credits include the *The Trials of Henry Kissinger*, *The Fifties* (based on the best-seller by author David Halberstam), and *The Pacific Century*.

ROBERT GORDON is author of *Can't Be Satisfied: The Life and Times of Muddy Waters*, *It Came from Memphis*, and two books about Elvis Presley. His documentaries include *Muddy Waters Can't Be Satisfied* and *All Day & All Night*. He was writer of the blues documentary *The Road to Memphis*.

PETER GURALNICK is author of *Feel Like Going Home*, *Searching for Robert Johnson*, *Sweet Soul Music*, and the novel *Nighthawk Blues*, along with a two-volume biography of Elvis Presley, among other books.

DAVID HALBERSTAM is a Pulitzer Prize–winning author whose most recent book is *Teammates*.

RICHARD HELL is the author of the novel *Go Now*. His most recent music release is the double CD *Time*, and his most recent book is *Hot and Cold*.

ELMORE LEONARD is the author of numerous books, including *Unknown Man #89*, *Get Shorty*, and *Tishomingo Blues*, soon to be a major motion picture.

MICHAEL LYDON, author of *Ray Charles: Man and Music*, has been writing about pop music for more than thirty years. He's also a singer-songwriter who performs regularly in New York City.

JAMES MARSHALL has written for *Spin*, the *New York Times*, and *High Times*, among other publications.

MACK McCORMICK is a cultural anthropologist who has been researching and writing about the blues since the 1940s.

CATHERINE NEDONCHELLE, a French journalist based in the U.S. for twenty years, covers the New York–Paris–Memphis axis.

PAUL OLIVER is the author of *Conversation with the Blues* and *The Story of the Blues*, among many other books.

PAUL OSCHER was the first white musician to become a full-time member of Muddy Waters' band. Oscher continues to perform at blues festivals throughout the U.S. and abroad. He sings and plays harmonica, guitar, and piano. "The Gift" is from Oscher's forthcoming book *Alone with the Blues*.

ROBERT PALMER has made several recordings with his band Insect Trust. His works include *Deep Blues*, *Rock & Roll: An Unruly History*, and numerous other projects.

SUZAN-LORI PARKS is a Pulitzer Prize–winning playwright.

DAVID RITZ, whose most recent book is *Faith in Time: The Life of Jimmy Scott*, is also the author of the novel *Blue Notes Under a Green Felt Hat* and the lyricist of "Sexual Healing."

LUC SANTE is the author of several books, including *Low Life* and *The Factory of Facts*. He lives in Ulster County, New York.

ROBERT SANTELLI is coeditor of *American Roots Music*, author of *The Big Book of Blues*, and the executive director of the Experience Music Project.

JEFF SCHEFTEL is an award-winning filmmaker whose most recent works are *Mahalia Jackson: The Power and the Glory*, *Welcome to Death Row*, and *Sounds of Memphis*. He also served as director of media production for NARAS, producers of the Grammy Awards. He is currently writing a book on the music business and directing a documentary about Irwin Wilder and Martin Scorsese.

JOHN SWENSON is editor of *The Rolling Stone Jazz & Blues Album Guide*. He has been writing about the blues since the late 1960s for publications including *Crawdaddy* and *Rolling Stone*, as well as UPI. He is the blues columnist for *OffBeat*.

JOHN SZWED is Musser Professor of African-American studies, anthropology, and music at Yale University, and is Louis Armstrong Visiting Professor at Columbia University in 2003–04. He is the author of *Space Is the Place: The Lives and Times of Sun Ra, Jazz 101*, and *So What: The Life of Miles Davis*, and is at work on a biography of Alan Lomax.

GREG TATE is a staff writer at the *Village Voice*. His books include *Flyboy in the Buttermilk, Everything but the Burden: What White People Are Taking from Black Culture, Midnight Lightning: Jimi Hendrix and the Black Experience*, and the forthcoming futuristic novel *Altered Spaydes*. He also leads the ensemble Burnt Sugar.

JEFF TODD TITON is professor of music at Brown University and author of *Early Downhome Blues: A Musical and Cultural Analysis, Powerhouse for God*, and *Give Me This Mountain*.

TOURÉ is the author of *The Portable Promised Land*, a collection of short stories, and the forthcoming novel *Soul City*. He is also a contributing editor at *Rolling Stone* and a contributor to NPR's *All Things Considered*.

PAUL TRYNKA is editorial director of *Mojo*, where he has worked in various guises since 1996. Trynka is also the author of *Portrait of the Blues* (with photographs by Val Wilmer) and *Denim: From Cowboys to Catwalks*.

JOHN EDGAR WIDEMAN, a novelist and essayist, is Distinguished Professor of English at the University of Massachusetts at Amherst.

VAL WILMER, the noted writer and photographer, is the author of *Jazz People, As Serious as Your Life, The Face of Black Music*, and *Mama Said There'd Be Days Like This*, an autobiography. Her photographs and writing have appeared in books, magazines, and newspapers worldwide.

PETER WOLF joined his first band, The Hallucinations, while attending the Museum School of Fine Arts in Boston. The band appeared with many of the great blues artists, including Muddy Waters, Howlin' Wolf, and John Lee Hooker. In 1967 Wolf formed the J. Geils Band, which combined blues and R&B styles with a rock & roll flair. They remained together for seventeen years, and since their breakup Wolf has released a series of critically acclaimed solo albums.

Photo Credits

Charles Sawyer (back endpaper: B.B. King, 1970); Ernest Withers/copyright © Ernest C. Withers/courtesy Panopticon Gallery, Waltham, MA (1, 37, 149, 151, 152, 278); David Gahr (Big Joe Williams's hands 2–3, 48, 49, 51, 89, 171, 183, 209, 240, 262); Peter Amft (front casing, back casing, 6, 7, 53, 153, 162, 166, 177, 217, 218, 220, 221, 275, 282); Russell Lee, Farm Security Administration, Library of Congress (9); Chicago Historical Society (12–13); Marion Post Wolcott, Farm Security Administration, Library of Congress (16–17); Courtesy Columbia/Legacy (19, 58, 62); Michael Ochs Archives/Venice, CA (20, 45, 115, 236); Frank Driggs Collection (22, 101, 117, 118, 120, 121, 122, 127, 140, 159, 199, 203, 215); FDR/Michael Ochs Archives (21, 109); Courtesy Yazoo Records/Shanachie (23); Sebastian Danchin Collection (26); Dixon Rohr (31); Don Bronstein/Chansley Entertainment Archives (36); Ray Flerage/Chansley Entertainment Archives (39); Joe Ciardiello (42, 181, 288); Jan Perrson (50); Chansley Entertainment Archives (52); Stephanie Chernikowski (55); Ken Settle (56, 254, 279); *Feel Like Going Home* (Otha Turner 60–61, Mali 64–65, 65, 66); Jim Marshall (68, 179, 193, 247, 261, 264); Courtesy Alan Lomax Archives (77); Dorothea Lange, Farm Security Administration, Library of Congress (80); Courtesy Jim Dickinson (left, 87); Ken Franckling (right, 87); Ebet Roberts (91, 94, 255); *Warming by the Devil's Fire* (98–99, 102, 103); Wayne Knight Collection/Chansley Entertainment Archives (112); Sylvia Pitcher Photo Library (124); James Fraher/Chansley Entertainment Archives (132); Val Wilmer (133, 244); *The Road to Memphis* (136–137), Zack Kenner (138, 139); Courtesy Yazoo/Shanachie/Eclipse Enterprises (144–145, 167); Damion Lawyer (150); *The Soul of a Man* (Chris Thomas King as Blind Willie Johnson 154, 268; Keith Brown as Skip James 155; top, 163; bottom, 163); Kenji Oda (164); *Godfathers and Sons* (184–185, 187); Gina Barge (186); Courtesy Peter Wolf (189); Mark PoKempner (190, 204, 207, front endpaper: Saturday night at Teresa's, Chicago, 1981); Terry Coyer (205); Courtesy Paul Oscher (227); *Red, White and Blues*/Jeremy Fletcher/ Redferns/Retna Ltd. (Zoot Money with Andy Summers, second from right 228–229); *Red, White and Blues* (233); © Brian Smith/Chansley Entertainment Archives (246); Adam Traum (250–251, 252); Paul Brissman (270, 281); Courtesy ABKCO (272)

Sister Rosetta Tharpe

EDITOR: Holly George-Warren
CREATIVE DIRECTOR & DESIGNER: Ellen Nygaard Ford
MANAGING EDITOR: Nina Pearlman
EDITORIAL/PRODUCTION CONSULTANT: Shawn Dahl
PHOTO RESEARCHER: Moira Haney
EDITORIAL RESEARCHERS: Andrea Odintz-Cohen, Robin Aigner,
Andrew Simon, Michele Garner Brown.

The Editors would like to acknowledge the following for their
contributions both to this book and to the larger project that
inspired it:
Dan Conaway, Executive Editor, HarperCollins Publishers
Alex Gibney, Series Producer, *The Blues*
Margaret Bodde, Producer, Cappa Productions & *The Blues*
Mikaela Beardsley, Supervising Producer, *The Blues*
Susan Motamed, Coordinating Producer, *The Blues*
Paul G. Allen, Executive Producer, Experience Music Project
Jodi Patton, Executive Producer, Vulcan Productions
Robert Santelli, Executive Director, Experience Music Project
Richard Hutton, Co-Producer, Vulcan Productions
Bonnie Benjamin-Phariss, Director, Documentary
   Programming, Vulcan Productions
HarperCollins/Amistad: Jill Schwartzman, Dawn Davis,
   Carie Freimuth, Laurie Rippon, Rockelle Henderson,
   John Jusino, Betty Lew, Dianne Pinkowitz, Lara Allen,
   Tara Brown, Laura Blost
The Blues Inc.: Dan Luskin, Agnes Chu, Salimah El-Amin,
   Susan Motamed

A companion book to the PBS documentary series
Martin Scorsese Presents The Blues: A Musical Journey

A Presentation of Vulcan Road Movies
Columbia
Universal Music Group
WGBN

HarperCollins books may be purchased for educational, business,
or sales promotional use. For information, please write: Special
Markets Department, HarperCollins Publishers Inc.,
10 East 53rd Street, New York, NY 10022.

FIRST EDITION

Printed on acid-free paper

Library of Congress Cataloging-in-Publication Data is available
upon request.

ISBN 0-06-052544-4

03 04 05 06 07 ❖/RRD 10 9 8 7 6 5 4 3 2 1